DEGREES OF MIXTURE, DEGREES OF FREEDOM

Genomics, Multiculturalism, and Race in Latin America

PETER WADE

D0907329

DUKE UNIVERSITY PRESS · *Durham and London* · 2017

Printed in the United States of America on acid-free paper ∞
Designed by Matthew Tauch
Typeset in Quadraat Pro by Westchester Publishing Services
Library of Congress Cataloging-in-Publication Data
Names: Wade, Peter, [date]—author.
Title: Degrees of mixture, degrees of freedom : genomics,
multiculturalism, and race in Latin America / Peter Wade.
Description: Durham : Duke University Press, 2017. | Includes
bibliographical references and index.
Identifiers: LCCN 2016047987 (print) | LCCN 2016052158 (ebook)
ISBN 9780822363583 (hardcover : alk. paper)
ISBN 9780822363736 (pbk. : alk. paper)
ISBN 9780822373070 (ebook)
Subjects: LCSH: Mestizaje. | Race—Social aspects—Latin America. |
Race—Political aspects—Latin America. | Human population ge-
netics. | Multiculturalism—Latin America. | Latin America—
Race relations.
Classification: LCC GN564.L29 W325 2017 (print) | LCC GN564.L29
(ebook) | DDC 305.80098—dc23
LC record available at https://lccn.loc.gov/2016047987

Cover art: Beth John, *Oxygenation*. Intaglio print.
Courtesy of the artist.

CONTENTS

PREFACE

This book emerges from an interdisciplinary and collaborative project called "Race, Genomics and *Mestizaje* [mixture] in Latin America: A Comparative Approach," which ran from 2010 to 2013. The project had two funding phases, each running for eighteen months. The project team consisted of myself, as overall director, and three teams, focusing on Brazil, Colombia, and Mexico, respectively. In each country, there was a senior coinvestigator (COI), who worked with a postdoctoral researcher (employed by Manchester University for the duration of the project) and a locally hired research assistant. The teams were as follows, listed in order as COI, postdoctoral researcher, and research assistant:

BRAZIL · *Ricardo Ventura Santos* (biological anthropologist at Fundacão Oswaldo Cruz, Fiocruz, in Rio de Janeiro); *Michael Kent* (PhD in social anthropology from the University of Manchester, now an independent development consultant based in Bolivia); and *Verlan Valle Gaspar Neto* (during the project he finished his PhD in cultural anthropology at the Universidad Federal Fluminense; he is currently a professor at the Universidad Federal de Alfenas).

COLOMBIA · *Eduardo Restrepo* (social anthropologist at the Pontificia Universidad Javeriana in Bogotá); *María Fernanda Olarte Sierra* (PhD in social sciences from the University of Amsterdam, currently a professor at the Universidad de los Andes, Bogotá) for phase one of the project, followed by *Ernesto Schwartz-Marín* (PhD in genomics in society from the University of Exeter, currently a research fellow at the University of Durham); and *Adriana Díaz del Castillo* (MA in medical anthropology from the University of Amsterdam, now a researcher at the Universidad de los Andes, Bogotá) for phase one, followed by *Roosbelinda Cárdenas* (during the project she finished her PhD in anthropology at the University of California, currently a visiting professor at Hampshire College).

MEXICO · *Carlos López Beltrán* (historian of science at the Universidad Nacional Autónoma de Mexico [UNAM] in Mexico City); *Vivette García Deister* (PhD in philosophical and social studies of science and technology from UNAM, where she is now a professor), replaced during her maternity leave by *Sandra González Santos* (PhD in sociology from the University of Sussex, currently teaching at the Universidad Iberoamericana, the Centro Nacional de las Artes, and UNAM); and *Mariana Ríos Sandoval* (MA in medical anthropology from the University of Amsterdam, now a PhD student at the same university).

In each team, the roles of the three members varied in terms of hands-on data collection, but in general the postdoctoral researcher was the main investigator. During phase one of the project, the focus was primarily on a small number of labs and scientists in each country and secondarily on the way genetic information circulated outside the labs; during phase two, the balance was the other way around, including data collection (e.g., through focus groups) on how nonscientists reacted to genetic information.

Although I appear as the sole author of this book, I have depended on the data collected by the other team members and am also indebted to the many discussions we had during the project, at the several project workshops we ran, and during the process of producing a number of collaborative publications, foremost among which are *Mestizo Genomics* (Duke University Press, 2014, coedited by Wade, López Beltrán, Restrepo, and Santos) and a special issue of *Social Studies of Science* (December 2015, coedited by Wade, López Beltrán, and Santos). In this book, I cite these and other publications where relevant. I extend my heartfelt appreciation to all the team members for what was an exhilarating intellectual experience—shared, I believe, by all.

The material in this book draws together the different strands of the project—plus some additional material (e.g., chapter 2)—into a single narrative, while also framing them in a new way, integrating them all into a single and, I hope, innovative argument about the relations and tensions between ideas of purity and mixture, and hierarchy and democracy. My aim has been to produce a deep analysis of the interweaving of ideas about the governance and imagination of cultural diversity/mixture with ideas about biological diversity/mixture. I use the concepts of assemblage and topography as conceptual tools in an analytical integration that seeks to avoid science–society dualisms, including the remnants of this opposition detectable in "coproduction" approaches. The main focus of *Mestizo Genomics*—which can be boiled down to the question of how much the practice of genomic science reproduces familiar race-like concepts—has been submerged in the broader question of how genetic science has been and is connected to nodes in an assemblage that encompasses ideas and practices around the governance and imagination of human diversity. In the process, the comparative view inherent in the project—across Brazil, Mexico, and Colombia, but also of Latin America in a global context—is sharpened, and the analysis is more sustained in an effort to grapple with both the insights afforded by comparison and the pitfalls it presents in terms of bringing some things into focus while moving others into the background.

ACKNOWLEDGMENTS

The project was funded by the Economic and Social Research Council (ESRC) of the United Kingdom through grant RES-062-23-1914; and by the Leverhulme Trust through grant RPG-044 (under the title "Public Engagement with Genomic Research and Race in Latin America"). My thanks to both organizations. I am very grateful for a British Academy Wolfson Research Professorship (2013–16), which has given me precious time to work on this book (among other things). I appreciate the support given by the School of Social Sciences at the University of Manchester. I would also like to thank all the scientists and others with whom the members of the project team worked in Brazil, Colombia, and Mexico; they were generous with their time and willingness to engage with the team. Thanks as well to the editorial and production team at Duke University Press, especially Gisela Fosado, Lydia Rose Rappoport-Hankins, and Susan Albury. The greatest thanks must, however, go to the team members themselves. On a personal note, I owe a debt of gratitude to my family, especially my wife Sue, for putting up with multiple trips abroad.

. . . .

INTRODUCTION

....

Mixture as a Biopolitical Process

This book is about mixture as a biopolitical process and how it has figured in science and society in Latin America—specifically, Brazil, Colombia, and Mexico. The immediate referent is "race mixture" or, in biological science, "genetic admixture," and the key location is Latin America. In this region, mestizaje (Spanish) or mestiçagem (Portuguese)—roughly translatable as mixture—is an important concept for thinking about history, politics, nation, identity, and human biology.[1] From colonial times onward, societies there have been conceived as formed from the biological and cultural mixture of Africans, Europeans, and native Americans. Especially after independence in the first half of the nineteenth century, mixture has been seen in most of the region as constituting the essence of the nation.

Taking race mixture or mestizaje to be a biocultural process means that, despite its focus on life sciences, and specifically genetics, this book is not just about biology and genetics, but rather about a complex assemblage of ideas and practices enacting mixture (and its relational counterpart, purity) in interconnected domains of social action, such as politics, genetics, and the constitution of identity. Although the focus is Latin America, by looking at mixture and purity, the book embraces broader themes of equality and hierarchy in liberal political orders, exploring how ideas about genetic mixture get drawn into the frictional tension between democracy and inequality, and what Latin America and its "admixed" populations mean for genomic science in general.

Mixture is attracting attention both as a set of sociocultural processes (whether phrased in terms of "interracial" or "interethnic" unions, or generally in terms of cosmopolitanism and the increased movement and exchange of people, ideas, and things) and as a genetic process (in terms of scientific interest in mestizo populations). I explore how genetic understandings of mixture, as the biological process of formation of national Latin American mestizo populations, operate in the larger biopolitical assemblage of mixture, becoming entangled with ideas about difference and sameness, hierarchy and democracy, and equality and inequality. Mixture in genetics insistently reiterates origins and (relative) purities, as well as reiterating the gendered, sexualized mixture that brings these purities together, and this insistence exists in variable relation with the tensions between hierarchy and democracy that pervade liberal democracies.

In this introduction, I first examine some key features of mestizaje and ideas about mixture and purity generally, before exploring their linkages to ideas about equality and hierarchy and describing how Latin American mestizaje has often been associated with democracy and equality, an association continuing through a recent turn to multiculturalism that appears to break with images of homogeneous mestizo nations. In chapter 1, I argue that population genetics has also been characterized by a tension between purity and mixture, which has run through its attempts to understand human diversity; in the genetic study of Latin American populations, that tension is especially evident. I go on to explore how these scientific and political practices and ideas are elements in a complex assemblage, rather than being two domains of "science" and "politics" that interact; I use the concept of topology to draw out the character of the relations involved in the assemblage.

Mestizaje, Mixture, and Purity

Mestizaje has deep roots in ideas of sexual reproduction between people of different "races," but it implies more than biological mixture. True to the biocultural character of race—which has always entangled nature and culture, and bodies and behavior, blurring the simple oppositions suggested by these binaries (Hartigan 2013d; Wade 2002b)—mestizaje is a biocultural concept that assembles many different meanings and elements, providing affordances for multiple practices in diverse clusters of thought and action. It is a concept, or rather an assemblage, that can organize practice in realms of politics and governance, demography, literary and artistic production, life sciences, identity politics, and kinship and family. The idea of Latin American nations and their peoples as mixed—as mestizos—runs deep and wide. Genetic scientists in Latin America today eschew explicit use of the concept of race, but they are certainly interested in mixture and its "original" ingredients, and the genetic data they produce about mestizos and their ancestral parents (indigenous,

European, and African populations) become part of the biocultural assemblage of mestizaje.

This book is about Latin America, but the idea of mixture has wider biopolitical connotations. It is fundamental to the notion of race: "bastard and mixed-blood are the true names of race" (Deleuze and Guattari, cited in Young 1995, 180). The tensions between ideas of purity and ideas of mixture have been recurrent in racial thinking in its varied forms (Monahan 2011). While in Latin America after the mid-nineteenth century, the idea of mixture was often embraced as a positive value—more ardently in some countries than in others, and always ambivalently—mixture has been a matter of concern in other regions. Within the theme of "purity and danger" and fears about contamination and classificatory conundrums produced when things are not in their "proper" place (Bowker and Star 1999; Douglas 1966), I focus on these matters as they pertain to societies characterized by what Foucault (1998) called the "symbolics of blood" and the "analytics of sexuality"—roughly speaking, "the West." Foucault traced major historical shifts from the symbolics of blood—in which a sovereign monarch ruled society and exercised direct control over people's bodies, having the power through law to decree life or death—to an analytics of sexuality, in which the aim of governance was to administer and invigorate the life force of the populace, through proper management of their bodies and behavior, especially in relation to sex.

In both regimes, purity and mixture were important for political order and governance. For royalty and nobles, the purity of bloodlines mattered greatly and had to be managed not through the avoidance of mixture—procreation requires mixture—but through the choice of appropriate mixtures: good marital alliances that would protect purity and property. For leaders and experts concerned with the biopolitical management of the life force of the nation's population, mixture was a process that should be channeled advantageously toward (relative) purity. In nineteenth-century thinking, mixture between "proximate" races could be acceptable, even beneficial; mixture with "distant" races produced degeneration for the "superior" race (Young 1995: 17). Animal breeders at the time saw carefully controlled mixture as potentially invigorating for purebred pedigrees (Ritvo 1997). As Foucault put it, ideas about regulating and optimizing the life force of populations and bodies "received their color and their justification from the mythical concern with protecting the purity of the blood and ensuring the triumph of the race," thus indicating that "the preoccupation with blood and the law has for nearly two centuries haunted the administration of sexuality" (1998: 149). Race and sex were integrally related:

sex was the means by which the biological and cultural purity of lineages, classes, races, and nations could be protected or threatened (Nagel 2003; Wade 2009).

Mixture/Purity, Democracy/Hierarchy, and Liberalism

Beyond a concern with race, it is clear that power, privilege, and hierarchy are fundamental to this tension between purity and mixture. Mixture does not *need* purity in the ingredients that make up the mix; it just needs difference, which allows the production of more difference in an endless proliferation. But, in the pursuit and maintenance of hierarchies of value and power, relative purities are carved out of the sea of mixtures, by dint of selective genealogical tracings of particular connections, the enforcement of categorical distinctions, and exclusive practices.

Mixture and purity are *relational* concepts, which mutually define each other: what is seen as pure for some purposes can be understood as mixed for others; behind every purity, a mixture can be revealed with sufficient digging; it is possible, with effort, to construct purity out of mixtures, even if "absolute" purity remains an asymptotic ideal. While in an abstract sense mixture might not need purity, in contexts of hierarchy, mixture is made meaningful only in relation to relative purities.

Maintaining purity is a matter of marking boundaries of inclusion and exclusion, which, when allied with the use of power, can easily be deployed to protect privilege and status and defend hierarchical orders. Mixture, when controlled by those defending such boundaries and purifications, can reinforce the hierarchy, but if it is not controlled, it can unsettle boundaries and hierarchies. Thus, marriage across class boundaries can reinforce the class hierarchy when it is restricted, is made conditional on assimilation, and is structured by ideas about "marrying up" that are gendered in ways that underline hierarchy (such that lower-class men who get rich can "marry up," but lower-class women might marry up because of good looks rather than wealth). But widespread marriage across class boundaries, in which every "up" might also be seen as a "down," might weaken those boundaries in the long term. In that sense, mixture can be claimed to possess a democratic dynamic, while purity is allied to hierarchy. Mixture has a dual aspect (Wade 2005a; Young 1995): when it exists in the context of hierarchy and purifications, it can reproduce these structures; when powered by difference as an endless proliferation, it can undermine them. The potential for mixture to enhance democracy has been made much of in recent social theory (see below): however, this potential is always truncated by the opposite tendency of mixture to reproduce hierarchy (Wade 2004, 2005a).

In liberal political orders, the tension between hierarchy and democracy is strong. The ideals of liberalism are fundamentally democratic, based on notions of equality and liberty and enshrined in such founding documents as the U.S. Declaration of Independence (1776), the French Revolution's Declaration of the Rights of Man (1793), and the Spanish Constitution of 1812, a model for independent nations in Latin America, such as the 1826 Bolivian Constitution, drafted by Simón Bolívar. Such ideals have always coexisted with hierarchies of one form or another, often involving dramatic inequalities. Women were deprived of the vote for centuries after the French Revolution's Declaration of the Rights of Man—until 1945 in France itself. Sexist beliefs deemed women to be unsuited to participate directly in politics. Liberal political orders also disenfranchised illiterates and non–property owners, measures that acted disproportionately to keep nonwhites out of the political system, as well as poor people (Engerman and Sokoloff 2005). Liberal ideals and political systems have coexisted easily with colonialism, slavery, and stark racial segregation. Many liberal nations practiced immigration policies that were racially discriminatory, either by intent or in effect, well into the twentieth century and, arguably, still today (FitzGerald and Cook-Martín 2014; Wade 2015: 113–16). Major theorists of liberalism, from the seventeenth to the nineteenth centuries, such as John Locke and John Stuart Mill, adhered to a theoretical ideal of the innate equality of all people, but also held that a proper education—not equally available to all—was necessary to cultivate the reason needed to rule (Mehta 1997). Whole categories of people—for Mill, the Indians or the Chinese, who had become "stationary"—needed the rule of people, such as Europeans, who were an "improving portion of mankind" (1859: 135). Recently, liberalism has eschewed such explicit language of hierarchical difference, but hierarchy itself remains, justified by criteria deemed to constitute good citizenship in a neoliberal world, such as personal or community responsibility, respect for "security," ethical and moral probity, accountability, enterprising self-improvement and organization, cultural tolerance, and maintaining a clean distinction between "public" and "private" spheres (Brandtstädter, Wade, and Woodward 2011; Rose and Miller 2008). In practice, hierarchy often retains strongly racialized dimensions, even if an explicit language of race is avoided (Goldberg 2008).

The inherent drive of liberalism toward sameness—all citizens are equal before the law and the state—is in friction with the inherent drive of the political economy, especially under capitalism, to generate hierarchical differences, typically those of race, class, and gender. This friction resonates with ideas about purity and mixture. The right to govern should be exercised by people selected for the job according to certain criteria. In theory, these criteria are determined by a bureaucratic rationality, which selects the best person for the job and allows a mixture of people. In practice, purifications take place that—directly, but mostly indirectly—select governors by race, class, and gender. The idea of mixture holds out the promise of crossing boundaries, of the rubbing of shoulders between different kinds and classes of people, and of the sharing of spaces, social milieux, and resources, as well as sexual intimacies, bodily substances, and lineage. The idea of purity betokens defensiveness, exclusiveness, fear of contamination and insecurity, the building of boundaries and maintenance of separation, and the channeling of bodily substances, such as "blood," into regulated lineages, races, and classes, a process that requires control of gender difference. Equality and hierarchy, and mixture and purity, exist in tension. Liberal political orders are characterized by processes that enhance equality of opportunity and mixing across social boundaries: access to education is widened and equality of opportunity is increased; discrimination is outlawed, "diversity" is recognized, and tolerance is valued. Simultaneously, other processes increase hierarchy and purifications, nationally and globally: immigration is controlled, "security" requires tighter regulation of movements of people, unwelcome aspects of "diversity" are proscribed, neoliberal economic measures increase poverty, and disparities of class and race persist and even grow, resulting in continued segregations.

The tension between democracy and hierarchy in liberalism is heightened by the fact that hierarchical processes of purification generate categories of excluded people who then use the categories on which their exclusion is based to self-identify, mobilize, and claim democratic rights. Purifications are bent to the service of democracy. This strategy of the oppressed is necessarily double-edged: political mobilizations based on categories of exclusion have historically made great gains (e.g., women's suffrage; the dismantling of Jim Crow segregation and apartheid); but they do so at the risk of reinforcing precisely the categories that were the bases of exclusion. A recurrent question for excluded people who mobilize politically is: What are we aiming for in the long term? Do we want a society in which categorical exclusions no longer exist (i.e., a society in which our political movement no longer serves a purpose)? Or do we want a society in which our difference continues to be recognized and perhaps given institutional space, but in a nonhierarchical and democratic way? This dilemma is part of the tensions inherent in liberalism.

Hierarchy always tends to utilize difference in the service of purification and more hierarchy, whether the difference comes from above or below. A truly democratic society, in which difference is only a process of endless proliferation, can only be achieved when hierarchy itself is banished.

Mixture and Democracy in Latin America

Latin American countries dramatize clearly the way mixture has been claimed to have a strong affinity with democracy, usually in terms of the potential of mestizaje to undermine racial hierarchy, often connected to the fact that mestizaje implies intimate relations and produces kinship. Latin American countries also dramatize the ambivalent meanings attached to mixture, which can simultaneously reenact hierarchy, even between sexual partners and within the family. As we will see, claims made about mestizaje and democracy do not always confine themselves to ideas about racial democracy, but refer to "social democracy" or simply "democracy." It may be that the commentators involved prefer to avoid the word race, but as they frequently use racialized terminology, it is likely that, for them, "democracy" and "racial democracy" are closely allied concepts. The broader purchase of the claims is worth noting: mestizaje is seen as a solvent for hierarchy in general.

The link between mixture and democracy was often forged in the middle to late nineteenth and early twentieth centuries, when Latin American elites bent on nation-building had to contend, on the one hand, with their majority black, indigenous, and mixed populations, and, on the other, with Euro-American theories, which argued that these populations were biologically as well as culturally inferior and that mixture was often a degenerative process. Latin American elites reacted in varying ways (Appelbaum, Macpherson, and Rosemblatt 2003; Stepan 1991; Wade 2010). One was to attempt the racial whitening of the population through immigration, allied with the belief that "superior white blood" would improve the mix, rather than itself suffer degeneration. Another was to declare that the new Latin American nations had embraced modern republican racial fraternity—much more so than the supposed beacons of democracy in North America and Europe, at least in the mid-nineteenth century (Lasso 2007; Sanders 2014). A related idea was to valorize mixture itself as a positive process, with the potential to generate physical vigor, cultural richness, and social democracy—albeit with a helping hand from projects of social hygiene and education. The last position gained ground in some countries in the early to mid-twentieth century, as the figure of the mestizo was resignified from being the illegitimate plebeian, or perhaps upstart, of colonial times, to embodying the dreams of national honor, of development and progress, of continental solidarity, and of modern democracy—contra the exclusivist purities of the global North. However, this glorification of the mestizo rarely divested itself completely of the superior value attached to whiteness; this meant that the possibility of linking mixture to democracy was always in tension with racial hierarchy.

In Colombia, as early as 1861, the writer and politician José María Samper optimistically wrote that "this marvelous work of the mixture of races . . . should produce a wholly democratic society, a race of republicans, representatives simultaneously of Europe, Africa and Colombia, and which gives the New World its particular character" (Samper 1861: 299). This did not stop him from characterizing indigenous people as "semi-savage," "of primitive race," and "patient but stupid" (1861: 88), nor from demeaning in racist terms the black boatmen (*bogas*) of the Magdalena River whom he encountered on his travels, whose "savage features, fruit of the crossing of two or three different races" betrayed minds for which "the law [is] an incomprehensible confusion, civilization a thick fog and the future, like the past and the present are confounded in the same situation of torpor, indolence and brutality"; these people "had of humanity almost only the external form and the primitive needs and forces." Typically of a liberal mind, Samper did not despair entirely of the black people he met, some of whom seemed to him "to form an energetic race, of excellent instincts and capable of becoming an estimable and progressive people with the stimulus of education, industry and good institutions," but the black boatmen he met earned his particular disapproval, and he thought they would "only be able to regenerate themselves after many years of civilizing work, fruit of the invasion of these jungles by agriculture and commerce" (Samper 1980: 88–94). In abstract terms, mixture should produce democracy; in practice, it could produce a barely human type, like the boatmen, product of the mixture of "races debased by tyranny," with little or no European input.

Later, another Colombian politician and writer, López de Mesa, took a similarly ambivalent stance on mestizaje. In one 1927 essay written for church and government officials, he said "the mixture of impoverished bloods and inferior cultures [by which he meant African and indigenous people] brings about unadaptable products" (cited by Restrepo 1988: 380). In another essay, written for general consumption, he said optimistically that Colombians were "Africa, America, Asia and Europe all at once, without grave spiritual perturbation," and that the country was no longer "the old democracy of equal citizenship only for a conquistador minority, but a complete one, without distinctions of class or lineage" (López de Mesa 1970 [1934]: 14, 7). Like Samper, López de Mesa thought indigenous and black people occupied lower rungs on the racial ladder, so that mixture with them was deleterious, yet he still thought mixture in general held democratic potential.

López de Mesa contributed a speech to a 1920 conference organized by a student association in Bogotá to debate the question of race in Colombia, the proceedings of which were published under the title *Los problemas de la raza en Colombia* (The problems of [the] race in Colombia) (Jiménez López et al. 1920).[2] In his text, López de Mesa makes repeated reference to "our love for democracy" and the "incessant desire" of "*la raza [colombiana]*" for "culture, liberty and democracy." Although he does not make an explicit causal link between mixture and democracy, it is understood that la raza is a mixed one—this is precisely the "problem" under debate. And the two concepts are often juxtaposed. Thus the "rapid mestizoization" of the people of the Antioquia region of northwestern Colombia is immediately followed by the claim that they have "the most democratic government in the world" (Muñoz Rojas 2011: 160–61, 181, 201). Another contributor, Jorge Bejarano, was more explicit: "What is the result of this variety of races? Politically [it is] the advent of a democracy, because it is proven that the promiscuity of races, in which the element socially considered inferior predominates, results in the reign of democracies" (Muñoz Rojas 2011: 245). Here, democracy results from a process of mixture powered from below and not controlled by the elite.

In Mexico, especially after the Revolution (1910–20), mestizaje was promoted as a means to national unity and a way—always double-edged, however—to erase old hierarchies of race (Moreno Figueroa and Saldívar 2015). The intellectual and author Andrés Molina Enríquez (1868–1940) placed his faith in the "mestizo liberals" as the ones who could modernize and indeed create the nation, a task the indigenous peoples and the *criollos* (Mexican-born descendants of the Spanish conquistadors) were not suited to, but which the mestizos, with their "egalitarian" tendencies, could achieve (Molina Enríquez 2004 [1909]: 42). Such a view by no means dispensed with racial hierarchy in the sense that Molina Enríquez saw mestizos as a "race," which was "inferior" in its inception, even if superior to the criollos and the *indígenas* (indigenous people) in its long-term capacity to forge the nation. But mixture was clearly linked to progress, equality, and modernity.

A similar view of mestizaje as holding the potential to dissolve racial hierarchy was held by the politician and intellectual José Vasconcelos (1882–1959), who, like Molina Enríquez, was nevertheless guided by the racial hierarchies and eugenic theories of his day. He foresaw the global dominance of a fifth "cosmic race," a mestizo race, additional to the existing four races, which would disappear, having had their day. The cosmic race was the "mission of the Ibero-American race": because of its history, Latin America was the crucible for racial democracy. The heroes of Latin American independence had declared "the equality of all men by natural right [and] the social and civic equality of whites, blacks and indios"; in this, they formulated the "transcendental mission assigned to that region of the globe: the mission of uniting [all] people ethnically and spiritually." Vasconcelos stated that global history was divided into three stages—material/warlike, intellectual/political, and spiritual/aesthetic. Together, this made "five races and three stages, that is, the number eight, which in Pythagorean Gnosticism represents the ideal of the equality of all men." This future of racial mixture and equality did not prevent Vasconcelos from seeing black people as a "lower type" of the species who would be gradually absorbed by a "superior type": blacks would be able to "redeem themselves . . . through voluntary extinction, [as] the uglier breeds will gradually give way to the more beautiful" (Vasconcelos 1997 [1925]: 59, 72, 79). Alongside this expression of racial hierarchy, the overall link between mixture and democracy was central to his approach. In the prologue to the 1948 edition of his book, Vasconcelos noted that UNESCO had recently "proclaimed the necessity of abolishing all racial discrimination and educating all men in [conditions of] equality," and he saw this as a return by dominant powers to "the recognition of the legitimacy of mixture and interracial fusion," which Vasconcelos had lobbied for twenty years earlier, with Latin America in mind as an exemplar (1997 [1925]: 43).

In the first half of the twentieth century, the Mexican government used claims that the country was a racial democracy as a way of taking the moral high ground in relation to the United States and its racially segregated society. An 1890 proposal for a new immigration law declared that Mexico was based on "the dogma of universal fraternity; believing that racial differences in the human family do not establish inequality before the law, all races . . . have the doors of the country open to them." The immigration law passed in 1909 restated this principle of "the most complete equality of all countries and races," noting that, although the law followed the U.S. example in some respects, the United States was "famously different" from Mexico, which was more racially tolerant. In practice, there was pressure from various sectors in Mexico to restrict Chinese immigration; anti-Asian racism was common (as was anti-Semitism). By 1927, a presidential decree banned the labor immigration of Middle Easterners. The rationale for these discriminations was partly economic, but also partly eugenic: Chinese and Arabs were seen as inferior additions to the Mexican mix, likely to provoke degeneration. Despite this, the Mexican government insisted that, because Mexico was based on mixture, it could not be racist: in 1933 the Foreign Ministry denied that the government had "any racial or class prejudice, all the more because the great Mexican family comes from the crossing of distinct races." Not mixing was deemed in itself evidence of racism: Mennonites and Jews were seen as minorities who refused to mix, believing themselves superior; their immigration was considered problematic and subjected to restriction, often through confidential directives to consulates that also restricted Asians, Arabs, and blacks, among others. During World War II, Mexican government protestations of antiracism gained force, attacking Nazism but also U.S. racial segregation. By criticizing U.S. racism against Mexican immigrants, the government effectively opposed an image of Mexican mestizo racial democracy to one of racial hierarchy. World War II and its aftermath were a time of global antiracist pronouncements (see chapter 2), and Mexico helped shape the discourse by emphasizing the role of mixture in fomenting democracy (FitzGerald and Cook-Martín 2014: 225–26, 227, 236, 251).

Brazil is probably the country best known for acting as a counterpoint to racism, especially of the U.S. variety. Brazilians and North Americans alike counterposed the idea of a Brazilian racial fraternity to the racial segregation of the U.S. South (Seigel 2009). In the 1920s, there was a public debate about proposals to create a statue in Rio de Janeiro commemorating the Mãe Preta (black mother) of slave times. Diverse opinions were expressed—for some the mother figure represented black resistance, for others the authority of the white-led patriarchal family—but the idea of racial fraternity was common ground. Washington Luis, elected president in 1926, wrote: "Fraternity, the sentiment that unites all men as brothers, with no distinctions whatsoever, will be the work of the South American peoples . . . [and] in South America, Brazil is the country foreordained to make this fraternity real" (cited by Seigel 2009: 217). Like Vasconcelos, Luis saw Latin America as destined to usher in racial democracy to the rest of the world. The statue was "conceived as a performance on a global stage to demonstrate Brazil's racial harmony and spiritual superiority." Its supporters all "rejected the notion that racial mixture in Brazil had weakened the nation . . . [and] championed this history as the nucleus of Brazilian moral superiority" (Seigel 2009: 207, 208). It is notable that the idea of racial *fraternity* depended on the image of a black *woman*. This encapsulates the way racial hierarchy articulates with sexism in Latin American: the existence of racial hierarchy is sublimated by the oppression of women, which involves dynamics of intimacy and love, as well as control and exploitation (see chapter 8).

In the 1930s, these ideas were developed influentially by Gilberto Freyre in his writing on Brazilian history and the formation of the nation. In his classic work, *Casa-grande e senzala*, first published in 1933 and translated into English in 1946 as *The Masters and the Slaves*, he wrote,

> The fact of the matter is that miscegenation and the interpenetration of cultures—chiefly European, Amerindian and African culture—together with the possibilities and opportunities for rising in the social scale that in the past have been open to slaves, individuals of the colored races and even heretics: the possibility and the opportunity of becoming free men and, in the official sense, whites and Christians . . . the fact is that that all these things have tended to mollify the interclass and interracial antagonisms developed under an aristocratic economy. (Freyre 1986: xiv)

In his view, the "social effects of miscegenation," the contributors to it, and its *mestiço* products all "exerted a powerful influence for social democracy in Brazil," with the result that "perhaps nowhere is the meeting, intercommunication, and harmonious fusion of diverse or, even, antagonistic cultural traditions occurring in so liberal a way as it is in Brazil" (1986: xxx, 78). Although Freyre did not use the term *racial democracy* at this time, others concerned with race in Brazil began to use it by the 1940s: the image of Brazil as racial fraternity had become official and was actively promoted as part of the nationalist policies of the Getúlio Vargas administration (1930–45) and during the military dictatorship (1964–85). The term *racial democracy* was also given currency in publications arising out of the large-scale research project on Brazilian race relations sponsored by UNESCO in the 1950s (Guimarães 2007). This was undertaken in the antiracist climate of the post–World War II Western world, symbolized by the UNESCO declarations on race, which attacked any scientific basis for racism (see chapter 1). As in the past, Brazil appeared here as a counterpoint to the United States, and as an example of a place where the problems of racism were relatively minor—an image not fully endorsed by the results of the UNESCO studies (Fontaine 1985; Maio 2001; Wade 2010: 52–59). Freyre himself continued to espouse ideas linking mixture to racial democracy. In the 1970s, he developed the concept of a *moreno* (brown) "meta-race": "The concept of meta-race [is] linked to that of brownness, as a Brazilian response—beyond sectarian or archaic racist ideologisms—to whitenesses, blacknesses and yellownesses" (cited by Hofbauer 2006: 252).

Mixture, Multiculturalism, and Democracy

The idea of a Latin American racial democracy has been severely dented by studies documenting the realities of racial inequality and racism, first in Brazil from the 1970s and subsequently in other countries, including Colombia and more incipiently Mexico.[3] Studies have also highlighted the powerful elements of hierarchy that pervade ideas about mestizaje and that denigrate blackness and indigeneity (De la Cadena 2000; Hale 1996; Wade 2005b). Latin America dramatized for the world the fact that racism can coexist with intimacy across race lines—which in the long term became blurred by those intimacies—and can exist within the families that those intimacies establish (Hordge-Freeman 2015; Moreno Figueroa 2008).

Partly in reaction to these studies, a wave of multiculturalist reform has swept Latin America since about 1990, recognizing indigenous and, to a lesser extent, Afro-descendant identities and rights, although not always explicitly recognizing the existence of racism as an issue (Hooker 2009; Sieder 2002b; Wade 2010: ch. 6). I explore this in more detail for Brazil, Colombia, and Mexico in chapter 4, and we will see there and in later chapters that multiculturalist reform does not necessarily dispense with mestizaje as a set of ideas and practices that enact the mestizo nation and the mestizo individual. Ideas about mestizaje, rather than simply holding up the image of a homogeneous nation, have always had room for commentary on black and indigenous people (in the past usually seen as inferior inputs to the mix) and on white people (usually seen as a redemptive force): venerating the mestizo did not exclude denigrating blackness and indigeneity, nor valorizing whiteness; in fact, it depended on these opposing valuations. In the twentieth century in some countries, ideologies of *indigenismo* and, incipiently, *negrismo* created conditional spaces for indigenous and black peoples; the ideologies cast them (or idealized versions of them), in primitivist mode, as embodying admirable values.

More significant in creating a space for indigeneity and blackness, and in the turn to multiculturalism, was the role of black and indigenous social movements in struggling for recognition and rights. Although such movements came into their own from the 1960s on, they built on long histories of resistance and struggle by black and indigenous people, often mobilizing around the identities that formed the basis of their exclusion from equality. As with such mobilizations from below, during the nineteenth century the question emerged of the long-term objective—integration into a liberal mixed society versus continuing separateness but on equal terms—and was answered in varied ways (e.g., Helg 1995; Sanders 2004). The question itself was a product of the dilemmas of liberalism, which put equality, democracy, and inclusive mixture in tension with hierarchy, inequality, and exclusive purification.

Multiculturalism, as an approach in liberal democracies, is one way to address these dilemmas (Barry 2000; Lentin 2004; Lentin and Titley 2011; Modood 2007; Modood and Werbner 1997). Whether official state policy or community-based endeavor, multiculturalism is based on the concept of separate, bounded "cultures"—notionally "pure," although this language is rarely used—each existing as a constituent element of the wider society, each having equal rights to respect and recognition. It holds out the promise that these notionally separate cultures can interact and mix on equal and inclusive terms, thus increasing democracy and perhaps resulting in an endless and nonhierarchical proliferation of hybrids. However, multiculturalism stands accused of merely masking inequality by pretending different cultures are of equal standing, rather than acknowledging the hierarchies of race and class that attach to cultural difference. The idea of the equal interaction among different cultures is undermined by the hierarchical ordering of difference. In addition, multiculturalism entrenches these hierarchies with its objectification of cultural difference and the encouragement of exclusive behavior in the policing of cultural boundaries, whether from inside or outside. This has opened multiculturalism to cutting critiques about essentialism, reification, divisiveness, and exclusive purifications. Multiculturalism's defenders argue that it can highlight inequality by pointing to its structural dimensions and colonial roots, explicitly recognizing racism and providing the basis for reparative justice. They say the recognition of difference does not necessarily lead to exclusive behavior. They maintain that multiculturalism can also create space for minorities to defend themselves and publicize their disadvantaged position; minorities can take the categorical distinctions used to discriminate against them and retread them for purposes of political solidarity and mobilization.

In Latin America, multiculturalism in theory neutralizes or even reverses existing valuations—black and indigenous groups are at least equal in value to mestizo and white (and may even be considered superior in some respects). But the debates about how multiculturalism works in practice show it cannot escape the frictive tension between democracy/mixture and hierarchy/purity that affects liberal political orders. Like mestizaje, multiculturalism is a variation played on the theme of sameness and difference, and it does not evade the play of power that always operates between these two (Hale 2002; Speed 2005).

Alongside these changes toward multiculturalism, Latin American mestizaje continues to be seen in some circles as an antidote to racism and racial divisions (see Hooker 2014; Jiménez Román 2007; Wade 2004). Indeed, mixture may be cast as a way to contest what some people see as the counterproductive essentialist and absolutist identities encouraged by multiculturalism. For example, the historian Gary Nash uncovers the "hidden history" of mixture in the United States, which existed despite its mestizo products being subsumed into the strict categories of U.S. racial segregation: a possible "mixed-race American [i.e., U.S.] republic" was blocked by "prejudice and violence"—which implies the frankly incredible corollary that mixed-race republics south of the border somehow managed to escape racial prejudice and violence. Far from being a solution to racialized hierarchy, multiculturalism simply fuels the "interethnic and interracial tensions that give more powerful groups opportunities to manipulate these divisions." "Racial absolutism [is] the enemy of mestizaje," and "racial blending is undermining the master idea that race is an irreducible marker among diverse peoples" (Nash 1995: 960, 961). In his view, "only through hybridity—not only in physical race crossing but in our minds as a shared pride in and identity with hybridity—can our nation break the 'stranglehold that racialist hermeneutics has over cultural identity'" (1995: 962, citing Klor de Alva).

In Mexico, novelist Carlos Fuentes, in his book *El espejo enterrado*, also gives a version of this argument, highlighting the supposed exceptionalism of Latin America: "Is there anyone better prepared than us, the Spaniards, the Hispanic Americans, and the Hispanics in the United States, to deal with this central theme of encounter with the other in the conditions of modernity of the coming century? We are indigenous people, blacks, Europeans, but above all, mestizos. . . . That is to say: Spain and the New World are centers where multiple cultures meet, centers of incorporation and not exclusion" (Fuentes 1992: 379).

The Chicana poet, scholar, and activist Gloria Anzaldúa is well known for her portrayal of the "new *mestiza*" as a figure who inhabits the ambiguous border zone between the United States and Mexico, and between racial binaries; the mestiza's liminality and mixedness has the potential to unsettle boundaries and hierarchies (Anzaldúa 1987). Within the United States, many commentators have observed that the simple black–white binary that has dominated racial classifications—although other categories such as Native American and Asian have historically been vital as well—is being increasingly complicated by the growing presence of Latinos and Asians. This has led to a process of "browning" that may, according to some, be bringing the United States into a convergence with Brazil, as the latter also changes toward a clearer political division between black and white (Bonilla-Silva 2004; Daniel 2006; Skidmore 1993). Browning—the product and, more importantly, the acknowledgment of mixture—can also represent a kind of liberation: according to the writer Richard Rodriguez, recognizing the brownness of the United States is a belated "last discovery": brown is the "complete freedom of substance and narration," and it "marks a reunion of peoples, an end to ancient wanderings . . . [which will] create children of a beauty, perhaps a harmony, previously unknown" (Rodriguez 2002: xi, xiii). This reference to the aesthetic appeal of brownness is strongly reminiscent of Vasconcelos.

Beyond regional notions of mestizaje, the idea of mixture or *hybridity*—a term usually used to connote cultural processes, but which inevitably retains its biological origins—has been often considered in the social sciences and humanities as a force undermining hierarchies and promoting cosmopolitan tolerance and democracy (Kapchan and Strong 1999; Wade 2005a; Young 1995). This is evident in the work of Caribbean commentators such as Edouard Glissant on *créolité*, a process of mixture that involves "a non-hierarchical principle of unity [and] a relation of equality" (Murdoch 2013: 875; see also Tate and Law 2015: 53–60). The work of Stuart Hall, Homi Bhabha, and Gayatri Spivak has been interpreted as suggesting that "at the broadest level of conceptual debate there seems to be a consensus over the utility of hybridity as antidote to essentialist subjectivity," and thus as a challenge to hierarchies that depend on such essentialisms (Papastergiadis 1997: 273). For Gilroy, identities that have formed through diasporic processes of movement and exchange are "creolized, syncretized, hybridized and chronically impure cultural forms" (Gilroy 2004: 129), and, as such, they pose a challenge to what he calls the "camp thinking" that separates people into rigid groups and categories, often based on race or ethnicity. Gilroy's project is to encourage "a larger set of loyalties: to humanity and to the idea of a world stripped of racial hierarchy," and to act in solidarity with a "new planetary network in pursuit of a more thoroughgoing democracy than was offered earlier in color-coded forms" (2004: xii–xiii). All these people remark on the dual aspect of mixture, which means that it can work in conservative mode to reinforce hierarchy and notions of purity, or it can operate in a more radical, rhizomic mode to undermine boundaries and hierarchy, increasing democracy. But they choose to highlight its disruptive potential.

Critiques of these optimistic visions of mixture and hybridity look at this duality in a different way. Hybridity and mixture may have destabilizing and unsettling—democratizing—potential. But this potential is insistently hampered by the other side of the coin of mixture and hybridity: in contexts of hierarchy, they also inevitably entrain concepts of purity and wholeness, as the notional bounded antecedents that give rise to the mixture that crosses the boundaries that would not otherwise exist. The imaginary of mixture persistently invokes a founding notion of relative purity, or of original ingredients. Against this, rhizomic models of hybridity emphasize that any mixture can be understood as a mixture of anterior mixtures. This is the logic of the cognatic kinship that acts as a (usually unspoken) model for these theorizations of hybridity: parents, each of whom is a mixture of their own parents, give rise to a child who is also a mixture. There is an endless proliferation of difference: children are similar to their parents, but also always different (Strathern 1992: 14). But therein lies the duality: mixture is meaningless, because all mixtures are generated from mixtures, so there is no origin and there is only the proliferation of difference; and mixture is meaningful, because the concept depends on the combination of identifiable wholes or origins (Kapchan and Strong 1999; Wade 2005a; Young 1995: 25–26).

This duality has long been evident to theorists acquainted with Latin America, who are aware of the potential of ideologies of mestizaje as both liberatory and yet host to virulent racism. Mestizaje simultaneously undoes purities, yet recreates them; it unsettles racial hierarchies, but reproduces them; it foments democracy, and still depends on inequalities. The possibility of marrying across racial boundaries and creating racial diversity within a single family blurs stark racial hierarchy by articulating it with sexual relations, which means people of the oppressed category living with and loving people of the oppressor category, a practice that also tends to blur the racialized dimensions of both those categories. But this possibility provides an arena in which to reenact boundaries and differences within the marriage and the family. The idea of a common mestizo identity for the nation creates a ground for racial democracy, but simultaneously provides a space within which blackness, indigeneity, and whiteness are hierarchically valued. Part of that valuation includes relegating black and indigenous peoples, at least in their "purer" forms, to the peripheries of the nation and associating them with the past, outside of modernity and development (Hordge-Freeman 2015; Moreno Figueroa 2010, 2012; Radcliffe 1990; Stutzman 1981; Wade 2009: 158–59). In fact, an important part of the way the tensions between equality and hierarchy are mediated in ideas and practices of mestizaje is by defining relatively pure nodes of indigeneity and blackness and locating them in the past; this temporal othering allows racial hierarchy to coexist with the democracy of mestizo modernity. In sum, then, seeing Latin American–style mixture as a model for facilitating racial democracy is a deeply problematic position, as it only focuses on one dimension of the inherent duality of mestizaje and of mixture more generally (Seigel 2009; Tate and Law 2015: 145; Wade 2004).

Structure of the Book

In chapter 1, I argue that, like liberalism and mestizaje, human population genetics has been characterized by a tension between purity and mixture, which has run through its attempts to understand human diversity; in the genetic study of Latin American populations, that tension is especially evident, and is part of what constitutes Latin America as an interesting site for global genomic science. I then address the issue of the "relation" between "science" and "society," outlining a perspective that avoids this dualism and sees scientific and political practices and ideas as elements in a complex assemblage, rather than as two interacting domains; I explore the concept of topology as a way to characterize the networks involved in the assemblage.

In chapter 2, I look at genetic studies carried out from the 1940s to the 1970s. These focused mainly on indigenous peoples, but necessarily explored processes of mestizaje. The studies took place at a time of a global shift toward antiracism, which depended on a strict divide between biology and culture, heralded by Franz Boas in the 1930s, and which undermined the authority of the concept of race (without abolishing it altogether). This divide, so necessary to the antiracist agenda, was, however, routinely confounded in Latin American eugenics. Eugenic discourse varied in how explicit it was about race—the concept was deployed openly in Colombia and Brazil, but not in Mexico—but like eugenics elsewhere, only more so, Latin American eugenicists emphasized the role of social hygiene, as well as manipulation of biological heredity, and did so into the 1950s. A familiar discourse was established during this period of seeing the mestizo as the norm and the indigenous and black populations as distinct entities that were backward and peripheral, in need of assimilation to modernity; Europeans and whites were seen as the most desirable and advanced types.

In the blood type studies that began in the 1940s, the divide between culture and biology was again confounded insofar as cultural and biological mixture, while at one level recognized to be distinct processes not necessarily in synchrony, were, at another level, seen to go hand in hand, opposing biocultural purity to mestizaje. The concept of race itself, as a biocultural entity, continued to be used in the early part of this period; it did not disappear over time, but instead became reconfigured toward the simply biological, without, however, losing its entanglement with cultural dimensions. In any event, the interest in mixture entrained the concept of relatively pure foundational populations. This chapter gives historical depth against which to compare the genomics of the 2000s: despite the new technologies used from the late 1990s, there is a great deal of continuity in the way human diversity within the nation is presented and the social implications of mixture drawn out.

Chapters 3–7 are an extended examination of genomic science and its participation in multiculturalist assemblages in each nation, drawing on data collected during a three-year research project "Race, Genomics, and Mestizaje in Latin America."[4] The first, chapter 3, describes the changes in genetic science from the 1990s, and then outlines the shifts toward multiculturalism in Brazil, Colombia, and Mexico, highlighting the higher public profile of race in Brazil, with its state-driven, race-based affirmative action program; the conflation of racial and regional diversity in Colombia and its relatively radical multiculturalist policies; and the lower public profile of race in Mexico, where a top-down multiculturalism is organized around the classic division between indígenas and mestizos.

Chapter 4, on Colombia, starts with a look at the Great Human Expedition (1988–93), a university-based multidisciplinary initiative, led by geneticists, which coincided with the beginnings of multiculturalist reform in the country. The project sought to map the biological and cultural diversity of the nation by focusing on its peripheral—indigenous and black—populations, described as "isolated communities." These were seen as the opposite of mestizaje and thus implicitly pure (although the language of purity was not used) and in need of salvage anthropological and genetic research before mestizaje wiped out their distinctiveness. This project also reproduced the connection between region and race, which is a powerful characteristic of Colombia. Although the term race was rarely used in the publications of this project, racialized terminology was employed (negro, indígena, mestizo, and, occasionally, Caucasian). These features were particularly evident in the work of a pioneer geneticist, Emilio Yunis, who used a language of race and talked about the regional-racial fragmentation of the country, which he saw as a problem. While he thought mestizaje had historically created exclusion and oppression in Colombia, this was because it was incomplete: he also saw it as a force for future democracy and national unity.

More recent genetic studies reproduce the correspondence between racialized category and region, and even use local indigenous and black communities as proxies for parental Native American and African populations, thus linking these communities to the past. The chapter then explores the case of a regional population—the Antioqueños—described by geneticists as an isolate and as having specific genetic characteristics, a description which tallies with historical and popular descriptions of them as culturally distinctive. The chapter ends with an example from forensic genetics that clearly shows how ingrained ideas about race and region are reproduced in scientific work, despite their technical redundancy. This chapter explores key themes of the book in concrete contexts—the entanglement of the biological and the cultural (genetics and region) to enact racialized concepts of the nation, the tension between purity and mixture (isolated communities as being the opposite of mestizaje and as representative of parental populations; certain regional populations as isolates), and mestizaje as having the potential to democratize, but also to hierarchize.

Chapter 5 moves to Brazil, where multiculturalism has been much more controversial, primarily when it takes the form of policies establishing race-based quotas for admission to higher education, but also when it shapes state-driven health care programs. Critics of quotas recognize that Brazil has a very unequal society, and the democratizing aims of multiculturalist policies were not necessarily challenged—just the particular way in which the state chose to implement them, which went against the grain of Brazilian reality by emphasizing inequality of race, rather than class. A prominent critic of quotas is the geneticist Sérgio Pena, who uses genetic data to argue that race has no biological reality and therefore cannot form a basis for social policy; other critics also deploy his data to affirm the commonality of all Brazilians as mixed and to challenge the existence of a collective category of Afro-Brazilians, who are the object of affirmative action policies. Pena wants genetics to act as a mandate for social policy, entangling biology and culture in two ways: at a general level, the nonexistence of racial categories in genetic terms should mean their nonexistence in terms of social policy; yet at an individual level, DNA tests were seen as having the power to define the reality of a person's identity. Defenders of the quotas argue that biology is irrelevant to social policy, that the nonexistence of race as a genetic object does not prevent racial classifications from driving racial discrimination, and that social policy should address this.

Multiculturalist policies in the area of health provision have been less controversial because these aim to collect data using racial categories (an established census practice), sensitize health workers to issues of racism and racial difference, and involve black social movement activists in the design of health policy. The link between racial classification and access to state resources is thus less obvious than in the quota system, which individualizes this link. Overall, in Brazil, genetics has been used to challenge state multiculturalism and reassert the shared mestizo character of all Brazilians, providing the basis for an image of Brazil as a racial democracy.

The next chapter, on Mexico, focuses on the top-down, state-driven character of genomic research, channeled by a state health institute, INMEGEN (National Institute of Genomic Medicine), with a public health agenda and a goal of genomic sovereignty (Mexican control over Mexico's genetic resources, seen as unique). Issues of multiculturalism were not directly addressed in genomic research, but were tacitly implied in the representation of the country as mainly mestizo, with a defined number of indigenous communities located within the nation as bounded units. Genomic sampling practices enacted indigenous communities as bounded and relatively pure, and assumed that other subjects were mestizos. Evidence of genetic mixture among indigenous people did not mean they were mestizos, because cultural criteria were used to define the mestizo/indigenous boundary. But this boundary also shaped the way genetic data were collected and interpreted, and the genetic data could then be seen to reaffirm the cultural boundary. In other words, Mexican genomics practice reiterated the basic elements of indigenismo (a state practice that venerated the indigenous past and tried to protect present-day indigenous populations, while also guiding them toward assimilation) and mestizaje (which saw Mexico as built on mixture and the assimilation of difference into a shared mestizoness). Unlike Brazil, where the basic character of the nation was up for discussion—should there be separate racial categories or not?—in Mexico there was a broad consensus on what the nation looked like: a dominant mestizo majority (suffering from problems of obesity and diabetes), with isolated indigenous groups (whose genetic inheritance was possibly part of the reason for mestizos' health problems).

Chapter 7 sums up the preceding four chapters by looking at Colombia, Brazil, and Mexico in comparative perspective and assessing the continuities between the earlier and later periods described in chapters 2 and 3. Common to all three countries and both time periods is the reiteration with genetic data of the image of a mestizo nation, with relatively pure original components—black and indigenous communities—encysted in the national territory, and associated with the past and the periphery. This is the way the tension between democracy and hierarchy has traditionally been handled in Latin America: it allows the coexistence of these opposite elements by locating the subordinate categories outside of modernity.

The idea that a highly racialized society gives rise to a highly racialized genomics—which could be a conclusion drawn from focusing on the United States alone—is nuanced by the material from Brazil, Colombia, and Mexico: in Brazil, arguably the most racialized of the three, genetics has been deployed to contest that racialization and genetics itself is more deracialized than in Colombia, where race has a lower institutional profile than in Brazil. The dynamic tension between purity and mixture is played out in different ways in each country, with mixture being attributed a democratizing power and also being defined in relation to (relative) purities, which symbolize hierarchy and inequality.

Chapter 8 turns to the gendered aspect of mestizaje, exploring narratives which describe European men having sex with indigenous and African women. Genomics addresses this with data about mitochondrial DNA (mtDNA, inherited via the maternal line) and Y-chromosome DNA (inherited by men from their fathers). The fact that many mestizos have African-origin and Amerindian-origin mtDNA in their genomes is taken as proof of interbreeding between European men and indigenous and African women at some time in the distant past, and this evidence of early mestizaje is used to promote antiracism. Yet the data paint a picture in which European men are given sexual agency and assumed to be dominant, while indigenous and African women are seen as passive recipients, and black and indigenous men (and European women) are placed in the background. This highlights the fact that mixture always involves sexual relations, which automatically places family and kinship at the center, but the democratizing and inclusive potential entailed by locating questions of racial difference in the context of family relations is undermined by the fact that families also provide a context in which racial difference and exclusion can be dramatized and accentuated.

Chapter 9 uses data drawn from focus groups and interviews with "ordinary" members of the public (in practice, mainly university students), who had little vested interest in DNA ancestry testing, although a subset of them were volunteer participants in an international genomic research project that included a DNA ancestry test. These people were often motivated by "curiosity" about their ancestry. The aim of this chapter is to assess whether and to what extent people's understanding of ancestry, race, health, and diversity in the nation is being transformed by the public presence of a genomic idiom in which to talk about these things. The conclusion is not only that people assimilate new data about genetic ancestry to existing ideas about genetics, which have long formed part of the basic conceptual tool kit of many people in Latin America, but also that they tend to see the data as confirming things they already knew or thought. Genomic data simply provide an additional idiom to talk about things such as mestizo, black, indigenous, white, European, African, race, nation, population, ancestry, and heredity, which are all resilient categories that have circulated around science, politics, education, and everyday knowledge for a long time.

1 · PURITY AND MIXTURE

1

....

Purity and Mixture in Human Population Genetics

In this chapter, I argue that the life sciences' understandings of human diversity—and biological diversity more widely—have been characterized by a version of the same tension between concepts of (relative) purity and mixture that I outlined in the introduction. This may sound counterintuitive for recent biology, in which the word purity is anachronistic, but I argue that, although the word itself may not be used, an underlying concept of *relative* purity can be found in debates about how to sample populations, in which "isolates" are counterposed to "grids," and about evolution, in which "trees of life" are counterposed to "nets." In a final section, I address the question of how to conceive of "relations" between "science" and "society" in ways that might avoid an implied dualism.

It may seem that, in the nineteenth century, the concept of purity was an accepted one, principally in relation to theories about race. Young contends that the concept of hybridity, as used in recent cultural theory, "has not slipped out of the mantle of the past," in which nineteenth-century theorists of race posited pure, fixed races, which were the antecedents that produced the hybrids (Young 1995: 25). In fact, even for these theorists, the "pure, fixed race" was an ideal type, not observable in reality, but instead inferred from the multiplicity of mixtures that scientists confronted in the present, which were shaped by "chance, variation, migration, intermixture and changing environments" (William Z. Ripley, cited by Stepan 1982: 62). For Nott and Gliddon, authors of *Types of Mankind* (1854), a racial type could "outlive its language, history, religion, customs and recollections"; it was an underlying and fixed structure, a kind of purity. But they also recognized that contemporary populations were shaped by "climate, mixture of races, invasion of foreigners, progress of civilization, or other known influences," which meant the underlying type was an abstraction that had to be inferred from the observable diversity produced by various processes of mixture (cited by Banton 1987: 41).

At this time and into the early twentieth century, soft theories of inheritance held sway. These proposed that the physical substance passed on through the mechanisms of heredity could be shaped by the environment within a single generation, implying that racial type was not fixed, but had to be maintained through constant regulation. For example, a European's racial status—understood as a biocultural constitution in which the moral and the physical were entangled—could be altered by the influence of a tropical climate and cultural environment (Stoler 1995: ch. 4; 2002: ch. 3, ch. 4). Purity was not a simple matter: it existed in a precarious relationship with mixture (Wade 2015: 76–78). The same was true for animal breeding: the notion of pedigree was based on purity, and breeders controlled the purity of their breeds and took care to avoid "mongrelization." Yet new pedigrees could also be founded by intentional and controlled cross-breeding, and pedigrees could be reinvigorated by the careful introduction of wild strains. Not surprisingly, disputes abounded about the purity or otherwise of the pedigree of particular animals. The concept of pure pedigree existed in constant tension with the concept of mixture. The former could not do without the latter; the latter made little sense without the former. The key was in the regulation of mixture, which entailed the hierarchical evaluation of different types. Unwanted mixture—with animals deemed of inferior type— was to be avoided (Ritvo 1997: ch. 3).

Populations and Isolates

After World War II and in the wake of Nazi theories of race and eugenics— which had been critiqued by some U.S. and European scientists, including German ones, from the 1930s (Barkan 1992; Lipphardt 2012)—there was a broad turn toward antiracism in science and society (see chapter 2). This involved an attack on the idea of racial hierarchy and a discrediting of the racial science that had legitimated hierarchy, but it involved an ambivalent and uneven challenge to the concept of biological race as a way of describing human diversity. The great critic of the "fallacy of race," Ashley Montagu, wrote that "in the biological sense there do, of course, exist races of mankind"—he identified the four distinctive "divisions" of Negroid, Australoid, Caucasoid, and Mongoloid—while also emphasizing the characteristically human history of migration and hybridization, and highlighting that these races were all "much mixed and of exceedingly complex descent" (Montagu 1942: 2–5). Ideas of pure races were put into question: the 1951 UNESCO statement, "The Nature of Race and Race Differences," drafted by life scientists, said, "There is no evidence for the existence of so-called 'pure' races" (UNESCO 1952: 14). But race remained as a way of describing human diversity, understood as a dynamic product of evolutionary processes and migrations, which could be appreciated in terms of statistical variations (Reardon 2005). Thus the earlier 1950 UNESCO statement, "The Race Question," said that "the term 'race' designates a group or population characterized by some concentrations, relative as to frequency and distribution, of hereditary particles (genes) or physical characters" (UNESCO 1950), and the influential geneticist Theodosius Dobzhansky said that "race differences are objectively ascertainable biological phenomena" (Livingstone and Dobzhansky 1962). However, there was also a tendency to drop the tainted terminology of race and talk instead of "populations": "Humans were no longer divided into races with typical traits, but instead into populations that differed in allelic frequencies" (Lipphardt 2013: 57). Populations could be large—and coterminous with the classic races. Or they could be small and more local—not dissimilar from the many subraces and racial variants identified by previous racial scientists, such as John Beddoe in his book *The Races of Britain* (1862) or William Z. Ripley in *The Races of Europe* (1899).

Alongside this shift toward a dynamic view of human diversity, driven by the convergence of evolutionary theory and the empirical study of genetic variation, including the study of blood type systems (see chapter 2), there was a continuing concern with studying the genetics of "isolated" populations and endogamous groups—which often turned out to be minority indigenous or ethnic groups, located at the bottom of colonial and/or national political hierarchies and in the geographical peripheries of the nation. The construct of the isolate—or the endogamous community, the breeding unit, or the reproductive community—derives directly from evolutionary theory, which posits that local populations biologically evolve within their local environment (through natural and sexual selection, genetic drift, founder effects, and endogamic mating), thus creating a dynamic relationship between geography and genetics (Nash 2015: 21–25). Scientists thought this process could be observed best in a population that seemed relatively isolated in a reproductive sense. Among humans, such reproductive "isolation" can be caused by environmental barriers (rivers, mountains, seas, etc.), but also by cultural factors, such as language, religion, class, marriage rules, and so on. This meant that human isolates did not have to be geographically isolated; they could also be, for example, religious or cultural groups that had strong endogamic tendencies. The population isolate figured in genetic science as a kind of natural laboratory. Postwar genetics institutes, such as the Cancer Research Centre in Bombay, the Institute for the Study of Human Variation at Columbia University, and the Laboratory of Human Genetics in Paraná, Brazil, shared a "preoccupation on the empirical and conceptual level . . . [with] 'endogamous groups,' 'isolates,' 'inbreeding' and 'consanguinity'" (Lipphardt 2013: 58–63). Not surprisingly, many of these isolates—for example, Basques and Australian Aborigines— had been the focus of scientific attention in the past, but now they were being studied using genetic techniques. In the United States, Native Americans were likewise considered to be scientifically interesting isolates that could shed light on human evolution, history, and "race" (Iverson 2007). The study of "isolates" was thought by geneticists at the 1950 Cold Spring Harbor Symposium in Quantitative Biology to contribute to a "genetical definition of race"; isolates seen as geographically insulated from the mixings and movements caused by modernization were of particular interest—for example, Amazonian indigenous groups (Reardon 2005: 65, 67; see also Santos 2002; Santos, Lindee, and Souza 2014).

Defining an isolate was not easy, in large part because geneticists were also aware that movement and mixing were the norm among humans. But isolates could still be defined for genetic purposes, and in relative terms: human populations were rarely completely isolated for long periods, but they could be considered isolated enough for long enough to make them genetically interesting (Lipphardt 2012). To determine whether a given population could be considered an isolate, geneticists had to depend on historians, ethnographers, demographers, and the self-perceptions and oral histories of population members themselves (Lipphardt 2013: 66). Given the perceived importance of cultural factors in creating reproductive isolation, geneticists necessarily used cultural criteria to define the populations they sampled.

The Human Genome Diversity Project

From its inception in 1991, the Human Genome Diversity Project displayed a similar concern with isolated populations, apparently less affected by mixing and migration. As with 1950s life sciences, the underlying agenda was humanist and antiracist: the exploration of human genetic diversity was seen as a contribution to this mission, and key figures in the HGDP, such as Luigi Cavalli-

Sforza, had impeccable antiracist credentials. Yet the plan to sample indigenous peoples, who often had histories of colonial and postcolonial subordination, ran into accusations of imperialism and racism, alleging that indigenous people's blood and genes would be used—perhaps commercialized—for the benefit of others, especially in the West (Reardon 2005). A project conceived as fomenting (racial) democracy ran up against the frictions caused by the insistent tension between democracy and hierarchy. To those who foregrounded the role of hierarchy—its victims, or those who claimed to speak on their behalf—an apparently democratic mission appeared to be racist because it was targeting "isolated" populations, and this evoked "archaic racialist language and thought, clearly loaded with astonishing archaic assumptions of primordial division and purity of certain large segments of the human species" (Marks 2001: 370). Later projects that have also aimed to map global genetic diversity—such as the Genographic Project and the HapMap Project—have not run into the same level of opposition, but they have been accused of reifying, and often tacitly racializing, the populations they sample (Bliss 2009; Nash 2015; Reardon 2007; TallBear 2007).

Issues of hierarchy also insistently arose because of the way the HGDP scientists dealt ethically with sampling subjects. In response to criticisms of the project as a form of biocolonialism, they introduced what they considered to be ethically progressive, group-based informed consent protocols. But these initiatives seemed to cede to the scientists the right to define a group and to make the assumption that it was fairly homogeneous, such that a group-based consent would speak unproblematically for everyone in the group, in the same way that a sample from the population would speak genetically for the whole population (Reardon 2005, 2008). Later initiatives, such as the HapMap Project, while claiming to avoid these ethical problems by including the subjects/ objects in a collaborative and democratic way, still failed to address the underlying problem that it was the scientists and their priorities that defined what constituted a population in the first place (Reardon 2007). Concepts of isolation, purity, and homogeneity became entangled and, by evoking hierarchies of race and power, haunted projects focusing on diversity, which aimed to foment democracy and antiracism.

One issue that exercised HGDP scientists early on was the question of how to sample humans; this was a general expression of the question of how to define an isolated population. The most common technique adopted to define a population—and the one that prevailed in the HGDP and still does in most genetic studies of human diversity today—is to choose a population defined by cultural and historical criteria: an ethnic group, a nation, a regional group, and so on. The alternative is to use a random grid, paying no initial attention to social divisions (Reardon 2005: 77–78). Geneticists know that genetic variation is clinal, characterized by gradual changes in the frequency of certain genetic variants over geographical space; there are no clear boundaries because humans are a recent species that has moved across the globe in a continuous fashion—and quite quickly in evolutionary terms—and people have constantly moved and mixed with their neighbors. A grid method of sampling is best suited to capturing this clinal variation. A population-based method of sampling also reveals such clines, insofar as it is possible to see shared genetic traits that have different frequencies in different places, but it also carries an inherent logic of dividing people into populations, which then inevitably take on an appearance of homogeneity: the population in question is defined by criteria of language, culture, history, and so on, which *by definition* are implied to characterize the whole population and demarcate it from other populations, evoking some kind of separating boundary. If the population is then characterized genetically, on the basis of a sample, its members then also logically and *by definition* appear to share a genetic profile, which differentiates them from other populations.

Of course, geneticists know that all populations share the vast majority of DNA and that differences are mainly in the frequency with which certain variants appear. Yet sampling "populations" tends to mask that basic reality and create what Pálsson calls an "island model" of insular populations (Nash 2015: 80–81; Pálsson 2007: 179–81). Population becomes reified: "Merely to offer a genetic description of a population in terms of frequencies of various alleles, perhaps to make predictions about future evolutionary changes or hypothesize about past evolutionary history, assumes the existence of an entity with discernible boundaries and determinate parts" (Gannett 2003: 998). The island model glosses over the fact that the concept of population is "not epistemologically tidy," as Zack puts it: "There are no generally accepted answers to the following questions: How many generations of isolation are necessary to form a population? How large must a population be? What proportion of population members must reproduce in a given generation for it to qualify as a breeding unit? How much gene flow into or out of a population can take place before the population is a different population?" (Zack 2002: 69). In talk of populations, there is little or no explicit reference to purity—the word is at odds with everything we now know about human population genetics. But we can see the tension at work between polar concepts of purity and mixture: insular populations inevitably represent a relative degree of purity; a population-based sampling strategy inevitably tends to "purify" populations, compared to a grid-based strategy.

DNA Ancestry Testing and Parental Populations

The island model tendency is especially evident in recent techniques of DNA ancestry testing, which assign proportions of a population's or a person's genetic ancestry to notional parental populations located in the past (see chapters 3–9). Typically, these parental populations are biogeographic continental populations that indicate African, European, Asian, and Amerindian genetic ancestry, although more geographically specific assignations are also made. Such measurements of "racial mixing" go back to the 1940s (see chapter 2), but at that time it was done for populations. Advances in DNA analysis have allowed measurements of "admixture" to be made for individuals, although the margin of error is greater, and tracing a person's ancestry to specific geographical locations or ancestral populations is fraught with uncertainty. Today, the terminology of race is rarely used, having been replaced by terms such as "biogeographical ancestry" (BGA) or sometimes "ethnic origin" (Gannett 2014).

The quantification of genetic ancestral origins is done using AIMs (ancestry informative markers); these are genetic variants or alleles that are mostly widely shared among humans, but have different frequencies at different locations across the globe. Geneticists use sample populations located in key locations (such as Ibadan, Nigeria, or Beijing, China) as standard reference populations, with known frequencies of AIMs, which are used to statistically estimate the BGA proportions of a sample population or individual. Naturally, the claim that a population or a person has, say, 28 percent European ancestry logically entails the idea that it is possible for a person/population to have 100 percent European ancestry—the reference population used to calculate European BGA is by logical definition "purely" European (although this statement is never actually made). Yet most AIMs occur in all populations, so the idea of purity, though only an implicit artifact of statistical extrapolation, is completely unrealistic (Duster 2011; Fullwiley 2011; Long 2013).

The idea of a continental ancestral population reveals the same tension between purity and mixture—or admixture—that I noted above. Contemporary populations are used as a proxy for populations that existed in the distant past—for example, before major events causing population mixing, such as the conquest of the Americas and transatlantic slavery. The concept of ancestral populations derives from an evolutionary narrative in which continental-scale human diversity emerged at some notional time between the migrations out of Africa, dated about 85,000 to 100,000 years BP, which eventually led to all the world's regions being populated by 15,000 years BP, and the "moment"— usually around AD 1500 in this narrative—that the continental populations started to mix more intensively. In the intervening period, continental populations formed and became genetically differentiated by natural and sexual selection, founder effects, genetic drift, and endogamic mating shaped by geographic and cultural barriers. Some scientists argue that major population differentiation developed in the wake of tight population bottlenecks, which occurred worldwide following the devastating volcanic winter caused by the Toba eruption around 71,000 years BP (Ambrose 1998). The "general rule" is said to be that, as the Old World and Antipodes became settled, there was "little if any further inter-regional gene flow" until about 15–25,000 years ago, when humans spread across the Bering Strait and into the Americas, forming a further relatively isolated continental population (Oppenheimer 2003: 113). In this narrative, the migration, movement, and exchange that have characterized human history from the start are put in the background for this period (Hunt and Truesdell 2013: 94, 103). Contemporary populations seen as genealogically rooted in these biocontinental evolutionary formations can represent them in their pre-1500 state and elucidate the ways in which continental populations mixed together after 1500. For the purposes of ancestry testing, all the genetic changes that have taken place in the reference populations in the last five centuries are deemed irrelevant.

This view creates an image of relatively pure continental populations, which then mixed after 1500: "Admixture approaches . . . take as an assumption the reality of parental populations; that is, it is assumed that there are, or were, such 'pure' human populations" (Weiss and Lambert 2014: 17). It is relevant that genetic ancestry testing generally relies on reference populations that have been sampled in a selective way: they include only people whose grandparents were members of the population under study or were born in the locality. This avoids the statistical "noise" created by recent migrations: the technique selects people who are genealogically rooted and works to "purify" the sample genetically (see chapters 4 and 5; see also Nash 2015: 130).

But the tension between the image of relatively pure continental populations and what we know about the history of movement and mixture in human evolution is evident among geneticists themselves. Some protest the "selective de facto typological sampling and the assumption of statistically homogeneous source populations" involved in measurement of admixed ancestries (Weiss and Lambert 2014: 24). Another prominent scientist states: "Yes, there are differences in genetic variation at the continental level and one may refer to them as races. But why are continents the arbiter?" He does not answer the question directly, but poses another instead: "If humans have had this single continuous journey disobeying continental residence—and as evidence we have the continuous distribution of genetic variation across the globe, not discrete boundaries like political borders—where do we divide humanity and why?" (Chakravarti 2014a: 9). Referring to the population versus grid sampling strategies noted above, he states:

> Human evolution has always been studied with respect to such populations defined by language, geography, or cultural and physical features. Consider instead what we could decipher if we could sample a million humans (say), without regard to who they were, across a virtual grid across the world. . . . These types of global surveys of diversity have been performed for other species and may provide the first objective description of ours, bereft of race and other labels. (2014a: 11)

These same disagreements are apparent in the debates among evolutionary biologists about whether to describe the peopling of the world, or more widely evolution itself, in terms of a tree-like branching process—"the tree of life" (figure 1.1)—or the connections and flows of a reticular net (Sommer 2015). For humans, the tree metaphor assumes the spatiotemporal narrative I outlined above, in which *Homo sapiens* evolved in Africa and migrated to other regions, displacing archaic humans with little genetic exchange, and forming continental populations—the branches of the tree—between which there was insignificant gene flow (figure 1.2). After divergence from the common trunk, each branch (or indeed twig) retains a relative purity. In contrast, the metaphor of a reticulated net, or "braided stream" (figure 1.3) points to recent evidence of important gene exchange between anatomically modern and archaic humans (Neanderthals) and assumes constant and important gene flows between populations: "It's mixing all the way back" (Hawks 2015; see also Templeton 2012) (figure 1.4). As a model for the evolution of life in general, not just humans, the tree is seen as inadequate by some theorists—"the history of life cannot properly be represented as a tree" (Doolittle 1999)—because it cannot adequately encompass phenomena such as lateral gene transfer, hybrid species, and polygenomic organisms, which are now seen to be common, especially among microbes (Arnold 2008; Dupré 2015; Raoult 2010).[1] These theorists argue that reticulate or rhizomic models are truer to Darwinian principles

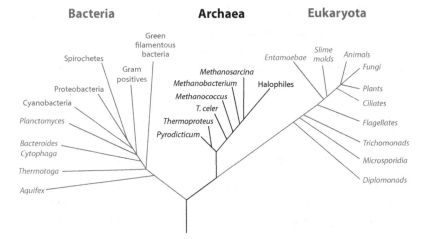

Bacteria   **Archaea**   **Eukaryota**

Green filamentous bacteria

Spirochetes

Gram positives

Proteobacteria

Cyanobacteria

Planctomyces

Bacteroides
Cytophaga

Thermotoga

Aquifex

Methanosarcina
Methanobacterium   Halophiles
Methanococcus
T. celer
Thermoproteus
Pyrodicticum

Entamoebae   Slime molds   Animals
Fungi
Plants
Ciliates
Flagellates
Trichomonads
Microsporidia
Diplomonads

FIGURE 1.1 A phylogenetic tree of living things, based on RNA data, as proposed by Carl Woese.

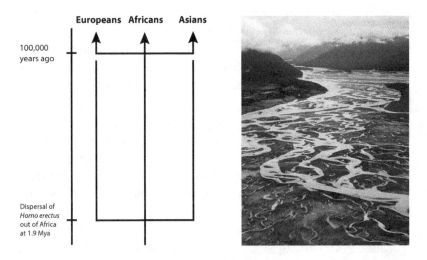

Europeans Africans Asians

100,000 years ago

Dispersal of
Homo erectus
out of Africa
at 1.9 Mya

FIGURE 1.2 The out-of-Africa replacement model of human evolution. The broken vertical lines represent the replacement of Eurasian populations by the expanding African population. (Alan Templeton, "Gene Flow, Haplotype Patterns and Modern Human Origins." *eLS.* © 2012, John Wiley & Sons, Ltd. www.els.net. By permission.)

FIGURE 1.3 A braided stream, Stikine River delta. Photo by Sam Beebe, Ecotrust.

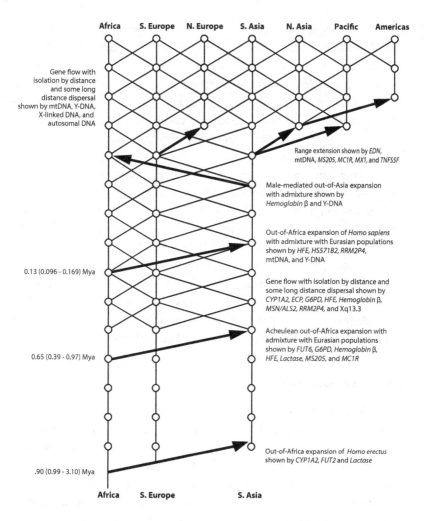

FIGURE 1.4 Reticulated net image of human evolution. Bold arrows show major expansions of human populations, with their estimated times. Thin vertical lines indicate regional descent, and thin diagonal lines show gene flow between regions. (Alan Templeton, "Gene Flow, Haplotype Patterns and Modern Human Origins." *eLS.* © 2012, John Wiley & Sons, Ltd. www.els.net. By permission.)

than the tree model that, they say, became the accepted way to visualize and spatialize the temporal processes of evolution (Grosz 2004; Helmreich 2003; Mikulak 2007), as well as family genealogies (Bouquet 1996). Tree metaphors imply a certain teleology (the "determinate natural teleology" involved in a seed-to-plant trajectory), whereas Darwinian evolution involves at best only "unbounded" or "contingent" teleology (a chance process giving rise to features that can nevertheless be partly explained by their function), or no teleology at all (Ayala 1970; Nissen 1997).

It is obvious that the continental ancestral human populations of the trunk-and-branch model often map straight onto familiar categories of race, and there has been much debate about whether genomics is resurrecting racial science (Chakravarti 2014b; Frank 2015; Hartigan 2013d; Koenig, Lee, and Richardson 2008; Krimsky and Sloan 2011). If we grasp the tension between purity and mixture in perspectives on evolution, it is not surprising that some genetic scientists today see race as a genetically meaningful concept that captures continental patterns of diversity seen as relevant for medical purposes, while others deny this, emphasizing shared DNA, genetic clines, and heterogeneity (see Bliss 2012: ch. 4; Bolnick 2008; Burchard et al. 2003).

Purity and Mixture, Hierarchy and Democracy

Geneticists are antiracist: they adhere to humanist values of racial and social democracy and inclusion (Bliss 2012). Mixture and the commonality it produces are a clear expression of these values: the fact that humans share most of their DNA has been frequently heralded as disproving the existence of race, and this, it is hoped, will foment racial equality. Yet, as with the Human Genome Diversity Project, hierarchy reappears, as it always does in liberal political orders that pursue democratic objectives and capitalist growth at the same time, and it may be subject to racialization. The reification of populations as genetic objects, the tendency to use an island model that evokes ideas of purity, the possibility of mapping continental ancestral populations onto familiar categories of race, the use of a tree model—all these are caught up in the tension between purity and mixture that characterizes both genetics and liberalism. The purifying tendencies of genetic science do not themselves necessarily connote hierarchy—this would be anathema to the geneticists' humanist values—but they provide underpinnings and legitimations for hierarchical thinking.

This problematic is evident in the way the "inclusion" agenda has worked out in medicine and health in the United States and other Western countries.

This agenda has been driven by the democratic motive of improving access to health care for women and various disadvantaged minorities, including racial and ethnic groups. This objective involves counting those who are seen to be excluded: counting is done using racial, ethnic, and other categories. This allows disparities to be monitored and disadvantaged categories to be targeted for inclusion in a democratic definition of well-being. It also obeys a multiculturalist logic of identifying and recognizing the special needs of minority groups. But, critics contend, this reinforces those categories as social realities, hardening boundaries, and it encourages the possibility of seeing these categories as biologically different—for example, as genetically predisposed to certain disorders—and masking the role of social factors in causing group-based health disparities (Bliss 2012; Ellison et al. 2007; Epstein 2007; Montoya 2011; Smart 2005). Liberal polities are caught, as ever, between democracy and hierarchy, between the aim of ensuring a mixed society in which racial and other categorical distinctions have no impact on life chances, and the purifications that assign people to categories, whether to discriminate against them or to overcome that discrimination. The medical sciences also experience the tensions between inclusion and exclusion, racism and antiracism, and universalism and multiculturalism.

Purity and Mixture in Latin American Genomics

Just as mestizaje in Latin America—especially in Brazil—has been associated with (racial) democracy on the global stage, making the region an interesting space in which to explore how democracy and hierarchy work together, especially in relation to race, so the ambivalent tension between mixture and purity in genetics is dramatized in specific and interesting ways in genomic research on Latin America. This is because Latin American genomics has a dual focus on mestizo populations as the national norm (statistically and symbolically) and on indigenous peoples. These native people figure as parental/ancestral populations, who are easily identifiable as indigenous groups today and, for genomic research purposes, can be seen as relatively pure and able to stand in for the ancestral populations of 500 years ago.

The importance of indigenous peoples relates to the evolutionary narrative outlined above. If a trunk-and-branch metaphor tends to evoke distinct continental populations without significant gene flow between them, then this "island model" appears to apply clearly to the peopling of the Americas. The narrative that held sway for most the twentieth century was that the

Americas were peopled 12,000–13,000 years ago by populations from East Asia that crossed the Bering Strait after the Last Glacial Maximum (LGM, when ice sheets were at their greatest extension, dated at 26,000 years ago), as a corridor opened up through the ice sheets; these people then fanned out through the rest of the Americas. In the 2000s, this simple theory—which emphasizes the "isolation" of the Americas—was rejected, but no consensus has been reached among competing alternative theories, too complicated to detail here. One synthetic view proposes that several migrations—with diverse origins in Asia, including East Asia, western Eurasia, and possibly Australo-Melanesia—populated the Beringia region before the LGM; some groups perhaps entered the Americas during that period, over land and along the coast. Then the LGM isolated the Beringian groups from both east and west for thousands of years until a corridor reopened and allowed migration flows in both directions. North and South America were not colonized in a simple fanning out from north to south of the founding populations, but in complex multidirectional flows (Dziebel 2015; Oppenheimer 2003: ch. 7; Raghavan et al. 2014; Skoglund et al. 2015).

Although this account challenges a trunk-and-branch model and suggests more reticular processes, the end result is still that indigenous Americans can figure in genomic science as relatively distinct: "The Native American populations have lower genetic diversity and greater differentiation than populations from other continental regions" (Wang et al. 2007); or, as a university press release put it: "Native Americans possess the least-diverse genomes. As a result, searching for disease-causing genes should require the fewest number of genetic markers among Native Americans and the greatest number of markers among Africans [who harbor the greatest genetic diversity]" (Erickson 2008). Another report described how the long isolation of a small group of people on the Beringian land bridge "brewed the unique genetic diversity observed in the early Americans" (University of Adelaide 2016). As the chapter on Mexico shows (chapter 6), this underwrites claims to "unique" genetic variants and "risk" genes that are common among Amerindians, but absent or infrequent among Europeans and Africans.

If Latin America's indigenous populations offer valuable opportunities to genomic science, the same is claimed for the mestizos. For example: "Brazilian populations make ideal material for genetic studies since, for instance, the high incidence of infectious diseases in genetically heterogeneous populations makes them favorable to certain types of investigation" (Salzano and Freire-Maia 1970: 178). Similar claims are made about "admixed populations" in general (those formed from the relatively recent mixture of previously geographically distant populations), which are said to be interesting and useful objects of study in the global mission to identify health-related genetic variants via techniques of admixture mapping (Bertoni 2011).

There are two main approaches for identifying genetic variants that may underlie complex diseases: genome-wide association studies (GWAS) and admixture mapping. The former compares the genomes of people with a disorder (cases) to people without it (controls), examining a million or more loci at which variations are known to occur (single nucleotide polymorphisms, or SNPs). Variants that are more frequent among the cases are possible candidates for predisposing people to the disease. These associations need to be controlled for possible confounding factors, such as sex, age, and biogeographical ancestry (BGA, often glossed as race or ethnicity, which causes "population stratification").[2] The admixture mapping approach works on case and control samples in "admixed populations" and is "based on the hypothesis that differences in disease rates between populations are due in part to frequency differences in disease-causing genetic variants. In admixed populations, these genetic variants occur more often on chromosome segments inherited from the ancestral population with the higher disease variant frequency" (Winkler, Nelson, and Smith 2010: 65). Thus loci on the genomes of cases that show large amounts of a given ancestry, compared to controls, can give clues about the location of candidate disease genes. Compared to GWAS, admixture mapping uses smaller samples and just thousands of genetic loci: it is quicker and cheaper.

In the vast majority of cases, the populations used in admixture mapping are African Americans, Latinos, and Latin Americans. Strictly speaking, virtually all human populations are "admixed," due to long-standing patterns of mobility and interbreeding, but admixture mapping is facilitated by populations formed from the relatively recent mixture of previously geographically distant populations. Hence, while it is certainly possible to explore the genetic ancestry of Asians and Africans, few such populations have been used for admixture mapping of disease-related genes (Gurdasani et al. 2015; Xu 2012). For Latinos and Latin Americans, although fewer data have been available than for African Americans, this situation is rapidly being rectified, and Latin Americans offer interesting opportunities because they often have three continental genetic ancestries, not two. The U.S. Latino geneticist Esteban Burchard says that, because "Latino populations represent different admixtures of 3 major racial groups," they "present a unique opportunity to disentangle the clinical, social, environmental, and genetic underpinnings of population differences in health outcomes" (Burchard et al. 2005: 2161, 2163). An advantage of Latin American mestizos is their Amerindian heritage, which is seen to offer interesting possibilities—particularly in the search for genetic variants potentially linked to diabetes (Acuña-Alonzo et al. 2010; Seldin 2007; SIGMA Type 2 Diabetes Consortium 2014).

Latin America offers a further opportunity for genomic science: the coexistence in one location of a mestizo majority with contemporary indigenous peoples, who can represent a main ancestral population. No other region of the world offers a similar scenario, though a partial exception is South Africa with its "coloured" people (less than 10 percent of the population), whose "unique" mixture is said to be very useful for medical genomics (Patterson et al. 2010). In the United States and Canada, Native Americans are parental populations in situ, but the majority population is not defined as mestizo; the classic locus of admixture in the United States is the African American population, but their main parental populations are located in Europe and Africa, not within the national territory, and they have little Amerindian ancestry. If we turn to, say, Great Britain, ancestral populations are located in continental Europe (Vikings, Saxons, etc.), and "native" ancestors ("ancient Britons") are not seen to have readily identifiable modern counterparts: the British are seen as genetically mixed, but they are not defined as mestizos (Nash 2015: 101–35). The Latin American scenario allows geneticists to disaggregate mestizo and indigenous populations, relating particular indigenous groups to local mestizo populations in terms of specific genetic ancestries, thus fine-tuning the admixture mapping process: "Ideally, admixture maps should therefore be developed for each Mestizo population studied" (Wang et al. 2008).

On top of all this, the mixed ancestry of Latin Americans is seen by some scientists to presage a global future: "interethnic admixture is either common or increasing at a fast pace in many, if not most populations": for this reason, findings based on Brazilian samples—which indicate that "extrapolation on a global scale of pharmacogenomic data from well-defined ethnic groups [i.e., data from studies in the United States or Europe] is plagued with uncertainty"—should be taken as a salutary lesson by geneticists attempting to tailor pharmaceuticals to categories of patients on the basis of ethnicity (Suarez-Kurtz and Pena 2006: 1649). More generally, some geneticists claim that focusing on mestizos will help correct the Eurocentric bias of global genomic science and democratically ensure a future in which more people worldwide benefit from its potential to improve health (Bustamante, De La

Vega, and Burchard 2011). Mestizos are positioned as people who can help the world solve its health problems, as well as its racial problems.

The tension between purity and mixture is dramatized in a particularly clear way in Latin American genomics: the emblems of the organizing poles of the tension—the Native American and the mestizo—are both seen as useful genomic resources. But these scientifically useful resources are also constituent elements of national populations that have been symbolically harnessed to nation-building projects, founded on the idea of the mixture of relatively pure ingredients. Even in Brazil, where European–African mixture has been the predominant trend and the indigenous population is now tiny, it is symbolically of huge significance (Ramos 1998) and has attracted a lot of genetic research. Although Latin Americans' genetic African ancestry does not offer the same "unique" genomic opportunities as their Amerindian parentage, in symbolic and social terms African ancestry is of great importance in some countries. The point is that the populations and ancestries that geneticists study have huge social significance; they are connected to complex networks of people and practices that run beyond the lab, but also through it. In genomics, the purity–mixture tension is expressed in the dual focus on indigenous (and black) populations and mestizos; this same dynamic is expressed in politics and culture as a tension between hierarchical racial difference and racial democracy. As this book shows, geneticists not only map the genetic characteristics of mestizos; some of them also intervene in public debates about national identity, racial inequality, and the health legacies of indigenous (and/or an African) ancestry and mestizo genomes. Latin America is the region of the globe where the question of what it means to be a mestizo nation—genetically and socially—is prominently discussed, thus highlighting the tensions between hierarchy/purity and democracy/mixture (Wade, López Beltrán et al. 2014).

Exploring mixture as a biopolitical process in genomic research and politics in Latin American countries is of special interest in view of the importance, noted above, attributed to processes of mixture in breaking racial barriers, fomenting racial democracy, and achieving a cosmopolitan "multiracial" society, in which many different racial groups, including various types of mixed-heritage people, might live on equal terms, or even a "postracial" society, in which race might have no social significance. Challenges to both multiraciality and postraciality, as concepts that risk ignoring the continued action of racism and racial hierarchy in society, can be strengthened by exploring the Latin American case and seeing how images of democratic mixture interweave with racial hierarchy (Da Costa 2016; Daniel 2006; Lentin 2011, 2014;

Sexton 2008). Focusing on the way genomic data are deployed in discussions about being mestizo highlights the way science is continuously entangled in these biopolitical debates.

Geneticists weigh in on debates about race, racism, and multiculturalism in Brazil and Colombia—usually to decry racism and assert the nonexistence of biological race, but meantime genetically reifying ancestral populations (which look similar to familiar images of African, European, and indigenous races) and local populations. The way genetic data are deployed in these debates about race and nation follows the tensions characteristic of liberalism, including in its multiculturalist variants. On the one hand, genetics highlights the medical value of mestizo populations and reasserts the importance of mixture as the central constituent of the nation; it reiterates the well-known narrative about mestizo nations having been formed by European men having sex with indigenous and African women, thus highlighting the way racial hierarchy is blurred by sexual hierarchy. Genetic data about mixture have also been used in Brazil to discredit social movements based on racial identity. On the other hand, genetics confirms the social and genetic existence of the different ingredients—especially black and indigenous groups—that make up that mixture. It supports narratives that, in relation to indigenous and to a lesser extent black populations, place the purest exemplars in the past (by using them as proxies for parental populations) and in peripheral spaces of the nation. These tensions are familiar, but now they are enacted using a scientific language of genetics.

Science and Society: Assemblage and Topology

The argument of this chapter and the introduction raises the thorny issue of how to conceive of the relations between scientific practice and politics or, more widely, society. Are the practices of scientists shaped by existing ideas "outside" those activities? Do the findings and theories of scientists, aimed at the internal world of science, impact on ideas in the wider society, whether to change or reinforce them? Or is there a circular relation of mutual constitution between these two domains?

To talk of a relation necessarily entrains the idea that there are two separate spheres of action, which encounter each other, albeit in complex and historically layered ways. The way social life is institutionalized in liberal democracies—with apparently discrete sets of institutions for science and politics, not to mention economics, religion, and family—gives this view experiential traction: the way we live our lives seems to be organized into distinct domains. Theories of coproduction in principle dispense with this dualistic approach, pointing out that science and society are inextricably interconnected and that they participate simultaneously in the development of objects such as population, mestizo, and race (Jasanoff 2004a; Latour 1993; Reardon 2005). The language of coproduction, however—like that of hybridity—tends to be haunted by the dualism it seeks to overcome: science and society risk reappearing as separate domains, albeit in a cooperative and mutually constitutive working relationship. Taking the idea of coproduction to its logical conclusion entails the more radical proposal that there is no separate sphere of the "social" that can be referenced as an external force that impinges on scientific practice. Instead, we should focus on how assemblages of relations and objects emerge—are "constructed"—through diverse practices, allowing certain relationships and meanings to be taken for granted (Latour 2005). One set of taken-for-granted meanings is the idea that society and science are separate entities: this is a process of "purification" that seeks to create classificatory and institutional order out of the multiple "hybridizations" that constantly crisscross classificatory and infrastructural institutional boundaries (Latour 1993). The mestizo, despite its proclaimed hybrid origins, can also be the result of a process of purification—a pure hybrid—insofar as it becomes an object that is taken for granted and made stable through the work of assembly.

Recently, the so-called ontological turn in social sciences has emphasized the need to grasp how a given object is "enacted"—brought into material existence—through the practices of different sets of actors, giving rise to multiple versions of that object (Henare, Holbraad, and Wastell 2007; Mol 2002; Woolgar and Lezaun 2013). Thus, society is not simply the wider context for scientific explorations of the mestizo, nor is science simply the factual context for social debates about that object; these figure/background images imply a reversible, perspectival approach, which reproduces dualism. Rather, in this approach, the mestizo is enacted in multiple ontological forms. As an object of knowledge, it does not have an identifiable essence that is viewed differently from different perspectives—scientific, political, literary—and is used in accordance with the priorities of each perspective; instead, it becomes a different object in each domain of practice. This view accords welcome importance to practice, and relativizes the idea of context, but it paradoxically threatens to reintroduce a divide between science and society, as distinct domains of practice, which construct multiple versions of the "same" object. Instead, we should think of objects/concepts (e.g., the mestizo) as acquiring different material realities in the various settings of institutional practice and knowledge-making, while also seeing these settings as part of a broader reticular network, which allows the object/concept to move between settings.

Assemblage theory offers a useful approach to thinking about society and its component parts in nonlinear, nonorganic, nondualistic ways that emphasize emergence, heterogeneity, and contingency, while still retaining some element of structure. Formally developed as a concept in philosophy by Deleuze and Guattari (1988) and DeLanda (2006), in social science the concept is often deployed in a metaphorical sense to express "a mix of the aesthetic and the structural in the current sustained revival of modernist thought" (Marcus and Saka 2006: 104). In brief:

> Assemblages are composed of heterogeneous elements or objects that enter into relations with one another. These objects are not all of the same type. Thus you have physical objects, happenings, events, and so on, but you also have signs, utterances, and so on. While there are assemblages that are composed entirely of bodies, there are no assemblages composed entirely of signs and utterances. (Bryant 2009)

And,

> An assemblage is the product of multiple determinations that are not reducible to a single logic. The temporality of an assemblage is emergent. It does not always involve new forms, but forms that are shifting, in formation, or at stake. (Collier and Ong 2008: 12)

Processes of territorialization or coding consolidate and rigidify assemblages, while deterritorialization and decoding introduce flexibility and contingency. Components of an assemblage are not in a necessary causal relation to other components, nor to the whole assemblage: the relationship is contingent and a component (e.g., "mestizo") can be taken out of one assemblage and plugged into another, where its interactions are different and it takes on a different materiality. Assemblage theory does not posit a necessary scalar hierarchy: while some assemblages are more widespread than others (e.g., international genomic science provides a global infrastructure of norms, practices, and databases), they are themselves made up of assemblages (e.g., the specific committees that define norms, the specific servers on which databases are held). "Mestizo" is both an assemblage in itself and a component in other assemblages, without these being in a scalar hierarchy.

All this sounds rather abstract, but the point is to conceive of society as a network of people, objects, ideas, and utterances, which are held together by contingent and changeable relations to form assemblages. These assemblages have a contingent structural dimension created by repeated acts and relationships, but they are inherently unstable and need constant work and regulation to make them look and act solid and institutional. They also overlap and interpenetrate, so it is difficult to draw boundaries around them: the assemblages that make up "science," for example, intersect with those that make up "politics." The same components can be plugged into different assemblages and have different interactions there. This gets us a bit further than the concept of coproduction, which, as noted above, only overcomes duality at the expense of reproducing it as a foundation.

The theory of assemblage has affinities with Stuart Hall's ideas about articulation. He states that the word *articulate* has a double meaning: to express and to connect. But any connection between two components is always contingent. "An articulation is thus the form of the connection that can make a unity of two different elements, under certain conditions. It is a linkage which is not necessary, determined, absolute and essential for all time . . . the so-called 'unity' of a discourse is really the articulation of different, distinct elements which can be rearticulated in different ways because they have no necessary 'belongingness.'" He uses the example of religion to illustrate the nature of a contingent relation. You can't simply detach religion from its historical embeddedness in a series of political, economic, and ideological structures that have "lines of tendential force"; but at the same time, a particular religious formation has no *necessary* connection to the specific structures it historically comes with; this means it is open to rearticulation. Thus, Rastas rearticulated Christianity as a language of resistance, connected to them as diasporic black people in the New World, and forged links between that and new forms of music (Grossberg 1986: 53–54). Hall's ideas evoke more structural solidity than does the concept of assemblage, but they both talk in terms of collections of components that can be articulated into changing patterns.

The image painted so far is rather flat: in theory, everything is connected to everything else; there is no indication of why certain structural configurations emerge and dominate, except by dint of repetition. Why does science *appear* to be separate from politics, for example? Why does the component "mestizo" resonate so well in Latin American nations? To explain this requires a theory of power. In brief, some assemblage configurations become dominant and look convincing, because people with resources at their disposal—and the power to use those resources to realize their own projects and senses of self—work to create and solidify connections and to privilege certain objects in ways that, collectively and as a result of aggregated foreseen and unforeseen consequences, create structuring tendencies. This results in certain aspects of the assemblage becoming "black-boxed"—that is, taken for granted and unquestioned in the normal course of events (Latour 1987)—and in certain objects becoming "immutable mobiles," able to function in a similar way in different assemblages (Latour 1990), although, in light of the ideas outlined above about enactment and materialization, such mobiles may be less "immutable" than Latour implied. These objects may also be "boundary objects," which operate convincingly across different classification systems (Bowker and Star 1999). The construction of "purity" out of "mixture" is an example of the emergence of a structure, usually driven by power relations.

The Mestizo Assemblage

If the mestizo is an assemblage, what kind of meanings and practices has it assembled? The concept of mestizo has circulated through different realms of practice, in the process accreting layers of meaning and offering diverse affordances. A few examples will serve as illustrations. In colonial times, mestizo was a complex category with multiple materializations. For example, the mestizo figured in the eighteenth-century Mexican and Peruvian paintings of *castas* (literally "castes," but better translated as sorts or kinds, with the implication of common descent), which were series of stylized portrayals of types of people. This mestizo was child, man, or woman in a mixed family, and was a component in a classificatory hierarchy that imposed an idealized order on what was surely a deeply unstable reality (Deans-Smith 2005; Katzew 2004). The same mestizo was also conceived by medics and scientists of the era as a body that displayed a blend of characteristics drawn from a suite of known Hippocratic humors or "temperaments," which characterized the indigenous as mainly melancholic and the Spanish as choleric; this mestizo was seen variously as a testament to creole vitality (contra certain European denigrations of American-born populations), as a signpost indicating the possibility of whitening, and as an element tainted by indigenous or African blood, to be excluded from the white ruling elite (López Beltrán 2007). The colonial mestizo also materialized as an insult, a way to dishonor someone with imputations of illegitimacy, inducing the victim to bring to bear the apparatus of legal redress, possibly involving investigations into his/her parentage (Twinam 1999). The painting, the body, and the insult were elements in transnational assemblages that included, among many other things, art collectors and lawyers, governors and bureaucrats, priests and painters, medics and natural historians.

In more recent times, but drawing on some of the elements outlined above, the Mexican mestizo has been materialized by intellectuals (e.g., Vasconcelos) as a heroic exemplar of la raza cósmica and forger of the nation's destiny as a democracy; and also by the novelist Octavio Paz as a cursed and conflicted hijo de la chingada, who nevertheless was proud and defiant (and macho).[3] These two mestizos are distinct, but recognizable, versions of each other—mutable mobiles (Mol and Law 1994: 663)—assembled into and articulated with overlapping networks of political and literary practice. These versions morph into the mestizo who is materialized in procedures of DNA sequencing and data analysis as a variable combination of biogeographical genetic ancestries; this mestizo is normalized as a typical citizen and pathologized as a body predisposed by indigenous ancestry to certain health risks; s/he is part of an assemblage that connects scientists, doctors, politicians, and policymakers, but also, more distantly, Vasconcelos and Paz, among others (López Beltrán, García Deister, and Rios Sandoval 2014).

Topology

The concept of topology is related to that of assemblage.[4] Topology as an abstract concept highlights relationality and continuum; things are not separated but always related; boundaries connect as well as divide; it flattens social space and makes everything contiguous and equivalent; a frame does not separate an inside from an outside in a stable way, but is itself dynamic and remakes relations; change is immanent in continuity, they are not opposed (Lury, Parisi, and Terranova 2012). The most concrete way to think about topology is via a topological map: this is a map of the Metro or subway that, no matter which shape you distort it into—a sphere, a donut, an oblong—still allows you to see where the stations are in relation to each other and allows you to navigate from A to Z. Stations that are topographically distant can be brought into topological proximity to each other if the map is distorted in the appropriate fashion.

Releasing the topology concept from the map metaphor of a series of nodes in a fixed relation, where in order to get from A to Z you always have to go through the same intermediate nodes, one can see how twisting the map in a certain way introduces the possibility of getting from A to Z by "short-circuiting" the map and omitting the intervening nodes, although they still remain there and the possibility of their reconnection remains as an absent presence. "Points (which might be entities or events) that are distant can also be proximal (categorically as well as spatially and temporally); and transformations of the relations between points are not causal or linear, but open and immanent" (Lury, Parisi, and Terranova 2012: 12). Another way of seeing the difference between a simple Metro map and a more complex notion of topology is Mol and Law's distinction between "network" and "fluid" forms of space (Mol and Law 1994). In a network, "places with a similar set of elements and similar relations between them are close to one another," even if they appear far apart on a "regional" or topographic map. This is close to what I mean by topology, but for them a network involves a certain rigidity: all the elements of a network are interdependent, there may be obligatory points of passage, and if you remove one element the network is in danger of collapse; networks allow the possibility of immutable mobiles, objects that have a given structure and that work the same in topographically distant regions. In contrast, the fluid type of space, characterized by gradients, the absence of boundaries, and the presence of mixtures, robustly adapts to the disappearance of individual elements and works with mutable mobiles, that is, objects that transform themselves "from one arrangement into another without discontinuity" through "invariant transformation" (Mol and Law 1994: 649, 658, 664). This captures what I mean by a topological network, or understanding assemblages in terms of topological relations.

A recent application of topology to the study of race-making in Europe says the following:

> The topological approach allows us to appreciate four important aspects of the role of science and technology in these dynamics [of race-making]. First, it enables an understanding of race as a temporal and spatial relation that cannot be reduced to one singular entity (skin tone, DNA, religion, culture, nationality) or traced through a single, linear historical process. Second, and related to this, the topological approach, which is based on the presupposition that elements that are distant in time and space can become proximate and relevant in the here and now, helps us to understand how technologies that seem indifferent to racial differences contribute to the enactment of race. Third, it allows appreciation of the continual ambiguity, contestation and fluidity of notions of difference and belonging in contemporary Europe, and the specific ways in which race is done or undone. Finally, it takes us away from the familiar tropes for discussing border management and databases—as the panoptic gaze of the all-powerful state—to an appreciation of the ongoing technical, legal, and organizational challenges of bringing data about human difference to life. (M'charek, Schramm, and Skinner 2014: 472)

Thus, if mestizo is a mutable mobile object in an assemblage, we can see how it can be brought into various proximal relations with other components to materialize as transformed versions in a fluid way. It can be brought into proximity with ideas of "racial difference" to materialize a version of the mestizo as a racially marked body that emphasizes its foundational racial origins. And the topological network of the assemblage can also be fluidly moved to make the mestizo proximal to "racelessness" and generate a morphed version of the mestizo that emphasizes the mixture that overcomes the boundaries separating those original categories. Despite racial difference and racelessness being apparently distant, they coexist in the same assemblage and are available as possible connections that can participate in the materialization of the mestizo. Although, in a given situation, the mestizo may connote primarily either racial difference or racelessness, in both cases the topological character of the relation means that the second term does not disappear in the fluid distortion; it simply becomes submerged or grayed out (see chapters 7 and 8).

Conclusion

The material in this book shows how geneticists in their labs undertake projects that, at the level of stated aims, are aligned to the agenda of global medical genomics in seeking out genetic variants connected to complex disorders such as obesity and diabetes, or the agenda of evolutionary population genetics, which seeks to trace the peopling of the globe. They do this according to the standard procedures governing science and the production of knowledge that aspires to be scientifically valid. At the same time, their practices enact the mestizo—not to mention the indígena, the Afro-descendent, and the European—in ways that reaffirm the basic shape of the assemblage of mestizaje; the latter has long been plugged into the assemblage of scientific institutions (see chapter 2), and current genomic practice invigorates those connections and the scientific authority they provide to the mestizo as a key component of the nation.

This is not a question of how social definitions of the mestizo shape scientists' ideas and practices, nor of how scientific data on the mestizo reinforce or change ideas in the wider society; instead, it is a question of how multiple actors work to produce different but related mestizos that are all potentially connected in the same assemblage of diverse elements including scientists, policymakers, doctors, politicians, writers, journalists, and academics, among others. The genetic mestizo connects inevitably with other materializations of the mestizo, which is not to say that the precise contours of the connections are predetermined, but rather that connection of some kind is impossible to avoid, given the ontology of the assemblage.

Although there is no direct mention of purity, the genomic projects enact the tension between purity and mixture insofar as the latter necessarily entrains the former. In so doing, geneticists address questions of democracy and hierarchy, either directly in popular writings that present genomics as undermining the concept of biological race and valorize Latin American mixture as an antidote to concepts of racial difference and racism, or by implication with data showing that all Brazilians, Colombians, and Mexicans are mixed, but that in the national territory there exist populations that can be taken as representative of, or closer to, putative parental populations. Genetics is thus a set of practices that, for all the promise of technological revolution and new advances in medicine and historical knowledge, materializes a mestizo (and its associated components) that tends to support existing "lines of tendential force." These lines of force act to reduce multiculturalist policies to a superficial politics of recognition, in which minorities can be managed by according them a conditional space.

2

....

From Eugenics to Blood Types

In this chapter, I explore changes in the way Latin American scientists—medics, physical anthropologists, geneticists—conceptualized and studied the diversity of human populations, often focusing on their own nations, but also tapping into international currents in science and making comparisons with other populations. My focus will be on the middle period of the twentieth century, which has been treated in less depth than the first two to three decades of the 1900s, when the influence of eugenics was at its strongest. This period is of interest because it covers a major global transition away from an uneven but fairly broad scientific consensus endorsing race as a concept with which to theorize—and evaluate—human diversity toward a growing scientific consensus that rejected race as a fundamentally undemocratic way to evaluate and judge human diversity, even if the concept often remained as a way to theorize and categorize a diversity now seen as only biological and thus located outside political hierarchy.

In line with the idea that conceptualizations of human diversity—especially the concept of race—are biocultural assemblages, in which the "biological" and the "cultural" are not easily separated and tend to reentwine as they are pulled apart, I argue that Latin American scientists did not, indeed at some level could not, fully isolate the biological level of the populations they studied. The tension between biology and culture/society was evident not simply in the persistence of the term race as a way to talk about biological diversity—which brought the risk that an older baggage of meanings attached to the word could weigh it down with cultural associations and even evaluative judgments—but also in the conflation of social and biological definitions of populations. This tended to lend biological substance to social belonging and to freight an apparently purely biological definition of race with social meanings. As I argued in chapter 1, the possibility of this conflation is not limited to Latin America, but is integral to the biological study of human populations.

In Brazil, Colombia, and Mexico, scientific studies of human diversity tended to focus on mestizaje, showing or implying that these nations were mixed and becoming more so, while also reaffirming the existence of relatively "pure" original categories, some of which were still present. Social categories of mestizo, Indian/indio/indígena, black/negro, and white/blanco were given weighty biological substance and reified as biological razas, which nevertheless inevitably carried with them some of the social meanings attached to the social categories that defined them for sampling purposes in the first place. Mestizaje was mainly talked of in these studies as a biological process, but social meanings of acculturation and modernization—which could be seen as both devastating and progressive—were often present, thus implying equivalences between social and biological processes, which the scientists recognized were not always supported by their own data. The attempt to enhance democracy by conceptualizing mestizaje and race as purely biological phenomena, outside of politics and value judgments, was undermined by the insistent return of social meanings of hierarchy and evaluation.

Before focusing on some of the studies themselves, I start with an outline of the broad context in which these mid-century studies took place.

Global Transitions to Antiracism

In 1900 in Europe and the Americas, the concept of race continued to hold the pervasive currency it had had—in gradually changing forms—since the late eighteenth century as a way of understanding and explaining human diversity and attributing value to different human cultures on a normative hierarchy leading from civilization to savagery. Humans were conceived as belonging to one of a small number of basic racial types, understood as ancient and permanent entities that defined the biology and culture of individuals and populations. These racial types were admitted to be underlying realities, the clear characteristics of which had been blurred by the influences of environment, migration, and mixture, but they structured the diversity of humanity in a relatively—but not completely—fixed way and allowed scientists, in principle, to assign individuals to a race or subrace, even if such assignations might at times be ambiguous (Banton 1987: ch. 2; Conklin 2013: ch. 1; Hannaford 1996; Stepan 1982; Stocking 1982). This was an era of biological or racial determinism, but of a rather particular kind, because of the widely held Lamarckian belief in the inheritance of acquired characteristics, which meant that environment could shape racial essence (Stoler 1995; Wade 2002b), producing "a 'blind and bland shuttling' between race and civilization" (Stocking 1982: 265, citing A. L. Kroeber).

Eugenics, founded in the 1880s by Francis Galton, was based in principle on Galton's anti-Lamarckian theories about the immutability of "germ plasm," the inherited material, which stayed the same when passed between parent and offspring, but could be shaped at a population level by planned breeding programs. Eugenics focused on the "fitness" of individuals and populations, and it targeted the working classes as much or more than people defined in terms of race; but eugenic theories dovetailed closely with concepts of racial difference in the idea that some races were fitter than others and that interracial breeding was a degenerative process. Despite Galton's theories about germ plasm, during the heyday of eugenics—when the three International Eugenics Conferences took place between 1912 and 1932—it was a progressivist movement driven by medics and reformers who focused as much on social "hygiene" (i.e., an improved environment, especially for children) as on measures such as sterilization and prenuptial medical examination, which would regulate sexual reproduction and thus directly impact germ plasm (Condit 1999b; Kevles 1995; Paul 1995; Stepan 1991). Like the contemporary science of race, there was a certain indeterminism in the relation between biology and culture.

By 1930, the basic concept of race that underwrote scientific racism and eugenics had held global sway for well over a hundred years. But in the space of a few decades, that concept lost a great deal of its authority, as antiracism became a new globally hegemonic idea. Even as an ostensibly neutral way to simply apportion human biological diversity, the idea of race was also challenged and over time lost a great deal, but never all, of its ground. This uneven transition was driven by various factors, including reactions against Nazi racism, both before and after World War II, and growing anticolonial feeling among people subordinated by European and North American states. Also important was the input of key intellectuals, such as anthropologist Franz Boas, who directly challenged the theories of racial science, using the kind of anthropometric methods on which it was based, showing that skull shape and size—the gold standard of much racial science—was quite plastic and could change over a generation, affected by changes in diet. Boas, alongside contemporary anthropologists such as A. L. Kroeber, strove to separate (heritable or racial) biology from culture, following others such as black U.S. intellectual W. E. B. Du Bois (Baker 1998). This separation accorded with growing evidence from genetics, which, developing Galton's theories of heredity, was taken to indicate that inherited biological material was clearly separated from immediate environmental influence at the individual level (even if the genetic pool of a population was shaped by long-term environmental forces in evolutionary processes): inherited biology provided a baseline, which did not determine the culture that was built on top of it. Having defined culture as a realm not determined by (racial) biology, Boas, like Claude Lévi-Strauss and other cultural anthropologists, championed cultural relativism as an integral aspect of their antiracism (Barkan 1992; FitzGerald and Cook-Martín 2014; Lentin 2004; Müller-Wille 2010; Schaffer 2008; Smedley 1993).

The idea that race defined a hierarchy of human value and ability became unacceptable in most scientific circles, as well as more widely; the word and concept of race were increasingly seen as themselves connoting racism. They continued to be used in the institutional public sphere in countries such as the United States, Britain, Brazil, and postapartheid South Africa—although not in most other countries, where the word ethnicity was preferred (Morning 2008)—and this was justified in terms of contributing to antiracist outcomes (e.g., the need to measure racial inequality or target racially defined categories in order to combat racial inequality and racism). Meanwhile, in popular usage, the word and concept of race persisted and were obscured in a very uneven way: in some countries, such as the United Kingdom and the United States, it could be a fairly common way to refer to differences often understood as primarily cultural, albeit perhaps signaled by traits such as skin color; but even in these countries, in some contexts, and more so in other countries, such as France, Germany, and much of Scandinavia, the word itself could easily connote racist views.

In this transition, the concept of race by no means disappeared from scientific usage. First, many scientists simply redefined race as a population with certain genetic traits, in line with new approaches in physical anthropology and genetics, which emphasized dynamic evolutionary adaptation over static typologies. This can be seen in the UNESCO statement on race, issued in the aftermath of World War II (Maio and Santos 2010; Marks 2010; Reardon 2005). As the education, science, and culture arm of the newly formed United Nations, UNESCO—which had as its president the British physical anthropologist Julian Huxley—formed a committee to produce a scientific consensus on race, intended as a nail in the coffin of Nazi theories.[1] The first UNESCO statement on race insisted on distinguishing the "biological fact" from the "social myth" of race, and stated:

The term "race" designates a group or population characterised by some concentrations, relative as to frequency and distribution, of hereditary particles (genes) or physical characters, which appear, fluctuate, and often disappear in the course of time by reason of geographic and/or cultural isolation. (UNESCO 1950)

This understanding of race proved quite durable over subsequent decades. In 1962, the influential geneticist Theodosius Dobzhansky, a main figure in the shift toward a more dynamic evolutionary approach in genetics, commenting on an attack on the biological race concept by Frank Livingstone, said "race differences are objectively ascertainable biological phenomena" and argued that "to say that mankind has no races plays into hands of race bigots," who are then able to say what they like about racial difference. He continued:

Since human populations (and those of other sexually-reproducing species) often, in fact usually, differ in the frequencies of one or more, usually several to many, genetic variables, they are by this test racially distinct. But it does not follow that any racially distinct populations must be given racial (or subspecific) labels. Discovery of races is a biological problem, naming races is a nomenclatorial problem. (Livingstone and Dobzhansky 1962: 279–80)

In 1985, a survey showed half of the U.S. biological anthropologists questioned thought humans formed biological races, while a survey of articles published between 1965 and 1996 in the *American Journal of Physical Anthropology* showed that about 40 percent used the race concept, if not the word. In Poland in 2001, 75 percent of physical anthropologists accepted the biological validity of race, while in China's main biological anthropology journal, articles published between 1982 and 2001 used the race concept unquestioningly (Cartmill 1998; Kaszycka and Strzałko 2003; Lieberman and Reynolds 1996; Wang, Štrkalj, and Sun 2003). Many biological anthropologists do contend that the race concept has no biological validity (Brown and Armelagos 2001; Goodman, Moses, and Jones 2012; Lewontin 1972), but we can see that the consensus in the social sciences that race is a "social construction" from top to bottom has not been entirely in line with the views of many biological anthropologists, even if the latter concur that racist meanings given to so-called biological race have no foundation in science.

Second, although the UNESCO 1950 statement was drafted mainly by social scientists, there were two physical anthropologists on the committee, and a draft was also circulated to some biologists. Nonetheless, the statement attracted critical comment from a variety of physical anthropologists and geneticists, some of whom thought the document was driven too much by ideological views about the insignificance of race. In 1951 a second UNESCO statement was issued by a panel composed of physical anthropologists and geneticists, restating the idea that biological race was a valid concept and adding: "It is possible, though not proved, that some types of innate capacity for intellectual and emotional responses are commoner in one human group than in another" (UNESCO 1952: 13). This reflected the comments made by some geneticists that the relationship of race to intelligence was a matter of investigation and had not yet been decided. Later, in 1961, the Mexican physical anthropologist and codrafter of the 1950 statement, Juan Comas, wrote a scathing critique in Current Anthropology of an article in Mankind Quarterly, a new U.K.-based journal funded by U.S. segregationists, which provided a venue for authors expressing scientific racist views (Schaffer 2008: 142). In a comment on Comas's article, caution was expressed again by a Danish anthropologist, Kaj Birket-Smith, who argued there was "a possibility that some mental traits may be racially distinctive" (Comas 1961: 314). Notoriously, a small minority of hereditarian psychologists have continued to argue that intelligence is linked to race (e.g., Lynn 2006).

Third, sociobiological arguments have contended that humans have evolved a biological preference for others whom they identify as being like them. Sociobiological arguments do not make any claims about racial hierarchies or intelligence; they simply say that similar appearance is taken as an indication of shared genetic material and acts as an evolutionary spur for altruistic or preferential behavior toward those who seem similar (van den Berghe 1979; Yudell 2014: ch. 10). Such arguments depend on a notion of appearance that is not necessarily racialized—it could refer to many different aspects of appearance, including cultural ones, which could still be correlated with a propensity to interbreed and thus share genetic material. But it is easy to see how racialized dimensions of appearance, which have become historically significant, such as skin color, hair type, and facial structure, could act as important cues. These sociobiological ideas are therefore technically different from, but dovetail easily with, segregationist arguments deployed in the southern United States and in apartheid South Africa—and frequently made in the pages of Mankind Quarterly in the 1960s—which contended that racial segregation was natural and a result of human instincts (Schaffer 2008: 144).

Sociobiological arguments depend on a concept of race as a real dimension of biological variability and see racial consciousness as a biological trait:

such approaches are a minority trend. But the central idea that it is natural for people to want to be with others "like them" has a much broader appeal, especially when the likeness is phrased in terms of culture. This notion underlies the "new racism" (Barker 1981), "cultural racism" (Taguieff 1990), or the "cultural fundamentalism" that relies on "organicist" notions of belonging (Stolcke 1995). The discourses characteristic of these trends eschew explicit reference to race or biology, but a sense of belonging and a preference for "one's own kind"—which frequently follow racialized lines—are naturalized and often construed as facts that science can attest to. If people instinctively prefer their "own kind," they will breed with them, such that culture, appearance, and biology will tend to coincide (Gilroy 2000: 32–34). As in sociobiology, appearance is likely to be an important cue for judging who is of "one's own kind," even if the discourse refers to cultural traits such as values, tastes, and so on.

There is, of course, more to say about how concepts of race persist in various and reconfigured ways in scientific accounts of human diversity, but the outline above gives us enough context to look at some Latin American material. The point is that the separation of biology and culture, so important to establishing the mid-century and postwar democratic antiracist agenda, has been beset by ambiguity and the reentanglement of the two realms. The antiracist agenda depended on an idea of differing frequencies of genetic variants spread across the world in clinal distributions, which in theory is at odds with the idea of biological "populations" (which implies some measure of boundedness of each population and distinction in relation to others): from this perspective, group boundaries are merely social. An implicit idea of mixture followed on from this: such clinal distributions must have been caused by mixture across social boundaries, and antiracism entrained the possibility of ever-greater rates of the mixture that had been anathema to scientific racist thinking. Against this, the sticky persistence of a natural-cultural version of racial thinking reintroduced the possibility of hierarchies of power and value.

Eugenics in Brazil, Colombia, and Mexico

Eugenics was popular in Brazil, Colombia, and Mexico, with early roots in the first two decades of the twentieth century—the Eugenics Society of São Paulo was founded in 1918—but only emerging in earnest in the 1920s, and consolidating in the 1930s and 1940s. In Europe and North America, the movement began to lose some authority in the late 1930s, when Nazi uses of eugenics became evident, but it was in the 1930s that central institutions in the eugenics movement were founded in Latin America—for example, the Mexican Eugenics Society and Brazil's Central Eugenics Committee both date from 1931. And the reverberations of eugenic thinking were felt into the 1950s and even the 1960s. Part of the reason for this is that the social hygiene and public health aspects of eugenics, noted above, were particularly strong in Latin America, for a number of reasons.

First, countries such as Brazil, Colombia, and Mexico had substantial indigenous, black, and above all mestizo populations. While many thinkers and scientists agreed with the Anglo-American science of the early twentieth century, which held that race mixture generally brought degeneration and weakness, too close an agreement with such a view could only condemn Latin American nations to perpetual inferiority. All three nations were intent on a program of modernization and reform, often instigated by authoritarian populist governments, and, as noted in chapter 1, this drive for progress was allied to ideals of (racial) democracy, underlain by mestizaje past and present. The attempt to build a modern and unified nation based on "mestizophilia" was particularly pronounced in Mexico after the 1910 Revolution (Basave Benítez 1992; Stern 2003), and was also strongly present in Brazil under Vargas (1930–45) (Burke and Pallares-Burke 2008; Skidmore 1974). It had a good deal of resonance in Colombia too, but less so, riven as that country was by regional and political differences (Bushnell 1993; Safford and Palacios 2002; Wade 1993). The nation-building drive for progress and a postcolonial sense of resentment toward northern powers were reflected in a countertendency to mainstream eugenics, which affirmed that mixture could be a positive process—what Stepan (1991) calls a belief in "constructive miscegenation"—by which a healthy mestizo population could emerge, aided by social hygiene. This was complemented in all three countries by a preference for European immigrants to "whiten" and "civilize" the population, although it was only in Brazil that such immigration assumed major proportions. Meanwhile, the immigration of black people, Jews, and Chinese was restricted in Brazil and Mexico, usually by covert means (FitzGerald and Cook-Martín 2014).

A second reason for the strength of social hygiene was the influence of the Catholic Church, which tended to be pronatalist and against the profaning of the sanctity of marriage with measures such as forcible sterilization. A third factor was the influence on Latin American intellectual circles of French scientific thought, which tended to be more environmentalist and Lamarckian, in contrast to the more hard-nosed hereditarian approaches of many Anglo-American theorists.

Together these factors meant that eugenics in Latin American tended to emphasize "preventive eugenics" (Stepan 1991: 87), with a focus on public health—Brazilian eugenicists defended the slogan "to sanitize is to eugenicize" (Kobayashi, Faria, and Costa 2009)—and on the need to cleanse the population of "racial poisons," such as alcoholism, sexual diseases, and drug addiction. Eugenic approaches were often channeled through a concern with *puericultura*, that is, the study of techniques to improve child development. Matrimonial eugenics included prenuptial examinations and certificates to advise people about the "fitness" of prospective partners, but heavy-handed sterilization policies were very rare: only one sterilization law was passed in Latin America, in Veracruz, Mexico, in 1932 (Stern 2011).

Colombia did not have a powerful eugenics movement compared to Mexico or Brazil, but eugenic thinking was influential and pervaded the ponderings of intellectuals on the state of the nation (Gómez 1970 [1928]; Jiménez López et al. 1920; López de Mesa 1970 [1934]). Thinking was characterized by, on the one hand, highly pessimistic views that saw black and indigenous peoples as a source of irredeemably inferior hereditary material, whose presence could only be offset by extensive white immigration. On the other hand, there were more optimistic views that envisaged the possibility of environmental campaigns to improve the population by hygienic measures, such as the control of alcohol (especially home-brewed varieties, such as *chicha*); the building of paved roads, sewers, hospitals, and housing; sanitary controls on food production, and so on (Castro-Gómez and Restrepo 2008; Helg 1989; Muñoz Rojas 2011; Noguera 2003; Restrepo 2007; Villegas Vélez 2005; Wade 1993: 14–17). The way environmental interventions were thought to actively shape hereditary material, thus blurring the apparent divide between hereditarian and environmental approaches, was evident in the importance attached by some medics to the idea that "race enters through the mouth" and that interventions in diet could improve the bodies of workers and, over the long term, enhance la raza colombiana—the Colombian people conceived as a biocultural entity (Pohl-Valero 2014).

These eugenic analyses of race and nation reiterated the categories of negro, indio, and blanco, both as historical foundations of and as contemporary presences in the nation, alongside their mixed products, principally the mestizo, and also the *mulato* and the *zambo* (referring, respectively, to a person of white–black and black–indigenous ancestry). Eugenic sanitary campaigns were nationwide and aimed at the working classes (Noguera 2003), but the attention paid to the country's Caribbean coastal region focused on its tropical climate, its role as a key maritime entry point, and the presence of significant black, dark-skinned mestizo, and indigenous populations, seen to need special attention (McGraw 2007). Thus, racial difference was constantly re-inscribed and, while race was often framed in terms of regional difference, it was nevertheless quite an explicit discourse.

In Mexico, racial difference was less explicit in eugenic discourse. The stage was set for eugenicists of the 1930s by thinkers such as the writer Andrés Molina Enríquez, the anthropologist Manuel Gamio, and the philosopher and politician José Vasconcelos (see introduction). These men promoted the mestizo as an icon of national unity and identity, although with varying emphases. Gamio promoted a state-driven indigenismo that sought both to catalogue and protect indigenous cultural traditions, particularly ancient and glorious ones, and also to assimilate present-day indigenous groups, whereas Vasconcelos held up the image of a future global hybrid "cosmic race," of which the Mexican mestizo was a precursor (Brading 1988; Gómez Izquierdo and Sánchez Díaz 2011; Knight 1990). Both distanced themselves from Anglo-American theories of the degenerative effects of mixture and adhered to ideas of the improvability of la raza mexicana. Eugenicists likewise saw mestizaje as a means to achieve homogeneity and national unity. Stern (2003: 192; 2009: 163) argues that they "invoked the figure of the mestizo without reference to any other 'race,'" generating a "generic mestizo," who was an "unraced subject." It is clear that an explicit discourse of racial categories was less evident than in Colombia, but Stern (2003: 194) herself cites the eugenicist Rafael Carrillo, who insisted in 1932 on the need for a study of the anthropometric traits of "the Indian, the Creole and the mestizo," which would allow eugenicists to "distinguish the races from one another." More generally, for the eugenicists, as for precursors such as Gamio and Vasconcelos, the idea of the mestizo was always dependent on the foundational categories of the indio and the blanco (and, to a much lesser extent than in Colombia and Brazil, the negro), and indeed indigenous populations remained important as an object of scientific attention and as a counterpoint for imagining the mestizo.

One indication of the evasion of race was the popularity in Mexico—as well as in Brazil and Argentina—of biotypology, which was being developed in Europe and the United States (Stern 2003; Uribe Vergara 2008; Vimieiro-Gomes 2012). Biotypology focused on measuring a whole host of physical characteristics—not just the classic traits of anthropometry, but also blood type, endocrine function, visual acuity, and so on. Using statistical methods, scientists tried to objectively classify people into biotypes, which were supposedly associated with particular aptitudes, pathologies, and predispositions, but which were not racial categories. A major proponent of biotypology, José Gómez Robleda, claimed in 1947 that the approach would change Mexican scientists, who he said "were so incredibly insistent on perpetuating techniques of racist physical anthropology" (cited by Stern 2003: 204), yet biotypology sought to establish a statistically normal type, and the studies Gómez Robleda did of Mexican indigenous groups showed, in his view, not only that they departed from the norm, but also that they were mostly "deficient" and exhibited traits such as "stupefaction" and sexual deviance (Stern 2003: 202–3). This sailed very close to the wind of racial stereotyping.

In many respects, eugenics in Brazil followed the same basic trends as in Mexico and Colombia, especially in the links between eugenics and hygiene. It was more akin to Mexico in the degree of institutionalization of eugenic activity, although Brazil started earlier, when Renato Kehl founded the short-lived São Paulo Eugenics Society in 1918, followed in 1922 by Gustavo Reidel's more durable League of Mental Hygiene, and in 1929 by the First Brazilian Eugenics Congress. Brazil was also similar to Mexico in the development, especially from the 1930s, of a strongly positive discourse about the mestizo as the essence of national identity. Edgard Roquette-Pinto, anthropologist and director of the National Museum, although a proponent of eugenics himself (Stepan 1991: 52), rejected pessimistic versions of eugenics that saw mestizos as racially degenerate, contending in 1929 that the characteristics of the "different types of Brazilian populations" were "the best that could be desired" (cited by Santos, Kent, and Gaspar Neto 2014: 41). As mentioned in the introduction, in the 1930s, Gilberto Freyre developed the image of Brazil as a tolerant, racially mixed country, which benefited from a combination of European, African, and Amerindian cultural elements. This version of Brazilian national identity—which underwrote claims about the country as a "racial democracy"—became strongly institutionalized by the authoritarian populist president Getúlio Vargas (1930–45) and remained influential thereafter.

One way Brazil resembled Colombia more than Mexico, however, was in the relatively explicit discourse about race. Some eugenicists were vocal about the need to restrict the immigration of those deemed unassimilable, which included black people and, according to some, other nonwhites, such as Chinese. In effect, in 1934 Brazil imposed an immigration quota system, referring to the need "to guarantee the ethnic integration and physical and civil ability of the immigrant." In 1938, a decree was passed that allowed the state discretion to exclude "individuals from certain races or origins for economic or social reasons" (legislation cited by FitzGerald and Cook-Martín 2014: 284, 285). Black Americans had been secretly excluded prior to this, and although the new laws did not exclude them specifically—and indeed the quota system had a greater impact on Japanese immigration, which was more numerous—the legislation reflected eugenicists' concern with restricting the entry of nonwhites and instead encouraging European immigrants, who had been arriving in large numbers since the 1870s (Skidmore 1974: 197; Stepan 1991: 54). Meanwhile, Brazilian officials laid claim to an image of racial harmony, contrasting their own country to the United States, despite the fact that their immigration quota system was modeled on the U.S. Immigration Act of 1924. It is worth noting that Brazil, having dropped a color question from the census after 1890, reintroduced it in 1940, with a specifically antiracist intent (to measure inequality in order to address it). Meanwhile, in its 1930 census, Mexico dropped the race question that had appeared previously and replaced it with a question about language; Colombia, on the other hand, dropped the race question after the 1918 census, in which several provinces refused to return racial data (Smith 1966; Telles 2004: 31, 81; Wade, García Deister, Kent, and Olarte Sierra 2014: 187).

Race was also more explicit in discussions among biotypologists in Brazil than in Mexico, where it was used as a way to avoid talking about race. Isaac Brown in his 1934 book *O normotipo brasileiro* (The Brazilian normotype) departed from the ideas of the Italian biotypologists, who held that there were no constant relations between constitutional biotypes and races, and instead thought that certain individual biotypes might predominate in certain races. Brown denied that there was such a thing as a single *raça brasileira*—contrast the frequent references to la raza mexicana—because there were many types of Brazilians, who could nevertheless be classified in broad terms, using Roquette-Pinto's categories of *melanodermos* (blacks), *faiodermos* (mulatos), *xantodermos* (*caboclos*, descendants of whites and indigenous), and *leucodermos* (whites), bearing in mind that each race would contain diverse biotypes. Another biotypologist, Waldemar Berardinelli, affirmed that to classify the diversity of Brazil's population one would need "sound knowledge of raciology, that is, of racial characteristics." As in Colombia, ideas about racial difference were framed by Brown and others in terms of regional difference, with specific regions having greater or lesser concentrations of morphological, physiological, and psychological types (Vimieiro-Gomes 2012: 714).

As a way of conceptualizing the diversity of the nation, eugenics was characterized by two key tensions. There was a tension between the power of hereditary biological determinations and the influence of environmental interventions, which were believed to shape the heredity material. In that sense, the diversity of the nation could be seen as more or less manipulable, with racial difference being more or less recalcitrant. This dovetailed with a second tension between, on the one hand, envisaging mixture in a hierarchical frame as evidence of the racial burdens of blackness and indigeneity inherited from the past but still present today as distinct populations, which would hold back the nation's progress, and on the other hand, seeing mixture as leading to a desirable future, in which indigenous and black people could be effectively assimilated, preferably alongside a growing proportion of white immigrant blood, all shaped by hygienic interventions, which could actively enhance the racial stock and produce democratic outcomes. Indigenous peoples in particular might even contribute valuable elements drawn from their own cultural traditions, which were being paternalistically nurtured, especially in Mexico, by state *indigenista* policies. African cultural contributions were generally seen as less valuable, although in Brazil, some culinary and musical traditions, seen as African influenced, were valued positively. Black, indigenous, and white people were thus conceived both as distinct racial categories, past and present, and as future mestizos among whom racial difference would be superseded. Reference to racial difference invoked past purities, which might hold the nation back, ensuring the persistence of old hierarchies and obstructing progress toward a mixed democratic future.

Blood Studies

Eugenics and biotypology provide the context for exploring a specific manifestation of scientific interest in a nation's diversity, sometimes conceptualized explicitly in terms of race, and sometimes, increasingly in later decades, phrased in more neutral terms. This involved the studies of human blood types done in Brazil, Colombia, and Mexico between the 1930s and the 1970s, carried out first by physical anthropologists and increasingly by specialists in the growing field of human genetics.

The existence of the main blood groups (A, B, and O) had been discovered in 1900 by the Austrian biologist Karl Landsteiner. Genetic studies suggested that blood type was inherited in Mendelian fashion, that all humans had a blood type, and that blood types were ancient, as they also occurred in apes. The study of blood types and compatibility between them went hand in hand with the massive use of blood transfusion during World War I, while the presence in the European armies of soldiers from colonial territories became a source of blood samples (Suárez Díaz and Barahona 2011: 71). The fact that blood type seemed to vary across different human populations soon suggested that it could be a useful way to study human variability and to help in the definition of races in terms of purely biological traits (e.g., Ottenberg 1925), although no consensus emerged on how to define racial categories using these criteria (Iverson 2007; Marks 1996; Santos 1996: 127).

Studies of blood types spanned several mid-century decades and took part in a shift of emphasis from the morphological to the molecular; from the anthropometrical measurement of bones by physical anthropologists, which, especially in forensic work, continued attempting to attribute individuals to typological categories, to the measurement of frequency of genetic traits in the attempt to characterize dynamic populations in stochastic terms. But over these decades, race did not disappear completely so much as become reconfigured (Iverson 2007; Santos 1996).

Colombia

In Colombia in the 1940s, a small series of studies by anthropologists explored blood types mainly among indigenous peoples, but also among some mestizo and black populations. These were studies in physical anthropology, but at the time the boundaries between this speciality, archaeology, and social anthropology were quite permeable. The studies were carried out under the aegis of the Instituto Etnológico Nacional (IEN), the beginnings of institutional academic anthropology in Colombia, founded in Bogotá by French anthropologist Paul Rivet in 1941 and funded by the Colombian state with some support from France. Many of the studies were published in the IEN's *Revista del Instituto Etnológico Nacional*. The key data presented in the studies showed the percentages of types O, A, and B found in various different samples, which were labeled by ethnonym (e.g., "*indios páez*"), by locality, and occasionally by racialized category ("mestizos," "negros"). The authors often contextualized the data with some geographical, historical, and cultural descriptions.

The rationale for the studies was not always explicit, but one can infer that the point of investing considerable time and resources into collecting and analyzing thousands of blood samples was partly to contribute to the field of "racial studies" (Duque Gómez 1944: 623), with serological data on indigenous peoples and on processes of biological race mixture. More particularly, the point was to address the "real problem" presented by indigenous peoples such as those in the province of Caldas, who were the same as those "encountered by the Spanish conquistadors," that is, unassimilated and in need of being incorporated "into the social and political orbit of the nation" (Duque Gómez 1944: 625, 627), which was in the midst of rapid agricultural and industrial modernization in the wake of the Liberal party's "revolution on the march" (1930–45). On the other hand, the problem was also that these "pure" indigenous people were undergoing "a devastating mestizaje" as "whites" encroached on their lands, often following in the wake of road-building projects designed to modernize the country's infrastructure (Arcila Vélez 1943: 8). There was a strong element of salvage anthropology at work, in the sense that indigenous groups were disappearing as a biological type. Milcíades Chavez and Gerardo Reichel-Dolmatoff were sent by the IEN to undertake studies of the Chimila because news had been received of the survival of various groups of them in the northern Magdalena region.

In line with this, the researchers all operated with a schema, which, in his account of these studies, Eduardo Restrepo (2014) describes for Luis Duque Gómez, but which can be generalized to other authors as well.[2] They all operated with

> a mode of racial thinking in which distinctions between negro, blanco, and indio were thought of in terms of "races." . . . The indicators of these racialized populations were blood types, but also embodied expressions and behaviors that the observers could read. An original correspondence was assumed between ideal and pure populations of indios, blancos, and negros and blood types O, A, and B. A gradient of mestizaje, or more or less mixed people, could be established corresponding to greater or lesser distance from these original racialized populations. (Restrepo 2014: 35, my translation)

There was a strong emphasis on "pure" indios, seen as a baseline, virtually unchanged from the pre-Columbian period, against which one could measure the amount of mestizaje that had occurred with blancos, and in some cases with negros. The degree of mixture was assessed by the relative presence of blood groups O, A, and B, with type O associated with indigenous people, type B with Africans/blacks, and type A with Europeans/whites. These populations were routinely referred to as razas by most authors; an exception is Gerardo and Alicia Reichel-Dolmatoff (1944), who nevertheless used terminology such as "undoubtedly negroid type." These races and the racialized categories indio, blanco, negro, and mestizo were thus given biological meaning in terms of blood type, even if the association between blood type and race was understood to be a tendency rather than a strict correspondence. Thus, the "purest" indigenous samples had very high percentages of blood type O, and lower percentages were always explained in terms of the mixture with white or black blood, sometimes referred to as *contrabando* (smuggling in) (Duque Gómez 1944: 627; Lehmann, Duque Gómez, and Fornaguera 1944: 206). Whites and blacks were not spoken of in terms of purity or its absence: this concept was reserved for indios. Whites were not sampled in these studies, but blacks were in a few cases, and their blood types were explained in terms of mixture with whites and indigenous people (Arcila Vélez 1943; Duque Gómez 1944). The concepts of race and of racial purity were not addressed or critiqued as such in the studies, despite the fact that Paul Rivet—a key figure in Colombian anthropology and teacher of most of these researchers—had instructed them that, while there had originally been three major races in the world, these had mixed to such an extent that it was an "absurd error" to speak now of "pure race" (Duque Gómez 1961: 359).

As Restrepo notes, the way these studies deal with the category of mestizo shows us how biology and culture were both separated and brought together by these scientists. In several cases, the researchers drew a distinction between indios and mestizos *within* the indigenous community. That is, mestizos were not always conceived as nonindigenous people who lived outside indigenous communities, which is a common meaning given to the term in Colombia and in Mexico (Bonfil Batalla 1996). Instead, they were seen as people who were culturally indigenous, while being biologically mixed compared to their "pure" cousins. Thus Arcila Vélez (1943: 14) said that, in the territories of the Paéz, intensive crossing meant that there were "indigenous people who behave in all their other ethnic manifestations like autochthonous Paéz indios, but who have in their veins the blood of white or black mestizaje." Duque Gómez (1944: 624) noted that some groups in the Caldas province were "almost completely incorporated into civilized life and only retain, more or less clearly, the anthropological characteristics of their race." Thus researchers perceived that there was no clear "correspondence between [cultural] tradition and biology" (Restrepo 2014: 32).

Yet biology and culture were continuously pushed back into alignment by the expectation that greater proportions of blood type O would correspond to greater cultural "purity." Thus, individual indios were identified as mestizos for sampling purposes on the basis not only of their reported parentage and their physical appearance, but also by their language use (e.g., not speaking Paéz) and their "mentality," which might show the influence of "the Spanish language and civilization" (Arcila Vélez 1943: 11–12), or their "psychology," which could be that of the mestizo, "frank, happy, active, progressive and confident when they have occasion to deal with whites" (Duque Gómez 1944: 632–33). Cultural indicators of mestizaje were expected to correlate with biological ones.

Mestizaje was generally spoken of as a biological process by which white (and black) blood entered indigenous bodies, but it retained a powerful sense of acculturation into the modernizing nation. As we saw, Duque Gómez (1944: 635, 639) spoke of a "devastating mestizaje" affecting the indigenous communities of Caldas, and he talked of the links between the "very obvious mestizaje" found in one community and its virtual "dissolution," implying a total biocultural transformation. He also referred to the more "open character" and "advanced mentality" of another community as being linked to frequent sexual contact with blancos and more biological mestizaje. Arcila Vélez (1943: 8) referred to "the civilizing action of white penetration which will possibly cause this indigenous group to lose its autochthonous racial character as a result of mixing with the colonists." Again, biological and cultural change were assumed to work in tandem, despite the recognition that many indios, defined in terms of their community residence and their behavior—which might appear "autochthonous"—showed biological mixture in terms of blood types.

The conception of Colombia that emerged from these studies was of a nation divided between indios, blancos, and negros. Whites were "civilized," and indigenous people (and implicitly blacks) were an obstacle to "civilization"; indios (but not blacks) were vulnerable and liable to be crushed by its march. Although mestizaje was broadly associated with modernity and progress (and implicitly with democracy), mestizos were—unusually for Colombia— lumped in with the indios. Even in a study that sampled "mestizos from Pasto [an urban center of some 30,000 people]," these people were included with indios in the presentation of blood type data (Páez Pérez and Freudenthal 1944). This inclusion of mestizos with indios was partly because the studies focused on indigenous communities, but it was also probably because many of them concentrated on the southwest region of the country, where the indigenous presence has been powerful. Overall, it is striking how the studies reiterate the black–white–indigenous triad not just as the formative basis for the nation but also as a salient aspect of its contemporary reality. Mestizaje was certainly a central interest, but it was seen as a process that affected indios and blacks, rather than whites: the biological mestizos (actually defined also in cultural terms) were part of communities identified socially as indigenous or black; even people classified in what were presumably social terms, such as "the mestizos from Pasto"—we are not told how these people were identified—were classed with indigenous people.

The blood studies of the early 1940s diminished during the civil conflict, known as La Violencia, that exploded in 1948, but they did not disappear entirely. In 1971, a foreign physical anthropologist published a study of "the black race of the Chocó," a province in the northern Pacific coastal region (Pujol 1970–71), which included data on blood types. Race was described as a purely biological matter, defined by fixed inherited traits, although the overall morphology and physiology of a racial group was also shaped by the immediate environment. While Pujol recognized that "the three races" could be found in the Chocó region, in practice she constantly used *chocoano* and *negro* as synonyms—and also referred to the chocoanos as examples of black people "of pure race"—thus creating the same slippage between social and biological profiles that was evident in the 1940s studies (Restrepo 2014: 40).

Brazil

In studies of blood carried out by Brazilian physical anthropologists, physicians, and early geneticists, we can see concerns with purity and mixture that are similar to the Colombian case; we can also detect similar ways in which biology and culture are entangled with one another. One difference is that mixture is seen in these studies as more central to the entire Brazilian population: mestizos are not included with indigenous populations in the way the Colombian anthropologists classified them (albeit this was a rather atypical usage in Colombian society). As we saw above, by the late 1920s, Edgard Roquette-Pinto had already begun to define the Brazilian mestizo in favorable biological terms, laying the ground for the broader characterization of Brazilian mestiçagem as a positive national feature, which was evident in the publications of Gilberto Freyre in the 1930s and became officialized under President Vargas.

Studies of blood groups in Brazil date back to the 1920s, when they figured alongside the anthropometric approaches as a way to characterize racial types and processes of mixture (Faria 1952: 47). Such studies became more common in the 1930s and 1940s, and some of them were connected to a concern with sickle-cell anemia as a public health problem, which had been studied for some time as a supposedly "black disease" in the United States (Cavalcanti and Maio 2011). Brazilian physicians saw Brazil as different from the United States, because of its history of mixture, which could be seen as a solution to the disease. The process of blacks mixing with whites could lead to the disease not expressing itself so frequently within the population, even if the trait was being carried by a variety of people, black and nonblack. Studies in Brazil indicated that the trait was found most commonly among darker-skinned people of African descent. Mixture seemed to be an answer, whereas in the United States, mixture was seen as a threat to the health of white people, which helped justify a ban on interracial marriage.

Brazilian scientists questioned the U.S. notion that the sickle-cell trait was purely African, because their data showed that mixed and white people also had the trait, but their studies still drew on ideas of purity and mixture. The hematologist Ernani Silva "developed a haematological anthropology of Brazilian 'racial types.' The logic behind the studies was to identify 'pure' white, black, or indigenous groups as well as mixed groups" (Cavalcanti and Maio 2011: 388). Silva studied indigenous groups, not only to explore blood group distribution, but also to prove that the sickle-cell trait was not present among them, except when they were highly mixed. The categories used by scientists varied, depending in part on whether they were publishing in English or not. Some classified their samples using Roquette-Pinto's categories of melanodermos (blacks), faiodermos (mulatos), xantodermos (caboclos), and leucodermos (whites), but with the blacks and mulatos subdivided into darker and lighter skin colors. Others referred to mixed people as *pardos* (browns), a category used in the 1940 census. Silva, publishing in English, labeled his samples as "white, negro and mulatto," and also as "Indians" and "white-Indian mixture." As in Colombia, scientists used polar racial categories (white, black, indigenous), but they gave much greater scope than their Colombian counterparts to mixed categories.

As in the Colombian studies, Silva conflated biological and cultural data: indigenous racial purity was judged both by behavior (e.g., use of imported vs. traditional items) and by hematological data, which were assumed to be roughly concordant. Cavalcanti and Maio (2011: 390) interpret this "confusion" as reflecting a transition in which social scientists shifted from "the concept of race to the concept of culture in their endeavor to understand race relations in Brazil." It is true that the conceptual apparatus used by scientists to understand human diversity was changing, and race was becoming a more contested and uncertain term, but in my view Silva's conflation reflects a deeper-rooted feature of racial thinking, in which nature in general and biology in particular are constantly entangled with culture and behavior, including at those moments when scientists strive to separate them out.

The concern with race mixture was evident in the numerous studies measuring degrees of mixture in Brazilian populations, carried out by doctors and by scientists in the burgeoning field of genetics, which was being developed from the early 1940s with Rockefeller Foundation funding and influential visits from geneticists such as Theodosius Dobzhansky and, in the 1960s, James Neel and Newton Morton (Souza and Santos 2014). The German-born medic Friedrich Ottensooser pioneered a serological method based on blood groups to estimate the contributions to "racial mixture" (mistura racial) from two parental populations (Ottensooser 1944). This was refined in the early 1960s to deal with "trihybrid" populations, allowing the calculation of the "racial composition" of a mixed sample population in terms of "Negro, White and Indian" ancestries or "genes" (Ottensooser 1962). Ottensooser's trihybrid populations were simply samples taken from several cities, with no further details given.

In the 1950s and 1960s, the geneticist Pedro Henrique Saldanha used similar techniques to calculate gene flow between white and black populations in Brazil, concluding that "White admixture accumulated in the Negro population is about 40%." For his purposes, the Negro population consisted of the Brazilian categories of "full Negroes (called Negroes) and the lighter Negroes (Mulattoes)," and he used previous studies of genetic frequencies of blood antigens and other genetic markers for the Negro population of the states of Bahia, São Paulo, and Rio de Janeiro (Saldanha 1957: 301, 303). For a later article, written while a Rockefeller Fellow at the University of Michigan, he sampled migrants from the northeast of Brazil living in a hostel in São Paulo, deemed to be a "tri-racial group," and used "racial markers"—defined as "genes whose frequency is relatively high in one base group but very low (or absent) among the other base populations"—to calculate proportions of race mixture (Saldanha 1962: 754). Saldanha showed that, although they varied regionally, rates of race mixture were higher in Brazil than in the United States, concluding "that 'the Brazilian black is twice as white as his North American counterpart,' which apparently resulted from different 'degrees of racial segregation' in the two countries," related to the greater propensity of Portuguese colonists to make "hybrid marriages" (Souza and Santos 2014: 103, citing Saldanha 1965).

These studies later formed part of a synthesis of Brazilian population genetics published by Francisco Salzano and Newton Freire-Maia, which traced the process of mixture that formed the Brazilian nation and summarized the "racial components" analysis of its "trihybrid" population (Salzano and Freire-Maia 1970: 172), emphasizing the country's high level of genetic heterogeneity (Souza and Santos 2014: 103). The authors recognized that racism did exist in Brazil, and cited as evidence the existence of the 1951 law banning racial discrimination. But they said Brazil was distant from the situation in South Africa,

Rhodesia, and the United States, because "Brazil's history shows more understanding," due to having been colonized by the Portuguese, which meant that "the unfair prejudice against the Negro that is present is not poisoned by hate." They noted that marriage patterns in Brazil tended toward endogamy within color categories and thus departed from racial "panmixia" (random mating). However, they insisted that a preference for marriage between social and racial equals was justified and natural in a context of hierarchy. But this preference had nothing to do with racism, unless it was specifically motivated by racial hatred. The authors emphasized high levels of mixture, while recognizing that racial endogamy still structured social relations; yet the latter was not evidence of racism (Salzano and Freire-Maia 1970: 56, 60). They established a distinction between "racism," which, fueled by hate, presumably aimed to establish purity, and "prejudice," which, although unfair and contributing toward racial endogamy, was symptomatic of a mixed and more democratic society.

The aim of establishing Brazilian mixture as a sui generis feature, which distinguished it from the United States, fitted with long-standing approaches to race in Brazil (and elsewhere in Latin America), which contrasted the two countries in terms of greater and lesser degrees of racism, or even its nonexistence in Brazil (FitzGerald and Cook-Martín 2014; Seigel 2009). However, the focus on mixture was counterbalanced by the imagination of relative purity, which might be located outside Brazil, in parental populations in Africa and Europe, but was also located inside Brazil, most notably in the form of indigenous peoples—who were the parental population for estimating the Amerindian "racial component"—and as relatively unmixed black people and "pure" whites (albeit Saldanha marked this purity with scare quotes). In his book on Brazil as a "racial laboratory," the idea of racial purity was challenged by Freire-Maia (1973) as part of an antiracist agenda, but a "racial components" analysis inevitably sets an admixed population in contrast to the relative purity of the parental components.

This dual perception of mixture and purity was not confined to Brazilian scientists. Santos, Lindee, and Souza (2014: 724) argue that U.S. geneticists James Neel and Newton Morton, who carried out research in Brazil with Brazilian colleagues, saw Brazil as an "idealized field site . . . [in which] Neel saw purity [and] Morton saw admixture." Both saw Brazil as hosting "primitive" populations—although Morton sometimes avoided that word—seen to be fast disappearing under the influence of social change.

Neel focused on isolated indigenous populations, which could illuminate the evolutionary starting point of the human species (see also Santos 2002).

His aim was to construct an uncontaminated baseline for calculating muta-tion rates, which related to the post-Hiroshima and Cold War concern with the effects of atomic radiation on heredity (the Atomic Energy Commission funded Neel's research); it would also allow insights into the long-term im-pact of "civilization" on health. Morton focused on mixed populations from the northeast—the same migrants to São Paulo that Saldanha had studied—perceived as having a premodern demographic regime (high rates of fertility, mortality, and close-relative marriage), which allowed the tracking of delete-rious mutations and, more generally, insights into the effects of modernization and demographic transition (Santos, Lindee, and Souza 2014). Morton was also interested in the effect of racial mixing on mortality and morbidity; with Brazilian colleagues, he received funding from the U.S. Public Health Service, the University of São Paulo, and the Department of Immigration of São Paulo. He carried out typical race mixture calculations—now using seventeen blood group and blood marker systems—on his sample, which was divided by eye into "white, light mestizo, dark mestizo, light mulatto, medium mulatto, dark mulatto and negro" categories (Krieger et al. 1965: 116). His conclusion was that mixing had no effect on biological fitness (Souza and Santos 2014: 103).

These studies of Brazil's human diversity show some common features. First, there is a marked focus on mixture as constitutive of the Brazilian na-tion. This focus made of Brazil both a genetic and a racial laboratory: as Souza and Santos argue (2014: 105, citing Warwick Anderson), Brazil was a "signifi-cant site of cognition." It was a location for interesting research in medical and evolutionary genetics, given its high levels of genetic mixture and hetero-geneity and the presence of nonmodern populations. It was also a place where racism and racial difference could be studied, a project that involved drawing a distinction between the United States, seen as the site of rampant and in-stitutional racism, and Brazil, not unaffected by racism, given its history of colonialism and slavery, but where extensive mixture meant less segregation and more potential for the democratic overcoming of racial prejudice.

Second, these studies of blood and diversity gave much room to catego-ries, both in Portuguese and English, which labeled mixed people, such as mulatos, caboclos, pardos, white–Indian mixtures, light and dark mestizos, light, medium, and dark mulattos, and so on. However, alongside the reitera-tion of mixedness, there was the constant reference to its relative absence. The calculation of "racial components" depended, as it always must, on the use of parental populations: Ottensooser (1962) used "Sudan Negroes," "Mediter-ranean Whites," and "Brazilian Indians"; Saldanha (1962: 752) used "South

African Bantu, northern Brazilian Indian, Portuguese, and/or 'pure' Whites in Rio de Janeiro"; Morton and colleagues agglomerated many existing studies into three basic categories: Negro, Indian, and Caucasian (Krieger et al. 1965). While it might be argued that, in global terms, no human population was pure, the binary of mixture and its relative lack was a key organizational frame. This meant that in Brazil, as in Colombia, the basic triad of black, white, and indigenous was constantly reinscribed within the nation, in the very act of announcing the country's fundamental mixedness: the latter took its meaning not only from distant parental populations, but from the presence in the national territory of "full Negroes," " 'pure' Whites," and indigenous populations.

Mixture was seen as a basis for substantial progress toward a racial democracy. Purity was an explicit referent early on, but by the 1960s, it was rarely mentioned or was placed in scare quotes. However, it was implied, first, by the opposition between Brazil and the United States, where segregation was associated with what Brazilians perceived as a concern with racial purity, and, second, by the persistent reiteration of the original categories that formed Brazil's mixture.

Mexico

Mixture was also central to the study of biological diversity in Mexico, but the key categorical distinction for Mexican scientists was between indigenous and mestizo. From the early decades of the twentieth century, in the context of post-Revolutionary nation-building, a powerful indigenismo, which marked indigenous people as a category for historical glorification, state protection, and future assimilation, combined with an equally powerful elevation of the mestizo as the prototypical Mexican citizen to consolidate the conceptual divide between indigenous and mestizo with greater clarity than in Colombia, where indigenista currents were not as developed.

Blood type studies in Mexico date back to the 1930s, carried out by Mexicans and foreigners (Comas 1941). An early contribution was made by Juan Comas, a Spanish physical anthropologist who escaped the Franco regime in 1940 and moved to Mexico, where he had a major impact on the discipline in Mexico and beyond, becoming noted for his antiracist stance (Comas 1951, 1961). In a 1942 article, Comas argued that blood types O, A, and B could be found all over the world and that "in establishing a racial classification of man," blood type was "a factor to be considered and taken into account, but by no means the only or the decisive one" (Comas 1942: 73). Listing blood type data for various indigenous groups in the Americas, using samples that were "the purest possible," he argued that the variation refuted the thesis that "by origin and in a state of purity the American Indian belonged to group O" (1942: 70). This did not challenge the idea that a racial classification of humans was possible; it just said that blood group data were not enough, on their own, to accomplish it. While Comas rejected the typological concept of race, according to which "all members of a race partake of its 'essence' and possess its 'typical' features," he adhered to a Dobzhanskian idea of race as a population with distinctive frequencies of certain genes, which corresponded to observable differences distinguishing "a white from a black, a Pygmy from a Chinaman . . . a northern European from a Sicilian [and] a Maya from a Tarahumara" (Comas 1977, cited by Vergara Silva 2013: 246–47, 249). This biological definition of race squared perfectly well, in Comas' view, with an antiracist stance, but it shared with scientific racist theories the common idea that races were real, natural, and easily observable entities (Vergara Silva 2013). In addition, the easy conflation of genetic, phenotypic, and social categories of difference—down to the very specific ethnic distinction between the indigenous Mexican Mayans and Tarahumarans—maintained a continuity with older ways of understanding human diversity.

Other Mexican scientists doing blood group studies were less interested in racial classifications and, in the context of Mexican indigenista agendas seeking to protect and assimilate indigenous groups, were more concerned with "the identification of indigenous variations that, eventually, could lead to specific strategies suitable for treating the maladies that affected indigenous Mexican populations, such as malaria, anaemia and paludism" (Suárez-Díaz and Barahona 2013: 106). Still, early studies did address issues of classification. The physician Mario Salazar-Mallén and his colleagues, for example, sampled various indigenous groups and mestizos from Mexico City and compared them with each other and with other populations around the world—labeled as Negroes, Pygmies, English, Hindus, and so on—as a contribution to "the study of human races." They noted that "while the groups of people to be investigated were carefully chosen for purity of breed, we are not convinced of having studied in all cases populations without some degree of European mixture." Indeed, one indigenous group resident near Mexico City itself was "a very heterogeneous lot, in which pure white people, pure Indians and mixed individuals" were present (Arteaga et al. 1951: 351). The indigenous groups were measured against a sample of people from Mexico City, about whom no details were given and who acted as taken-for-granted examples of nonindigenous Mexicans, even though the word mestizo was not used in this English-language publication.

Rubén Lisker, a student of Salazar-Mallén's and a major player in the development of genetics on Mexico, undertook a series of blood studies in the 1960s, focusing on hematological abnormalities in Mexican indigenous groups, but sampling Mexican mestizo populations as well. Like the physicians and anthropologists before him, his work was shaped by a state-driven indigenista medical-anthropological project to improve indigenous health and by the state's postwar ambition to create a medical establishment providing health care to the population at large. For example, the National Campaign to Eradicate Malaria provided the context for research on hematological traits among indigenous people (Lisker, Loria, and Cordova 1965). This public health agenda was supported by U.S. funding in a context in which areas of the "Third World" were battlegrounds in a Cold War waged with development aid as well as military hardware: poverty and ill health were seen to create seedbeds for communism. The Cold War context was obvious in the links between a colleague of Lisker's, León de Garay, and the Atomic Energy Commission, which funded his research. In 1960, de Garay established a research program in genetics and radiobiology in Mexico to study the effects of radiation on health; he also carried out studies on the genetic diversity of Mexicans. The infrastructure supporting Lisker's and de Garay's blood sampling was thus provided by state institutions such as the Instituto Nacional Indigenista (INI) and the Ministry of Public Education, both of which had networks that extended into indigenous communities and facilitated obtaining blood samples (Suárez-Díaz 2014; Suárez Díaz and Barahona 2011). The INI provided protection and support for indigenous communities, while the everyday practices of its workers at the local level reinforced the basic hierarchy of indigenous communities and the mestizo majority, and conveyed the overarching message of the need for eventual assimilation (Saldívar 2011).

Lisker emphasized the diversity of indigenous groups: he sampled each of the five major language groups defined by linguistic anthropologists. The criteria for deciding who was indigenous were simpler: in some areas, the scientists relied on indigenous schools, which selected monolingual indigenous-language speakers from recognized indigenous communities; in other areas "the people sampled lived in Indian villages, could speak the particular dialect and had the physical appearance of Indians" (Cordova, Lisker, and Loria 1967: 58; Rodriguez et al. 1963: 352). Biological diversity among those identified as indigenous was explained in two main ways: first, as a result of successive waves of ancient migration, with the possibility of pre-Columbian mixture between different groups; and second, as a result of admixture with Spaniards and, to a lesser extent and in particular areas, black people. In relation to the second factor, Lisker used the language of purity—although, like Saldanha in Brazil, he generally qualified this with scare quotes (Lisker, Loria, and Cordova 1965: 179; Lisker, Zarate, and Loria 1966: 824; Rodriguez et al. 1963: 358).

Lisker thus tended to distinguish between "Indians"/indígenas and nonindigenous people, with the latter identified mainly as Spaniards and mestizos, with some mention of "Negroes." In his work on hematological abnormalities in Mexican indigenous groups, for example, "Negroes" were mentioned as the main source of G6PD deficiency,[3] and a discussion of African slavery in Mexico ensued (Lisker, Loria, and Cordova 1965). Despite Lisker's interest in descendants of African slaves in Mexico, sparked by the pioneering work of physician-turned-anthropologist Gonzalo Aguirre Beltrán (1946), black people were not always accorded an immediate place, as when Lisker wrote that the "Mexican population is essentially composed of three groups: the Indians, the descendants of the Spanish and their mix," with black people only named as a secondary input (Lisker 1962, cited by Suárez-Díaz 2014: 113). More informally, Lisker recounted that he had spent thirty-five years of his life studying "genetic markers in indigenous and later mestizo populations" (interview data, cited by Barahona 2010: 104). In this sense, Lisker's genetic studies reproduced familiar racialized categories of black, white, indigenous, and mestizo (Suárez Díaz and Barahona 2011: 93), while also "reinforcing the dichotomy between the backward indigenous peoples and the mestizo modern nation" (Suárez-Díaz 2014: 115). The science of this period "confirmed popular common sense: when all the postrevolutionary institutions (the school, the hospital, the political party) were run by and for mestizos, when any random Mexican walking down a city street was almost certainly a mestizo, one would expect scientific scrutiny to confirm the presence of mestizo characteristics in the majority of the population" (López Beltrán, García Deister, and Rios Sandoval 2014: 91).

In sum, for Mexican scientists, the ideological combination of indigenismo and mestizaje—which, although not unfamiliar in other areas of Latin America, held particular sway in twentieth-century Mexico—meant that the key classificatory divide for thinking about diversity in the nation was between indigenous people and mestizos (with the latter including people nowadays sometimes tellingly called "Afro-mestizos"). The triad of white, black, and indigenous, which informs the notion of mestizaje found in Brazil and Colombia, is more skewed in Mexico, as blackness has typically been marginalized, almost to the point of invisibility in some domains. In these blood studies,

Lisker paid some attention to blackness, but even he tended to sideline it and locate it only in regions where it was traditionally perceived to be most evident (the Costa Chica region of the southwest Pacific coast).

Conclusion

The assemblages of which these mid-century studies of blood formed a part were complex and fluid networks. It would be possible to outline the context in which these studies took place—the postwar antiracist turn, the Cold War science-funding scenario, Latin American agendas of indigenismo, nationalism, and modernization—and pose these as independent social forces that impinged on the scientists. This dualistic approach reifies "science" and "society" as separate spheres. The assemblage perspective instead traces sets of connections and practices, infrastructures and concepts. Thus, Mexican scientists such as Lisker and de Garay depended in part on state indigenista institutions, which not only provided basic census information about indigenous people, but also provided the infrastructure for the scientists to collect blood samples; these institutions enacted dominant concepts of what indigenous people were and how they figured in the mestizo nation. How the scientists collected samples and what they did with them, in terms of analysis, necessarily followed the shape of the infrastructure in place, and simultaneously sustained it. On the other hand, some scientists in Mexico and Brazil were also funded by the U.S. Atomic Energy Commission and the U.S. Public Health Service, themselves linked to networks designed to combat communism in the "Third World" by addressing issues of health and welfare. In Colombia, anthropologists doing blood studies worked in the IEN, a new state-funded infrastructure founded by a French anthropologist, who helped link them into European debates about "race" in the era of Nazism, in which racial hierarchy was being rejected as the supposedly neutral gaze of science was applied to human biological diversity, still phrased as "racial." The IEN, like other institutions in Mexico and Brazil, including science departments in universities, enacted the state's nationalist drive to compete on the world scientific stage by building up national infrastructure in knowledge production. Tracing these complex networks of connections helps us to see how scientists had to work between protecting indigenous people, as more or less primitive isolates useful for genetic and "racial" studies, and promoting their integration into the mestizo nation, which was on the road to modernity and (racial) democracy on a global stage. The pursuit of studies about blood inevitably proceeded by means of these complex connections, while the data generated flowed along them as well, producing new connections.

These assemblages included material and administrative infrastructure, embodied in a network of public institutions, and conceptual schema of underlying ideas about the nation and its diversity, ideas which were not confined to the national sphere, but were linked into wider notions of race and civilization. Both infrastructure and conceptual schema built on existing connections of ideas, practices, and materials—for example, the geographical expeditions and data collection exercises of the previous century, which had mapped the new nations.[4] Nor was one simply the mirror of the other (Harvey and Knox 2012): the infrastructure was the materialization of the conceptual schema, but its concrete existence also enabled the schema, motivating new interventions—in this case, the collection and analysis of blood—and resulting in new and possibly unintended effects—in this case, the geneticization of notions of cultural diversity.

The conceptual components of the assemblage had several key features. First, at the most taken-for-granted level, the perspective underlying the scientists' practices posited the existence of parental categories of blacks, whites, and indigenous people, located in the past on separate continents and in the present within the nation, and the existence of the products of their mixture—mestizos. This conceptual apparatus implied ideas of purity and mixture, which were linked to similar ideas in the life sciences more globally and to governance in Latin America and elsewhere (see introduction and chapter 1). The language of purity appeared in many of the publications emerging from the blood studies—interestingly, often hedged about with scare quotes.

The use of scare quotes around the words pure and purity was a way to distance the author from the notion of absolute purity, associated with racist ideologies, while holding onto the idea that some people could be understood as relatively more pure genetically (and culturally) than others. The idea of purity worked in a relational way with particular efficacy for indigenous populations: by implicitly deploying a familiar time frame, derived from an evolutionary narrative (see chapter 1), that used the "discovery" of the Americas as a chronotope, the indios could be imagined as having been "untouched" by European and African ancestry, even if in evolutionary terms all these populations shared and share still a huge amount of genetic material. Using scare quotes suggested that many indigenous populations were by now actually "impure," due to 500 years of colonial contact, but that they would once have been pure, and thus that some would still be purer than others. Thinking topologically about the assemblage that involved ideas of purity and mixture, we can see how a particular route (the process of mestizaje) mapped out a series of intermediate steps along the way (degrees of mixture). Purity, without necessarily being named as such, was relationally made proximate to mixture as a route end-point, which remained an absent presence (signaled by scare quotes). The "pure" indigenous person or community was materialized as a ghostly presence, an intangible and temporally distanced morph of the actual indigenous people being sampled.

Second, genetic purity/mixture was normally expected to correlate to cultural purity/mixture—for example, being monolingual in an indigenous language or being bilingual—even if the scientists were aware that these two dimensions were not always concordant. As the Reichel-Dolmatoffs remarked of the Pijao people in Colombia (1944: 512): "It is interesting to observe that the indigenous group that is most pure in its customs, traditions, physical type and even language is the one which seems to have the greatest influence of a foreign element in its serological constitution." Despite the recognition that biological and cultural criteria and processes of change might not correlate, there was an expectation that they would usually go together. Overall, the connections the scientists had to ideas, practices, and infrastructures of social change, driven by the modernization that the governments of the three countries were intent on, were part of an assemblage in which the scientists were also linked to theories of evolution and associated scientific practices of designing projects and working in labs: these diverse connections together made it seem obvious that, overall, cultural change would lead to biological change and that more modernity meant more mestizaje, and vice versa.

Third, the biological and social were brought together because, as usual in this type of population-based genetics and physical anthropology, the populations under study were defined using social criteria—geographical or national location, ethnicity, perceived appearance—that operated in diverse institutional spheres (e.g., governance and policymaking, education, demography, literature, and the visual arts) and that were thus an obvious way to isolate samples. These populations were then used to identify genetic traits, thus tending to conflate social and biological profiles, when only a tiny portion of the genetic profile of the population in question was being used. Thus, the diversity of Brazilian, Colombian, and Mexican populations was parceled into categories at different scalar levels—from the broad transnational scale of black, white, indigenous, and mestizo, to the finer resolution of particular indigenous ethnic groups—which then materialized as both social and biological entities, even if biologically they had huge amounts in common and, from a different perspective, could not be clearly separated out.

Finally, it is evident that, into the 1960s and 1970s, many medics and geneticists had little trouble using the concept of race as a way to describe and classify biological variation: it was used above all to talk about racial mixture, thus apparently sidestepping any notion of purity. In Colombia, physical anthropologists in the 1970s, while decrying racism and notions of racial purity, were happy to use race to refer to biological diversity, usually distinguishing among the Caucasoid/European, Negroid/African, and Mongoloid/Asian races (Restrepo 2014; Suárez Díaz 1973: 127). But such categories were never simply biological, precisely because of the use of social labels to talk about biological profiles, because social and biological change were assumed to correlate, and because biological mixture was linked to the potential resolution of social issues such as racism. Thus, biology and culture were reentangled even as they were apparently separated, and race remained, as ever, a biocultural concept lodged in an assemblage the network connections of which could not sustain the clean separation of biology and culture that would allow scientists to define the indígena, the mestizo, the negro, and the blanco as merely biological figures: the assemblages in which the scientists operated insistently made these figures materialize in biocultural forms.

Although the scientists did not write about issues of democracy and hierarchy—except in Brazil, where occasional reference was made by some geneticists (in books, rather than scientific papers) to the perceived contrast between their country and the United States in terms of race relations—these issues were part of an ongoing conversation about modernization and progress toward democracy, and expanding programs of health care supported by U.S. Cold War funding. The use of the race concept and the entangling of biology and culture meant social issues were connected to the biological questions that geneticists studied—connected in the topological sense of making proximate elements that, from another perspective, seemed distant. Mestizos were connected to modernity and thus also to democracy. In contrast, indígenas were connected to the past and to social subordination, whether that made them liable for protection or assimilation; black people, insofar as they were not seen as mestizos themselves and were seen as a more or less pure parental population, were also connected to the past and to slavery. The mixture that was seen as typical of the nation and leading it toward democracy inevitably implied the idea of purities and the hierarchies associated with them.

II · GENETICS AND MULTICULTURALISM

3

....

Changing Practices

This chapter sets the scene for chapters 4, 5, 6, and 7. First, I lay out a sketch of the changes in genetic science leading to the so-called genomic era, which are necessary to understand the kind of genomic research being carried out in Brazil, Colombia, and Mexico. Then I give a brief overview of the shifts in the political discussions surrounding cultural diversity in each nation. This provides a basis for grasping the way genomic research and diversity politics are entangled through participation in assemblages connecting diverse components, which is examined comparatively in the following four chapters.

Changes in Genetic Science

The basic structure of DNA was revealed as a double-helix by Francis Crick and James Watson in 1953. Around this time, geneticists exploring human diversity focused on a limited number of markers associated with the blood, such as blood types, proteins (e.g., hemoglobins), enzymes, and antigens; fewer than 100 polymorphic loci in the DNA chain had been documented by the early 1970s.[1] In the ensuing decades, a number of technological changes have transformed genetic science and given rise to "genomics" and the "new genetics" (Barnes and Dupré 2008; Richardson and Stevens 2015; Rubicz, Melton, and Crawford 2006).

During the 1970s and 1980s, scientists found ways of purifying DNA more easily; they were also able to isolate specific segments of the DNA chain and reproduce these segments quickly, to provide more material for analysis and, above all, to determine the sequence of "letters" or nucleotides that make up the segments. DNA sequencing became automated in the 1980s, initiating the era of genomics, and in the late 1990s "high-throughput" sequencing massively increased the speed with which DNA could be analyzed, as well as lowering the cost. Famously, these developments led to the Human Genome Project's publication of the sequence of a whole human genome in 2001, and to global studies of human genetic variation, such as the International HapMap Project, initiated in 2002. Currently, some 10 million SNPs (single nucleotide polymorphisms or common genetic variants) have been located, vastly expanding the way geneticists can explore human population diversity. For example, geneticists can use AIMs (ancestry informative markers), which are genetic variants found more frequently—or occasionally exclusively—in the populations of particular areas of the world; the presence of such markers in an individual's DNA or a population's gene pool *may* indicate ancestry that derives from that area (Long 2013). The "new genetics" is characterized by the use of mapping and related visual techniques to represent DNA and its diversity (Haraway 1997: ch. 4; Pálsson 2007: 12). It is also characterized by the use of bioinformatics: the computing power needed to handle the massive datasets produced by rapid sequencing, and to run the complex software developed to analyze them, means that as much work is in the "dry lab" of computer terminals as in the "wet lab" of sequencing machines and chemical reagents.

Genomic science has been deployed in areas such as mapping human evolutionary history, improving forensic identification of persons, and allowing individuals to trace ancestors for "recreational" purposes, but a major driver—as in previous decades—has been the field of biomedicine and the search for genetic variants that influence health, especially "complex disorders" (i.e., not ones directly determined by a specific genetic trait). This dimension has meant a strong interest in genetic research by global companies seeking to develop new therapies and "personalized medicine," in which treatments are tailored to the genetic profile of an individual, or more likely a population category, the members of which have, or are assumed to have, relevant genetic traits in common and can be targeted as a niche market (Fortun 2008; Kahn 2013). The commercial or even scientific utility of the enormous amounts of genetic data that have been produced in the last decade or so has been questioned by some. Why decode an entire human genome when vast regions of it do not directly influence the development of the human phenotype (Barnes and Dupré 2008: 43)? Why focus so much on genetics when the environment could be a more important influence on disorders such as obesity and diabetes (Montoya 2011)? And where are the much-heralded genomic therapies (Richardson and Stevens 2015)?

The impact of genomics on social life has been widely debated. The increasing public presence of knowledge about genetics and of the "icon" of the gene (Nelkin and Lindee 1995) has spurred theories about new forms of biological or genetic citizenship, built on senses of belonging—inclusive and exclusive—and entitlement that people might feel because of genetic traits they think they share with others, such as fellow sufferers of a genetic condition, or fellow bearers of a common ancestry seen as conferring a social identity. Knowing about one's genes and the health risks they are perceived to entrain may stimulate a deliberate fashioning of the social self (Heath, Rapp, and Taussig 2004; Rose 2007). People's ideas about kinship relations can be affected by knowledge about genetic links or their absence, creating new senses of connection and disconnection (Edwards and Salazar 2009; Finkler 2001; Pálsson 2007; Wade 2007). There has also been debate about whether genomics reinforces or undermines familiar concepts of race.

Overall, some people identify a trend toward "geneticization," in which people think increasingly about being and belonging in terms of genetics, which may entail thinking in increasingly biologically deterministic ways, linked in part to the popular status of genetics as a producer of reliable truth (Brodwin 2002; Byrd and Hughey 2015; Lippman 1991; Lynch et al. 2008). But other evidence indicates that people use genetic knowledge—which they may in any case find ambiguous or hard to interpret—in selective and strategic ways, which fit in with the narratives they want to weave about themselves (Condit et al. 2004; Nelson 2008; Schramm, Skinner, and Rottenburg 2012; Wailoo, Nelson, and Lee 2012). In short, the ways in which genetic knowledge gets drawn into social life and in which social life shapes the production of genetic knowledge remain an area of debate, in which we have to examine specific cases.

Changes in Political Context

At the same time as genetic science was undergoing radical changes, with important consequences for the way genetic knowledge flows through social relations, many Latin American countries were witnessing major changes in the definition of the national political body, especially in relation to the presence of indigenous and black or Afro-descendant peoples—that is, the issues of being and belonging that genetics was being drawn into. All over Latin America, there was, from the late 1980s, a turn toward a more or less official "multiculturalism," shaped in part by pressure from indigenous and black social movements, which, drawing on a long history of resistance to co-lonial and republican rule, had been increasingly active since the 1960s, lobby-ing for recognition and rights, and occasionally using violence. The turn was also influenced by an increasing recognition of ethnic minority rights globally (e.g., the International Labour Organization's [ILO] Indigenous and Tribal Peoples Convention 169 of 1989, and the adoption of multiculturalist policies in several Western countries), which associated such measures with the image of modern democracy. Multiculturalism could be seen by various state and non-state actors as part of a solution to social inequality and the violence and conflicts often associated with it.

Latin American multiculturalism has been varied and has involved, among other measures, constitutional reforms recognizing a country as pluriethnic or multicultural and new legislation giving special rights to indigenous and/or black communities, including access to collective land titles, rights to mul-ticultural and/or bilingual education, new kinds of fiscal and political auton-omy, and affirmative action programs for access to higher education (Greene 2007; Postero 2007; Rahier 2012; Sieder 2002b; Van Cott 2000; Wade 2010). The pros and cons of multiculturalism are outlined in the introduction: as else-where, multiculturalist policies in the region have been criticized from left and right as potentially divisive, exacerbating ethnic and racial difference and ten-sion, and as tools of control and domination, extending state rule at the grass-roots level and obliging ethnic minority communities to actively participate in forms of self-governance that are highly constrained and may be subordinated to development priorities of a "neoliberal" bent (i.e., fostering corporate ac-cumulation, mobility and flexibility of labor, globalized markets, and state decentralization) (Hale 2002; Speed 2005). As ever when considering Latin America, it is important to recognize internal variation: in practice, multicul-turalism has worked out in different ways in Brazil, Colombia, and Mexico, and this creates different possibilities for the way genetic research into human diversity can circulate through assemblages nationally and transnationally.

Colombia
Colombia's multiculturalist reforms started with the new constitution of 1991, which defined the nation as pluriethnic and multicultural. The constitutional reform process had not initially envisioned multiculturalist provisions as part of its remit. The problem was one of long-standing civil conflict involving left-wing guerrillas, state forces, and right-wing paramilitaries who were often linked in clandestine ways to the state. These armed actors were involved in

disputes that centered around social inequality, control of resources, especially land, and power. Issues relating to indigenous and Afro-Colombian peoples entered the arena as a result of the election to the constitutional assembly of indigenous delegates, some of whom also championed Afro-Colombian rights with the support of a few other delegates (Van Cott 2000: 2–90; Wade 1995).

Indigenous people had long had access to special land rights, via state-recognized *resguardos* (reserves), but the new constitution and subsequent laws reaffirmed these land rights, recognized indigenous languages, gave some juridical and administrative autonomy to "indigenous territories," which also began to receive fiscal transfers from the central government, and provided for indigenous senators and representatives to be elected by a special electoral process. By 2013, legally constituted indigenous resguardos numbered 715, with an area of about 32 million hectares, representing 30 percent of the national territory, although about 80 percent of this reserve area is home to a mere 5 percent of reserve-dwelling indigenous people. This 80 percent is located in the Amazon region, where the resguardos are not numerous but very big; many smaller resguardos are located in the Pacific region and in the Andean highlands (Salinas Abdala 2014).

The 1991 constitution included—at the last minute—a transitory article relating to "black communities," which recognized them as an ethnic group and led to Law 70 of 1993 and a raft of subsequent decrees. This legislation permitted rural black communities in Colombia's Pacific coastal region—a region historically 80 percent black—to gain collective title to land. By 2013, collective land titles for black communities numbered 181, encompassing over 5 million hectares, or about 4 percent of the national territory and over 20 percent of the land mass of the Pacific coastal region, where over 95 percent of these lands are located (Salinas Abdala 2014). The definition of "black community" in Law 70 was restricted to rural, riverine communities, which were "ancestral and historic settlements" made up of families of "Afro-Colombian descent"; which possessed a shared history, a conscious identity, and distinctive "traditions and customs"; and which used "traditional production practices" (Law 70, cited by Wade 1995: 349). This focus on rootedness and ancestrality was a powerful stimulus for the "ethnicization" of blackness (Restrepo 2013a), but it has weakened a little over time, as legal challenges led to judgments recognizing a black community in an urban context, and recently a small number of black community lands have been titled outside the rural, riverine zones of the Pacific coastal region (Salinas Abdala 2014; Wade 2002a), although this tendency is still limited by Law 70 (Engle 2010: 254–73). "Black communities" can be used colloquially to refer to Afro-Colombians in general, and the state holds a register of thousands of "black community organizations," but as a legal entity a black community is still tied restrictively to land. In effect, Law 70 presented an image of Colombia as a nation in which blackness is located in the Pacific region, even though traditionally the Caribbean coastal regions have also been associated with blackness in the Colombian national imaginary (Wade 2000).

Official statistics have made increasing use of self-declared indigenous and Afro-Colombian (and Rom) ethnic identity in the collection and analysis of data—nonminority people identify themselves as "none of the above." The 2005 census counted 3.4 percent of the population as indigenous and 10.5 percent as Afro-Colombian or black (DANE 2006), and such data have allowed detailed analysis of racial inequality (Rodríguez Garavito, Alfonso Sierra, and Cavelier Adarve 2009). The census also revealed that most Afro-Colombians live outside the Pacific region, including in the major cities, a tendency that has increased as the violence devastating that region has displaced large numbers of Afro-Colombian (and indigenous) people from their land and into the big cities. This has complicated, but not displaced, the strong link between the Pacific region, rurality, and blackness.

In addition, between 1993 and 1997 and from 2001 (after a lapse due to constitutional complications), two special seats were reserved for elected delegates of black communities in the House of Representatives, while black community representatives now participate in state bodies such as INCORA (Colombian Institute of Land Reform), Ministry of Mines, Ministry of the Environment, Ministry of Education, and the Office of Black Community, Afro-Colombian, Raizal, and Palenquero Affairs (part of the Ministry of the Interior).[2] Recent legislation has promoted Afro-Colombian studies in the national curriculum and given black students special access to grants for university studies (Hernández 2013: 114–18; Mosquera Rosero-Labbé and León Díaz 2010; Restrepo 2013b: 207–68; Wade 2012a). Although there are certainly important elements of affirmative action in public policy, Colombia does not have Brazil's racial quotas (see below). In the field of health, for example, while providers are now sensitive to the ethnic and racial diversity of their clientele, the reaction is to emphasize lack of discrimination and equality of treatment, rather than to enact differentialist policies (even if racial stereotypes actually influence the delivery of services on the ground) (Viveros Vigoya 2006; Viveros Vigoya and Gil Hernández 2006).

The features that stand out from Colombia's experience of multicultural-ist reform are: (1) the powerful linking of blackness and indigenousness to specific locations in the nation, associating blackness with the Pacific region and linking indigenousness to regions such as the Amazon jungle and the An-dean highlands; these traditional links are reinforced by the importance the reforms give to land title claims by rooted ancestral communities; (2) the way blackness was construed initially as a less valid form of difference than indig-enousness and yet also conceived as parallel to it, in terms of being connected to land and ancestral community; this bias has lessened recently as blackness has become more legitimate as a form of cultural difference and as the urban dimensions of black experience—so central to Brazil—have received more attention (Barbary and Urrea 2004; Wade 2013c); (3) the relatively low pro-file of the idea of race and racism in public discourse, compared to Brazil (see below); the word *ethnicity* was preferred, and racism has only recently become a feature of political and policy debate, precisely as attention has shifted a bit toward black urban life, and as activists and academics have brought to bear their knowledge of Brazilian race-based affirmative action and the Durban 2001 United Nations World Conference against Racism (Mosquera Rosero-Labbé and Barcelos 2007; Mosquera Rosero-Labbé and León Díaz 2010).

Brazil

In 1988 Brazil passed a new constitution, which made racism a crime; en-sured the free exercise of religious beliefs (including Afro-Brazilian religions such as Candomblé, which had previously been defined as a threat to public order); protected expressions of popular, indigenous, and Afro-Brazilian cul-ture; required educational curricula to take account of contributions made by different ethnic groups; and recognized the land ownership of communities descended from—labeled as "*remanescentes*" (remnants) of—*quilombos* (maroon communities), which could apply for formal title to the lands they occupied. The constitution abandoned the assimilationist approach that former con-stitutions had had toward indigenous peoples and recognized their right to continued difference; the terms of the Indian Statute of 1973, which provided for the demarcation of indigenous territories but saw this as a step on the road to assimilation, were altered by recognizing indigenous land claims as aris-ing from original and traditional occupation. In practice, making a land claim is long-winded and difficult, but to date indigenous people, who form about 0.4 percent of Brazil's population, have about 700 demarcated territories (cov-ering over 117 million hectares or 14 percent of the country's land mass); the vast majority of this land is in the Amazon region (Instituto Socioambiental 2015).

The Palmares Foundation—named after a famous historical quilombo— was created in 1988 to oversee land title claims by remanescentes, but progress was slow, as the definition of eligible communities was restricted by the need to prove historical and genealogical links to an actual fugitive slave settlement. After 1994, this definition was relaxed, and a wider range of rural black communities—already a familiar category in Brazilian social science—was included (French 2009: 95–98). The language of being historically linked to a former quilombo faded away and communities could even become quilombos, populated by people presumed to descend from slaves, who lived a subsistence lifestyle and whose cultural forms were seen as linked to a history of popular resistance (Arruti 1997). This definition—a good deal broader than "black community" in Colombia—increased the number of officially certified quilombos to nearly 2,500 in 2014 (Fundação Cultural Palmares 2014); of these only 129 have had land titled, covering just over 1 million hectares (INCRA 2014). The wider definition also meant that quilombolas (quilombo dwellers) were not necessarily "black" in a straightforward way, even by Brazilian standards. French (2009) shows that people of mixed ancestry in rural northeast Brazil constituted themselves, at different moments, as an indigenous community and as a quilombo in order to lodge land claims. But the idea of a presumed genealogical connection was still there—almost certainly these people had indigenous and African (and European) ancestors somewhere along the line—a connection reflected in darkness of skin and other phenotypical traits associated with black and indigenous people.

Most of Brazil's black and brown population lives in urban areas, and multicultural reforms targeting them have been about access to markets and services, such as health and education, rather than land titles. In the mid-1990s, President Fernando Henrique Cardoso officially recognized that racial inequality and racism were issues in Brazil. Since the 1950s, social scientists, including Cardoso himself, had been amassing evidence in this direction. From the 1980s, statistical studies added weight by using the color classifications in Brazil's census and national household surveys to prove that pretos (blacks) and pardos (browns) were not only socioeconomically subordinate to brancos (whites), but that this difference was in part explained by race, as well as by other factors (rural–urban location, migratory status, age, education, etc.) (Hasenbalg 1985; Silva 1985; Telles 2004). These statistical studies tended to create a categorical division between negros (pretos + pardos) and brancos, a divide supported by black social movements and, nowadays, the state. In the early 2000s, presidential recognition of racism laid the ground for affirmative action programs aimed at negros: in 2001, some state universities reserved 40 percent of places for negro students (alongside other places reserved for applicants from the state public school system), but soon reduced this to 20 percent for negros and 5 percent for indigenous applicants. Despite great controversy over the rights and wrongs of race-based quotas (Fry et al. 2007; Htun 2004), by 2010, seventy public universities had adopted similar measures (Daflon, Feres Júnior, and Campos 2013). In 2012, the Law of Social Quotas was approved, instituting quotas for all public universities based on a combination of public school background and self-declaration as preto, pardo, or indigenous. Meanwhile, the National Policy for the Promotion of Racial Equality had been launched in 2003, under the aegis of a Special Secretariat, and a Statute of Racial Equality was finally passed in 2010 (after ten years of debate had watered it down into not much more than an antidiscrimination law), followed by Law 12.990 of 2014, reserving 20 percent of federal civil service positions in the executive branch of government for negros (Conceição 2014).

Policies aimed at negros also addressed health inequalities, culminating in the 2006 National Policy on the Health of the Black Population, focusing on disorders seen to be more frequent among black people and on what the then-minister for health called institutional racism in the health care system. The policy included training for health workers, money for projects targeting black communities, and the collection of health statistics by racial category. Sickle-cell anemia was a disorder of special interest from the mid-1990s, as it has long been associated with people of African descent (although it is also found among other populations), and there was a tendency, especially among black activists, to see it as a "black disease." However, the genetic trait behind the disorder can be carried by nonblack Brazilians as well, so in 2001 the Brazilian state instituted a universal neonatal screening program. Although the health problems confronting negros were recognized as affecting others too, and as mostly having social causes rather than simple genetic ones, the creation of health policies for negros evoked the idea that this broad social category shared some specific biological or genetic characteristics (Fry 2005; Maio and Monteiro 2010).

These measures constitute the most developed system of race-based affirmative action in Latin America, outdoing even Colombia. Notable is the very public and political discourse about raça (race), which is unusual in Latin American politics and policy. This is a result of the long-established debates about racial inequality and racism in academic circles, culminating in the official recognition of the existence of racism. It is also partly due to the use, since 1940, of a "race" question in the national census, although the question inquired about "color" until 1991, when the term *race* was added at the same time as *indigenous* was included as a response option. A second important feature is the attention given to black people and to racial discrimination, compared to the emphasis on indigenous people and land rights that is characteristic of much of the multiculturalist policies in other areas of Latin America.

Mexico

The Mexican version of multiculturalism has been strongly marked by the combined weight of state-backed ideologies of indigenismo and mestizaje. Both ideologies have been present in twentieth- and twenty-first-century Brazil and Colombia, but not with the institutional elaboration and support that has been evident in Mexico. After the 1910 revolution, there were limits to the formal recognition of indigenous communities. The words *indio* and *indígena* did not appear in the 1917 constitution, and legal figures such as the *ejido* (a parcel of communally owned land allotted by the state to landless farmers) and the *comunidad agraria* (communal lands owned by an existing agrarian community) were generic and not ethnically specific. However, in practice many ejidos and comunidades agrarias were indigenous and were allowed to manage their own affairs, including nominating municipal authorities, in accordance with their *usos y costumbres* (custom and practice) (Velásquez Cepeda 2000). By the middle decades of the twentieth century, indigenous communities and their governing structures and leaders were bound tightly to the state, while also being given some highly constrained autonomy in a "particularly enduring form of authoritarian clientelism" enacted by the corporatist character of the hegemonic PRI (Institutional Revolutionary Party) (Sieder 2002a: 188). State-backed indigenismo meant not only the symbolic glorification of an ancient and rich indigenous heritage, but also the practical recognition of usos y costumbres and the creation of institutions—such as the Instituto Nacional Indigenista (INI 1948)—and programs for indigenous communities, covering land distribution, education, health, and other infrastructural services. At the same time, these programs were designed to guide indigenous communities through a process of mestizaje, which would assimilate them and transform them into Mexican mestizos (Saldívar 2011).

Educational programs aimed at indigenous communities helped to produce an indigenous elite, some of whom, in the 1970s and 1980s, became strongly critical of state indigenismo and lobbied for more formal recognition and autonomy, to which the state reacted by encouraging further participation of indigenous people in its programs, under the banners of "ethno-development" and bilingual education, and promoting higher education for indigenous people, although the INI's budget plummeted during the 1980s as Mexico submitted to neoliberal measures imposed by the International Monetary Fund. In 1991, a constitutional reform defined Mexico as multicultural, and formally recognized and protected indigenous usos y costumbres. This move was prompted in part by ILO Convention 169, ratified by Mexico in 1990, but it also acted as a sweetener to counterbalance the state's eagerness to lubricate the mobility of capital and labor by facilitating the privatization of communal land, a process begun in 1982 and pushed further in the 1991 constitutional reform (De la Peña 2006; Saldívar 2011; Speed 2005).

Multicultural reform had been top-down in Brazil and Colombia as well, but there was even less input from ethnic minority groups in Mexico. In Brazil, the 1988 constitutional reform was shaped by the demise of the military dictatorship in 1986 and the mobilization of black organizations during the *abertura democrática* (democratic opening) of the dictatorship's waning years; Colombia's 1991 reform was driven in part by the need of the government to address long-standing left-wing guerrilla mobilizations, but indigenous organizations managed to win seats in the constitutional assembly. In Mexico, the 1991 reform involved only a cursory consultation by the INI with some indigenous organizations, with the result that the new text was heavily criticized by many other indigenous organizations as not going far enough. In fact, negotiations over the laws needed to implement the promises of the new constitution had barely begun when events were overtaken by the 1994 armed rebellion in Chiapas of the Ejército Zapatista de Liberación Nacional (National Zapatista Liberation Army, EZLN), consisting mainly of indigenous people. The confrontation was defused in 1996 with the signing of the San Andrés Accords, which enshrined quite far-reaching principles of indigenous autonomy with regard to territory, politics, and culture. Autonomy was based on the community, although other proposals focused on the municipality: indigenous municipalities already existed in practice in some areas and were rapidly multiplying under the influence of EZLN ideology, albeit subject to government counterinsurgency operations and paramilitary harassment; in 1995, the Oaxaca state legislature passed a bill legally recognizing the usos y costumbres of indigenous municipalities for local electoral purposes (Sieder 2002a; Velásquez Cepeda 2000). Other proposals focused on whole regions as the relevant unit of indigenous autonomy.

The uneven and conflictive implementation of the 1996 accords was made evident in the 2001 law on indigenous rights, which, while it evoked many of the principles of the accords, left most aspects of autonomy to be decided by state legislatures, opening the way to local watering down of the principles. In practice, too, the federal and state governments have used the language of human rights to limit indigenous community autonomy, raiding indigenous communities and imprisoning leaders on the basis that local usos y costumbres are causing the violation of individual human rights protected by federal law (Speed and Leyva Solano 2008). Thus, Mexico has "managed to avoid making any real changes in the direction of real recognition of cultural difference and cultural rights." This is perhaps less because ideologies of mestizaje are proving highly durable—after all, this is also true of Brazil and Colombia—and more because in Mexico indigenous rights are associated—in contrast to Brazil and Colombia—with a major armed insurrection that challenged the entire apparatus of state governance (Speed 2005: 39–42).

For Mexico, in relation to Brazil and Colombia, various key features are notable:

1. The state has been more resistant to conceding legal recognition and rights to ethnic minorities, and has tried to maintain some of the paternalistic control that characterized its former indigenista policies; there is no equivalent of Colombia's indigenous resguardos and fiscal transfers, and nothing like the affirmative action programs of either Colombia or Brazil (Hoffmann and Rodríguez 2007).

2. The key conceptual divide in terms of categorizing diversity within the nation continues to be between indígena and mestizo.

3. Black or "Afro-mestizo" people, while recently receiving some cultural recognition as representatives of Mexico's "third root," have been in the past and are still today seen as very marginal to the nation and confined to specific areas on the Caribbean and Pacific coastlines; there is no formal or legal recognition of black communities (Cunin and Hoffmann 2013; Hoffmann and Rodríguez 2007; Sue 2013; Vinson and Restall 2009).

4. The issues of race and racism get little airtime in Mexico, compared to Brazil or even Colombia; the term la raza can certainly be heard, including in relation to la raza negra, but it refers mainly to "the Mexican race," conceived as a people sharing a history of biocultural mixture (Hartigan 2013c). The difference between indigenous and mestizo people is conceived in terms of culture (language, dress, etc.), in part because, as we saw in chapter 2, many mestizos, especially of the poorer classes, are physically the same as many in-

digenous people; while black people are seen as more physically distinct, the common view is that racism is not an issue (Moreno Figueroa 2012; Saldívar 2014; Sue 2013), a view only partially unsettled by the state National Council for the Prevention of Discrimination (CONAPRED, founded 2003), which deals with all forms of discrimination. Instructive in this respect are the controversies surrounding the cartoon character Memín Pinguín, a heavily caricatured black boy who has been a favorite comic-book figure since the 1940s, with little sense that his depiction might be considered racist. His commemoration in a national postage stamp in 2005 drew criticism from black activists in the United States, and in 2008 Walmart withdrew the comics from their shelves. Although some commentators recognized the potential for racism in the caricature (Fernández 2014), officials and the public at large defended the comics, complaining that Mexican culture had simply been misunderstood by the *gringos* and that Memín could actually be seen as a symbol of Mexico's racial tolerance (Moreno Figueroa and Saldívar 2015; Sue 2013: 154).

Comparing Contexts

The preceding sections have shown that, while Brazil, Colombia, and Mexico have all been through processes of multiculturalist reform, parallel to many other Latin American countries, they did so in particular ways, shaped by their particular histories, demographies, and politics. It is important to avoid relying on a methodological nationalism, which would see each country as a separate case study that can be compared to the others, because this glosses over the fact that they are all connected to each other, especially through transnational networks and processes, manifest in such things as the ILO Convention 169, or the United Nations Declaration on the Rights of Indigenous Peoples (2007), the Inter-American Court of Human Rights (established 1979), as well as in such processes as structural adjustment programs imposed by the International Monetary Fund, the funding provided by the Ford Foundation for research into and support of Afro-descendants all over Latin America, and the grants provided by the Rockefeller Foundation to support science and medicine (including genetics) in the region. The three countries are also connected by a common reliance on a grammar of mestizaje or mestiçagem as the basis for the emergence of the nations, in cultural and biological terms, and on the associated idea of human diversity within the nation as structured by the triad of European/white, African/black, and indigenous. But the way that grammar has been conjugated in each country has been quite distinctive, and this has been reflected in their multicultural reforms and in the way genetic science has addressed issues of the genetic character and diversity of the nation.

Genetic science is not by any means determined by the social and political "contexts" in which it works, whether national or transnational. Talk of contexts implies a clear line between science and social context, which does not exist. Instead, as we will see, the way genetics is structured as an institutional enterprise, the focus of its research, and the way genetic knowledge gets drawn into public policy, whether related to health, forensics, or social inequality, are all practices that are elements in complex and fluid networks of connections that assemble diverse actors, ideas, and objects.

4

....

Colombia, Country of Regions

Early genetic research in Colombia focused on medical genetics, but, as with the blood studies of the 1940s, the biological diversity of the nation was both included in that remit and of interest in its own right. Pioneering genetic researchers, such as Emilio Yunis, Jaime Bernal, and Helena Groot, were attached to university departments, from which they established institutes dedicated to genetics, which developed research in forensic, medical, and population genetics starting in the 1960s, but more firmly in the 1980s (Barragán 2011; Restrepo, Schwartz-Marín, and Cárdenas 2014).[1]

La (Gran) Expedición Humana

A key project in which the diversity of the Colombian nation was explored in its genetic dimensions was the Expedición Humana (EH, Human Expedition), later titled the Gran Expedición Humana (GEH, the Great EH). The EH began formally in 1988, and with its successor, GEH, lasted until 1993, spanning precisely the period during which Colombia started its multicultural reforms. The EH had its roots in the Pontificia Universidad Javeriana's Institute of Human Genetics, founded in 1980 by Jaime Bernal. By the late 1980s, the research carried out by Bernal and his colleagues crystallized into the idea of an interdisciplinary expedition to go "in search of the hidden Americas," in the words of the EH's subtitle. The research was primarily genetic, medical, and also populational, but, in an innovative move, the EH explored cultural diversity as well: the well-known anthropologist Nina de Friedemann was an *expedicionario* (expeditionary), and her colleague Jaime Arocha—like Friedemann, a pioneer of Afro-Colombian studies—was involved with the project. Many of the scientific outputs of the EH were based on blood samples, which also fed into a Biological Bank, but

FIGURE 4.1 Cover of the journal *América Negra*, showing the logo of the Expedición Humana, with three faces representing indigenous, African, and European heritage.

other EH publications—those listed on its website, for example—included many cultural anthropological texts.[2] The EH journal *América Negra*, edited by Friedemann, Arocha, and Bernal, published more articles in history, linguistics, and cultural anthropology than in genetics (figure 4.1).

The aim of the EH was to "respond to the needs of the indigenous, black and isolated communities of Colombia . . . describe [their] multiethnicity, make an interdisciplinary diagnosis of their needs and provide a solution." Needs were seen primarily in terms of health, both particular (e.g., the skin disease actinic prurigo)—some of which might have a genetic component—and more general (malnutrition, parasites, infectious diseases, etc.). As the project's subtitle suggested, the aim was also to reveal a hidden dimension of the country, especially its marginalized indigenous and black populations and their historical roots: the expeditionaries "return from their journeys with a new vision of Colombia, which slowly unfolded before us."[3] The EH's leaders saw themselves as heirs to the nineteenth-century expeditions, such as the Chorographic Commission, which had explored distant domains and mapped the new republic's diversity and resources (Gómez Gutiérrez, Briceño Balcázar, and Bernal Villegas 2007: 166). This vision was seconded by a dean of the Universidad Javeriana, who wrote that the EH sought "the rediscovery of the contemporary national self" by means of constructing "a new map of the true country" (cited in Restrepo, Schwartz-Marín, and Cárdenas 2014: 72). The press reported the EH's results in a similar fashion: "Kilometer by kilometer, [the EH expeditions] have traversed the various corners of the country in search of profound roots. . . . From the findings [of the EH] the country's genetic map and human geography will be outlined, enabling us to develop a clear idea of the other nation that is also Colombia" (Ortega Guerrero 1993). Bernal saw positive consequences emerging from this endeavor: "[we] need to know ourselves if we want to live in reasonable harmony, because we cannot love that which we do not know" (cited by Restrepo, Schwartz-Marín, and Cárdenas 2014: 67).

What kind of picture of Colombian diversity did the EH produce? First, the emphasis was squarely on indigenous and black minorities; within that focus, although the launch of the journal *América Negra* was important in highlighting Colombia's black population, the EH itself studied many more indigenous communities than Afro-Colombian ones. The GEH covered nearly 6,000 indigenous people and about 1,600 Afro-Colombians, compared to some 550 mestizos and 600 "*colonos*" (colonists; see below for a definition of these categories).[4]

Second, indigenous and black communities were construed as isolated and peripheral—and vice versa: as one lead researcher said, "The Expedición Humana frequently travels to meet with our country's isolated populations, mainly black and Amerindian ones" (Alberto Gómez, cited by Restrepo, Schwartz-Marín, and Cárdenas 2014: 74). The indigenous communities studied were located mainly in the Pacific region, the rural Caribbean coastal region, the Amazon region, or relatively remote spots in the Andean highlands. The urban indigenous population—measured at 12 percent of all indígenas in the 1993 census (Molina Echeverri 2012)—did not figure. The black communities studied were mostly in the Pacific coastal region (principally in the northern Chocó province), with one other on the small Caribbean island of Providencia—populated originally by English-speaking black people—and another in the village of Palenque de San Basilio in the Caribbean coastal region, a former maroon settlement famous in Colombia for having retained a distinctive culture and language. The association of blackness with the Pacific region and with specific localities traditionally linked with Afro-Colombians was very strong. Absent were the black people who lived in the cities of the Andean interior and the Caribbean coast: by 2005, 73 percent of Afro-Colombians lived in urban areas, and 30 percent of these resided in Cartagena, Cali, Barranquilla,

Medellín, and Bogotá (DANE 2006: 20; Hernández and Pinilla 2010). Overall, the notion of diversity was almost exclusively linked to regions traditionally associated with ethnic and racial otherness.

Third, this focus on peripherality and isolation aimed to uncover the "hidden" and "other" Colombia and salvage it from the homogenizing impacts of mestizaje (Schwartz-Marín and Restrepo 2013). As a statement by the Universidad Javeriana put it, "The conservation of all this biological patrimony is truly urgent, given that the different ethnic groups run the risk of being diluted amid the progressive mestizaje of these cultures" (cited by Restrepo, Schwartz-Marín, and Cárdenas 2014: 69). According to Bernal, the survival of these communities, which had been undergoing a gradual process of extinction for 500 years, was crucial because they were "the supreme representatives of the biological and cultural diversity of our country" (Bernal Villegas 2000: 19). Diversity was linked to racial and ethnic otherness, seen as rooted in an ancestral past when local gene pools were relatively "undiluted." Although there was little direct reference to "purity"—in contrast to the 1940s blood studies—the idea of isolation played a similar role (Barragán 2011: 53; see also Santos 2002; Santos, Lindee, and Souza 2014). The notion of indigenousness and biological otherness implicitly invoked an evolutionary narrative about the peopling of the Americas (see chapter 1).

A senior researcher, recalling the EH in a 2010 interview, said "Mestizaje is the opposite of the isolate; it is what is not isolated. When we talk of isolated communities, typically what we are looking for are the sources of mestizaje. We wanted to get away from urban communities to see what genetic *fondos* [foundations] could be found by virtue of their isolation in the most peripheral zones of the country." In fact, things were not so easy because, while they sought "geographic isolation to try to limit the option of mestizaje and then try to find a cultural identity, which could correspond to a genetic identity and isolation," they found unexpected genetic links between widely separated indigenous communities, and they discovered that genetically speaking "it is very difficult to speak of an original indígena," because all of them had some degree of mixture with nonindigenous people. In that sense, the difference between an indígena and a mestizo was only "cultural isolation." Still, they had been able to locate people who were effectively "original indígenas" for particular purposes, because "it depends on what is under [genetic] analysis."[5] As with the 1940s blood studies, there was equivocation about the fit between biology and culture: on the one hand, there was not an exact fit, as indígenas were not genetically perfectly isolated; on the other hand, for particular genetic purposes, some of them were as good as perfectly isolated; and overall, cultural and biological mestizaje was the opposite of cultural and genetic isolation.

Isolation created productive diversity, whereas mestizos, by comparison, were not "diverse," or at least not in interesting ways. Isolated indigenous and black communities housed useful genetic diversity that could be used to trace prehistorical migrations.[6] Because of its geographical position, Colombia had become home to populations from "all four compass points from prehistoric to colonial times, [creating] a kaleidoscope of very varied human groups," which formed "one of the few living 'laboratories' in the world where we can still study human biological history" (Keyeux 2000: 347). Biological diversity was seen to be under threat in the same way as cultural diversity. Strictly speaking, genetic variants do not "disappear" through mixture in the same way that cultural practices might, but local gene pools with characteristic frequencies of genetic variants could be "diluted." Thus, cultural and biological mestizaje were seen to go hand in hand—much as they were in the 1940s blood studies.

A fourth aspect of the EH's portrayal of diversity related to the concept of race, which was ambiguously located, in comparison to the 1940s blood studies. It was occasionally mentioned explicitly, as when one researcher said that the project's Biological Bank would provide a safe storage place for samples of "the three races that make up this program" (Alberto Gómez, cited by Restrepo, Schwartz-Marín, and Cárdenas 2014: 75). Surveys carried out during the GEH included a question on what the researchers called the respondents' "racial group," which was deemed to be indígena, mestizo, negro, or colono: "All individuals who had an indigenous ancestor in the first degree of consanguinity were classified as mestizos, and individuals who had no knowledge or documentation of indigenous relatives were classified as colonos" (GHE publication, cited in Restrepo, Schwartz-Marín, and Cárdenas 2014: 75). The colono was a colonist: "he leaves an urban group already mestizado [mixed] and travels to the periphery."[7] They were mestizos, by definition, but at some historical remove, meaning they had no knowledge of indigenous ancestry. Race could thus include the apparently nonracial category of colono, but the category was clearly related to ancestry and degrees of mixture. Such overt references to race were unusual, and the language of the EH was about isolated groups, ethnic groups, black and indigenous communities, mestizos, and, occasionally, "Caucasians" (Keyeux 2000: 353). The idea of race was present in the naming of racialized categories and racialized ancestries, but it was rarely made explicit.

In sum, the EH's representation of Colombia's diversity fitted quite neatly with the reconfigured version of the nation emerging out of its multicultural reforms. The focus in the EH and the reforms was on indigenous and (some) black communities as the locus of diversity, understood both as a rich resource for the nation and as needful of protection. The mestizo majority was taken for granted both by the EH and, for example, by Colombia's 2005 census, adapted to a multicultural nation, which asked people to identify as black/Afro-Colombian, or indigenous (or Rom), or "none of the above." Mestizos were seen as much less diverse, or diverse in less significant ways, and this constituted them as a threat to the true genetic and cultural diversity of the nation. Compared to mestizos, isolated black and indigenous communities were relatively "undiluted" (i.e., pure, although this language was never used), although they were losing this quality through mestizaje. Although the EH sampled some mestizos and colonos, and although the Colombian state did explore and support the diversity of mestizo "popular culture" (see, e.g., Triana 1990), this was submerged by the role of black and especially indigenous communities as "the supreme representatives" of diversity within the nation. The geographical location of this diversity was also similar in the EH and the reforms: the strong association of blackness with the Pacific region in Law 70 of 1993 was also made by the EH, albeit a few other black communities were also visited. The legal reforms did not explicitly locate indigeneity in a specific region in the same way, but the EH's selection of communities reinforced the de facto association, which emerged from the land-titling legal process, between indigenous people and the Pacific, the Amazon, the far northeast, and various highland Andean zones. The EH was driven by humanitarian, democratic, and antiracist motives, seeking to protect isolated communities, provide for their medical needs, highlight their existence in a multicultural nation, and defend their right to difference. The idea was that this difference could persist alongside greater integration into the nation, in a spirit of multiculturalist tolerance. But the EH also reinscribed a national hierarchy in which black and indigenous people were linked to isolated and underdeveloped areas, while mestizos belonged to urban modernity. Moreover, the EH now described these communities in genetic terms, as reservoirs of useful and interesting genetic difference.

Emilio Yunis Turbay: An Analysis of Mestizaje

Having studied medicine, Emilio Yunis Turbay began his research into genetics in the late 1950s at the Universidad Nacional de Colombia, where he was based for many years and where he founded the Institute of Genetics. He also established a private company, providing medical and forensic genetic diagnostic and testing. In addition to his scientific articles, Yunis has published

MAP 4.1 Colombia's "natural" regions, as defined by the Instituto Geográfico Agustín Codazzi.

several popular science books, on genetics and on Colombia, and been interviewed many times in the press (e.g., Fog 2006; Gutiérrez Torres 2012).[8]

In the early 1990s, he and his students used a set of some 60,000 samples, covering much of the country, collected over fifteen years for paternity tests by the Colombian Institute of Family Welfare (ICBF), to analyze patterns of genetic mestizaje in Colombia (Yunis Turbay 2009: 94). The first scientific article on this theme used a subset of these samples to establish the idea of Colombia as a "racial mosaic" that underlay Yunis's later, more popular writings on the theme of Colombian national identity. Drawing on the mainstream genetics literature, the article used data on "racial groups" labeled negro, indígena, and *caucásico* as ancestral reference points to estimate the "indigenous, Caucasoid and Negroid [also labeled 'black'] contributions" in the Colombian samples. These samples were classified into "natural regions"—the Pacific, Caribbean, Andean, Orinocan, and Amazon regions—and into political divisions, based on the country's administrative "departments" (see map 4.1). For continental Colombia, the data showed that the negro contribution was highest in the Pacific region (nearly 55 percent), followed by the Caribbean region (about 25 percent); the indígena contribution was lowest in the Pacific region (under 20 percent), and varied between about 25 percent and 30 percent for other natural regions, with higher levels (over 40 percent) in the southwest Andean departments of Cauca and Nariño; the caucásico contribution was lowest in the Pacific (under 30 percent), followed by the Caribbean (about 55 percent) and the other regions (65 percent to 68 percent) (Sandoval, De la Hoz, and Yunis 1993). Of course, these patterns were shaped by the nature of the samples, which were donated by people for judicial paternity cases, which involved going to the offices of the ICBF or a family judge, located only in towns and cities; the "isolated" communities of the EH were less likely to be represented.

These data informed Yunis's popular books (Yunis Turbay 2006, 2009), and would be no surprise to Colombians: the division of the country into natural regions is standard,[9] as is the account of the regional variations of mestizaje (Olarte Sierra and Díaz del Castillo H. 2013; Wade 1993). What Yunis adds is a genetic and scientific dimension to what would be a vision based on history and common sense: he phrases this explicitly in a language connecting race and genetics, identifying the "regionalization of race" and the corresponding "regionalization of genes," resulting in a "racial mosaic" in Colombia (Yunis Turbay 2009: 19, 94). This has been a historical process in which "culture determines genes" (Sandoval, De la Hoz, and Yunis 1993: 8), in this case a culture of discrimination and segregation, which has given "a differential value, a racial value" to the "existence of regions which are distinguished by the [varying] genetic-racial contributions" (Yunis Turbay 2009: 94). Race here is explicit, but it is ambiguously both the genetics itself ("genetic-racial contributions") and the social valuation imposed on the genetics ("racial value").

Yunis's work presents diversity in an ambivalent way. On the one hand, he presents Colombians as all mestizos, who have varying amounts of ancestral genetic contributions. On the other hand, in the same book, he produces three maps that, although they are all depictions of the ancestral proportions of mestizo populations, are labeled separately "Black Colombia, Afro-American" (see figure 4.2), "Mestizo Colombia (Caucasian component)," and "Indigenous component of the mestizo population" (Yunis Turbay 2009: maps 9–11). Mestizos with their Caucasian and indigenous ancestries are effectively opposed to "Black Colombia." In more specialist publications, aimed at audiences in forensic genetics (and usually written in English), he and his son, Juan Yunis, divide the Colombian population into three categories—sometimes called "ethnic groups"—labeled as "Caucasian-mestizo," "Black" or "African-descent," and "Amerindian" (Yunis et al. 2005, 2013; Yunis and Yunis 1999).

In relation to multiculturalism in Colombia, the striking thing about Yunis, who is writing for a nonspecialist audience as well, is that he does not mention it at all, despite his popular books being published more than ten years

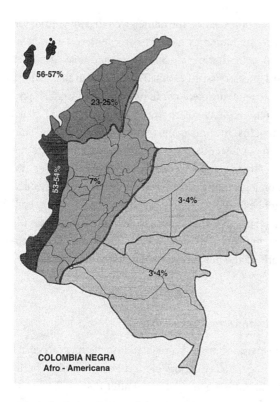

56-57%

23-25%

53-54%

7%

3-4%

3-4%

COLOMBIA NEGRA
Afro - Americana

FIGURE 4.2 Map of "Black Colombia, Afro-American." The percentages refer to the proportion of African genetic ancestry in the samples from each region. From Yunis Turbay, 2009; with permission from Editorial Temis.

after the 1991 constitution. His work both reinforces multiculturalist perspectives by separating black and indigenous peoples from mestizos (who, in Yunis's terms, are "Caucasian" to boot) and presenting them as distinct biocultural groups, and challenges these perspectives by presenting all Colombians as mestizos, with varying ancestral proportions. Overall, the main emphasis is on mestizaje, which for Yunis is a positive force for the future, although it has historically produced negative results in Colombia. According to him, the central problem Colombia suffers is its historical tendencies toward regional fragmentation and autarky, with some regions being deemed racially inferior and consigned to the margins. Mestizaje, instead of producing "the cosmic man"—a reference to Vasconcelos's *raza cósmica* (see chapter 1)—has been "exclusive and oppressive" (Yunis Turbay 2009: 311–12). On top of the regional diversity that is characteristic of many countries, Colombians "added a racial mosaic, with a good dose of exclusion," making the regions very unequal. Nowadays, "rather than abandoning the regionalization of race and 'the purity of blood,' we go deeper into and persist in them" (2009: 19–20):

Yunis cites the regional pride of the *paisas*, the name given to people from the province of Antioquia, who are famed as hard-working, enterprising, colonizing go-getters, who also claim that the so-called *raza antioqueña* has rather little black and indigenous ancestry (see below). The answer to this "failure of the nation," which has generated violent conflicts—which now affect precisely the excluded peripheral regions—is to "favor the exchange of genes and goods" between the regions, to warn against "cultural endogamies," and "to propose actions that do not foster them" (2009: 17–18). In contrast to the views of the EH, mestizaje—if practiced effectively—is seen as an answer, not as a threat. Cultural and biological diversity, based on difference, is a valued resource, which should not be disdained, but it has to be harnessed to overall national unity (2009: 18, 337). Yunis sees that mestizaje can be persistently exclusive and hierarchical, but this is because it has gone wrong (succumbing to regional fragmentation) and not gone far enough: the solution is more mestizaje.

Mestizos, Indigenous People, and Afro-Colombians

The ambivalent view of diversity—both as segregated into distinct categories and as spread across a heterogeneous category of mestizos—is evident in the work of other geneticists, of Yunis's generation and after (Olarte Sierra and Díaz del Castillo H. 2013). Delving into what the category mestizo means to these researchers reveals that, while they generally consider all Colombians to be mestizos, they see some people as more mestizo than others, or in different ways. For one researcher, the real mestizo—the "mestizo mestizo"—is a mix of the three classic ancestral components; for another, a mix of any two will do; for a third, the presence of African ancestry creates a slightly different form of mestizo from the mix of European and Amerindian ancestries, which creates the most typical Colombian mestizo; for another, most people in the world are mestizos from a genetic point of view, although in Latin America the mestizo has become most consolidated; for another again, mestizos are typically urban, with rural people being less mestizo (Olarte Sierra and Díaz del Castillo H. 2013: 238–40). This is a nice illustration of the relational character of mixture (and its unwanted cousin, purity, shut away in the attic).

The strongest sense in which Colombian mestizos are differentiated by these geneticists is in relation to region. As one lead researcher in a Bogotá lab stated in an interview:

For me, there are four big regions: Andes, which is everything on top of the mountain range. Chocó, which is a different group owing to the influx of Afro-descendants and its peopling process, which was different from the Caribbean. The Caribbean, which has five different influxes: Arab, Indigenous, Afro, and one or two types of Europeans (Spanish, Iberians, Italians, French, Dutch, Germans), and then you have the [Amazon] rainforest, which is mainly Indigenous people but there are also the colonos of different types [of European and Indigenous ancestry]. (Olarte Sierra and Díaz del Castillo H. 2013: 241)

This researcher produces, in conversation, a very typical account: the major regional-racial divisions he specifies are very common currency. In the quotation above, the regional diversity of the mestizo is strong enough to produce a three-way categorization similar to that outlined by Yunis: mestizo, indigenous, and black, with the latter two most evident in particular locations such as the Pacific coast region (Chocó) and the Amazon rainforest.

A clear example of regionalization is a paper on the genetic structure of Colombian populations, which aimed to show the diverse ancestries of different populations of mestizos within the country. The study starts with a typical description of Colombian regionalized diversity: "The population of mixed ancestry concentrates mainly in urban areas, particularly on the Andes [sic]. African-Colombians live predominantly on the Caribbean and Pacific coasts and islands. Native American populations concentrate mainly in the East (on the vast Orinoco and Amazon river basins) and in rural areas of the SouthWest and North of the country" (Rojas et al. 2010: 13). The study then reinforces this by labeling samples as either mestizo (also identified as urban) or Native American or Afro-Colombian (also called Afrodescent). The Afro-Colombian sample came from Chocó, while the indigenous samples came from the Amazon, the Pacific, and the far northeast Caribbean region, locations that reiterated both peripherality and a standard racialization of region. This differentiation by space was mirrored by a distancing in time: when calculating proportions of admixture, the indigenous and the Afro-Colombian samples were used "to infer the parental putative Native American and African populations" (Rojas et al. 2010: 15). These samples represented ancestral founding populations, consigning to irrelevance, for the purposes of this paper, all the genetic changes that might have taken place in these populations over several centuries. As with Yunis, then, there is a tension between seeing all Colombians as a heterogeneous set of mestizos and categorizing them into distinct categories of mestizo, black, and indigenous, with the latter two linked to specific regional locations.

The Paisas as a Regional Genetic Isolate

A different configuration of the Colombian mestizo mosaic emerged from the research of a group of geneticists based in the city of Medellín, capital of the province of Antioquia—mentioned by Yunis as a glaring example of the regionalism of which he disapproved. One focus of their research was precisely the paisas, a term which can be a synonym of *antioqueño*, referring to anyone born in the province, but more usually labels people seen as emerging from a particular regional history. This history is rooted in the highland zones of the province, which were the launching pad in the nineteenth century for a large-scale colonization movement of small-scale agriculturalists and traders toward the south, into the provinces of Risaralda, Quindío, and Caldas. This successful and productive movement, fed by a late nineteenth-century coffee boom, helped establish the reputation of the paisas as dynamic go-getters, a fame consolidated in early twentieth-century Medellín by rapid industrialization, fueled by coffee money. Antioquia has hot lowland zones toward the Cauca valley to the northeast of the province, and toward the Caribbean coast in the far northwest; these areas have historically been home to dark-skinned populations. In the highland areas of Antioquia, although in colonial times there was a significant black population, these people became assimilated or excluded and did not demographically shape the main colonization movement to the south, with the result that the image of the stereotypical paisa is that of a rather light-skinned mestizo or even white person, a proud member of la raza antioqueña, a trope which emerged in the late nineteenth century in response to accusations of Jewish ancestry and is still current today (Quintero Restrepo 2013; Twinam 1980). The combination of economic success—of small-holders, merchants, and industrialists—and European looks have fueled a regionalist mythology and a strong, almost ethnic identity, built around a stereotypical image of the paisa (Wade 1993: 66–78).

Some of the research into the genetics of the paisa population has focused on the idea of the paisas as a genetic or population "isolate," that is, a population located in a geographical space, with little gene flow in from outside. In general, Colombia's regionalized genetic diversity is talked about by many geneticists—for example, Yunis—in terms of histories of regional formations between which communication was slow and difficult, leading to patterns of endogamy, which might also be fueled by social motives related to control of lands and resources. But it is the paisas who have been most strongly tagged with the label of isolate in genetic research (see also Carvajal-Carmona et al. 2000, 2003), and this label, which fits neatly with existing images of the paisas as special and different, has been taken up more widely. Colombia's Caracol radio network, for example, headlined an interview with one of the geneticists involved in the research in the following terms: "Confirmed: Antioquia is a so-called genetic isolate; the Antioqueños are 80 percent European" (Caracol Radio 2006). Yunis and colleagues, in their earlier paper, separated out samples belonging to a subregion called "Antioqueño colonization," seen as somehow specific, although in fact the ancestral proportions they found—64–71 percent Caucasian, 17–24 percent indigenous, and 12 percent black—were similar to their estimates for other subregions; the proportion of African ancestry was, if anything, relatively high (Sandoval, De la Hoz, and Yunis 1993).

One research paper on the Antioqueños as a genetic isolate aimed to demonstrate the great genetic diversity of Latin American mestizos, making the general point for medical genetics that admixture mapping techniques need to be "adjusted to the specific admixture history of the population from where patients are being ascertained" (Bedoya et al. 2006: 7238). As far as the Antioqueños were concerned, the paper analyzed samples from six towns in a small area of Antioquia, called Oriente, known to be the location of early founding settlements and the heartland of paisa identity: the research sampled individuals whose great-grandparents were also from the Oriente area to ensure a sample with strong local ancestry. The paper explored why the samples drawn from this area had high levels (around 80 percent) of European ancestry in the autosomal DNA, inherited from both parents, while the mitochondrial DNA (mtDNA), inherited only through the maternal line, showed high levels of Amerindian ancestry (about 90 percent). This was explained in terms of colonial patterns of Spanish men mixing with the females of a relatively sparse indigenous population, which soon virtually disappeared: these early encounters left indigenous women's mtDNA in the genomes of their mestizo descendants (see chapter 8). Isolation was not the issue here, as Spanish men were immigrating into the area over much of the colonial period. Also, the authors recognized that there was nothing very special about such a pattern, which could be found in many areas of the Americas, where native populations declined quickly, while Spanish male immigration continued over several generations: "A similar phenomenon has now been described for several other

Latin American populations" (2006: 7234). They speculated that "a process of 'cultural' selection"—essentially increasing prejudice against marrying indigenous women as colonial hierarchies became consolidated (although they don't consider extramarital sex)—could have increased the European ancestry of the population (2006: 7238).

Isolation set in after the colonial period, they argue, and they support this with data showing the predominance of a small number of surnames in the Oriente area. But the odd thing is that the basic pattern they are trying to explain is accounted for by colonial processes—characterized precisely by lack of isolation. The postcolonial population may have been isolated (at least in the very small area where they study surname transmission), but this simply maintained the pattern established in the colonial period—again, this would not have been unusual in areas where there was little of the immigration of European women that would have lowered the proportion of indigenous markers in the mtDNA. The authors point to a major contrast between Antioquia and countries such as Brazil and Argentina, where there was massive European immigration in the late nineteenth and early twentieth centuries. But in these terms, the whole of Colombia—and many other areas in Latin America—was relatively isolated, not just Antioquia. The 90 percent figure for indigenous ancestry in the mtDNA of the Oriente samples is very high, but comparable with samples from other populations in Colombia, Costa Rica, Guatemala, Chile, and Argentina (Ruiz Linares 2014). The whole argument about isolation is, in a sense, surplus to requirements, and is not specific to the Antioqueños, yet it fits nicely with an image of the paisas as different and special (Wade, García Deister, Kent, and Olarte Sierra 2014: 201–2).

As I argued in chapter 1, the search for genetic isolates is linked to basic ideas about human evolution and the way human diversity develops through adaptation, founder effects, and genetic drift in local populations; the idea of the isolate as an object of genetic study is always in tension with the idea that people continuously move around and mix (Lipphardt 2012). Genetic research on the Antioqueños favored the idea of the isolate, and it did so by focusing on six towns in Oriente, all within fifteen miles of each other and where certain surnames were very common. If samples had included other areas of the province—the Caribbean and Cauca valley lowlands, for example—a different picture of the Antioqueño population would have emerged. Yunis and colleagues sampled more widely—at least into the lowland Caribbean zones of the province—and also did not confine their samples to people with local grand-parental ancestry. They found lower levels of European ancestry than Bedoya et al. (under 70 percent, compared to 80 percent) and double the proportion of African ancestry (12 percent as opposed to 6 percent).

The image of the Antioqueños as a genetic isolate generated some discussion on the Spanish-language version of Wikipedia, where an anonymous researcher from the Medellín genetics group defended the concept against criticisms from a commentator—a proudly self-declared paisa, who embraced his mestizo ancestry—who said the concept was biased and racist.[10] The researcher emphasized that the study focused on a specific subpopulation, taken to represent the founders of the region, rather than Antioqueños as a whole, and said that the results showed that even these Antioqueños were mestizos, not "pure" in some sense. The researcher defended the idea of genetic isolate in terms of Antioqueños having Basque ancestry and also showing the presence of the Y-chromosome haplogroup R1B, which s/he said was "almost unique" in Colombia.[11] However, many Latin American populations have Basque ancestry, and the R1B haplogroup is very common in Western Europe and parts of Africa, and thus is found in mestizo populations in Latin America, including in many populations in Colombia (Acosta et al. 2009). Interestingly, the researcher discounted the idea of significant Jewish ancestry among Antioqueños—an idea that has formed part of the mythology about the paisas because of their reputation as successful merchants—saying it had been scientifically disproved. In fact, the Medellín researchers had already published findings suggesting that about "14 percent of the Antioquian haplotypes could have a Jewish ancestry," while remaining agnostic on whether this represented an unusually high level in Colombia or Latin America more widely (Carvajal-Carmona et al. 2000: 1290, 1293). This caution about Jewish ancestry contrasted with a more general tendency among genetic researchers to characterize the Antioqueños as particular, in relation to traits that are actually quite widespread in Latin America.

In terms of representing Colombia and its diversity, this research on the Antioqueños powerfully reinforced the idea of Colombians as mestizos, but also as mestizos who were regionally distinctive in social as well as genetic terms: as usual, social identities were given a genetic counterpart. It also emphasized the relative Europeanness and thus whiteness of this particular mestizo population. In the end, then, the main emphasis was on Colombians as mestizos: this focus explicitly recenters the category that has been ignored and taken for granted for over twenty years in multicultural policies.

Forensic Genetics and Regional Reference Populations

An important strand of research concerns forensic genetics. Much of Yunis's work has been in paternity testing and the identification of human remains. The latter became a pressing issue as levels of violence rose from the 1980s onward, driven by a toxic mix of drug trafficking and conflicts between guerrilla, paramilitary, and government forces. The 1991 constitution, which aimed to ameliorate violence and conflict, failed to do so, as measures for political inclusion did not reduce economic inequality. Multiculturalist measures also failed to reduce violence, and conflict began to ravage new areas, such as the Pacific coast region, which had been relatively free of violence in the 1980s. As a result, forced displacement began to disproportionately affect black and indigenous people, despite their new legal land rights. Of the 4.1 million Colombians forced from their homes between 1999 and 2012 (CODHES 2012), it is estimated that some 17 percent are Afro-Colombians and 6.5 percent indigenous, although some estimates are much higher for particular years.[12] This is compared to the 2005 census figures showing Afro-Colombians as 10.5 percent and indigenous people as 3.5 percent of the national total.

Violence resulted in many unidentified human remains—of disappeared people, massacre victims—found singly or en masse, and sometimes severely mutilated, making DNA identification techniques especially valuable as a complement to the standard techniques of forensic anthropology. Organized training in anthropological techniques, focusing on the bones, teeth, skull, and so on, was led by the Physical Anthropology Laboratory of the National University of Colombia from the late 1980s, with training in genetics becoming more consolidated in the 1990s (J. V. Rodríguez 2004: 33–35). Questions of reliability and transparency—for example, of the chain of custody of evidence—were of concern, because state agencies were directly and clandestinely involved in violence, and were also tasked with carrying out the identifications. A famous case spanning the 1980s and early 1990s, involving the official identification of the remains of a disappeared person being contested by his mother, who brought in international forensic genetics experts, undermined public confidence in the state system (J. V. Rodríguez 2004: 215–17). This was one motive behind the post-1991 constitution restructuring of the National Institute of Legal Medicine and Forensic Sciences (INMLYCF), which included moving it from the Ministry of Justice to the Fiscalía (public prosecutor's or attorney general's office) to give it more autonomy, and adding a forensic genetics section.[13] In about 2000, the Institute established a DNA database, following the protocols of CODIS (Combined DNA Index System), a genetic database and software platform created by the FBI, based on a standardized set of thirteen genetic markers called STRs (short tandem repeats), which are loci on the DNA chain where significant allelic variation exists (Schwartz-Marín et al. 2015).

As part of the consolidation and standardization of forensic genetics, the director of the Forensic Genetics Group of the INMLYCF, Manuel Paredes, together with his colleagues, published in 2003 an important scientific paper that aimed to establish the profiles of reference populations for Colombia, using the thirteen STRs. This is a technical paper, but its importance lies in the fact that it established a standard working tool for forensic genetic *peritos* (expert technicians) all over the country, whose reports are routinely used in legal processes where DNA identifications form part of the evidence. At the same time, the paper painted a picture of the regional-racial diversity of the country, similar to that painted by Yunis and others.

The purpose of the paper relates to the role played by reference populations in DNA identification. When a sample of DNA (from a crime scene or body part) is tested against a suspect or a presumed relative, this is done in relation to a small number of markers—typically the thirteen STRs—not the entire genome. The test establishes a likelihood ratio (LR), which expresses the probability that the sample might belong to someone other than the presumed person, *within a given population* deemed relevant for these purposes. That is, the probability is calculated for a reference population to which the presumed person is thought to belong in terms of shared genetic profiles, defined using allelic frequencies for the reference population. That population is often national (e.g., in the Netherlands, Dutch people), but may be racial (e.g., in the United States, African Americans, Caucasians, etc.). In one case in the Netherlands, the defense lawyers for the accused contested the DNA identification of their client because the reference population used by the labs was made up of white Dutch people, when their client was Turkish. Using a different reference population reduced the LR—the probability that the sample belonged to someone other than the suspect—from one in 10 million to 1 in a million (M'charek 2000). The paper by Paredes and colleagues set out allelic frequencies at thirteen STR loci for Colombian populations, thus defining a reference population that could be used in DNA tests involving Colombians and would improve reliability: "the definition of specific reference databases is necessary for forensic purposes" (Paredes et al. 2003: 67).

The interesting thing about this paper, for our purposes, was that the authors thought it appropriate to create not a single reference population for

FIGURE 4.3 Map from Paredes et al. (2003). With permission from Elsevier.

the whole country, but instead four regional populations, because "each main region in Colombia seems to show different population contributions and degrees of admixture." Using some historical and social science sources, they defined the four regions, which conformed fairly closely to the standard regional division used by Yunis and others. They then used a clustering analysis on their genetic data and found a "complete correlation of the genetic data with the historical classification" (Paredes et al. 2003: 67, 68).

The authors described the regions they defined thus: "(a) African-descendants population inhabiting the North Colombian Pacific coast and the Caribbean island of San Andrés, (b) 'Mestizo' populations from the Colombian mountain range of Los Andes and populations settled in the Amazonian region and Oriental flats (Orinoquian region), (c) populations from the Southwest Andean region (with an important Amerindian component), and (d) African-descendant populations inhabiting the Colombian Caribbean coast" (Paredes et al. 2003: 68). Again, the racialization of these regions is pretty much standard, and similar to that found in Yunis and others (figure 4.3).

In fact, the genetic differences between these regions are very small in relation to the chosen STR markers. The Paredes paper did not include data about genetic distances between the populations—for example, fixation indices (F_{ST}) and other data regularly used by similar studies (Rubi-Castellanos et al. 2009;

Salazar-Flores et al. 2015)—but when the peritos came to calculate LRs using the four regional tables of allelic frequencies, they found that it barely made any difference which table they used. This is mainly because the STR markers used are highly polymorphic (i.e., highly variable), which allows them to overcome the kind of genetic differences commonly attributed to ethno-racial and biogeographical groupings on the basis of other kinds of markers, such as AIMs (ancestry informative markers). Yunis's regional picture was based on continental genetic ancestries, which show greater differentiation by region.

Despite the inability of Paredes' regions to capture significant genetic diversity in the STR data, the peritos still used—indeed were obliged to use—the table, assigning the cases that arrived on their desks to one of the four regions, making the appropriate calculation, and naming the relevant reference population in the reports they wrote for the legal teams. They could, of course, see that the table did not capture much genetic differentiation in the Colombian population in relation to the chosen markers, yet the table seemed an obvious and innocuous tool (Schwartz-Marín et al. 2015). This was because the peritos—like other geneticists and the general public—did not doubt that region was crucial to understanding human diversity in Colombia: as one said, "here we separate it [the DNA] by regions, Colombia by regions, for us it is easier to separate them [the samples] by region." And regions had racialized connotations: alongside the idea that everyone in Colombia was mixed, for the peritos it was clear that the coastal regions had more black people in them, while the southwest provinces had many indigenous people and mestizos with a lot of indigenous ancestry. As one perito said, "we are definitely not the same, I mean if you travel to the Pacific coast of Colombia you will find a totally different race, from what you find here in the center of the country, and the same will happen if you go to the eastern side of our country, you will find lots of indigenous population, the same in the southwest, and they are not the same . . . we are not the same."[14] The table thus resonated with their commonsense understanding of Colombia's racialized regions, even if its regions were redundant for their technical calculations.

The same peritos generally rejected the concept of race as a biological reality—although the word occasionally slipped in, as in the quotation above. The word race for them was associated with ideas about pure races, which they saw as inappropriate to thinking about Colombia, and a product of racist ideologies. They also thought the kind of markers that forensics genetics used had nothing to do with race, because they did not correlate to phenotype; they were neutral and thus ethically sound. Yet race was part of the more general forensic processes that surrounded the peritos. For example, the INMLYCF's manual for the forensic identification of corpses instructs technicians how to identify the "racial ancestor," "racial filiation," or "racial pattern" by examining the skull and, where possible, skin color to establish "which of the three main racial groups (Caucasian, Negroid and Mongoloid) predominates in the cadaver" (Morales and Niño Córdoba 2009: 78). Peritos in forensic genetics were not physical or forensic anthropologists, but this kind of classification formed part of their institutional infrastructure. They rejected the explicit use of the race concept, but race was a normal part of forensic practice, and the racialization of Colombia's regions formed part of the same common sense that shaped the production of the four reference populations in the first place.

This is similar to what Kahn (2012) found in U.S. forensic genetics practice, where racial categories are still used to calculate LRs, even though, *for legal purposes*, it makes no difference which racial reference population is used. Current technologies allow for extremely low probabilities to be calculated: for a judge or a jury it does not matter if the probability is 1 in 96 billion or 1 in 180 billion—the match is secure either way. Yet racial categories are still used because of the "inertial power" of race in U.S. culture: it matters in many domains of social life, so it continues to matter in DNA matching, even if its use is acknowledged to be a matter of "convenience, uniformity and clarity" rather than technical necessity (Kahn 2012: 123, citing an official report).

In Colombia, racialized regions continue to matter, even though they are virtually irrelevant to the calculation of probabilities in the peritos' labs. When the regional reference populations enter the courtroom, they disappear almost completely: the naming in the peritos' reports of the reference population used for the LR calculation is routinely ignored in light of the infinitesimal probabilities of mismatching: the simple number—a chance of 1 in millions or billions—suffices. Interviews with participants in the courtroom, such as lawyers, public prosecutors, judges, and police investigators, revealed that they did not grasp the technicalities of reference populations (Schwartz-Marín et al. 2015).

This effect can also be seen in the way forensic DNA identifications are reported in the Colombian press. When commenting on specific cases—often the identification of human remains—DNA is mentioned as the final arbiter, achieving confidence levels of 99.9 percent in linking remains to a family member. Race is almost never mentioned directly, and even region is tangential, although it may be inferred by the reader from the naming of specific locations where the remains were found. In contrast, reports on population genetics—such as the studies by Yunis—are much more outspoken about region, and use racialized terms such as *negro, mestizo,* and *indígena* (Díaz del Castillo H., Olarte Sierra, and Pérez-Bustos 2012).

The significance of Paredes's technical paper for Colombian multiculturalism may seem slight, but there is a twofold connection. First, like Yunis's work, the paper gave a biological idiom to talk about regional-racial difference in a way that chimed with multiculturalist constructions of the nation and the location of its ethnic diversity. Even if the particular markers used did not, in the end, really substantiate genetic difference, the way the tables of allelic frequencies entered into the daily practice of the peritos reinforced their existing perception that Colombia was divided regionally, and racially, in cultural and biological terms, with biology encompassing phenotype and genotype. Second, the creation of standard instruments such as these tables was part of a project to strengthen Colombia's democratic accountability and transparency, linked to the aim of resolving conflict and violence: restructuring the IN-MLYCF and improving forensic identification techniques were components in this larger project. Multiculturalist reforms were a related project in the broad drive to reduce inequality and conflict, and enhance tolerance and national integration. Paredes's article represented an interaction of these two projects by producing a version of Colombia that promised greater reliability in the legal process by marking racial-regional difference.

Conclusion

In Colombia, geneticists participated in complex networks in diverse ways that linked them to national forensics and political violence, global medical genomics and theorizing about evolutionary history, and popular discourses about the nation's characteristics and problems, including regional identities and the need to protect indigenous communities. The geneticists' practices and the knowledge they produced provided biological concepts and language that circulated through the nodes of these networks and allowed mutable mobiles, such as the mestizo, the indígena, and the Afro-Colombian, to be materialized in divergent ways. Geneticists themselves did not have to undertake these materializations (although EH researchers and Yunis, for example, did do some of this work), but they participated in networks where such materializations were already formed. On the one hand, indígenas and negros appeared as distinct racialized populations and cultures set in a modern multicultural mosaic-like nation—alongside a taken-for-granted mestizo majority—to form a democracy of difference. On the other hand, the mestizo was foregrounded and marked as constituting the nation as a single population, heterogeneous in biology and culture, to be sure, but essentially the forward-looking result of an ongoing mixture, which produced a democracy of sameness. In both cases, the promise of democracy was insistently undermined by the possibility of reassembling these figures into topological proximity with familiar ideas of hierarchical difference that located black and indigenous populations in the periphery and in the past, and associated progress with mestizos. Black and indigenous groups were used by geneticists as relatively unmixed samples able to stand in for parental populations; purity was not a term considered appropriate, but it was relationally implied as an absent presence by the simple concept of mixture. The language of race could be quite explicit, as in Yunis's case, or it could be implicitly lodged in the way people spoke about (Caucasian) mestizos, Afro-Colombians, and indigenous people (with the latter as both contemporary and parental populations). Or in specific contexts—the presentation of forensic DNA evidence in the courtroom or the press, when individual identifications predominated—the whole issue of race and region could virtually disappear. Here genetics did not add biological freight to collective social categories of nation and racialized region, but instead added biological certainty to individual relations of kinship and responsibility.

What can Colombia tell us about the concept of mixture in genomics? Colombia is an example of geneticists emphasizing a relatively negative vision of mixture. Like the anthropologists of the 1940s blood studies, Expedición Humana researchers materialized mestizos as threat and predator; they were linked to modernization, but they spelled the end of cultural and biological diversity understood as a set of more or less isolated gene pools, twigs at the ends of the branches on the tree of life—in the case of indigenous Americans, potentially very interesting twigs due to their evolutionary history. Yunis saw mestizos as an expression of mixture gone wrong: they were people obsessed with hierarchy and exclusion, which had led to the fragmentation, conflict, and violence that had wracked Colombia for so long and which defined its global image. Other geneticists, who did not venture into popular writing, avoided these value judgments, but they all confirmed the racialized, regional fragmentation of their mestizo country. Genetic portraits that reinforce a picture of molecular difference provide fuel for exclusions that operate on those differences as they are materialized in social relations. This much is evident from India, where DNA data have been drawn into debates about the origins of castes: researchers argued that ancient mixtures suddenly stopped about

1,500 years ago when endogamic rules were imposed, creating castes as social and genetic entities (Kapila 2007; Newitz 2016). In Colombia, when the very tools developed to aid processes of restitution—DNA identification of victims of violence—also reiterate the racialized regional differences that have been argued by many to contribute to the country's conflicts, then there is reason for pessimism.

On the other hand, different materializations can emerge from assembling connections in a different way, creating topological proximities between elements that appeared distant in a previous formulation. Yunis optimistically reconfigured more mestizaje as the solution to regional fragmentation; research arguing that Antioqueños were a genetic isolate drew a critical response from at least one commentator, who detected the possible racist connections of such an argument; and in the courtroom, the regional differences of DNA disappeared, because for legal purposes—which have more weight than simple genetics when dealing with violence—they are irrelevant. In this positive view, mixture need not lead to dull homogeneity as the opposite of hierarchy: instead, it can lead to a different kind of diversity, understood as the rhizomic and endless proliferation of heterogeneous mestizos.

5

....

Brazil, Race, and Affirmative Action

In Brazil, genetic data circulated through complex networks traversing labs, genomic projects, scientific journals, popular science publications, funding bodies, state institutions and policymakers, mass media, and social movement activists.[1] The data were articulated with other elements in varied and indeed contradictory ways—materializing mestizos, blacks, browns, indígenas, and whites—but the dominant trend in the way genetic data were drawn into public debates produced a biologically raceless Brazilian mestizo (and indeed a raceless human being); this was also a mestizo who did not fit into a multiculturalist nation, at least when multiculturalism was perceived as reinforcing racial division. The social and the biological were separated out and reentangled in complex ways—more so than in Colombia—and as they became entangled, the boundaries separating them became blurred. Vociferous denials of the biological reality of social categories of race and color went hand-in-hand with claims that social policy should be guided by the biological facts of mixture, and genetics was asserted as both relevant for social issues and totally irrelevant. The "bare facts" of DNA were seen as unrelated to social identity, and as themselves social facts weighted with meaning.

Sérgio Pena and the Critique of Race

The geneticist best known in Brazil for commenting publicly on the intersection between genetic science and society is Sérgio Pena, who has become a kind of media-savvy public scientist-intellectual, not unlike the case of Emilio Yunis in Colombia, but with a higher profile (figure 5.1). Like Yunis, he was trained in medicine, much of his work is in medical genetics, and he works in a university-based research context (currently in the Federal University of

FIGURE 5.1 Sérgio Pena.

Minas Gerais), and also owns a commercial DNA testing lab; like Yunis, he has been interviewed in the press numerous times and, alongside his scientific papers, has published a number of popular books about genetics in general and about his own country's history, demography, and identity.[2] Unlike Yunis, Pena has campaigned energetically against the use of the concept of race and race-based categories in genetics, medicine, and social policy.

From the mid-1990s, Pena started publishing with colleagues on the ancestral origins of American populations (e.g., Pena et al. 1995), and in 2000 he was lead author for an article titled "Molecular Portrait of Brazil" in a popular science magazine, summarizing some key results about "how much is there of the Amerindian, the European, and the African in each one of us" (Pena et al. 2000: 16). The article used data from a sample of 200 "white" people, according to the self-identified color/race classifications of the Brazilian census, spread across four of Brazil's official five major geographical regions: Southeast, North, Northeast, and South. Data presented analyzed the geographical origins of the haplogroups found in Y-chromosome and mitochondrial DNA and showed that some 90 percent of Y-chromosome haplogroups were of definite or probable European origin, with very few having clear sub-Saharan African or Amerindian origins. In contrast, the mtDNA haplogroups were fairly evenly split among European, African, and Amerindian origins: the 60 percent contribution of the latter two was seen as "surprisingly high" (2000: 25). These average patterns varied between major regions, in accord with their demographic histories: mtDNA haplogroups of Amerindian origin were more common in the North, for example; ones of African origin were more frequent in the Northeast, and those of European origin were a majority in the South. The data demonstrated the well-established idea that early sexual encounters between European men and indigenous and African women had been important in shaping the early colonial population (see chapter 8), while massive immigration of European men and some women in the nineteenth century, mostly to the South and Southeast, had brought more European-origin haplogroups to the mix, including in the mtDNA.

The article mentioned the race/color categories used in the national census, but was careful to point out that race was "more a social and cultural construction than a biological one": there was no biological foundation for the idea of human races, and biologically homogeneous human groups did not exist either (Pena et al. 2000: 20). The language of race was thus only used in relation to social and census categories ("black Brazilians," "whites") and the definition of the study sample ("the white population"). Otherwise, the language was geographical—"European genes," "African Y-chromosomes," "Amerindian haplogroups"—but, as usual in this kind of genetic diversity research, it was deployed in a way that resonated very easily with racialized categories, such as white, black, and indigenous. The language also gave geographical categories a genetic weighting: shorthand use of terms such as *African Y-chromosomes*, again common in this kind of research, suggests entire chromosomes could be labeled African, rather than specific genetic variants on the chromosome being historically traceable to Africa.

The take-home message of the article came back to race as a social issue: while Brazil was "certainly not a 'racial democracy,'" the authors liked to believe that, naïve as it admittedly might seem, "if the many white Brazilians who have Amerindian or African mitochondrial DNA were to become aware of this, they would value more highly the exuberant genetic diversity of our people and, perhaps, would construct in the twenty-first century a more just and harmonious society" (Pena et al. 2000: 25). Here we see the idea that awareness of genetic realities might impact on people's social attitudes: there was no genetic basis for race as a social identity, but there might be one for a raceless and tolerant democracy.

Soon Pena added a wrinkle to this molecular portrait, in the form of the genetic uniqueness of the Brazilian population (Kent et al. 2015). Editing a book with chapters by anthropologists, linguists, historians, and geneticists on the

Brazilian people, Pena and colleagues coined the term *Homo brasilis* to represent, "a little irreverently," the idea that in Brazil "a process of genetic mixture was initiated that is unique in the entire history of Humanity, generating the contemporary Brazilian" (Pena 2002b: v). The notion that Brazil's population was special was important in ways—which will become apparent below—connected to arguments about the nonexistence of genetic race and to claims about the inappropriateness of global (read U.S.) medical and social policies for Brazil.

The theme of the nonexistence of genetic race—already clear in the "Molecular Portrait"—has been a constant concern for Pena in his scientific and popular publications. Brazilian mixture helped emphasize the nonexistence of biological race; if it was generally impossible to classify humans into biological categories of race, this was made emphatically clear in Brazil, where the social conventions of race/color, which divided people into white, black, brown, yellow (meant to capture Asian Brazilians), and indigenous, had no biological basis due to the country's history of intensive mixture. Successive publications by Pena and colleagues made this point in diverse ways, with different implications drawn out:

1. A 2003 paper used a variety of samples—rural and urban, black, white, "intermediate," and indigenous—to measure an "African ancestry index (AAI)" for individuals. The study found that color classifications in Brazil—whether assigned clinically on the basis of phenotype (skin color, hair type, nose and lip shape), or by self-identification—had little relation to AAI. This was because the ten "population-specific alleles" that defined the AAI were designed to pick up African ancestry in general; only a small part of this would be related to the phenotypical traits that socially prompted the Brazilian color classifications, which had been shown by demographic studies to influence mating and marriage patterns; thus it was possible to have a white group and a black group, in Brazilian color terms, which had similar AAIs. The paper sought to make clear "the hazards of equating color or race with geographical ancestry . . . as is often done in scientific and medical literature" (Parra et al. 2003: 181). It is no good looking at someone's face (especially in Brazil) to ascertain relevant medical facts about their biogeographical ancestry.

2. A later article, published in a social science journal special issue on race and affirmative action, used these and other data to show that nearly 90 percent of Brazilians have more than 10 percent African ancestry and that whites, browns, and blacks did not differ very markedly in this respect; many whites had significant African ancestry and many blacks and browns had a lot of European ancestry. This meant that it was not possible genetically to define who should

be eligible for university quota places for "black" applicants (Pena and Bortolini 2004). Pena and Bortolini argued that genetics could not take on "an explicitly prescriptive role" in political decisions, but that "the genetic profile of the Brazilian population should be taken into account" in such decisions (2004: 46).

3. The same conclusion inspired another piece coauthored with a philosopher and published in a journal special issue about racial quotas. Here Pena argued that "the only way of dealing scientifically with the genetic variability of Brazilians is individually, as singular and unique human beings in their mosaic genomes and in their life histories" (Pena and Birchal 2006: 19). Any collective categorization did not work genetically—although Pena himself had used collective categories of region to organize genetic data in the "Molecular Portrait." In any case, quotas for "black" students could not be legitimated in terms of genetics, and this scientific fact was important because, while science did not generate moral rules, it did play "an important role in instructing the social sphere by showing 'what is not,' it liberates, that is, it has the power to avert errors." With Birchal, Pena now took a stronger line than before, saying that "science could contribute to a prescriptive position in favor of a nonracialist society." In this respect, the "scientific fact of the nonexistence of 'races' must be assimilated by society. . . . Awareness of this [fact] meets the utopian wish of a nonracialist, 'color-blind' society, where the singularity of the individual is valued and celebrated" (2006: 13, 20).[3]

4. Pena applied this kind of reasoning to medical genetics. In a history of science and medicine journal special issue on race, genetics, identity, and health, he argued that "color and/or geographic ancestry have little or nothing useful to contribute to medical practice, particularly when it comes to caring for an individual patient" (Pena 2005). Even disorders such as sickle-cell anemia, which is often seen as particular to people of African descent and, in Brazil during this period, was being claimed by some as a doença de negros (a black people's disease), was for Pena a disease related to certain evolutionary adaptations to malarial environments, not color categories or continental origins (see also Tapper 1999; Wailoo and Pemberton 2006). For Pena, race was "toxic," used to foster oppression; it had no role in a clinical context.

5. The irrelevance of collective color or ancestry-based categories for medicine was reiterated in relation to pharmacogenomics by Pena and other colleagues (see Santos, da Silva, and Gibbon 2015). Because the way people classified themselves in Brazil in terms of race or color had been shown to correlate only weakly with genomic ancestry, it made little sense in Brazil to use the criteria of "skin color and self-reported ethnicity [that] have systematically

been used in the pharmacogenetic/-genomic literature as phenotypic proxies for geographical ancestry." Brazil's population admixture challenged "the appropriateness of this approach" and showed that "admixture must be dealt with as a continuous variable, rather than proportioned in arbitrary subcategories" (Suarez-Kurtz et al. 2007: 765). In other words, the kind of racial-ethnic categories that a U.S. medic might use to infer genetic ancestry and inform diagnosis or dosage regimes would not work in Brazil (Suarez-Kurtz 2011). In fact, this was a more general lesson about the dangers of relying on collective categories based on phenotypic proxies: "Because interethnic admixture is either common or increasing at a fast pace in many, if not most populations, extrapolation on a global scale of pharmacogenomic data from well-defined ethnic groups is plagued with uncertainty." In general, it was better to look at the genetic profile of each individual in terms of a continuum of ancestral contributions, rather than use population-based categories (Suarez-Kurtz and Pena 2006).

6. A similar concern with collective categories based on race and color lay behind the cautions expressed by the authors of a paper on genomic ancestry and color in Brazil written by five social scientists and two geneticists, of which Pena was one. The data showed "closer biological proximity between browns and whites" rather than browns and blacks, meaning that any health policies directed at a politically defined category of negros (encompassing browns and blacks) could be misdirected if it assumed that all these people shared some medically relevant genetic profile (Santos et al. 2009). As noted in chapter 4, in 2006 the government had published a National Policy on the Health of the Black Population.

7. A later paper took another swing at the use of collective categories—this time, the region—to organize genetic data on ancestry. Although in the "Molecular Portrait" Pena had used regional categories himself, he and his colleagues now challenged their usefulness in making significant genetic distinctions in Brazil. They noted that color categorizations were subjective and varied between regions: someone identifying as white in the North could have a very different genetic ancestry profile from a white person in the South. To allow for this, they created a "color-independent total ancestry" measure by multiplying "the proportions of a given ancestry in a given color category by the official census information about the proportion of that color category in the specific region." That is, to measure total European ancestry in the North, they weighted the amount of European ancestry of whites, browns, and blacks according to the relative demographic share of each category in the North's population. This was different from looking at the average European ancestry of a random sam-

ple of people from the region. The results showed that there was less regional variation than had appeared previously, and that, because of the large influx of immigrants from Europe, all regions showed a predominance of European ancestry, ranging from 61 percent in the Northeast to 78 percent in the South (Pena et al. 2011). These results were again held to show that, in a pharmacogenetic context, "each person must be treated as an individual rather than as an 'exemplar of a color group,'" not only in Brazil but also in other countries with admixed populations. Furthermore, "the introduction of public policies favoring the non-White population," based in part on the fact that nonwhites were a demographic majority, could not be supported by genetic data, which showed that, "for instance, non-White individuals in the North, Northeast, and Southeast have predominantly European ancestry and differing proportions of African and Amerindian ancestry" (Pena et al. 2011). Again, then, public policy was supposed to take its cue from genetic realities.

The publications above were all scientific and academic papers, but Pena also wrote several more accessible texts, such as the book À flor da pele: Reflexões de um geneticista[4] (Pena 2007), which had a chapter titled "Recipe for a Deracialized Humanity," and the short book Humanidade sem raças? (Humanity without Races? Pena 2008). As noted above, he has contributed to online and print media, in the form of interviews, articles, and blog posts. In 2012, he kicked off a media campaign called "We R No Race," which coincided with the London Olympics and used a spot in the Brazilian Embassy in London, where free DNA tests were given to some 800 people, with which they could find out about their ancestry and which would underline the fact that all humans are biologically very similar; the offer was part of the Brazilian government's promotion of the 2014 World Cup, where the same free DNA test offer was planned, but did not materialize (Herbert 2012; Portal da Copa 2012). The campaign was accompanied by an online video, which outlined how the genetics of human biological diversity gave no basis for the idea of races, and ended with statements about the mixed ancestry shared by all Brazilians, the country's multicolored population, and the cordial welcome that would be extended to visitors to the 2014 World Cup and the 2016 Olympics (Pena 2012).

Pena, Genetics, and University Racial Quotas

The genetic data described above became an important component in public debates about race-based affirmative action in education and health. These policies, pushed forward by the state and favored by black activists and a sec-

FIGURE 5.2 A group of students at the University of São Paulo demonstrate in support of racial quotas. The slogan reads "Those against quotas are racists."

tor of the academic community (Carvalho 2003; Lobato and Santos 2003; Nascimento et al. 2008), were opposed by significant numbers of politicians, academics, and influential parts of the mainstream media (Daher et al. 2008; Fry et al. 2007). The debates varied according to who was talking—left-leaning academics opposing the policies made arguments different from those made by right-leaning newspapers—but the key issue was whether it was right to address social inequalities, which had a clear racial dimension, with policies that explicitly recognized racial or color groups in the society and accorded them special rights (figure 5.2).

This issue—whether phrased in terms of race, ethnicity, or culture—is central to all debates about affirmative action as a forceful manifestation of multiculturalism (Fraser and Honneth 2003; Taylor and Gutmann 1994; see also introduction). One view holds that social inequalities are best addressed by redistribution policies that target poverty generally, not in a differential way; institutionalizing differences of race (or ethnicity or culture) will only reinforce these differences, embedding them more deeply into society, when the ultimate aim is to achieve a society in which racial (or ethnic or cultural) differences are irrelevant to a person's life chances in the public sphere, even if the recognition of such differences may be acceptable in "private" spheres that are seen as not impinging on public life. The opposing view argues some combination of the following points to support differentialist policies: (1) Racial inequality is caused by past racism, which has put particular racialized categories of people at a disadvantage, which needs to be corrected by differential action. (2) Current racism reinforces existing racial inequality and creates disadvantages for subordinate racialized categories of people, which need to be directly addressed. (3) Policies aimed at poor people will by default help poor black people, but they cannot correct racism, which may affect the implementation of these very policies and which shapes life chances outside the remit of these policies (e.g., for middle-class blacks). (4) The divide between "public" and "private" which the anti–affirmative action position relies on is unrealistic, because the very differences deemed acceptable in the so-called private sphere (e.g., indigenous language, black cultural practices) actually operate in public ways (e.g., language impinges directly on schooling, and negative stereotypes about black cultural practices can shape employment prospects). (5) Policies favoring racialized categories give these groups greater public visibility, which helps to affirm group solidarity and identity, thus empowering individual members to fight racism and giving them the self-confidence to pursue their own life goals. These points all underlie the idea that an unfairly disadvantaged group needs to be given a special "leg up" in the competition of life in a stratified society.

These moral and political debates mobilized genetic data considered to prove the nonexistence of biological race, and used them to reaffirm the political stance that racial divisions, while they unfortunately did exist in Brazil, should not be the basis of an even-handed and fair public policy. As Pena had argued, social policy should take the genetic facts as a mandate. Another related use of genetic data asserted that "black" was not a real (i.e., genetically meaningful) category in Brazil, because everyone was mixed, and therefore a social policy directed at this category was not justifiable (Kent and Wade 2015).

At first, however, genetics was used in a slightly different way. In 2003, Rio de Janeiro State University (UERJ) opened 40 percent of its places to people declaring themselves to be negro or pardo (brown). Claims were soon made that some apparently white students from privileged backgrounds were applying for black quota places, on the basis that, as Brazilians, they had some African ancestry. This led to other universities establishing controversial vetting procedures, based on interviews and photographs (Maio and Santos 2005). In a magazine interview, Pena reported that some light-skinned pardos, whose applications were rejected because they looked white, had DNA tests done by his lab to prove their African ancestry (Gomes 2007: 72). Although this looks like an affirmation of blackness, in fact genetic data were being used to underwrite a view that any Brazilian with some African ancestry was eligible for a racial quota place, even if they looked more or less white and thus were likely to escape the racism—aimed at people who actually *looked* black or dark-skinned—which the quota system was designed to compensate for. The message was ambivalent: "We are all genetically mixed, so we are all eligible for the resources on offer; university places should not be reserved for particular racial categories"; but also, "even if we don't look black, we are genetically Afro-descendant, so we are eligible for black quota places." In either case, genetics was seen to define social identity.

These challenges presaged the use of genetics to challenge the whole idea of racial quotas. This was evident in various ways. First, the media presented genetic data that attracted a lot of attention: the Globo TV and press network, *Folha de São Paulo* newspaper, and *Veja* magazine widely publicized Pena's work (Kent and Wade 2015). Reports on the "Molecular Portrait" and on the 46th National Congress of Genetics, which in 2000 had the theme "Brazil—500 Years of Genetic Mixture," focused on genetic data showing the simple prevalence of mixture, sometimes linking this to classic statements about Brazil's mestiço character by such writers as Gilberto Freyre (Azevedo 2000a, 2000b; Leite 2000). A couple of years later, the same message was complemented by statements about the genetic nonexistence of race (Azevedo 2002; Pena 2002a).

A widely reported event was the BBC Brazil project on Afro-Brazilian Roots, which commissioned DNA tests by Pena's lab on nine Afro-Brazilian celebrities. An iconic figure of Brazilian black culture, the dark-skinned samba dancer and musician Neguinho da Beija Flor, was revealed to have 67 percent European ancestry (Salek 2007). This finding was widely used to challenge racial quotas. For example, the lawyer Roberta Kaufmann, attorney general of the Federal District of Brasilia and author of a comparative study of affirmative action (Kaufmann 2007), who submitted a petition to the Supreme Court in 2009 challenging the constitutionality of the racial quota system in the University of Brasilia, commented on her blog that "it is more probable that Neguinho da Beija-Flor is a descendant of a person who owned slaves than of a black person who was enslaved. . . . For this reason, there is no way you can justify racial quotas [as a reparation for descendants of slaves]" (Kaufmann 2011). In an interview she quipped that Neguinho should have been called "Branquinho [Whitey] da Beija-Flor," while also asking "if we did an ancestry test to see who is black, which one of us is not black?" (Marques 2012). In her publications arguing against racial quotas, Kaufmann cited the Neguinho case (Kaufmann 2010: 28), making the point that, because it was impossible to prove genetically who was and was not black, it was impossible to operate a racial quota system. In interviews with black activists, many reported that it was through the Neguinho incident that they first encountered the use of genetic data to challenge quotas.[5] Ana Honorato of the Movimento Negro Unificado, for example, reported that "people started telling us 'you're not black, you're just a bunch of white guys [um bando de brancos].'" Many activists recounted that they had been challenged with genetic data simplified into bite-sized headlines, such as "according to genetics we are all equal," "genetics has proven that race does not exist, therefore it is impossible to have racial quotas," and "if even Neguinho da Beija-Flor is 67 percent European, it is impossible to define who is black in Brazil" (Kent and Wade 2015: 824–25).

Pena's 2011 research was reported by the press, with a front-page article in the leading daily O Globo carrying the headline "A More European Country" and coining the term brasipeus (a combination of brasileiros and europeus) to describe Brazilians (O Globo 2011b). Inside, a full-page spread confirmed that Pena's research showed that Brazil was "above all a country of mestizos" and that "the only thing one can say is that we are all Brazilians" (Jansen 2011). A blog linked to the major weekly magazine Veja trumpeted, "It's nothing to do with Mama Africa! It's Mama Europe, in fact!" (Azevedo 2011). Meanwhile, an editorial in O Globo made explicit the link between science and policy, asserting that "now it is science that proves the nonexistence of the 'Afro-Brazilian'"— as well as the white and indigenous person—and concluding that any social policy based on color could not be justified (O Globo 2011a).

The press reported the publication of an anti-quota manifesto, signed by "113 antiracist citizens against racial laws," in which the signatories cited Pena—also a signatory—to the effect that "we have to assimilate the idea that the only coherent biological division of the human species is into billions of individuals and not a handful of 'races'" (Daher et al. 2008).

A second use of genetics to contest the racial quotas was in legal challenges to the policies, which deployed genetic data as part of the case. The petition presented to the Supreme Court to have racial quotas declared unconstitutional, authored by Kaufman and put forward by the Democratas political party, cited Pena on the impossibility of biologically defining racial or color categories and included as an appendix an expert opinion by Pena on "the nonexistence of races and the consequences for Brazilian society" (Kaufmann 2009: 31, 131–73). In 2010, at public Supreme Court hearings on the constitutionality of the racial quotas, Pena was called as an expert witness.

In sum, then, genetic data circulated through labs, scientific publications, popular science, diverse media outlets, and legal documents in an attempt to invalidate any racial division as a basis for social policy, and specifically to challenge the validity of a black or Afro-Brazilian category. These challenges did not succeed: the Supreme Court judges decided that quotas were constitutional, with the reporting judge, Ricardo Lewandowski, noting that "racism persists as a social phenomenon" and that it was "necessary, for the purpose of this discussion, to remove the biological concept of race" (2012: 19–20). As noted in chapter 4, the 2012 Law of Social Quotas was passed, which reserved 50 percent of federal university places for applicants from public schools, with half of these reserved for students from low-income families; of these quota places, a proportion is reserved for those declaring as preto, pardo, or indígena, corresponding at a minimum to the combined demographic weight of those categories in the state population. This was followed by Law 12.990 of 2014, which reserved 20 percent of the federal executive's civil servant jobs for negros. State multiculturalism won the day.

Pena, Genetics, and Health Policy

In keeping with their position that race has no genetic basis, Pena and others have argued that the race-color categories used in Brazil do not define populations that share medically meaningful genetic characteristics. The way genetic data have been drawn into debates about health policy has been different from their role in discussions about higher education. There has been less public controversy about health policies, because they have not involved racial quotas, which are seen by many as creating blatant unfairness and division because they distribute significant public resources to individuals based on acts of racial identification, which in Brazil were notoriously vague and subjective.

Affirmative actions in the health sector have had two strands. The first is similar to the policies in education, aiming to correct social inequalities caused by racism, past and present. This is the thrust of the 2006 National Policy on the Health of the Black Population—finally implemented by a 2009 decree—which seeks to correct disparities that exist in terms of black people's access to health care, and their rates of mortality and morbidity, all considered to be influenced by the impact of racism on broad areas of social life such as work, housing, education, and environment. The policy included measures for collecting and organizing health data by race-color categories in Brazil's Sistema

Único de Saúde (SUS, Single Health System); creating "sensitization" programs for health workers; involving black social movement activists in health policy; directing extra resources at programs (including medical research) targeting a wide variety of disorders seen to affect black populations—as well as many other poor people—such as hypertension, infant and maternal morbidity and mortality, tuberculosis, sickle-cell anemia, colon cancer, and mental problems; and ensuring access by quilombo dwellers and other rural black communities to the health system (Batista, Monteiro, and Medeiros 2013; Maio and Monteiro 2010; Ministério da Saúde 2010). These measures targeted black people as a category (and, in some cases, poor people), without quotas that channeled valuable resources toward individuals.

The second strand linked black people to specific disorders by virtue of their African genetic ancestry. This strand is included in the National Policy, but is different from the first strand and from education policy: targeting health problems caused by racism and poverty is qualitatively distinct from targeting problems caused by genetic inheritance, even if the two interact (e.g., if a genetic condition affecting black people does not get as much investment as a genetic condition affecting white people; or if poor environmental conditions affecting black people create epigenetically heritable health problems). The main disorder here has been sickle-cell anemia (SCA), which, as noted above and in chapter 2, was construed by some people as a doença de negros (a black people's disease). Hypertension and diabetes were also mentioned as diseases that, while they affected many people, might be linked to African ancestry in some way (Ministerio da Saúde 2001), but these are disorders with complex genetic and environmental causes, unlike SCA, which has simple Mendelian inheritance. Fry (2005) argues that, in the late 1990s and early 2000s, as a Programa de Anemia Falciforme (SCA program) was being developed, government health agencies, black activists, and the media all made strong connections between SCA and black people, seen as an ethnic or racial group, sharing genetic traits (see also Laguardia 2006). Genetic explanations, linking SCA to Africa and the African ancestry of black people, were reiterated in pamphlets, policy documents, and information posters—a process that has continued (e.g., Pinto and Lupinacci 2008). This created a powerful "naturalization of the 'black race'" (Fry 2005: 365), which glossed over the facts that SCA can be found in historically malarial areas outside Africa; that, in Brazil, people who do not look black can carry the trait and even suffer from the disorder; and that rates of SCA vary widely among different quilombo communities (Fry 2005: 368).

How were genetic data deployed in debates about health policy? Such data were deployed openly in relation to SCA, both to link the disorder to Africans and black Brazilians, and to contest that link (Calvo-González and Rocha 2010: 290–92). But the challenge to the geneticization of race in this field was principally academic: there were no legal challenges and, although the media certainly reported on SCA and public health policy (Diniz and Guedes 2006), there were not the heated debates that surrounded racial quotas in universities. In the end, though, the SCA screening programs begun in 2001 and extended to the whole country by the SUS in 2009, as part of the National Policy on the Health of the Black Population, were universal, even as the link between blackness and SCA was repeated (Fernandes 2009; Iervolino et al. 2011). The idea of instituting screening programs directed only at black people never became an issue.

Genetic data have been used much less to address the health issues that the National Policy saw as linked to "institutional racism," on which the policymakers laid more emphasis than on inherited disorders, such as SCA. This muted use of genetic data in relation to race-based health policy might be because the health problems at issue are often clearly related to poverty. But the same is true of racial inequalities in education. The key difference is that no one has suggested that the health issues be addressed by quota policies. The policy measures to organize SUS's health data by racial categories are justified by the need to monitor racial inequalities, not to define individual beneficiaries of quota benefits. Interviews with health professionals working in a local health center in Brasilia showed they felt that the National Policy was unnecessary—everyone suffered health problems—and that it simply fostered racism because it threatened to privilege blacks over others in access to health care (Santos and Santos 2013). These fears were quite speculative, however, because no system for enacting such privilege in everyday treatment was actually in place. In short, health policy has never generated the intense controversy that the quota policies did.

This indicates the uneven way genetic data circulate through networks that connect scientists, the press, politicians, policymakers, and activists. The data were drawn into the debates about university quotas not only because they could be used to challenge these policies, but because the policies were so controversial. The quotas were widely seen by critics as importing a foreign model of race into Brazil in a way that was quite inappropriate to the racially mixed character of the nation: quotas were often tagged by critics as involving U.S.-style racial segregation or South African apartheid. Genetic data on

Brazil's "unique" mixture and the impossibility in Brazil of defining who was black and who was white were perfect for addressing the apparent racial divisiveness that quotas dramatized so clearly. Genetic data could certainly be used to challenge health policies—particularly when those policies targeted genetic disorders. And indeed they were used, but in a much more muted fashion.

Pro-Quota Reactions

The main reaction by those in favor of race-based affirmative action in social policy, whether academics or activists (or both), has been to deny the relevance of genetic data to what they see as fundamentally a social domain (Kent and Wade 2015). Faced with arguments that race does not exist genetically, that Neguinho da Beija Flor's case shows it is impossible to define who is black, and that therefore racial quotas are unjustifiable, pro-quota people have insisted on the radical separation of society and genetics. This constitutes a Latourian purification (Latour 1993), or an attempt to materialize the negro and the mestizo as figures in a network in which connections with the practices of geneticists have been cut and topological proximities have been reconfigured as topographical distance—a segregation that, ironically, accords closely with the presentation by scientists of their methodology as immune to "the social."

One black university professor, for example, commented that DNA tests showing that apparently white Brazilians have African genetic markers means that everyone can say they are Afro-descendants, but this is for him "a political decision." If a white person decides to declare himself black and claim his right to a quota place, "there can be no dispute" (Munanga 2004: 52). Restating the standard social science position on race as a social construction, he observed that the nonexistence of race at a molecular level has not impinged on the continued existence of race as a social idea and racism as a social force. Attempts to create a negro category, encompassing blacks and browns, is a political project, in which the black social movement had been engaged long before quotas; it has nothing to do with creating a biological definition of race, as some critics have implied when they say that quotas reinforce a belief in the existence of biological race (Munanga 2005: 52–53). Another university professor remarked that the people in the University of Brasilia who were vetting applicants for racial quota places presumably knew that race had no biological meaning, but that is not what they were testing for—they were trying to see if an applicant was black in Brazilian cultural terms, and thus a possible victim of racism (Anjos 2005: 235).

A similar line was taken by Frei David Santos, a priest and director of the NGO Educafro (Education and Citizenship of Afro-Descendants and the Poor), who had also been tested in the BBC's Afro-Brazilian Roots project (Kent and Wade 2015). Evoking the oft-cited quip in Brazil that if you want to know who is black, ask a policeman, he used the example of police harassment to illustrate the social definition of race: "I have never seen any police raid on a bus, for example, where before discriminating, they ask a person what percentage of Afro genes he has." He went on: "Discrimination and the discriminator . . . do not see in genetics any arguments to stop discriminating. However, they want the discriminated to stop fighting for their rights because 'we all have Afro genes'" (Glycerio 2007). The authors of the pro-quota manifesto, first published in 2006 and reissued in expanded form in 2008 in response to the anti-quota manifesto, likewise stated that it was "totally irrelevant" for their opponents to marshal genetic data showing some self-declared browns and blacks had no African ancestry, while many self-declared whites did: "this has nothing to do with racism." They said that pro-quota and anti-quota people agreed on the nonexistence of biological race, but the young black dentist who was shot by police in São Paulo in 2005, having been mistaken for a mugger, was being judged on his "black appearance not his genetic baggage" (Nascimento et al. 2008: 18)

The key point was that racial identity in Brazil was typically assigned on the basis of appearance: whoever is in a position to discriminate makes a subjective judgment based on what another person looks like—skin color, hair type, facial features, and so on—and also on how they act in relation to cultural definitions of black, brown, white, and indigenous—this could include how they dress, their musical tastes, their religious practices, and so on. It was these judgments that reproduced existing racial inequalities and created new ones. As the black district attorney Indira Quaresma put it when addressing the Rio Grande do Sul state legislative assembly: "I'm the daughter of a black woman and an Indian man. My parents divorced, my mother remarried and my half-sister is as white as can be. My white sister is as Afro-descendent as I am, but she has never suffered, nor will she ever suffer, situations of prejudice, discrimination or racism because of this" (cited in Kent and Wade 2015: 829). Pro-quota people thus emphasized evidence about the socioeconomic position of the black population—typically using well-known statistics that combined the census categories pardo and preto and, comparing them to brancos, demonstrated significant inequalities in which racial discrimination could be shown statistically to play a role. Affirmative action was justified by the size and persistence of racial inequalities and the role of racism in reproducing them.

Black movement activists generally preferred to consign genetics to irrelevance, in part because they too wanted to emphasize that there was no genetic reality to race—without, however, concluding that race should therefore be discarded as a relevant category for social policy. But some black activists used the genetic connections that could be made in relation to SCA in a different way (Kent, Santos, and Wade 2014). First, as we have seen, black social movement organizations were instrumental in constructing the concept of SCA as genetically a doença de negros, even if the disorder was generally seen as more frequent among black people, rather than exclusive to them. This genetic connection, however, cut both ways: the more the SCA–black connection was emphasized, the more a case could be made for special treatment for black people; but the greater the emphasis on the presence of the SCA trait among the wider population, the more likely that health policy would direct resources toward coping with a disorder seen to affect more than just a subsection of the population. The black activist health organization Associação de Anemia Falciforme do Estado de São Paulo (AAFESP, Sickle Cell Anemia Association of the State of São Paulo), for example, links the condition strongly with the black population and places itself firmly within the black social movement, but also takes care to state that the "mutation of the HbS gene also occurred in the Arab peninsula, central India, and northern Greece" and that because of prehistoric and historical migrations out of Africa, SCA is "a prevalent genetic disease of global dimensions" (AAFESP 2007). Health policy has struck a genetically logical balance in the end: neonatal screening for SCA is universal, but the connection between SCA and Afro-descendants or negros is commonly reiterated (Ministério da Saúde 2001, 2010; Pinto and Lupinacci 2008).[6] In contrast to the branding of genetics as "totally irrelevant," it has emerged here as a way to underwrite and specify black identity.

Second, the fact that different variants of the HbS gene are associated with different regions of Africa, and given names such as Benin type and Bantu type, has been used by AAFESP to promote identification with African ancestry and roots among the people who attend the classes and social activities that the organization offers to people affected by the disorder (AAFESP 2007; Cardoso and Guerreiro 2006). However, this strategy, as explained by AAFESP's founder, the black nurse and health administrator Berenice Kikuchi, was not directed only at black people. White people were also encouraged to be aware of their African ancestry. Kikuchi observed: "these [patients] weren't able to affirm themselves as white anymore. So it's really interesting, this re-reading of history that sickle cell anemia permits" (cited by Kent, Santos, and Wade 2014: 743). In relation to SCA, then, the racial diversity of the nation is constructed in very uneven ways: on the one hand, blackness is represented as a specific identity, by virtue of genetic connections; on the other hand, Brazilians of various colors are genetically linked to Africa and share a common mixedness (Calvo-González and Rocha 2010).

De- and Re-Racialization, De- and Re-Geneticization

Geneticists producing data about human diversity (and sometimes making pronouncements on social policy), policymakers, politicians, judges, and black activists working in the field of affirmative action and multiculturalist policies in Brazil all participate in an assemblage, the networked connections of which can be configured or articulated in varied and even contradictory ways, shaped by power relations. On the one hand, geneticists and others use genetic data to deracialize Brazil, configuring the embodied (genetic) mestizo as the true Brazilian, democratically including everyone in his/her heterogeneity: self-identified "brancos" and "negros" are in (genetic) reality mixed. This Brazilian mestizo insists on the meaninglessness of biological race and highlights the problems around defining racial categories in a reliable way (e.g., for clinical or administrative purposes). This mestizo, however, also produces a re-geneticization of the social order, because as a genetic body s/he is seen, either implicitly or explicitly, as a mandate for society: the racial categories that the mestizo's existence show cannot be defined genetically, and should therefore not exist socially either. Of course, it is recognized that they do—an unfortunate reality—but they should not form the basis of social policy.

This stance became increasingly clear. At first, Pena and Bortolini (2004) said that genetics and politics were separate, but that genetics could at least inform social policy, if not take a prescriptive role. In their view, genetics could not decide who should get a quota place and who should not, because genetics could not validate what were fundamentally political identities: categories such as negro had no genetic meaning, and quotas could only be based on self-identification. Two years later, Pena and Birchal were saying that science could indeed "effectively contribute to a prescriptive position acting in favor of a nonracialist society" by showing policymakers "what is not"—namely, genetic race (2006: 13, 20). Genetics had become a directive for society: the biological and the social, at one moment configured as disconnected in line with scientists' view of themselves as neutral, had become reentangled as connections that had once been severed, or rather denied, were reinvigorated.

The prescriptive role allotted to genetics had an important effect in terms of defining individual identities. Pena would still say that genetics could not decide who was "really" black, but this stance was not entirely clear. For example, in a magazine interview, Pena himself, while saying that quotas had to be based on self-declaration, also said that the case of light-skinned applicants turned down by a university, who used DNA tests to prove their African ancestry, showed that "the test can help to maintain the *sanidade* (sanity, health) of the racial quota programs" (Gomes 2007: 72). This remark—which attributes a decisive power to DNA tests—is inexplicable if Pena really believes that quota programs can only operate via self-declaration. This might be a case of poor journalism, but a similar tendency can be observed in the use of genetic data by Roberta Kaufmann in her petition to the Supreme Court contesting the University of Brasilia's quota system. After citing Pena to the effect that the amount of African genetic ancestry in individuals has little correlation with their race-color categorization, she went on to say that relying on "objective criteria of genomic ancestry, by means of DNA tests, in order to identify who is in fact 100 percent white in Brazil—and thus not eligible for the benefits of the [UB quota] policy—would be the only way to implement the racial quotas without any doubts," a strategy that she said was impractical rather than scientifically invalid (Kaufmann 2009: 31). She attributed to genetics the power to define who is white and who is not—a power Pena has explicitly denied.

A journalist did something similar when she noted that the quota debate could become even more complex if students chose to use DNA tests to prove African ancestry. Citing geneticist Francisco Salzano, she noted that black Brazilians could have up to 50 percent European ancestry, so the issue was "how much African or Amerindian ancestry would be necessary for a candidate to declare himself *negro* or *índio*?" As before, genetics seems to be able to provide the tools to decide racial identity, even if, in the Brazilian case, it is complicated by mixture (Guedes 2006). Hovering ghost-like behind the genetic mestizo in these remarks are figures of the pure black, white, or indigenous person—the one who has 100 percent African, European, or Amerindian ancestry, the logical entailment of mestizaje.

Paradoxically, the same tendency is evident in remarks made by the black pro-quota university professor cited earlier: having said that if a white-looking applicant declared himself black for quota purposes, there could be "no dispute," he goes on to say, "the only way would be to submit this person to a DNA test." But then "all Brazilians would have to take tests"—again an impractical plan, but it seems not epistemologically problematic (Munanga 2004: 52). This defining of social identity by genetic criteria was very obvious in the case of Neguinho da Beija Flor, when his identity as a black man was challenged in terms of his hidden European genetic ancestry; or in O Globo's quip about brasipeus, whose European genetic ancestry made them European-like in identity. Genetics is given the power to define racial identity, despite the fact that both anti- and pro-quota proponents agree that, in principle, it cannot do so.

The result here is an overall process of re-geneticization—using genetics again to talk about and guide social issues—which is used apparently to deracialize society, but which has the paradoxical effect of re-racialization because genetic discourse creeps into the definition of the social identities of race that are logically entailed by the mestizo. While the genetic mestizo is used to recommend that racial categories not be used in social policy—because they are not "real" and policy should respect reality—the same racial categories, admitted to exist as social entities, are lent genetic meaning. There is a temporal shift here: social policy is future-oriented, and the anti-quota proponents are imagining a future without racial categories, a future imagined to converge with current genetic reality; but racial categories are also a feature of past and present Brazil, where they exist as a powerful social force, and the defining of the mestizo in genetic terms inevitably freights these categories with genetic cargo, as the close connections between the mestizo and its component categories may be denied, but are impossible to cut. The attempt to topologically create an unbridgeable distance between elements normally in close connection does not fully work. This is unsurprising when the genetic science used to deny the existence of biological race anywhere in the world still depends on defining genetic ancestry in biogeographical terms—African, European, Amerindian—which resonate quite closely with familiar racial categories and allow Kaufmann to talk in terms of a DNA ancestry test deciding who is "100 percent white." Genetic ancestry data are used to define the Brazilian population as heterogeneously mestizo, a powerfully racialized concept, now given genetic meaning even as genetic race and racial difference are denied.

Defining the mestizo in genetic terms (re-geneticization) in order to deny the existence of race (deracialization), but with a paradoxical reappearance of genetic racial categories (re-racialization) is only one side of the story. The other side, represented by the pro-quota proponents and black activists, is about re-racialization, allied—mostly, but not completely—with de-geneticization. This perspective materializes the figure of the negro (and logically the índio, although this does not appear much in practice) to highlight racial categories as part of a broader multiculturalist strategy to correct racial inequalities. But the figure of the negro, for which the body (as racialized appearance) is central, is resolutely de-geneticized—except when it is linked to genetic disorders. Contrary to the fears of the anti-quota camp that affirmative action reinforces naturalized concepts of race, the pro-quota camp insists on the entirely socialized character of race. Biology is important—skin color, and so on—but it is a completely culturalized biology in which skin color, despite being controlled by genetic inheritance, only becomes an active force in relation to Brazilian cultural classifications. This perspective agrees with the geneticists that there is no genetic reality to race, but blocks the move that uses this to support the argument that racial difference cannot form a basis for social policy. The thrust of this perspective goes against the notion of the pervasive geneticization of society and citizenship: the negro is a material, corporal being, but one constituted entirely through his/her connections with assemblage components defined as social—racial stereotypes, racist exclusions in education, the structure of the job market, the history of slavery and black resistance, and so on.

On the other hand, in the health field, there has been a concerted action, not just by black health activists but also by the Ministry of Health, to use the Mendelian genetics of SCA to configure new connections between black individuals, and between Brazilian blacks and their African heritage. This work of reassembly can generate unexpected topological proximities as people who identify as mestizo or even white, but who carry the recessive allele or suffer from the disease, are linked via the genetic variants in their DNA to labels such as "Bantu" and "Benin."

On this side of the story too, then, we can see contradictory tendencies: re-racialization is a common theme, but it may be accompanied by both de-geneticization and re-geneticization, depending on the context. Faced with genetic data used to attack the legitimacy of affirmative action, the main reaction has been to deny the relevance of genetics; given the genetic connections between Africa, blackness, and SCA—albeit probabilistic, not exclusive—one reaction has been to capitalize on them to gain visibility for black identity. We can see "strategic naturalizing" (Thompson 2005: 145)—or rather geneticizing—at play here, but also strategic culturalizing (Wade 2012b: 86) operating to tactically configure parts of the assemblage network, making diverse connections with genetic data, or erasing them altogether in some contexts.

In Brazil, the genetic mestizo has mainly been ranged against state multiculturalism. Geneticists working mainly out of public universities, funded by state research councils (as well as income from private labs, such as Pena's), collaborating with each other and with overseas colleagues, gathered data in the course of research on medical and population genetics—much of it following long-standing research interests in admixture—which were then used by some of them directly and by other interested parties to challenge key planks in the state's multiculturalist agenda. In the end, the challenge failed, insofar as quota policies and differential health policies have gone ahead: the state, far from buying wholesale into geneticized definitions of citizenship, mostly deemed them irrelevant to social policy (with the exception of sickle-cell anemia, where policy mainly followed a medical genetic logic). But in the process, the overall assemblage of the Brazilian nation, which already afforded the possibility of divergent configurations, orthogonal to each other and structured by power relations, became open to new articulations. One such was Brazil as a multicultural, multiracial nation, seeking to overcome past racial hierarchies; genetic data only participated in a limited way in this set of connections. Another configuration, for which new genetic data helped strengthen the existing connections and provide new ones, reinforced a robust network in which Brazil was materialized as a pervasively mixed nation, in which racial difference was muted and ambiguous, or at least could not be the basis for social policy that it had been in other countries. In the process, race was claimed and disavowed, genetics was privileged as a true guide and relegated to irrelevance, and the social and genetic were radically separated and constantly reentangled.

Conclusion

In terms of the relation of mixture to democracy and hierarchy, it is clear that geneticists and others see mixture as a powerful democratizing force: it can lead to a raceless future, and the job of science is to provide accurate data and even prescriptions to policymakers to help achieve this. They believe insisting on racial difference as a basis for the future is a retrograde step, reinforcing old hierarchies, which are better tackled in a color-blind way. Geneticists and others are keen to present Brazil as an example to the world—for genomic science and race relations. The Brazilian mestizo holds lessons for medical genomics and pharmacogenomics (racial categories are not effective tools in the first place; they are less so in a mestizo nation; the world is rapidly becoming more "admixed," i.e., mestizo). And Brazil's official image on the global stage as a convivial, tolerant, mixed society is held up as an object lesson in how the mestizo—whose ubiquity is now attested to by genomic science—can help overcome racial division. In contrast to Colombia, Brazilian genomics gives a much more positive spin to mestizaje: the violence that is a major feature of Brazilian society (and that has important racialized dimensions) does not "stick" to the country as it does to Colombia.

It is relevant in this context that genetic data were integrated into a version of the Brazilian nation that rejected affirmative action as an inappropriate expression of state multiculturalism. It is interesting to compare this with India, which has long had a well-developed affirmative action program for Scheduled Castes and Tribes. The definition of castes and tribes who may benefit from the programs is based on cultural criteria but also on physical anthropological data collected by the Anthropological Survey of India (AnSI). In the genomic era, the Indian state is funding research on the historical genetics of castes and tribes, which "is set to sit alongside the ethnographic research produced as evidence for constitutional reclassification [of claimant groups as entitled to the benefits of affirmative action]" (Kapila 2007: 247). Brazilian geneticists have already developed a powerful argument that such a use of genetics is deeply flawed in a mestizo society, but by extension elsewhere as well, insofar as the geneticists see Brazilian mestizaje as the future for the world.

However, this argument and the positive spin put on mestizaje in Brazil are undermined by the fact that deploying the idea of mixture in an already hierarchical context necessarily entrains the concept of (relative) purities, which provides grist to the mill of hierarchy. Genetics reinscribes this by (1) using concepts of continental biogeographic genetic ancestry (allowing educated commentators to talk about being "100 percent white") and (2) providing the tools that permit people to define social identities in terms of genetics (Neguinho is not "really" black).

Black activists and their allies—and the state itself—see insistence on racial difference as enhancing democracy, by acting as the basis for reparative justice—a view supported by other states that have implemented affirmative action programs. In this view, mixture, as it exists in Brazil, threatens black identity and masks racism and racial inequality. This view highlights the hierarchical and exclusive aspects of mixture, in which whiteness, blackness, and indigeneity coexist, as relative purities, with mixedness. This view either banks on the possibility that the categories deployed in the service of hierarchy can be retooled for a democracy in which continuing difference is recognized and yet not discriminated against (in my view, a utopian possibility in a capitalist society), or it aims at the more pragmatic objective, in the ongoing struggle against racism, of creating advantages for black people, who will then become more evenly distributed across the classes of an unequal society, unsettling stereotypes that link blackness to low status.

6

....

Mexico, Public Health,

and State Genomics

As we saw in chapter 4, the multiculturalist turn has had a rather lower profile in Mexico than in either Brazil or Colombia; it has been a more top-down affair, and questions of race and racism have taken a back seat, with the focus predominantly on indigenous people's rights to land, and political and cultural autonomy. Indigenismo, hand-in-hand with mestizaje, have remained powerful ideological influences, construing the nation as overwhelmingly mestizo—although a significant minority of people self-identity as "blanco" (Telles and Project on Ethnicity and Race in Latin America 2014)—with separate community-based indigenous populations located in specific places.

As genetic information has moved through networks connecting scientists, policymakers, and politicians concerned with multiculturalism, and diverse people interested in the ethnic and racial diversity of the nation, the effect has been to reinforce this dominant configuration of the nation, in a genetic idiom. Genetic data emphasize the conceptual divide between mestizo and indígena, while also tapping into the equivocations that the divide entails, when, first, indigenous people can become (and indeed are often seen as destined to become) mestizos in cultural terms and, second, there is not a clear boundary between mestizos and indigenous people in terms of genetic ancestry. The striking feature in Mexico is the very direct and centralized way in which the state has driven the genomics agenda, via the creation of INMEGEN (National Institute of Genomic Medicine), and the way geneticists and genetic data have been plugged into state-oriented networks, in which public health and genomic sovereignty are key concepts. This contrasts with the decentralized networks characterizing geneticists' practices in Brazil and Colombia, and the way genetic data were deployed against state-driven affirmative action in Brazil. This is not to say that public health and genomic sovereignty were not issues in Colombia and Brazil: public health is a key justification for genomic projects everywhere, and geneticists certainly mooted the ideas that Brazil had a unique population and that medical treatments developed by and for countries with "well-defined ethnic groups" were not necessarily appropriate for Brazil. In Colombia, this discourse was less evident, but was present in the idea that medical genomics had to take account of diverse kinds of mixture among Latin Americans. But in neither country were these themes as publicly elaborated as in Mexico.

Also striking is the work the indígena/mestizo divide could do in the global genomics assemblage. It tapped into dominant evolutionary narratives (see chapter 1) about the peopling of the Americas, the special genetic characteristics of indigenous Americans, and what Latin America, with its indigenous populations and their mestizo descendants, could offer global genomic science.

The Creation of INMEGEN and the Mexican Genome Diversity Project

INMEGEN was created by presidential decree on July 19, 2004.[1] Its purpose was to enable Mexican expertise in genomic medicine to compete at global levels. Lobbying for the institute had started in 1999, initiated by Gerardo Jiménez Sánchez (a medical doctor trained in pediatrics, with a PhD in human genetics from Johns Hopkins) and Antonio Velázquez, both of whom had been involved in failed attempts to set up a genetics research unit in the National Pediatrics Institute. They met with senior figure Guillermo Soberón Acevedo (trained in biochemistry)—whose career included terms as rector of the National Autonomous University of Mexico (UNAM, 1973–81) and secretary of health (1982–88)—to tell him that Mexico could not afford to stay outside the genomic revolution being ushered in by endeavors such as the Human Genome Project. Soberón Acevedo, then executive director of FUNSALUD, an influential privately funded institution promoting public health, backed the idea of a new institute. Early meetings drew FUNSALUD together with key state bodies: the Ministry of Health, UNAM, and the National Council of Science and Technology (CONACYT, the main state funding agency for scientific research). These bodies funded a feasibility study, published in 2001, and in the same year a Consortium for the Promotion of the Genomic Medicine Institute was created to lobby for INMEGEN, directed by Jiménez Sánchez, with the backing of influential political figures such as Juan Ramón de la Fuente (rector of UNAM and former minister of health) and Julio Frenk (minister of health), and supported by corporate figures such as Antonio López de Silanes, head of a Mexico-based international pharmaceutical company (and president of FUNSALUD). The consortium also sponsored lectures, produced educational brochures, and helped launch new postgraduate programs in genomic medicine at UNAM (Jimenez-Sanchez 2003; López Beltrán and Vergara Silva 2011: 107; Schwartz Marín 2011a: 86–87). Notable here—in comparison to Colombia and Brazil—is the way INMEGEN was deeply embedded in government institutional networks from the start.

The flagship project undertaken by INMEGEN, under the leadership of Jiménez Sánchez and with initial funding of over US$125 million from the government, plus private-sector support, was to map the genomic diversity of the Mexican population, in a project explicitly compared to the Human Genome Project and the International HapMap Project, titled the Mexican Genome Diversity Project (MGDP or, in Spanish, Diversidad Genómica de la Población Mexicana). The first phase of the project, 2005–6, sampled three hundred "self-identified Mestizo individuals" from six states in the country; a second phase in 2006–7 extended sampling to another four states (INMEGEN 2009a; Silva-Zolezzi et al. 2009). This sampling was carried out by well-publicized *jornadas* (workdays)—translated in English as sampling "crusades"—in which INMEGEN personnel visited state capitals. During an open event, based at a local public university, they gave presentations and distributed brochures explaining the project and its value, before collecting informed consent and blood samples from volunteers—who were mostly local university students—and rewarding them with a commemorative T-shirt or mug. The ground had been laid for the jornada through negotiations with the local state governor, other state officials, and the local university administration; Jiménez Sánchez and his team advertised the jornada via local TV, radio, and press (García Deister 2014; Silva-Zolezzi et al. 2009: Supporting Information). INMEGEN had its own Educational and Dissemination Unit, which produced publicity materials (see figure 6.1). After the project's main scientific paper was published in May 2009, INMEGEN teams returned to some states, gave presentations of the results, and handed over a commemorative package with the scientific paper—in English and Spanish—and a DVD encased in an impressive box, designed in colors that evoked the nation: Mexican pink and colonial blue (García Deister 2014: 167; López Beltrán, García Deister, and Rios Sandoval 2014: 97). The sampling process involved a large-scale mobilization of state resources and publicity. The overall frame of the recruitment drive was public

FIGURE 6.1 Front cover of INMEGEN public outreach pamphlet for the MGDP. (*Mapa del Genoma de Poblaciones Mexicanas, Libro de Divulgación del Proyecto de Diversidad Genómica de Poblaciones Mexicanas*. By permission of Instituto Nacional de Medicina Genómica, México, www.inmegen .gob.mx.)

health: people were being asked to donate blood to help improve the nation's well-being, and they were apparently eager to participate (García Deister and López-Beltrán 2015).

Although the MGDP focused on mestizo populations, in phase two of the project (2006–7), they also sampled indigenous populations. Initially, these populations had been avoided, because of fears that the project could run into the type of problem that the Human Genome Diversity Project had run into, when activist groups accused it of biopiracy and the unethical appropriation and exploitation of indigenous people's blood samples (Reardon 2005). Indeed, similar accusations about MGDP were made in the Mexican press (S. Ribeiro 2005). But indigenous populations had already been sampled by scientists such as Rubén Lisker in the 1960s and 1970s, and, as early as 2005, Jiménez Sánchez started meeting with local officials to assess the possibility of sampling indigenous people. In due course, MGDP collected samples from Maya, Zapotec, and Tepehuano communities, among others (Schwartz Marín 2011a: 188). Recruiting indigenous people was different from recruiting mestizos: it depended less on relations with state governors and more on local rural doctors, anthropologists, and community leaders, whose contacts extended into areas where high-level state authorities had less leverage. As usual, recruitment was framed in terms of contributing to the future health of the nation, including indigenous peoples. INMEGEN staff believed that indigenous people saw the sampling visits as similar to the vaccination programs with which they were familiar, and they reported that indigenous people participated willingly. The state was powerfully present in the recruiting of mestizo populations, but it was far from absent when it came to gathering indigenous samples. The links were not with high-level state officials, nor did the sampling take place on a public university campus, but INMEGEN depended on the kind of connections that Lisker and others had used in previous decades, based on state health institutions and quite possibly state-funded anthropological networks, although the latter are not acknowledged by INMEGEN (Silva-Zolezzi et al. 2009: 8616).

In the end, recruiting indigenous people turned out to be very useful, as in 2008 the peer reviewers of the scientific paper arising from the MGDP insisted on the inclusion of data from an indigenous sample as a comparative reference population to assess Amerindian ancestry, in addition to the Hap-Map populations used to assess African, European, and Asian ancestry. Apparently, the global status of Amerindian populations as genetically special could not be ignored. For this purpose, the Zapotec sample was considered the most appropriate, as it had low levels of mixture compared to, say, the Maya samples (García Deister 2014: 165–67, 173–74).

The MGDP reached a milestone on May 11, 2009, when Jiménez Sánchez formally delivered the first results of the project—the Map of the Genome of Mexican Populations—in its blue and pink box, to President Felipe Calderón. The event had been extensively publicized—INMEGEN was the only one of Mexico's eleven national health institutes with its own publicity unit—and the DVD in the commemorative package included nearly thirty newspaper clippings, some 120 photos, INMEGEN's own promotional song, and other audiovisual material (Schwartz Marín 2011a: 244). The ceremonial culmination of MGDP happened to coincide with Mexico's swine flu crisis—people at the event had to wear surgical face masks. Despite this, the MGDP had no trouble hitting the headlines. One newspaper report said: "Only a story as strong as the decoding of the Mexican Genome could compete in Geneva, Switzerland, with the attention that the World Health Organization (WHO) had given to the health alert for AH1N1 flu" (cited by Schwartz Marín 2011a: 241). Indeed, INMEGEN's reputation—which had been tarnished by some criticisms that it was a badly run white elephant (Schwartz Marín 2011a: 168)—drew sustenance from the flu crisis. After accepting the MGDP box, Calderón commented that "in the twenty-first century Mexico faces sanitary challenges that cannot be ignored, and to tackle and overcome them we need scientific research and medicines tailored to the specific needs of every person and every social group, [we need] a more predictive and preventive medicine; this is precisely the advantage offered by genomic medicine. . . . This effort in health will allow us to swiftly and efficiently deal with emergencies like the one we have experienced in the last days" (cited by López Beltrán, García Deister, and Rios Sandoval 2014: 98). The relevance of genomic medicine for the flu epidemic was unclear, to say the least, but the overall message was unmistakable: the government was investing in the health of the nation and could be trusted to take timely and effective action, using the most up-to-date technologies.

The main results of the MGDP were conveyed in a 2009 paper (Silva-Zolezzi et al. 2009). The paper framed its contribution in terms of global, rather than just Mexican, health, saying that "the diversity of Latino populations" made them "a powerful resource for analyzing the genetic bases of complex diseases," and that the sixty Amerindian groups contributing to Mexico's "complex history of admixture" made it "an ideal country in which to perform genomic analysis of common complex diseases." The Latin American combination of mestizos and Amerindians—in a specifically Mexican configuration—was touted as a special resource for global genomics.

Comparing SNP frequencies for HapMap populations and the six Mexican state samples, plus the Zapotec sample, the article presented data on heterozygosity (a measure of genetic heterogeneity in a population), and the results of principal components analysis (PCA), a way of clustering and visualizing data that highlights their internal variance. Following common practice, the paper used the HapMap samples from Utah, Nigeria, and Beijing/Tokyo, plus the MGDP's Zapotec sample: these represented the ancestral populations that had contributed to the present-day Mexican population. The PCA graphs showed these reference points as very tight clusters, widely separated from each other, with the Mexican mestizos spread between the European and the Zapotec clusters. Analysis with STRUCTURE—a software package for analyzing population structure—used 1,814 ancestry informative markers (AIMs) to assess the proportions of European, African, Amerindian, and Asian ancestry in individuals and population samples, showing that Mexican mestizos had mainly European and Amerindian ancestries, with the latter ranging from 66 percent in Guerrero to 36 percent in Sonora. One key message was the internal diversity of Mexican populations, but the payoff for genomic medicine more widely was that the availability in global datasets of information on Mexican populations, with their Amerindian ancestry, would reduce costs for future studies of Latin Americans and Latinos that had previously relied on datasets, such as the HapMap, which did not include such ancestry. Thus internal diversity was balanced with the idea of Mexican mestizos as a national population, and as representative of Latinos in general, and thus as a useful resource for global genomics. Indeed, the concept of a national mestizo population had been present in INMEGEN from its inception, expressed in the concept of genomic sovereignty.

Unique Mixtures and Genomic Sovereignty

The rationale for INMEGEN had two major elements. One was an economic case based on predictions of reduced public health costs. The 2001 feasibility study, for example, compared the cost of creating INMEGEN to the savings made by applying genomic medicine to diabetes, predicted to reduce current costs by 36 percent (similar calculations were made for hypertension and for carrying out clinical trials of new medicines). These predictions were guesswork, given the rudimentary state of knowledge about the genetic components of diabetes and, even more, any gene-based therapies for the disorder, but the economic case was important in garnering the support needed in Congress to fund the new institute. Genomic medicine was touted as a way of saving public money, but also as a means of generating profits for the private sector—represented by FUNSALUD, and by corporations such as Applied Biosystems and IBM, which in 2005 began collaborations with INMEGEN. In the growing global biomedical industry, INMEGEN was a way of staking a claim in the market (Taylor-Alexander and Schwartz-Marín 2013).

The second element was clearly nationalist in orientation: as Jiménez Sánchez put it (2003: 295–96), Mexicans had "a unique genetic makeup and a characteristic set of disease susceptibilities" resulting from "an admixture of more than 65 native Indian groups with Spaniards," with the result that "genomic medicine in Mexico needs to be based on the genetic structure and health demands of the Mexican population, rather than importing applications developed for other populations." The idea of national genetic particularity depended on an unspoken but self-evident evolutionary narrative that saw Amerindians as a continental isolate, unlike any others (see chapter 1). It was a constant theme in the promotion and early agendas of INMEGEN. The official title, Mexican Genome Diversity Project, was often rephrased in public pronouncements, and in some technical papers, with more overtones of singularity: Map of the Genome of Mexican Populations (Mapa del Genoma de las Poblaciones Mexicanas), Map of the Mexican Genome (Mapa del Genoma Mexicano), or simply the Mexican Genome (el Genoma del Mexicano) (Granados Arriola et al. 2011; INMEGEN 2009b). The results of the project were reported in ways that reaffirmed this impression of a singular genome. One newspaper article headlined with "Mexican Genes: Mixture of 35 Races"; the reporter continued that "the map of the human genome of Mexicans" showed that "the genes of the Mexican population" are "different from those of Europe, Asia, and Africa" and that "65 percent of the genetic make-up of Mexicans is unique and has been named 'Amerindian'" (Alcántara 2007; López Beltrán and Vergara Silva 2011: 121).

By 2008, Jiménez Sánchez was more circumspect, and in an article for *Genome Research* there was only mention of Mexico's "unique history" of mixture, involving "more than 60 local Amerindian groups, Europeans and, to a lesser extent, Africans." Still, the data showed that "although there are some regional genetic differences between Mexican subpopulations, they are similar enough to be analyzed as a single group" (Jiménez Sánchez et al. 2008: 1192, 1195). INMEGEN was mobilizing an "ideology of homogeneity characteristic of centralized nationalist discourse" (García Deister 2014: 164). By the time the main scientific paper from the project was published, there was no mention of uniqueness, and regional diversity was highlighted—alongside, as we saw, the idea that Mexicans could also be considered in national terms, and used in global datasets. The project did identify a number of "private alleles"—genetic variants not found in the HapMap samples from Africa, Europe, and Asia—and these were found mostly in the Zapotec sample, although also in one regional mestizo population. But this did not lead to any statement about the singularity of the population at large (Silva-Zolezzi et al. 2009). The idea that Mexicans might be described in terms of a single genome circulated alongside the idea that Mexicans were genetically diverse: Mexican mestizos were materialized as both heterogeneous and homogeneous, depending on whether one was looking from the bottom up or the top down.

Closely associated with the concept of a singular genome was the idea that Mexico needed to develop its own genomic medical capacity, in order to better control its "unique" genomic resources, shielding them from external exploitation, and to reduce dependence on medical treatments controlled by researchers and corporations outside Mexico (notably in the United States). As one commentator affirmed, "we believe that if we do not carry out studies to understand our genomic patrimony that we possess, well, no one else will because they will be interested in their own populations. Secondly, should the interest exist and they [other countries] come to get this information, they make us dependent on this information and then it will cost us. We have to develop our own genomic information" (cited in Seguín et al. 2008: s5–s6). A report on Jiménez Sánchez's presentation to an international workshop on advancing technologies summarized his views that a Mexican genomic platform was "considered key to discouraging non-Mexican research and development of Mexican-specific products and services." Jiménez Sánchez suggested that U.S. field workers had collected blood samples from Mexican indigenous populations and taken them to the United States, where he speculated that "polymorphisms could be identified and genomic-specific medicines made and sold at US prices," unaffordable for most Mexicans. He apparently even made the slightly paranoid suggestion that "the same knowledge and technology could be used to make Mexican-specific bioweapons" (National Academy of Sciences 2005: 10–11; Taylor-Alexander and Schwartz-Marín 2013: 342). In short, the idea of the genetic specificity of the Mexican population was constructed in a network that connected it closely with dense clusters of existing dominant ideas, people, and practices enacting postcolonial national pride and autonomy.

This was encapsulated in the concept of "genomic sovereignty," or control by the nation-state over its country's genetic resources (Benjamin 2009; López Beltrán, García Deister, and Rios Sandoval 2014; Schwartz Marín 2011a, 2011b). The concept was ill-defined: did it encompass *any* genetic material taken from human and nonhuman biomes found on Mexican territory, or did it refer to genetic material deemed *particular* to Mexico? Clearly, the idea of genetic uniqueness was not logically necessary for proposals that genetic material located in Mexican territory should be under Mexican control. But uniqueness and sovereignty went hand in hand, especially for a resource that is ubiquitous (unlike oil, for example): if Mexican genetic material was the same as everywhere else, there was less reason to protect and control it as a national resource.

The concept of genomic sovereignty was disputed, insofar as many geneticists did not subscribe to the idea of a specific Mexican genome (Guerrero Mothelet 2006). As the head of the ELSI (ethical, legal, and social issues) unit of INMEGEN's lobbying consortium said, "Genomic sovereignty is an exaggeration . . . [to say] that a country geographically and politically [defined] represents a different genome, as if we were a different species—no! We are the same species! Politics is what defines countries . . . it has nothing to do with genes" (cited by Schwartz Marín 2011b: 165). But these critiques were rather muted in the public domain, and the idea served very well to marshal support across a wide political spectrum; reactionary nationalists and postcolonial critics could connect to the idea from very different starting points

(López Beltrán and Vergara Silva 2011: 118, 139). The concept circulated in political networks and produced enough "cooperation without consensus" (Schwartz Marín 2011a: 264) to support the creation of INMEGEN. It became enshrined in law in 2008, when the General Law of Health was amended to address human genomic population studies, making it a crime to export human samples without official permission. The decree itself did not mention "sovereignty," but the proposals preceding it did, in terms of reducing dependency on other countries, defending Mexican patrimony against foreign exploitation, and improving public health (Cámara de Diputados 2008).

Mestizos, Indígenas, and Race

In contrast to Brazil and, to a lesser extent, Colombia, the discourse of race was very muted in INMEGEN and the MGDP. Early on, two science journalists, writing a note for the U.S.-based journal *Nature Biotechnology* on Mexico's "bold genome project," described it as a "race-based" project to determine if a genetic basis existed for the country's growing health crisis (Guerrero Mothelet and Herrera 2005). Also, the press occasionally used the term in relation to the MGDP, talking about "35 races" or genetic differences between "races" (Alcántara 2007; Cruz Martínez 2006). In general, however, explicit use of the term was rare and often appeared in disavowals: INMEGEN geneticists themselves "repeatedly affirmed in conversation and interviews that race does not exist" (Kent et al. 2015: 853) and "steadfastly denied there was anything 'racial' about their work" (Hartigan 2013a: 148). Nevertheless, one geneticist from the Faculty of Medicine at UNAM criticized the MGDP for using terms such as mestizo and indigenous, which were "obsolete and anachronistic," because "races do not exist" (El Universal 2009).

The overt disavowal of race alongside the use of racialized terminology and concepts (critiqued by some) points to a central feature of many of these genomic projects, which I have noted before, to which the MGDP was no exception. The whole project can be seen as deeply racialized, precisely because of the use of categories such as mestizo and indigenous, which have roots in colonial hierarchies of race and class. In the early twentieth century, the idea of the mestizo was a "solution to the conflictive postcolonial racial situation of Mexico": it held out the promise of national unity and the resolution of inequalities and conflicts between indigenous and nonindigenous people (López Beltrán and Vergara Silva 2011: 110). While recognizing this, we need to recall that when people use the term race in Mexico—as in many other areas of Latin America—they generally use it in a specific sense, which differs from some other usages (such as in the United States): the idea that there are "35 races" in Mexico or that there is such a thing as la raza mexicana is an indication of this. The reference is to a biocultural lineage: breeds of animals and strains of plants are routinely called razas, but when applied to people, the term implies a shared history of language and culture as well as biological ancestry (Hartigan 2013a, 2013b). Race is always a biocultural construct (Wade 2002a), but in Mexico, culture and history weigh heavily, in part because mestizos and indigenous people overlap a great deal in terms of racialized physical differences, such as skin color (Telles and Project on Ethnicity and Race in Latin America 2014).

Bearing in mind this characteristically Mexican understanding of race, what is interesting is how the racialized differences between mestizos and indigenous people were perceived and enacted in the MGDP. We have already seen that the recruiting processes involved were quite different: they interpellated mestizos as public citizens, reachable through high-level state bureaucracies, capital cities, and public universities, while indígenas had to be approached with extra ethical caution and through more local networks of the state that reached into isolated rural areas. When it came to identifying individuals for sampling, the mestizo–indigenous distinction was also maintained. The mestizos were said to have "self-identified" as such (Silva-Zolezzi et al. 2009: 8611), but it seems that in practice this was simply assumed (García Deister 2014: 165; López Beltrán and Vergara Silva 2011: 126). Instead, mestizo donors were required to testify that they, their parents, and their four grandparents had been born in the state where the sample was being taken. This is common practice in population genomics of this type: it aims to sample a population genealogically rooted in the locality and exclude the genetic influence of recent migrants. The technique is a direct correlate of the concept of "population" and of making genetic ancestry the object of research—by definition, one wants to sample rooted populations. It inevitably "purifies" the local population by selecting only those with ancestral roots, whose genetic profile then appears to represent the local population as a whole (Nash 2015: 130).

For the Zapotec sample, the same criteria about state origins applied, but they and their four grandparents had also to speak Zapotec (García Deister 2014: 166). That is, mestizos were defined by geographic genealogy alone—their culture was taken for granted as national—while indigenous people were defined by specific cultural attributes. The criterion of language was at variance with census-taking practice in Mexico, which from 2000 has counted indigenous people using a self-identification question as well as a question about indigenous language speaking. INMEGEN applied a more exclusive definition of indigeneity than either the Mexican state or indigenous people themselves (cf. Reardon 2008). Once the samples had been taken, each tube was labeled with a bar code, which included details of the sample's state of origin, the sex of the donor, and the date. The tubes were then stored in boxes labeled to differentiate mestizo from indigenous samples (sorted by ethnic group) (García Deister 2014: 169). These practices all enacted the standard distinction between indígena and mestizo.

The Genotyping and Expression Analysis Unit at INMEGEN carried out the DNA analysis, identifying mitochondrial and Y-chromosome haplogroups for each sample and measuring genetic ancestries for the autosomal DNA. For most individuals, mitochondrial DNA showed the presence of haplogroups common to Amerindian populations, while the Y-chromosome DNA revealed haplogroups associated with European origins: this could not effectively distinguish in genetic terms between mestizo and indigenous samples. The autosomal DNA was a different matter: the more markers were used to make the analysis, the more it was possible to infer the presence of even small amounts of different ancestral origins. As lead INMEGEN scientist Silva-Zolezzi put it, "I know of no indigenous population that is 100 percent Native American or, in quotes, 'pure.'" But these people were not mestizos, despite being genetically mixed, because "that is the way they were defined . . . because indigenous populations are not only genetically indigenous; they are indigenous in culture, in usages and customs. They self-describe as such and this correlates with their genome" (García Deister 2014: 171). On the one hand, the social categories were given greater importance than the genetic data for organizing the data: a sample was either mestizo or it was not; the category was discrete in social terms. On the other hand, any individual could be more or less genetically mixed, from having mainly Amerindian genetic ancestry with a tiny proportion of European ancestry, to having a more balanced mix: the mestizo category was a genetic continuum (García Deister 2011). The idea of a continuum was later reiterated by two Mexican scientists, a geneticist and a physical anthropologist, based at Stanford, writing in a Mexican journal of anthropology and history: "How can we distinguish between an indigenous individual from Oaxaca with a certain amount of European ancestry and a Oaxacan mestizo with high levels of indigenous ancestry? . . . Genetically they are indistinguishable" (Moreno and Sandoval 2013: 270).

There is ambivalence here: the indígena/mestizo distinction is both reiterated (discrete mestizo) and unsettled (continuous mestizo). However, there was a tendency to bring the social and the genetic into line for the purposes of the MGDP, which was explicitly interested in genetic ancestry: this followed the idea that indigenous people "self-describe as such and this correlates with their genome." The relatively tight correlation observed between genome and social category was helped along for the Zapotecs by sampling only people who had four grandparents who spoke Zapotec. In addition, among some indigenous samples, especially ones with comparatively high degrees of admixture, those individuals who were genetically close to the mestizo samples tended to be excluded as "genomic noise"—they got in the way of using these samples as proxies for an Amerindian ancestral populations. Likewise, when those labeled as "mestizos" were genetically close to the local indigenous populations, this was taken to show "different qualities of mestizaje." Thus, the social categories of indigenous and mestizo shaped the way the genetic data were organized and interpreted, for the purposes of the MGDP. The indígena "resists the force of [genetic] mestizaje," as long as s/he is located in the community; s/he can also become a mestizo by leaving the community and changing culturally. But "there is no turning back from mestizo to indígena" (García Deister 2014: 171).

The ideologies of mestizaje and indigenismo both envisage a mainstream mestizo nation into which indigenous communities can in theory assimilate, but both ideologies also require there to be indigenous communities against which the mestizo is defined, and these are typically seen as rural, isolated, and having distinctive languages and modes of dress and behavior—despite the fact that, by 2005, 38 percent of indigenous people lived in urban areas, and nearly half of these lived in six major cities (Mendoza Mendoza 2010: 21, 23). The MGDP reinforced this image of the nation: people were by default mestizos; nonmestizos required special efforts to recruit; the choice of a Zapotec community as a reference population fit the bill of a relatively pure indigenous people; the indigenous sample stood in for an Amerindian ancestral population, thus linking indigeneity to the past, where ideologies of mestizaje and indigenismo already placed it; the foundational indigenous/mestizo distinction was reiterated in the recruitment of samples, and in the labeling and management of the data; this distinction was freighted with genetic meaning, aligning social with genetic difference and representing mestizos and indigenous people as genetically distinct. The particular character of Mexicans' genomic profile was said to be given by the indigenous ancestral contribution—visible in the private alleles—which reproduced the sense of indebtedness to the indigenous past that is evident in the indigenist celebration of ancient Aztec culture.

Forensics and Regional Diversity of Mexican Mestizos

The indigenous/mestizo distinction was reiterated in studies that fall into the field of forensic genetics: their primary concern was with forensic identification, and they used CODIS STRs as their source of data. (The Mexican studies are compared to Colombia and Brazil in chapter 7.) This research portrayed a strong image of Mexico as a basically mestizo country, with indigenous communities, identifiably apart from the mestizo majority, being used as reference populations for Amerindian ancestry. The studies represented Mexican regional diversity as structured by differing proportions of Amerindian and European ancestry, along a north–south gradient; African ancestry was a comparatively minor component, and, according to these data, did not vary much from region to region.

We have seen that the MGDP hovered between representing Mexican mestizos as "similar enough to be analyzed as a single group" in the words of Jiménez Sánchez et al. (2008)—an image buttressed by talk of "a Mexican genome"—and seeing them as a diverse set of populations, with different proportions of continental genetic ancestry according to the state of origin. Research that used CODIS STRs came to the conclusion that Mexicans could be sorted into regional clusters, and one study concluded that "in terms of human identification purposes in Mexican Mestizos, results compel us to employ the STR database of the relevant [i.e., regional] population when DNA matching is found in forensic casework or paternity testing" (Rubi-Castellanos et al. 2009: 292).

However, the study did less to indicate which would be the "relevant" population. The data from ten mestizo populations spread across the country showed different possibilities. First, using FST values, they identified a "clearly shaped differentiation" between a Central/Southeast region (Mexico City, Puebla, Campeche, Veracruz, and Yucatán) and a North/West region (Chihuahua, Nuevo León, and Jalisco). This linked to greater proportions of European ancestry in the latter region and more Amerindian ancestry in the Central/Southwest, features which accorded with colonial demography and history. However, to achieve this result they had to exclude a sample from Hidalgo, which had missing data, and a sample from the "Central Region (CR)," defined by a previous study, which included people from four different states (Morelos, Querétaro, Mexico City, and Puebla), meaning that the "definition of a single geographical origin of this [CR] population sample was rendered complicated"—as if they expected state boundaries to define genetically homogeneous populations. The data analysis included the CR sample in the North/West region, which was "closer to the European ancestor"; this was "unexpected, considering the geographical origin of this sample," which led them to predict it would cluster with the Central/Southwest region, because of the "clear North-to-South increase of the Amerindian component." A first clustering thus defined two clear regions, as long as one complicated sample was excluded.

Second, a different statistical technique, analysis of molecular variance (AMOVA), revealed that "the best grouping of Mexican populations suggested separation of populations into three well-differentiated groups . . . representing the North/West [same as before, but with CR included], Center (Mexico City, Hidalgo, Puebla, and Veracruz), and Southeast (Campeche and Yucatán)." The Central/Southwest region was now broken into two. The same issue with the CR emerged, however—"incorrect assignment" to the North/West region. So excluding it once again and using a slightly different technique, spatial analysis of molecular variance (SAMOVA), a third analysis identified "four groups as best-data predictors": the previous North/West region was now divided into North-Central and Northeast-West, while the Central/Southeast was now formed by the previous Center region, plus Campeche, leaving the southeastern state of Yucatán as a single-state region (Rubi-Castellanos et al. 2009: 288–89). A later study of samples classified as mestizo, involving some of the same researchers, used Y-chromosome markers to define three regions—"north-west, center-south and southeast" (Martinez-Cortes et al. 2012), while a third publication, again authored by many of the same people and using the CODIS markers, reiterated a basic Northwest and Center/Southeast division (Salazar-Flores et al. 2015); in both cases, because the studies used different sets of samples, the assignation of states to regions also varied.

In short, then, multiple versions of Mexico's regional diversity emerged, depending on which samples were included and which statistical techniques were used. Region was acknowledged as an important aspect of diversity, racialized in terms of continental genetic ancestry, but the boundaries of the regions were vague and shifting. Compared to Colombia, regional difference was markedly less noteworthy for geneticists: the mestizo/indígena distinction cross-cut all the regions.

The interesting features of INMEGEN and its flagship project the MGDP are the degree of state investment in the project and the degree of consensus that it generated. The profound engagement of the state has emerged clearly in the account given above; this distinguishes Mexico from both Brazil and Colombia. Of course, not all human population genomic research has been carried out by INMEGEN. Among others, the Molecular Genetics Lab in the National School of Anthropology and History (ENAH), the Genomic Medicine Unit in the Salvador Zubirán National Institute of Medical Sciences and Nutrition (INCMNSZ), and the Institute of Molecular Genetics at the University of Guadalajara have all been active in this kind of work, and, starting in 2008, the Coca-Cola Foundation funded UNAM's School of Chemistry to create a *genoteca indígena* (indigenous genome library) to help address health problems, especially diabetes. Scientists in these institutes have collaborated with each other and with INMEGEN scientists, among others (Acuña-Alonzo et al. 2010; Reich et al. 2012; Villalobos-Comparán et al. 2008). But it is relevant that ENAH, INCMNSZ, and UNAM are all major state institutions and that the research is located in the same field of medical genomics.

INMEGEN itself has also changed since the conclusion of the MGDP project (García Deister 2014: 176–77; García Deister and López-Beltrán 2015; López Beltrán, García Deister, and Rios Sandoval 2014: 100–103). Jiménez Sánchez left, after a government inquiry that cast doubt on administrative leadership in the institute, and was replaced in 2010 by Xavier Soberón, former director of UNAM's Institute of Biotechnology. The research agenda of INMEGEN shifted a bit: there was less emphasis on Mexican uniqueness and related ideas of genomic sovereignty, and on Mexico trying to command its own place on the global platform of genomic medicine; there was more emphasis on international collaboration—for example, with researchers at Stanford (e.g., Carlos Bustamante, Andrés Moreno-Estrada) and San Francisco (e.g., Esteban Gonzalez Burchard, Elad Ziv)—as well as domestic ones (e.g., with people from ENAH, UNAM, etc.). Some of the research priorities remain very similar: one collaborative study developed more refined panels of ancestry informative markers, using samples from all over the Americas, to allow more accurate calculation of ancestral proportions and improve the ability to control for population stratification in medical genomic studies (Galanter et al. 2012).[2] Another big international study used twenty indigenous samples, drawn from the project's "Native Mexican Diversity Panel" and from older MGDP samples, and eleven mestizo populations to show how the Amerindian ancestry of Mexican mestizo populations recapitulated the genetic characteristics of nearby indigenous groups (Moreno-Estrada et al. 2014).

These studies reflect a shift in interest toward the fine-grained analysis of indigenous DNA, which was already under way in international circles before the end of MGDP (e.g., Wang et al. 2008). In INMEGEN, this shift was reflected in a project, led by Soberón, to study the genomic diversity of "Native Mexican populations" by sequencing a complete genome (López Beltrán, García Deister, and Rios Sandoval 2014: 101). The overall aim is still to improve the health of the Mexican population, but there is now more emphasis on the goal—already present in the 2009 publication from the MGDP project—of making a contribution to international genomic medicine by factoring in Amerindian genomics, seen as Mexico's unique selling point. The point of exploring indigenous DNA in detail is the potential contribution to the health not only of mestizos but also of populations worldwide.

Some post-MGDP genomic projects reinscribe the basic indígena/mestizo conceptual distinction by pathologizing indigenous people as the bearers of high-risk genetic variants, building on existing tendencies in that direction. One example is a project to study the genomics of diabetes and obesity in the Yucatán peninsula. A university press report stated that the project sampled twenty-six rural communities, selecting Maya-speaking adults, and that the scientists had carried out a preliminary study on "the association of 10 genes related principally to diabetes" in the communities. The aim was to explore how these genetic variants influenced the intestinal flora that affected the digestion of food. The report said that one of the geneticists involved had "specified that a Mayan mestizo, or a person from the city, has a genome that is half Mayan and half mestizo. In this sense, the research carried out in [rural] Mayan communities explains 50 percent of the genes of [mestizo] people in this region" (Coordinación de Medios de Comunicación Universidad Autónoma de Yucatán 2015). This clumsily worded report clearly distinguishes Mayan genes (found in rural communities) from mestizo genes, reifying each set of genes and producing the local variant, the "Mayan mestizo," who is genetically half Mayan and half mestizo. The implication is that the "Mayan half" of the genome carries the variants that are associated with diabetes.

This implication is clearer in INMEGEN's research on diabetes, carried out in collaboration with the Slim Initiative in Genomic Medicine for the Americas (SIGMA), funded by Mexican billionaire Carlos Slim, and collaborating with the Broad Institute of MIT and Harvard (García Deister and López-Beltrán

2015: 800). A summary in the institute's bulletin said "there is evidence that the indigenous population is more susceptible to diabetes and in Mexico 10 percent of the population is indigenous, which is why . . . INMEGEN is identifying the genetic risk factors for diabetes among indigenous people." The report goes on to say that a genetic variant has been identified, which is involved in the metabolism of triglycerides and which is "very frequent in the indigenous and Mexican mestizo population." It is also "common among other Latin American populations, but infrequent or absent in European and African populations" (INMEGEN 2014). In fact, the technical paper behind this report focuses almost entirely on mestizos, using standard reference samples from Amerindian populations; it states that the "risk haplotype" is found at levels of about 50 percent in Native American populations and that, among Mexican mestizos and U.S. Latinos, there is a correlation between the presence of the risk haplotype and the amount of Native American ancestry (SIGMA Type 2 Diabetes Consortium 2014: 97, Supplementary Table 4).[3] Mestizos here are presented as very heterogeneous—indeed, about 3 percent of them had over 95 percent Amerindian ancestry—but conceptually the divide between indigenous and mestizo people is maintained, especially in the bulletin's summary, and indigenous populations are clearly identified as being the source of this particular risk haplotype.

Conclusion

For Mexico, during the MGDP and after, there has been a broad consensus on how human genome science figures in the nation: it is all about public health, seen as key to a democratic society, as it was also seen in the postwar decades. There were certainly voices critical of INMEGEN in its first phase (a white elephant, poorly administered) and of the idea of genomic sovereignty, insofar as this implied the genetic uniqueness of the Mexican population; a few voices were critical of the whole idea of genomic medicine, arguing that social factors were much more important and should be the target of investment, and that genomic medicine was of benefit primarily to global corporations (Ribeiro 2009). But the basic idea of supporting medical genomics in an effort to resolve Mexico's alarming rise in obesity and diabetes generated a high level of consensus.

The assemblage that linked Mexican scientists, policymakers, politicians, health sector officials and workers, and the press, among others, formed a relatively stable set of connections, with institutional infrastructure, that materialized the mestizo as a body predisposed to ill health. These connections gained solidity from links, again with institutional infrastructure, to global medical (genomic) science, which has increasingly produced the human being as a body constantly at risk and always a (potential) patient (Dumit 2012; Rose 2007). For these Mexican actors, the possibility of recruiting indigenous genomes into their networks—and the mestizos whose bodies carried diverse amounts of Amerindian ancestry—allowed them to carve a national space out of the network, and mobilize this as a resource for the wider assemblage. The attraction of indigenous genomes as a resource tapped into existing evolutionary narratives about the peopling of the world, which cast the original Americans as a continental isolate with particular biological traits.

In contrast to Brazil, genomics did not enter into public debates about the role race should play in the public domain. In Brazil, the very shape of diversity in society was up for debate—what should the nation look like in terms of racial difference?—and there was profound disagreement as to the answer, which drew genetic data into the dispute. Questions of race and racism in Mexico were muted in public debate. If the mestizo can be understood as a solution to the "conflictive postcolonial racial situation" in the aftermath of the Mexican Revolution—a key symbol for claims of racial democracy—then it was an effective solution: discussions of racism in the press in the 2000s, for example, focus on countries other than Mexico, or on the racism that Mexicans suffer when abroad—with a few exceptions (e.g., Camacho Servín 2014; El Universal 2011). While there was some coverage of the idea that genetics in general could undermine racism (El Universal 2003), racism was not seen as a national problem to which genetic knowledge could contribute an answer.

In Mexico, most people agreed on what the nation should ideally look like in terms of diversity—a country of (healthier, less obese) mestizos, proud descendants of indigenous civilizations. Issues of cultural diversity and democracy were a political hot potato—the Zapatista rebellion and associated indigenous movements are evidence of that—but genetic data did not get drawn directly into these debates. Instead, the role of genomics was indirect—as in Colombia—underwriting, and to some extent genetically reifying, a hegemonic version of the nation's identity as fundamentally mestizo, with indigenous populations encysted within it (with only passing mention of Afro-Mexicans). Democracy was linked to mixture in the shape of an institutional agenda of "health for all," which in practice meant mestizos. Hierarchy emerged in relation to the indigenous populations, seen not only as bounded communities distinct from the mestizo mainstream, but also as the source of genetic variants, which put mestizos at risk of poor health and which genomics could help identify and, it was hoped, address with appropriate therapies. As the afflicted inheritor of indigenous genetic ancestry in what was fast becoming a *país de gordos* (a country of fat people; see García Deister and López-Beltrán 2015), the mestizo who emerged in this Mexican assemblage was a morph of the traditional hijo de la chingada (see chapter 1) and, as such, a less promising figure than the Brazilian version (tolerant, inclusive), and more akin to the Colombian mestizo (violent, exclusive). But from this unfortunate mestizo could perhaps be extracted some benefit for the nation and for the world in terms of future well-being.

7

....

Genomics and Multiculturalism

Comparisons and Continuities

Making comparisons can be a tricky business, as noted in chapter 3. Isolating cases as separate entities risks erasing possible connections between them. The "cases" may shape each other, such that their characteristics are the products not just of local contexts and histories, but also of interactions with each other and with common third parties (Seigel 2005). Assemblages do not have natural borders; networks can connect endlessly. For example, multicultural reforms in Brazil, Colombia, and Mexico did not proceed in each country without some awareness of what was going on in the other countries. Brazil's affirmative action programs were reported by the press in Colombia and rather less in Mexico, albeit not widely in either place—allegations of racism on the football pitch or the fashion catwalk attracted more coverage. And many people in all three countries were aware of issues around racism in other parts of the world, especially in the United States, which was often seen as a nation marred by racism and obsessed by race. Genomic research in each country was integrally linked to international genomic science, even as national themes were being addressed in the science itself and genetic data were being drawn into national debates about health crises or multiculturalism. Many researchers routinely published in English in international—usually U.S.-based—journals and collaborated extensively with other Latin American, U.S., and sometimes European colleagues.

We need to be alert to the politics of comparison: who compares what and for what purpose (Seigel 2005; Stoler 2001). Comparing race in Brazil or Mexico to race in the United States has long been a technique to cast mestizo countries in a good light, as relatively free from racism or at least racial conflict (see chapter 1; see also Seigel 2009). In other words, as Stoler (2001: 863) says: "We might treat the comparisons as technologies that produced truth claims about normalcy and race that were predicated on what Michel Foucault called a 'will to knowledge.'"

In genomic science, we can see a politics of comparison at work. Geneticists constantly compare samples, and some of this involves comparing mestizo or Latin American samples to other samples. Claims are made about the specificity of mestizo populations, in terms of their difference from European or North American samples, or the fact that they do not correspond to "well-defined" ethnic groups: these features are said to predispose them to certain disorders, affect the way they respond to medical treatments, or make them useful or even necessary resources for medical genetic research. This is partly about getting Latin American and Latino populations onto the global genomic map (Burchard et al. 2005; Bustamante, De La Vega, and Burchard 2011), a project of ethnic inclusion for social justice (Bliss 2012). On the other hand, comparisons are also made within a country—witness the way the paisas in Colombia have been the focus of research and singled out as an "isolate."

In this sense, genomic research in the three countries shares many common features, starting with their common framing in medical genomics (and, secondarily, forensics and evolutionary history). Researchers in Colombia and Mexico used standard STRs to characterize populations for improved forensic identification; in Brazil, researchers were doing the same kind of thing (Dellalibera et al. 2004; Francez et al. 2011; Pinto et al. 2014). Researchers in all three countries were preoccupied with mixture and routinely assessed proportions of genetic admixture. In doing so, they all used similar reference populations to capture European, African, and Amerindian genetic ancestry, which by definition were relatively pure compared to the admixed population.

In all three countries, too, no matter how much democracy and liberal values were being undermined by antidemocratic practices, they still figured as ideals and as an organizing frame for political activity. The mestizo character of the nation was adduced as an integral part of that frame, while multiculturalism was added on as a new approach in which separate cultures could mix on equal terms. When geneticists highlighted mixture, they connected it to democracy, directly (Brazil's antiracist genomics) and indirectly (Mexico's public health agenda, or the idea that incomplete mixture was a factor in Colombia's regional-racial divisions). The tension between democracy and hierarchy was reflected in the reinscription of racial difference, with the implication of relative purity, located either in the nation or beyond, in parental populations.

Geneticists themselves did not hierarchize populations—in that sense, their practice underwrote multiculturalism by presenting indigenous, black, and mestizo populations as separate but equal—but implicitly, genomic projects linked black and indigenous populations to the periphery, to the past, and, in some cases, to disease.

Alongside these similarities, genomic research practices in each country had particular features that corresponded to the fact that the science connected to other network nodes, which were related to the country's preoccupations, organization, governance, and institutional infrastructure—for example, regional difference in Colombia, racial inequality in Brazil, indigenous ancestry and public health in Mexico. In each case, these configurations were not exclusive to each country, but took on greater prominence there. Network connections between geneticists' practices and national preoccupations could appear distant (as science presents its methods as insulated from "society"), but could be proximate (as scientists present their mission as socially useful), and could also be made topologically proximate by bringing together apparently distant nodes (e.g., genetic diversity and conflict in Colombia). Genetic data thus got drawn into public debates about social issues, although the degree to which this happened at all also varied—in Colombia, for example, genomic research has had a rather low profile in this respect, in contrast to the use of genetic data in discussions about affirmative action in Brazil or about public health in Mexico. The way democracy and hierarchy figured was also particular to each country—antiracism and black people in Brazil, public health and indigenous ancestry in Mexico, regional conflict in Colombia.

Race and Mixture

Race was generally denied by geneticists and other specialists, such as the Colombian forensic technicians. This denial could take several forms: (1) there were no superior and inferior races; (2) there were no pure races (although this often implied there once had been, but they had long since become mixed, a result which Latin America exemplified especially well); (3) race itself was not a genetically valid concept. Everyone agreed on the rejection of racist hierarchies, but things were not so simple in relation to (2) and (3). Sérgio Pena was the most outspoken about (3), but others took a similar stance. As one Colombian geneticist said, "I think it is not appropriate to continue to talk about race. From a genetic point of view, it is a concept that is not accepted; it has no basis."[1] The INMEGEN scientists also rejected the genetic validity of race. Nevertheless, the concept of race, and even the term itself, reemerged in the practice of human population genetics: it was disavowed and yet made present at the same time.

Some Colombian geneticists, for example, used the word quite frequently in interviews: when questioned directly on the topic, one said, "The term *race*—I don't think so," but earlier he had commented that "the purest race is the African, it is the original one" and had described a project in which he had tried to see if the "racial factor" influenced drug metabolism. Others commented on the resistance of the "African race" to malaria, and another mentioned a book which described "all the possible crosses—mulato, zambo—of all the possible races." Of course, merely using the word did not mean a belief in the genetic validity of the concept—it could describe a social category, as when one Colombian scientist noted "the stigmatization of some races." But references to purity, originary status, influences on metabolic processes, and resistance to malaria all impute some degree of genetic reality to race. We saw this in the ambiguous way Emilio Yunis talked about race, both as a social imposition of hierarchical value onto a neutral genetic basis, and as itself a way of describing genetic variation.

The most common way in which race seeped into the practice of genetics was the use of categories that evoked racial meanings, and the tacit genetic reification of these categories by implicitly aligning social categories with genetic data. This effect has been widely observed in other contexts (Duster 2015; Fujimura and Rajagopalan 2011; Fullwiley 2008; M'charek 2005); the effect is indeed "the trouble with genetic ancestry" (Nash 2015). In Brazil, Colombia, and Mexico, the process was evident in various ways.

First, social categories were used to define samples, which were then presented in terms of genetic data. Thus, Zapotecs and mestizos in Mexico, or Afro-descendants, indigenous groups, and mestizos in Colombia appeared in research publications—and media reporting of these findings—as distinctive entities. In Brazil, the effect was different precisely because Pena and others insisted on the genetic indistinctiveness of categories such as *pardo, preto,* and *branco*. But while "some contemporary White Brazilian populations can represent an extraordinary reservoir of Amerindian and African mtDNA genomes," other populations, such as the descendants of European migrants found in the southern city of Veranópolis, "are in fact [i.e., genetically] basically European" (Marrero et al. 2005: 505), and it was also possible to define "African-derived populations," identified by locality or appearance, which could then be genotyped (Bortolini et al. 1999).

Second, samples were routinely used to represent ancestral populations of Amerindians, Africans, and Europeans, whether using HapMap data, the HGDP-CEPH Diversity Panel (a widely used dataset of fifty-two populations), or other indigenous Latin American samples. Contemporary populations were used as a proxy for continental populations that existed before the conquest of the Americas, and, when geneticists use these proxies for ancestral populations to define African, European, Amerindian, and Asian genetic ancestry, it is no surprise that they can evoke racial meanings, as these continental categories have been at the root of racial constructs for centuries and remain the underlying basis on which some geneticists defend race as a genetically meaningful category (see chapter 1). Of course, these ancestral populations can be used precisely to deconstruct the genetic concept of race. Pena and colleagues, for example, use them to show how mixed Brazilians are and to argue that they have to be seen as 190 million individuals: the ultimate expression of the need for personalized medicine. But in the process he has to "racialize to deracialize": there is a "molecularization of race," in which ancestral populations are defined genetically, followed by its "de-molecularization" when racial categories in Brazil—and more widely—are shown to lack any genetic coherence (Santos, da Silva, and Gibbon 2015: 62).

There is an important shift here between the particular—Brazil or Latin America—and the general—the world as a whole. Saying that races do not exist in Brazil because everyone is so mixed can be seen as just one example of a general condition—everyone everywhere is mixed and always has been—or it can be seen as a historical outcome that is particular to Brazil, but that implies the existence, in some other place and/or time, of the (pure) races that created its mixture. (This is an expression of the duality of mixture, noted in the introduction, and the tension between mixture and isolation in genetics, noted in chapter 1.) The use of ancestral populations inevitably invokes the second scenario. The idea that there are no pure races in Brazil or Latin America today depends on the idea that they used to exist somewhere else in the past. However, the fact that *contemporary* populations, selected by social criteria—self-identification, location, ethnic identity, and so on—are used to represent ancestral populations then creates a double effect of racializing and genetically reifying these populations. Zapotecs thus appear as representatives of a past (pure) racial category, which has persisted into the present, retaining its genetic characteristics, but is still rooted in the past and thus temporally other in relation to mestizo modernity.

Geneticists would object—quite rightly—that, for genetic ancestry analysis, an ancestral population is nothing like a race, defined as the racial type of early twentieth-century racial science. Ancestral populations are defined in terms of frequencies of particular genetic markers—large numbers may be used, but they are a miniscule proportion of even the coding portion of the genome—which have been chosen precisely to differentiate as much as possible between populations. The markers are often unrelated to phenotype; they may be located in the noncoding portion of the DNA. There is no attempt here to typologize entire genetic profiles and sort them into distinct kinds. The fact that, on a PCA graph, Zapotecs appear separate from Mexican mestizos—and very distant from other ancestral populations chosen to represent African and European ancestries—is an artifact of these choices and the mode of statistical analysis and visual representation used. If people draw the wrong conclusions, this is because they do not fully understand the methods. This is partly true, although one could add that it behooves the scientists to pay greater ethical attention to the possible effects of their categories and methods (Bliss 2012: 204). But, as I argued in chapter 1, the very concept of ancestral population relies on a "genetic geography" (Nash 2015) of biocontinental populations, understood as emerging from evolutionary processes that bring environment, social groups, and genes into rough correspondence. Furthermore, a main reason that continental ancestry is analyzed in the first place is that it is seen by many geneticists as being potentially medically relevant: it is useful to control for population stratification in medical studies,[2] and it is studied for possible clues to predispositions to disease, the metabolizing of drugs, and so on. The easy alignment of ancestral populations with familiar racial categories thus goes deeper than simple misunderstanding by the layperson.

Third, and as a consequence, race was evoked in the figure of the mestizo, often seen as a living challenge to the idea of (pure) race, but whose existence depends on the notion of (relatively pure) races. The mestizo is a biocultural figure, defined as much in terms of historical cultural mixture as biological interbreeding, but there is no doubt that the idea of the mestizo is profoundly rooted in images of sexual reproduction (see chapter 8).

This account of the mestizo as a racialized figure is, however, too simple. It fails to grasp how the mestizo both invokes and disavows race at the same time. If the mestizo is connected historically to colonial race categories and to racialized categories today (negro, indio, blanco), it can also be imaginatively configured to connect with a future trajectory toward raceless universalism.

"We are all mestizos" is a familiar Latin American phrase, but several geneticists used it to describe the genetic reality of the human condition, which they saw as being unfortunately not recognized by those who made invidious distinctions. Like the mestizo, race is thus universal (the human race) and particular (different human races) (Balibar 1991). We can think of "mestizo," "racelessness," and "racial difference" as three points in a topological network (see chapter 1). Then we can see how "mestizo" and "racelessness" can be brought close together and made to connote each other, with the mestizo configured as a body that is generic, even universal. The mestizo is made apparently distant from "racial difference" without the latter ever becoming disconnected: it may be submerged, but its trace presence remains. And the network can twist again to bring "mestizo" into intimate proximity with "racial difference," so the mestizo embodies and displays its racialized origins, without the possible connection to "racelessness" being erased.

Something of these complexities can be seen in the way geneticists dealt with particular mestizo populations. Mestizos were always in some sense generic—most Latin Americans were mestizos—but they appeared in specific combinations of mixture. Genomic science provided the tools to understand that an "unlimited finity" of combinations was possible. The possibility of precisely measuring degrees of ancestral contribution, of locating ancestries in different kinds of DNA (autosomal, mitochondrial, Y-chromosome), and of identifying multiple ancestral lineages (e.g., from different indigenous populations) created a situation in which "a finite number of components yields a practically unlimited diversity of combinations" (Deleuze 2006: 109). All this distanced the mestizo from racial difference by multiplying difference almost limitlessly—the endless proliferation of difference—and approximating the mestizo to racelessness: this was Pena's Brazil as 190 million individuals. But the relation to racial difference was always there as an absent presence.

Take the genetic study of the paisas in Colombia (Bedoya et al. 2006). The paper suggested the take-home message was that genomic medical science should be aware that mestizos are not a homogeneous category: they are subject to endless variation, which genomic science can map. This casts the paisas as generic mestizos: like all mestizos they vary in their precise makeup; this is the character of the mestizo. Yet the paper also suggests that the paisas are special: they are an isolate; they have high levels of European ancestry, alongside the high levels of Amerindian ancestry hidden in their mtDNA. The research thus also provides the resources to understand the paisas as racially distinctive and rather white, which reinforces the myth of la raza antioqueña as a special breed of Colombians. The transnational assemblage into which the paper is plugged materializes a generic mestizo; in the national assemblage of the Colombian landscape, this generic version morphs into a racial exception.

Multiculturalism, Blackness, and Indigeneity

The previous section outlines commonalities in the use of the concept of race and the way it came into and out of focus, disappearing incompletely and reappearing without being fully present. There were also important differences between the countries in the way race entered into genetic practice and how blackness and indigeneity figured in ideas about the nation as a multicultural polity.

First, the way the concept of race figured in genomic discourse differed. In Brazil, the word *race* had an institutional life—in governance and in politics—but Pena and colleagues spent a good deal of time showing precisely that the official race/color categories had no genetic meaning. Although Colombian and Mexican geneticists also disavowed race as a genetic reality, the concerted genetic deconstruction of race undertaken by Pena was not a project that they undertook, even though racialized categories had an institutional life of sorts in their countries: the national census in Mexico has counted indigenous people, whether by language-use or more recently self-identification, and the Colombian census, after 1993, included questions to capture Afro-Colombians and indigenous people (Loveman 2014). Instead, geneticists there tended to reify these categories by using them as sampling frames. Meanwhile, the offhand and taken-for-granted use of the word *race* by geneticists—usually in interviews, rather than publications—was most common in Colombia, deriving, I argue, from the way regional difference was strongly racialized in the country, and especially the way blackness and region were perceived to coincide in the Pacific coastal region (see below). In Colombia, the word *race* does not have the institutional presence it has in Brazil, but blackness and African heritage certainly do—"black communities" and "Afro-Colombians" form part of the language of the state and of NGOs—and, as in many areas of Latin America, blackness, associated with visible, bodily inherited difference, evokes the idea and terminology of race (and racism) more strongly than indigeneity, which is often seen as more a matter of culture and language rather than of appearance and descent.

Second, while genomic studies in all three countries tended to portray the nation as basically mestizo with indigenous and black minorities on the side—thus both reproducing an official multiculturalism that focused on ethnic minorities and took for granted the mestizo majority, and also challenging that multiculturalism by explicitly recentering the mestizo majority as the core of the nation—this took different forms in each country.

In Colombia, genomics located black and indigenous people in the geographical regions typically associated with them in the popular imaginary, reinforced by multiculturalist legislation, which ceded them land rights mostly in these regions. Although multicultural legislation had focused first on indigenous people, Afro-Colombians made an important impact at this level and soon became an integral part of the multicultural nation, particularly via their visible presence in the Pacific coast region and the multicultural policies that targeted that region (despite the fact that a minority of Afro-Colombians lived there). This result was shaped by the differential positioning of blackness and indigeneity in Latin American "structures of alterity": in broad terms, indigenous people are located in the nation as more "other" in cultural and linguistic terms than black people, who tend to be seen as urban citizens, perhaps second-class, but less distinctive (Wade 2010, 2013b). In multiculturalist Colombia, "black communities" initially underwent a process of ethnicization, which made them look more indigenous (Restrepo 2013a; Wade 1995). Genomic studies reinforced this picture by locating Afro-Colombians above all in the Pacific coastal region, while indigenous people were sampled in a variety of classic indigenous locations (the far southwest, the far northeast, the Amazon plains, etc.). The Pacific coast region was important genomically, because of the high levels of African ancestry that were identified there. Although African ancestry was also important in the Caribbean region, it was the Pacific region that acted as the real locus of blackness and African ancestry.[3] Genomics thus reinforced the notion of a mestizo nation divided by region and race, with prototypical blackness and indigeneity being located in particular, rather peripheral places.

In Brazil, genomics painted a different picture, one already familiar to Brazilians. The nation was mixed, of course, but blackness was an integral part of the mixture: pardos (browns) were over 40 percent of the population, and, together with pretos (blacks), were a majority. Although there were concentrations of Afro-Brazilians in the northeast region, they were also found all over the country: there was nothing like Colombia's Pacific coastal region, with its majority population easily identifiable as black in Colombian terms. Politically, however, black social movements and a left-leaning state were keen on instituting a binary divide between negros and brancos, explicitly labeled as racial, legitimated by statistics on racial inequality, and reinforced by policy measures targeting black people: these actors and many sympathizers agreed that racial inequality and racism were important issues. However, many others, including some geneticists, while perhaps agreeing that racial inequality and racism were problems, were against the black–white divide as a basis for policy. Genetic data were widely adduced to attack the divide and the whole idea of biological race that was taken to underlie it. By contrast, in Colombia genetic data were not used to undermine the idea of blackness (or indigenousness) in the nation, but rather to reinforce it. Racism began to emerge publicly as a political issue in Colombia in the 2000s, but genetics were not deployed in discussions about it, except occasionally in general statements about the nonexistence of biological race.

In Mexico, genomics had a higher public profile than in Colombia, due to the PR machine behind INMEGEN, but, as in Colombia and in contrast to Brazil, genetic data were not drawn into a political debate about the multicultural nation. Instead, the portrait painted of the country resonated uncontroversially with the idea of a mestizo nation made particular by its indigenous ancestry and in which indigenous people still lived in bounded communities: this image was now readable in a genetic idiom, which reinforced the foundational divide between mestizo and indígena. In contrast to Brazil and Colombia, blackness figured low on the scale, for geneticists and politicians. Although, in the 1960s, Lisker had paid some attention to the genetics of black populations, the MGDP and other genomic studies had little to say about them. This genomic image of the nation was part of an assemblage in which political practices and networks configured multiculturalism as about the rights of indigenous people and issues of indigenous community autonomy. Racism was not a common theme in discourse about indigenous rights, and neither did it figure large in the incipient discussions about Mexico's black/African "third root." Genetic data were not deployed to adjudicate questions around racism—except again in generic statements about the nonexistence of genetic race. The public discussion involving genomic research was about public health: the figure of the mestizo, with his/her indigenous genetic ancestry, could help understand the etiology of obesity, diabetes, and cardiovascular disease.

Region and Race

Differences between the countries emerge in the way genomic research dealt with regional diversity and its relation to African, European, and Amerindian genetic ancestries. All geneticists were alive to the regional diversity of their mestizo populations, but the issue was handled differently in each country.

For Colombia, the question of region was central and strongly racialized. In forensic genetics, Paredes et al. (2003) confidently defined four separate regions, described in highly racialized terms, but having little practical forensic value. This version became a standard tool in forensic labs, despite the fact that its regional reference populations were ignored in courtroom practice and its validity was criticized by other geneticists. Its standardization and commonsense use attested to the power of region as an organizing conceptual frame. Using different markers, Yunis had previously produced a similar map, and in 2007 the geneticist William Usaquén was working on another map, using the CODIS STRs, which had regional divisions slightly different from those of Paredes (Barragán Duarte 2007). While different versions were produced by using different markers and methods, the regionalization of genetic difference was a persistent preoccupation.

In Mexico, regional differences were recognized and linked to racialized difference by means of the north-to-south gradient along which European ancestry decreased, while Amerindian ancestry increased. As in Colombia, different versions of the regional divisions emerged, not only across different studies, but from within the same study using a single set of CODIS markers. This study cautioned that "ancestral components at present could be observed as a cline throughout the Mexican Republic," thus putting into question the whole notion of dividing by region (Rubi-Castellanos et al. 2009: 292). Regional variation was of interest because the proportion of Amerindian ancestry was seen as potentially linked to health risks (Acuña-Alonzo et al. 2010), but there was a good deal less concern than in Colombia with dividing genetic diversity into regional clusters, and more attention to clines and gradients.

In Brazil, there was the least interest in regional variation. This is not to say it did not appear. In the "Retrato Molecular" (2000), Pena and colleagues presented data organized by the official macro-regions, defined by the national geography and statistics institute: North, Northeast, Central-West, Southeast, and South. Several studies used this regional classification to organize their data on the diversity of genetic ancestral proportions. The common knowledge that the South was whiter and more European, while the Northeast and North were home to many Afro-Brazilians and darker-skinned people with a lot of indigenous ancestry, was consistently borne out, but there was little concern with regional variation and no attempt to produce regional classifications different from the standard macro-regions. Some papers barely mentioned regional difference: one forensics paper presented allele frequencies for thirteen STRs, noting only that the samples came from various regions (Grattapaglia et al. 2001); another specified which regions its samples came from, but then evinced no more interest in the matter (Pinto et al. 2014).

Others took a little more interest, but not much. One medical genomics study of two hundred people, using ancestry informative SNPs, found a "low degree of genetic differentiation among the Brazilian geopolitical regions," although some samples from the South "were significantly different from all other samples" (Lins et al. 2010: 188). A larger forensics study, based on over twelve thousand samples and using fifteen STRs, concluded that "although the three Brazilian populations from Central West, Southeast and South are grouped together, the remaining populations from Northeast and North are quite distant from this group"; this was linked to differing proportions of European, African, and Amerindian ancestries (de Assis Poiares et al. 2010: e62). Finally, Pena and colleagues (2011) decided that "the genomic ancestry of individuals from different geographical regions of Brazil is more uniform than expected," because all the regions showed a majority of European genetic ancestry.

Brazilian geneticists showed much less interest in regional diversity than their Colombian and Mexican counterparts. This is in some contrast to some accounts by historians, which depict region and race as closely related (Blake 2011; Weinstein 2015). In that sense, Brazilian geneticists were particularly interested in the portrayal of Brazil as, above all, highly mixed: the population was seen as extremely heterogeneous, but it was not important to partition this diversity into regional categories, whatever historical importance region might have had. By contrast, in Colombia the history of the racialization of regions carried more weight and was seen by geneticists as fundamental to understanding the nation's diversity, with blackness especially partitioned into a recognizable region. In Mexico, regions were less important than the north-to-south gradient of increasing proportions of Amerindian ancestry, which might have significant health implications.

Geneticization

Some differences between the three countries can be detected in the degree to which genetic idioms permeated public policy domains—that is, the extent to which genetic data and arguments entered into public discussions about issues deemed to be of social concern. Genetic research was being carried out in all three places, and in Mexico was being supported strongly by the state, but the level of geneticization of the public sphere was quite uneven.

Brazil was the country where genetic data entered most into public debates about matters of national concern. Some geneticists, and some nongeneticists, thought public policy about university education should take note of genetic findings about the meaning of race: Pena and colleagues (in genetics and in the humanities) started by saying genetics should not take a prescriptive stance and could only provide (true) information; later they moved on to say that, in the quest for a color-blind society, science could be prescriptive, insofar as it could show social policymakers where they were going wrong. Genetic data were used by some nongeneticists to explicitly contest the existence of an Afro-Brazilian social category.

The state eventually ignored these claims and deemed genetics to be irrelevant to the social policies defining racial quotas, which targeted a socially defined category and aimed to correct social processes of discrimination. On the other hand, for policies related to health, genetics was given more of a say: the state retained a generally race-based affirmative stance by promoting policies to improve the health of the black population, but it was recognized that it made no genetic sense to do anything other than screen universally for the sickle-cell anemia trait. Black activists were also uneven in their responses: mostly they sidelined genetics as irrelevant to questions of racism and racial inequality, but some were prepared to use the idea of genetic connections with Africa—revealed through the carrying of the sickle-cell trait—to induce changes in identity, for both black and white people.

In Mexico, geneticization happened mostly in relation to health. With the MGDP, a genetic idiom became more widely available to think about what it meant to be a mestizo, to ponder regional diversity, and to consider the difference between indigenous people and mestizos. But this had little impact on multicultural policy and public debates about what form diversity in the nation should take. On the other hand, genetics was clearly an important element in thinking about the health of mestizos (and indigenous people) and how this could be improved, with the Mexican state directing the nation down a sovereign path. The idea that genetics was a key field of intervention and investment, and that Mexico had to control its own destiny in this respect, fired the entire state mission to create Mexican expertise in the field and secure its own share of the "promissory capital" that biomedicine was creating (Thompson 2005: 258).

In practice, however, genomic medicine was not yet making good on its promise to provide practical therapies, whether tailored to individuals or to the nation (assuming the latter made any genetic sense, which was questionable). Therefore, the Mexican government's diabetes prevention campaign emphasized healthy lifestyles and barely mentioned genetics. A poster campaign included the slogan "Do not inherit diabetes," but made no mention of genetic inheritance and the known risk factors of having close relatives with the condition, saying instead that "healthy diet and exercise from a young age are the basis for the prevention of diabetes." A Mexican health-related website, using the same slogan, clarified that genetic factors could predispose a person to diabetes, but then went on to emphasize lifestyle choices (Munguia 2009). In short, genetics again had a very uneven effect, galvanizing government policy guiding science investment, but hardly appearing when addressing the general public about health.

Colombia shows the lowest degree of geneticization of the three countries. The government was interested in, and funded, genomic research: genetics institutes pursued their research in medical and forensic genetics with state funds in the manner of normal science. But genetic data entered little into public debates about health. Despite the controversy over the Great Human Expedition's alleged exploitation of indigenous blood samples, the state showed scant interest in the idea of genomic sovereignty, compared to Mexico, and produced minimal legislation to promote it: the main bone of contention has been in relation to nonhuman genetic diversity, with indigenous communities taking up the cudgels to demand protection of the biodiversity harbored by their territories and communities (Barragán 2011: 46–48; Nemogá S. 2006). Finally, debates about multiculturalism, while an important feature of the political panorama, have not drawn genetic data into their purview.

Continuities and Changes

As part of the process of comparison, it is instructive to explore the differences and continuities between the material in chapter 2, on the mid-century studies of human diversity in physical anthropology and genetics, and the genomics studies that date from the late 1990s. The most obvious change over this period has been in the infrastructure of genomic science. Although the earlier studies were already concerned with health, the promise that medical genetics will deliver solutions to intractable health problems has meant the rapid development of the field in terms of public and private investment, technological innovation, and international collaboration. This has created a landscape in which established ideas of national autonomy are channeled into notions of genomic sovereignty, which gain traction in political and economic terms.

If we compare a blood type study from 1940s Colombia, or Lisker's studies from 1960s Mexico, with the MGDP or multinational studies such as those led by the Colombian geneticist Andrés Ruiz-Linares, based in University College London (e.g., Wang et al. 2008), the infrastructural differences are plain to see: the national and international dimensions of the data collection, the scale of the international collaborations, and the level of detail of the genetic information are on a completely different plane; the location of the studies in the domain of global medical genetics is also markedly different. The infrastructure in terms of recruitment remains very similar: to recruit subjects, researchers often use health networks, paternity suit samples, and educational establishments; they approach people in public locations and negotiate with specific communities. Perhaps the approach used by MGDP was innovative in recruitment for genomic studies: they advertised for subjects to attend their sampling jornadas at public universities. The multinational project CANDELA, exploring genetic ancestry, physical appearance, and social background, adopted a similar technique, advertising via university networks and social media (Ruiz-Linares et al. 2014).[4] In both cases, the inherent interest of the project—the status of the gene as cultural icon (Nelkin and Lindee 1995) and, in the case of CANDELA, the promise of individual DNA ancestry results—was enough to generate volunteers.

The way the material and administrative infrastructure of genomic science related to a conceptual schema of underlying ideas about the nation and its diversity shows some important continuities with the mid-twentieth century.

First, the consolidation of a move toward antiracism has been complemented by a turn toward multiculturalism, both global trends, which have been very evident in Latin America. Some have questioned the apparently radical nature of these changes in social terms, and certainly one can detect major continuities in genetics research into human diversity in Latin America: the figure of the mestizo and the measurement of mixture is still a fundamental preoccupation; the use of ancestral populations is very similar, whether sampled using contemporary proxies on other continents or in indigenous and black communities in the nation; the implied temporal displacement of these communities into the past is also an important continuity, as this temporal othering is a key mechanism for allowing the duality of mestizaje—the tension between hierarchy and democracy—to persist. Genomics continues to represent and describe both mixture and difference (especially in the guise of black and indigenous communities, although with some attention in Brazil to white or European immigrant communities).

A clear change is the fading of an explicit language of purity, used above all to describe indigenous populations; instead, genomic data indicate ever more clearly that everyone is mixed, although to different degrees. Explicit reference to purity and the associated framing of mixture in terms of overall processes of the assimilation, civilization, or modernization of indigenous people is no longer an overt part of genomic discourse. However, the idea of isolated populations stands in for relative purity under threat from mixture— for example, in Colombia's Great Human Expedition—while ancestral populations are also necessarily a locus of relative purity compared to the mestizo populations they have produced.

Along with the fading of explicit reference to purity, there is greater emphasis on the mestizo. The mid-century research included mestizos—more in Brazil and Mexico than in Colombia—but now the mestizo is a higher-profile object of biomedical attention. If anything, however, this focus restates the political and cultural emphasis given to mixture in the mid-twentieth century, which became slightly decentered when the multiculturalist turn put the spotlight onto ethnic minorities as constitutive of national identity.

Second, although there has been an obvious move away from explicit reference to race in genomic science, there is still an important sense in which the concept has not disappeared, and may be subject to genetic reification. In the 1940s in Colombia, many physical anthropologists referred to race unproblematically, even though their teacher Paul Rivet had challenged the validity of the concept. By the 1970s in Mexico, Lisker and his colleagues did not use the term, and by the 2000s, geneticists in Brazil, Colombia, and Mexico either campaigned against the genetic validity of race or disavowed it when directly questioned on the matter. But just as ideas that there might be a genetic basis to race did not entirely disappear from the life sciences in general—despite social scientists' confidence that life scientists all agreed that race was a "social construction"—so the idea of race did not always vanish from the practice of genomics, as we have seen.

It is undoubtedly true that genomics has complicated ideas of race: geneticists such as Pena openly deny the genetic reality of race; genomic data multiply the ancestries of a single person, by analyzing maternal, paternal, and biparental markers; populations are sometimes depicted with the ancestral profile of each sampled individual, breaking down the image of a homogeneous group; genetic markers are often clearly dissociated from classic social markers of race such as skin color. These changes mean that it is possible to claim that identity and race, when "rewritten at the genomic level, visualized through a molecular optic," are "both transformed" (Rose 2007: 179), that genomics "reconfigures both nature and society" (Reardon 2005: 16), and that the logic of reading race through a "molecular optic" which establishes "the correlation of disease risk and racial difference" is different from a twentieth-century genetic logic which, for example, linked blackness to sickle-cell anemia in a deterministic way (Abu El-Haj 2007: 287–88). These claims carry some truth, but the language of transformation needs to be quite significantly tempered with an understanding of how racialized categories continue to be routinely deployed as sampling frames and how, as I have shown, these categories tend to become freighted with genetic meaning.

This signals a third continuity, which is the tendency, then as now, to bring social and genetic categories into alignment by defining samples in social terms and then depicting them in terms of genetic profiles, often in ways that highlight genetic difference. We saw that, in the mid-twentieth century, scientists appreciated that mestizos and indigenous people could be socially distinct but genetically similar, but overall expected social and biological change to proceed roughly in tandem, and thus for social identities and genetic profiles to correspond in the long term. Similarly, post-2000, we have seen that Pena and colleagues can demonstrate that social categories of color do not correspond to coherent genetic profiles, in terms of African ancestry, while other geneticists in Brazil and elsewhere, by their practices of sampling, labeling, and data presentation, often state that social categories have a distinctive genetic profile, without it necessarily being clear that this distinctiveness is in relation to specific genetic markers, which constitute only a tiny part of the genome.

How can we assess this picture of continuity and change? I am struck by the strong similarities in the conceptual schemata underlying genetic science in the two periods. The—as yet unrealized—potential of genomics to intervene in health care constitutes a huge innovation (assuming it comes to fruition), but the way nation, population, and diversity figure in this science shows strong continuities with the previous era, despite the submerging of race in most cases. Approaches that explicitly frame mixture in terms of assimilation and modernization have been abandoned, but a link, direct or indirect, between democracy and mixture is still present, and still in tension with hierarchy and relative purity. In that sense, claims about the power of genomics to transform sociality need to be approached with caution.

Latin American Race and Genomics in a Global Frame

What can these three countries tell us about race, mixture, and genomics more widely? I will explore three themes: the way race and genomics become entangled in assemblages; the role of the nation as a framing device in the network; and the meanings of mixture.

Race and Genomics

One of the regions of the world where the debate about race and genomics is most heated and elaborated is the United States. While the issue of the genetic validity of race is a question debated in the global forum of international genomic science, it is notable that many of the actors and venues in the debate are U.S.-based. Equally, many of the social studies of how race figures in genomic science focus on the United States, although some concern Europe (M'charek 2005, 2013; M'charek, Schramm, and Skinner 2014; Nash 2015; Smart et al. 2008; Taussig 2009; Tutton 2007). The fact that race and genomics entangle so readily in the United States may be linked to the "inertial power" of race (Kahn 2012). Alongside the still open possibility entertained by some geneticists that racial categories do have some genetic validity, the "deep-seated American identification of violent crime and race" also facilitates the inertial power of race to enter into forensic genetics, despite its lack of "practical legal utility" in the calculation of likelihood ratios in DNA identifications (Kahn 2012: 136–37). The fact that race is a potent social force in the country means that it seeps into the categories of forensic and also medical genetics (Kahn 2013: 158). The pursuit of social justice has been powerfully racialized, leading to race-based social movements and affirmative action programs; this has included the federally mandated use of racial categories in scientific research and medical practice, with the aim of monitoring racial health disparities (Epstein 2007), an ethical practice that has been followed elsewhere (Smart et al. 2008). Geneticists in the United States generally support the use of these categories, and even more so the ethical agenda of social justice that underlies them; they vary on the usefulness of race as a relevant category in medical genetics, but a significant number do see it as relevant (Bliss 2012). In short, a highly racialized society correlates with a highly racialized genomics, whether the racial categories are acting in medical genetic or bioethical mode.

The material from Brazil, Colombia, and Mexico adds a good deal of nuance to this relatively simple picture. For example, Brazil is, compared to Colombia or Mexico, a country where race has an institutional presence and a public profile; state-driven racialized inclusion-style agendas are present in health policy and university admissions. Yet genomics is a realm where race has been vociferously denied both as a genetic reality and as a basis for social policy. In part this is because these ethical inclusions are very controversial and have often been seen by critics as the importation of U.S. models of race, judged inappropriate for Brazil. We cannot say that racialization in the public sphere in Brazil has led straightforwardly to a racialization of genomics. One could argue the opposite effect has occurred—genomics has been deracialized—but this would be too simple as well. Genetic data have been widely used to underwrite the idea of racial *mixture*, rather than separate racial categories; and this concept of mixture still depends on the idea of separate ancestral populations, which are racialized by their biocontinental origins. Mestiçagem is a racialized concept, even if it is being deployed to deny the existence of racial categories.

By comparison, both Colombia and Mexico are instances where the shape race takes in society at large is broadly reflected in the practice of genomics. Colombia has lower levels of institutionalized racialization than Brazil. Race is present indirectly, through the institutional recognition of blackness and indigeneity; race and racism, per se, have a lower profile. In the guise of indigeneity, and above all blackness, and through the conceptual vehicle of region, race is quite strongly geneticized, unlike in Brazil and more like in the United States. The powerful common sense of the nation's racialized regions is reflected in some genomic practice.

In Mexico, the powerful institutionalization of indigeneity and the mestizo by the state, alongside the minimization of race, racism, and blackness, is reflected in the geneticization of the indigenous/mestizo divide, together with a lack of interest in African ancestry and a disavowal of race as such. The geneticization of the mestizo, however, takes place primarily in relation to health, rather than multiculturalism.

The Nation as Framing Device

In all three countries, it is evident that the nation plays a key role in articulating ideas about race in genomics (Wade, García Deister, Kent, Olarte Sierra, et al. 2014). Although geneticists in the three countries often publish in English in international journals, the nation usually figures with little or no comment as the taken-for-granted frame for collecting and organizing data. But the nation is evidently an object of concern: Pena produced a "molecular portrait" of Brazil; INMEGEN produced a map of the Mexican genome; Yunis wrote a book asking "Why are we [Colombians] like this?" These projects sought to define the nation and address some of its problems, and in all of them mixture figured as a key—to overcoming racial conflict in Brazil, to grappling with health problems in Mexico, and to understanding racial-regional conflict in Colombia. The idea of the nation as originating in mixture and as a representation par excellence of mixture in the global panorama of human diversity means that race is always present, even when it is absent as such, or is being vocally disavowed. Black, indigenous, mestizo, and sometimes white people are named; European, Amerindian, and African ancestries are defined. The fact of their presence in the nation is obvious and taken for granted; the fact that the nation emerged from their mixture, equally so. Genomic research into mixture not only defines the specificity of the nation by mapping particular patterns of mixture, but also holds out the promise of solving some national problems—as well as putting mestizos, in their national variants, on the map of global genomic science.

In Latin America, the conceptual frame of the nation carves a space out of the assemblage in which race and genomics can become entangled, without race necessarily being mentioned as such. This strikes me as different from the United States, where social science studies of race and genomics have not generally emphasized the role of the nation (e.g., Koenig, Lee, and Richardson 2008; Krimsky and Sloan 2011; Wailoo, Nelson, and Lee 2012)—although this is less so for Canada (Hinterberger 2012; Kohli-Laven 2012). Latin America is perhaps more similar to Europe, where issues of race have frequently crystallized around questions of nationality, citizenship, immigration, and xenophobia, and this is reflected in the attention paid to the nation in studies of genomics and human diversity (M'charek 2005, 2013; M'charek, Schramm, and Skinner 2014; Nash 2015: ch. 3; Taussig 2009).

The Meanings of Mixture

In the previous chapters, we saw that geneticists had distinctive takes on what mixture and the mestizo meant for their country and for the world. These stances felt the pulls generated by the tensions between mixture and purity, and between democracy and hierarchy. In Colombia, Yunis was explicitly pessimistic: mixture had gone wrong; the mestizo was preoccupied with maintaining distinction, hierarchy, even purity of blood; in Colombia, for historical reasons, this had manifested itself in regional fragmentation, which had contributed to persistent conflict and violence. Other geneticists did not venture into this kind of reflection on their country's history and future, but they persistently reiterated the regionalization of Colombia and linked it to race and genetics, thus rooting it deep in history and biology. Yunis, perhaps perversely, maintained an overarching faith in mestizaje: more of it would solve the problem. Yet he was tapping into an insistent materialization of the mestizo in Colombian and Latin American history: the mestizo as predator, as abuser of indigenous (and black) people, as colonist (or usurper of lands), as a social climber who claims to be whiter than his/her ancestry warrants—in Mexican terms, an hijo de la chingada (see below). On this view, mestizaje was a mixed blessing: if the global future was more mixture, genetically and socially, the world had better watch out.

In Brazil, Pena was far more optimistic about mixture, befitting the way mestiçagem has historically been configured in Brazil. The mestizo as materialized in Brazilian genomics was a body in which racial difference disappeared in endless permutations of mixture, which confounded the drawing of biological and therefore, in the view of Pena and others, social boundaries of race. Without such boundaries, racial hierarchy would disintegrate. Brazil was seen as already some way toward this democratic future; it thus stood as an object lesson to the world. Race-based affirmative action was a backward step on this path. The use of commonsense, simple racial categories in medicine did not work clinically for Brazilians, and it behooved the rest of the world to take notice, as admixture was increasing in most places. If the global community agreed on the moral value of antiracism, they would do well to observe Brazil's example. In fact, this Brazilian mestizo also abused indigenous people's rights, but they were a tiny proportion of the population, and this behavior was not highlighted by most geneticists. In this genetic view, the mestizo was hard put to abuse black people, as they were themselves mestizos in this configuration.

This materialization of the mestizo connected to persistent ideas about sexual openness, tolerance, and social inclusiveness, which was also marked on/in the body, whether as the "Mongolian spot" that many Brazilians carried, according to Freyre (1986: 278), or the haplogroups of indigenous and African origin found in their mtDNA.[5] Far from being an hijo de la chingada, this mestizo bore the influence of "the mulatto girl" who "initiated [him] into physical love and, to the creaking of a canvas cot, gave [him his] first complete sensation of being a man" (Freyre 1986: 278). Despite Freyre's sexist language, this is a benign portrayal of the nation-forming sexual act (compared to the violent imagery of the chingada), which links to ideas about the power of sexual relations to transcend racial difference that resonate strongly with ideas about mixture all over the world.

In Mexico, the mestizo was made material in ambivalent ways. Mestizos had figured officially as the core embodiment of la raza mexicana for most of the twentieth century; they were la raza cósmica made flesh; they were the *raza de bronce* (the bronze race) through which Vasconcelos said the "universal spirit" would speak.[6] In contrast, Octavio Paz famously ruminated on the mestizo as an hijo de la chingada (see introduction), carrier of all the fucked-up-ness of a traumatic history—who could nevertheless be *chingón* (smart, cool, awesome). In everyday life, being mestizo became so taken for granted, almost banal, that most Mexicans only claimed the label when specifically asked about their raza. Genetic studies reproduced that taken-for-grantedness, but also assembled a more pessimistic morph of the mestizo as a medicalized body at risk (of obesity and diabetes), due in part to the burden of its indigenous heritage (its sky-high consumption of sugary drinks was noted in medical circles, but of course genes were what interested geneticists). The lesson for the world—rather than "don't drink so much Coke"—was that Mexico had populations of special interest for science: indigenous people who were the biological representatives of peoples who had populated the isolated Americas thousands of years ago, and mestizos who had inherited their genes and could be studied to identify some causes of disorders increasingly affecting the entire world.

III · NARRATING MIXTURE

8

....

Gender, Genealogy, and Mestizaje

In the previous chapters, I showed how genomic research on human populations put a strong emphasis on mixture as the core reality of Brazil, Colombia, and Mexico. The production and reproduction of mestizos—initiated by genetic and cultural exchanges between original populations of Africans, Europeans, and Amerindians—lay at the heart of these nations. In this chapter, I explore how genomic science reinforced this emphasis by presenting genetic data showing that many present-day Latin American populations have inherited Amerindian (and, especially in Brazil, African) genetic ancestry via the maternal line and European ancestry via the paternal line. This made connections with existing historical and popular narratives about early colonial sexual relations between European men and indigenous and African women. The genetic data were often popularized in terms of the national population's "indigenous mothers" and "European fathers."

Mestizaje is an assemblage with multiple connections to elements in networks of gendered and sexualized ideas and practices: although cultural exchange is central to mestizaje, the figure of the mestizo persistently evokes ideas of sexual reproduction and gendered kinship, which over the centuries have created genealogical connections that range widely in time and space. The DNA technologies used in genomic analysis open temporal frames that allow geneticists to make inferences about early colonial sexual encounters between populations originating on different continents and to highlight these as foundational moments. Such accounts resonate with familiar stories—fictional and otherwise—about the encounter between a Portuguese colonist and the indigenous woman, Iracema, in José de Alencar's eponymous 1865 Brazilian romantic novel (Devine Guzmán 2005; Sommer 1991); or that between the Spanish conquistador Hernán Cortés and the Nahua woman popularly known as La Malinche, who was given to Cortés in 1519—or more apocryphally "gave herself"—and now embodies multiple meanings, ranging from mother of the first mestizo and thus of the nation, to traitorous whore who sold herself to a dominant power (Paz 1950; Wood 1998).[1] The deep temporal frame underpins the representation, in genetic idiom, of a mestizo nation founded on three originally separate populations. The way gender and sex enter into the network, articulating with racial difference, puts agency and power into the hands of European men. However, this aspect is generally neutralized in genomics, which skirts questions of power and coercion when talking about sexual relations. Meanwhile, indigenous and African women appear as relatively passive figures, the sexual agency of indigenous and African men is marginalized, and European women are similarly sidelined. Such representations, not surprisingly, pose a challenge to important currents in today's race–gender politics in Latin America.

Gender, Genomics, and Uniparental DNA Analysis

Although genetic data can impinge on ideas about gender difference in multiple ways (Ettorre 2002; Fausto-Sterling 2000; Haraway 1989, 1991), here I explore specific technologies that allow geneticists to draw conclusions about the roles played by men and women in human evolutionary history. The analysis of mitochondrial DNA (mtDNA), using techniques dating from the 1970s, and the analysis of nonrecombinant Y-chromosome DNA (Y-DNA), which dates from the 1990s, provides data on the basis of which to make statements about sexual and gender relations—among other things—stretching back into the prehistoric past. This requires a bit of explanation.

Uniparental Analysis, History, and Genetic Genealogies

The DNA located in the mitochondria—subcellular units that generate energy for the body's cells—is passed from mother to offspring, without the genetic material being recombined, or "shuffled," in the process. Men and women inherit mtDNA from their mothers, but only daughters pass it on, thus establishing a single genealogical line connecting each person to her/his mother, mother's mother, mother's mother's mother, and so on, into the ancient past. As only men possess a Y-chromosome—some intersex individuals aside—the DNA in the nonrecombinant section of the chromosome is passed on in the paternal line alone, establishing a second unilineal genealogical connection into the distant past. Both mtDNA and Y-DNA are used to establish genetic relatedness for forensic purposes, usually over a short time span, for example, between family members. But relatedness can be traced over many generations, giving potentially vast historical depth. In the 1990s, there was a controversy in the United States over genetic data indicating that Thomas Jefferson had fathered a child with one of his slaves, Sally Hemings. The case was made by comparing Y-chromosome markers from the known descendants of Jefferson's paternal uncle and the known descendants of one of Hemings' sons (Palmié 2007). Going further back, mtDNA and Y-DNA allow inferences to be drawn about the prehistory of the human species.

Occasional mutations occur in the mtDNA, and these are passed from the woman in whom the mutation occurred down the maternal line to her offspring; her daughters will pass on the same mutation to their offspring, and so on. Mutations also occur in the Y-DNA—usually at a slower rate than in the mtDNA. The presence of these mutations allows an individual to be connected back, via an unbroken unilinear maternal or paternal ancestral connection, to the originator of the mutation: every person with this particular mutation in their mtDNA or Y-DNA will have this originator as a common ancestor. Particular mutations—sometimes a single one, sometimes as many as a dozen—define a "haplogroup," and each person will belong to a number of different haplogroups of varying genealogical depth: a man's patriline might have a distant ancestor who originated a given haplogroup and a less distant descendent of that ancestor, who originated another haplogroup, nested within the more ancient one. Thus haplogroups have a tree-like structure, starting with a very early Y-DNA "signature" that defines the widest level—in theory, all living males—and a series of more recent mutations that define smaller, less inclusive levels, usually called subclades. Working out the structure of the tree by comparing which haplogroups exist in different populations allows geneticists to order haplogroups chronologically in relative terms, by working out which mutations are more widespread and therefore more ancient. Assumptions about how often mutations occur allow geneticists to create a "molecular clock" to estimate in absolute chronological terms when a common ancestor lived. Data on the geographical distribution of people with given mutations permit inferences about where the haplogroup originated in the world—sometimes quite specifically, sometimes very generally—and how its carriers migrated in the process of peopling the world.

It is important to understand what data derived from mtDNA and Y-DNA can tell us. They tell us about unilineal or "uniparental" genetic genealogies, which are highly selective. Such genealogies trace the ancestry of specific genetic variants rather than whole persons; or rather, they trace the ancestry of a person, but only in relation to a very specific part of their DNA. If an individual reckons his or her genealogy, one mode of calculation—enacted in a cognatic or bilateral kinship system—produces an ever-greater number of ancestors as one goes back in time, all of whom will have contributed toward the genome of the individual: there are many ancestors, all connected to a single descendant today. If the same individual selects only one unbroken line of connection, s/he traces a specific path through all those myriad ancestors to reach a single ancestor—perhaps a famous historical figure, or simply the host to a random genetic mutation—who has passed on a small part of his or her DNA to many people alive today: there is a single ancestor connected to multiple descendants today, who may be seen as connected to each other via the common heritage of a genetic variant (M'charek 2005: 129).

A person has various ancestors of this kind—usually called the "most recent common ancestor" or MRCA—depending on the number of living people included as related descendants: a person will share a particular set of mtDNA mutation markers with a given set of people who can all trace their maternal ancestry in an unbroken line to a given female MRCA, but who will also share a different set of markers with a larger number of people, who have inherited mtDNA from a more distant MRCA. As noted above, each individual belongs to multiple haplogroups, which are in a nested hierarchy, structured by time and level of inclusiveness. Ultimately, all living humans can trace their mtDNA to a so-called Mitochondrial Eve (a name coined in the late 1980s, when researchers first estimated when she might have lived). She is a woman who, among all the other women alive at that time (estimated to be anywhere between one hundred and two hundred thousand years ago), has passed on mtDNA to all living humans today (or rather, those sampled to date by scientists). She is not a fixed individual: her existence is a logical entailment of the way mtDNA operates, but "she" varies according to the currently living population: as this changes over time—if, for example, certain matrilines die out because some women do not produce daughters—the position of Mitochondrial Eve in the genealogical tree changes, becoming more recent. The same applies to the "Y-chromosomal Adam," whose existence is also a logical entailment of the way Y-DNA is inherited (Oppenheimer 2003: 37–42). The point here is that mtDNA and Y-DNA allow geneticists to make statements about ancient male and female ancestors and to posit connections between sets of people who share some inherited trait from these ancestors: the definition of a given set depends on how far back in time the MRCA is located.

As noted, mtDNA and Y-DNA can be used to make inferences about the geographical origins of a person's ancestors, but they are not well suited to estimating percentages of biogeographical ancestry in an individual: this is better done using ancestry informative markers in the autosomal DNA (inherited in recombined form via both parents—"biparental"—and thus used to measure overall ancestry). But at a population level, mtDNA and Y-DNA data can be used to estimate ancestral percentages by measuring the frequency in a given population of haplogroups deemed to belong to specific continents. Again, it is important to understand what mtDNA and Y-DNA data can say about biogeographical ancestry. In a living individual, the presence in the mtDNA of haplogroups thought to originate in ancient Amerindians or their ancestors—which is very common in Latin American people—does not necessarily mean the person has a significant amount of indigenous ancestry: it merely means that, among all the thousands of ancestors s/he has—and going back only ten generations produces 2,048 ancestors—one of them was an Amerindian woman who happens to be connected in an unbroken maternal line of descent to him or her. Thus a population made up of people whose complete genomes show rather little indigenous ancestry may still have high frequencies of Amerindian haplogroups in their mtDNA. The Colombian paisas, who appeared in a previous chapter, were estimated to have about 80 percent European ancestry in the autosomal DNA, while about 90 percent of the matrilines found in the mtDNA were of Amerindian origin (Bedoya et al. 2006; Carvajal-Carmona et al. 2000). This uniparental genetic analysis reveals hidden ancestral connections and uncovers admixture in people who might seem quite "white" or "European," but it does so by picking out very specific parts of the DNA and highlighting very selective and possibly distant connections (TallBear 2007). The haplogroup tree traces selective connections carved out of a proliferating network of genetic links.

Uniparental Analysis and Gender Relations

Uniparental analysis allows historical arguments to be made about populations, but also about men and women. Because the analysis focuses on matrilineal and patrilineal connections, data which are actually about molecular lineages also allow inferences to be made about men and women as persons and about sexual relations between them, as mtDNA travels through reproductive acts of mothering and Y-chromosome DNA through reproductive acts of fathering. Even though men and women have mtDNA, the genetic lineage established by the analysis of mtDNA is a female one, just as the genetic lineage established by looking at Y-DNA inheritance is a male one: this kind of analysis is "a technology for producing sexualized genetic lineages" and, furthermore, an "enactment of sex difference" (M'charek 2005: 130, 137).

We already saw how ancient common ancestors, whose theoretical existence is deducible from genetic genealogies that trace the ancestry of particular genetic variants, in popular science become gendered individuals—Adam and Eve, no less. As persons they can absorb—better than molecular lineages can—the socially meaningful baggage associated with the kinship genealogies of persons, freighted with hopes, fears, nostalgia, and personal life projects. This tendency toward personification is very evident in the popular science writing of British geneticist Brian Sykes, who coined names and speculative life histories for the "seven daughters of [Mitochondrial] Eve," who he said were the maternal ancestors of all living "native" Europeans. Each ancestral mother was linked to a major haplogroup originating in Europe (although some analyses have defined more than seven of these). Sykes shifted from impersonal genetic links to emotional bonds, saying that the route by which mtDNA genetic variants reach people from their ancestors "has its own special importance, for it follows the same path as the bond between a mother and her child. It is a living witness to the cycle of pain, nurture and enduring love which begins again every time a child is born" (cited by Nash 2004: 19–20). Gendered links were made between mtDNA and images of maternity built around nurture and love. Sykes founded a DNA testing company, Oxford Ancestors, which, like similar enterprises, offers to link individuals to specific ancestral groups via their mtDNA and Y-DNA: thus British men can trace links to Celtic, Anglo-Saxon, and Viking origins, using the Tribes of Britain service (Oxford Ancestors 2015). These very selective genetic links—when attached to "tribal" names, some of which are associated with warlike and masculine qualities—can become freighted with a cargo of historical, cultural, and personal and powerfully gendered meanings, a network of connections articulated and coproduced by the DNA testing company and by the individuals who purchase the DNA tests (Sommer 2012).

Another illustration of this is the way Y-DNA becomes associated with masculinist images of domination and sexual competition (Nash 2015: 148–54). Specific Y-DNA haplogroups have been linked to historical figures, such as Genghis Khan. The relative frequency of a Y-DNA signature in populations living in areas once in the Mongol empire was speculatively attributed by scientists to Khan's reputed fathering of many children, while his military campaigns slaughtered many other men, ending their patrilines. Popularizers of science embellished this with tales of the penchant of Genghis Khan (and his close male relatives) for the rape of enemy women and the enjoyment of large harems of subservient females. His alpha male tendencies led to the proliferation of his Y-DNA in subsequent generations. A similar story emerged around a medieval Irish king called Niall of the Nine Hostages, another heroic, warlike, masculine figure. Various DNA testing companies offered services for people interested in tracing possible links to Niall. One press report at the time said:

> Fathers who believe they rule the roost can now discover if they are the descendent of a notorious Irish warlord. Ireland's oldest pub and New York's first Irish tavern will be offering DNA testing on Father's Day to identify relatives of the marauding king Niall of the Nine Hostages. . . . Customers revealed to be a descendant of Niall—who scientists suggest is second only to Genghis Khan in fecundity—will receive complimentary drinks and the house's food speciality. (Stack 2008)[2]

For geneticists, these cases represent examples of how particular human cultural tendencies, such as warlike and patriarchal male behavior, can shape genetic ancestry in populations, but these tendencies can also appear to be a natural part of human behavior in general. Thus the fact that Y-DNA haplogroup diversity is generally less than that for mtDNA is linked to a general model of human evolution in which the DNA of powerful, successful men tends to dominate local gene pools (Nash 2015: 154–61). This is part and parcel of a view of evolution as driven by masculine competition and sexual dominance, which has been criticized by a number of feminists—from quite different angles—as ignoring women's strategies and/or foisting a vision of Western gender relations and competitive individualism onto the evolutionary record (Haraway 1989: 279–367; McKinnon 2005). In another example, there is less emphasis on overt male competition, but ideas of male control over women are still invoked: relatively low levels of Y-DNA diversity in populations in northern Sinai were linked by geneticists to male polygamy and the way men controlled what the scientists called the "traffic in women" (M'charek 2005: 138).

These accounts, especially when popularized, depict "a naturally brutal or at best ordered world of male dominance, sexual competition and women's and men's profoundly different 'reproductive strategies' [and] dangerously legitimate and naturalize a whole range of reactionary 'truths' about the 'universals' of sex, gender and reproduction" (Nash 2015: 168). MtDNA and Y-DNA data allow inferences to be made about relationships between men and women, and this gives them multiple affordances in many overlapping assemblages, including ones involving mestizos and their ancestors. Before getting to that, we need some historical background about racialized relations between men and women in Latin America, in order to understand the connections that genomic accounts do and do not routinely trace out and highlight in these networks.

Mestizaje, Race, Nation, Sex, and Gender

Brazil, Colombia, and Mexico are countries said to be founded on a sexual act between men and women of different "races" or continental origins. It is well known that ideas of race, ethnicity, and nation all integrally—one could say intimately—depend on gender and sexual relations (Nagel 2003; Stoler 1995, 2002; Wade 2009).[3] This is for various interconnected reasons. First, many social group boundaries regulate things that are passed on, or are thought to be passed on, by inheritance in the broadest sense: belonging, land, resources, skills, moral qualities, and so on. Rights to donate and claim these things are thus mediated by social relations involving the production and raising of offspring, including sexual relations between men and women. Second, ideas about race, nation, and ethnicity all involve notions of connectedness through common origins, genealogy, "blood," birth, and upbringing; these connections are mediated by gendered processes of sexual and social reproduction, especially in the domain of the family (however that is thought to be constituted). Third, the first and second points coalesce in the idea, identified by Foucault as emerging in Europe from the late eighteenth century, that the strength and vigor of a society's population need to be promoted by active attention to sex and reproduction, individual and collective. Fourth, in contexts of hierarchy, relations of dominance can be enacted by policing sexual boundaries, such that the dominant group has sexual access to the subordinate group, while repressing the reverse exchange. Dominant men's power is expressed in their sexual access to women of their own and the subordinate class. The preceding points add up to elites' concerns with maintaining class or group boundaries in a way that creates "purity": "Efforts to regulate women's sexuality are endeavors to achieve purity qua patriline for a racial or ethnic group as well as for the nation. . . . Women must be sexually pure in order to preserve the purity of the race or nation" (Lee 2012: 36).

In Latin America, things were more complex, insofar as mixture was from the beginning an integral part of the colonial order, and ideas about purity consequently took a rather specific shape (Mörner 1967; Powers 2005;

Wade 2009). In the early American colonies, Spanish and Portuguese men had sex with indigenous and African women (usually slaves), whether by rape, more indirect forms of coercion, or consensual unions (albeit consensus in very unequal power relations). Indigenous people (usually women) also sometimes had sex with African or American-born black people (usually men), despite the authorities' rather inconsistent attempts to prevent it in the name of protecting the indigenous people. The offspring of these various unions, recognized as mestizos of diverse kinds, had sex with each other and with Europeans, Africans, American-born blacks and whites, and indigenous people.

Elites in Spanish America and Brazil did not abandon social and racial hierarchies in the face of mixture. On the contrary, they were concerned to maintain their elite position, based in part on a notion of genealogical purity. In colonial Spanish America, the so-called society of castas notionally ranked people, placing European and American-born whites at the top, black Africans and indigenous people at the bottom, and varied degrees of mixture in the middle, referred to by assorted labels (Katzew 2004; Martínez 2008). These labels suggested a ranking by degrees of mixture, but occupation, appearance, place of residence, and education played important roles in defining status or *calidad* (quality). A person's status could change according to context and over their lifetime. In short, it was a rather unsystematic and contingent social order (Cope 1994; Rappaport 2014).

Still, elite people had honor and strove to maintain it by behaving with propriety and keeping their family lineage pure and "untainted" by black or indigenous blood, or by religious heterodoxy. From the elite perspective, mestizos, blacks, and indigenous people generally did not have honor, by virtue of their birth, which was tainted by their inferior blood and their assumed illegitimacy. However, mestizos, blacks, and indigenous people often claimed to have honor by virtue of their good and proper behavior (Garrido 2005; Johnson and Lipsett-Rivera 1998; Twinam 1999).

Honor was strongly gendered. Elite men could have informal relationships and indeed families outside their marital households with lower-class, darker-skinned women, without this staining their honor; for elite women, the same was far from true. This classic sexist double standard provided a social climbing mechanism for women from the lower and middling classes: even if an extramarital relationship with a richer, lighter-skinned man meant no honor, it might mean access to resources and to lighter-skinned children, who could perhaps have some claim on their father. In some cases, a brown-skinned woman might aspire to marry a whiter, richer man, and, if his family opposed the match, the couple might elope to force the parental hand and permit marriage (Martinez-Alier [Stolcke] 1989 [1974]). Mestizo men who became wealthy might be able to "marry up" as well and, with time, draw a veil over their own and their children's mestizo origins, a process of *blanqueamiento/brancamento* or "whitening." In short, boundaries of class and race were constantly traversed by sexual relations, while elites simultaneously attempted to maintain some purity for themselves in a constant struggle to defend honor and status.

In postcolonial Latin America, some of these patterns retained their shape. The nineteenth and early twentieth centuries saw the advent of liberal ideologies, the abolition of slavery, the attempted disestablishment of indigenous communities (often unsuccessful), attempts to offset the perceived poor qualities of nonwhite populations by encouraging European immigration (successfully in Brazil, much less so in Colombia and Mexico), and the uneven valorization of the mestizo (less evident in Colombia than in Mexico and Brazil). Against this background, basic hierarchies of color, race, and sexual honor continued to operate (Wade 2009). In 1930s Brazil, white men could "deflower" young darker-skinned women (take their virginity under false pretenses of marriage—defined as a sexual crime at the time) with relative impunity, compared to darker-skinned men, who suffered the legal consequences more often. Legal authorities assumed that these young women had no honor or that they knew marriage to a well-off white man was not a realistic possibility for them and thus had consented to sex without the promise of marriage. In contrast, a white woman who accused a man of deflowering her stood a better chance of seeing the man prosecuted and punished (Caulfield 2003). In late nineteenth- and early twentieth-century Colombia, in the flourishing economy of the coffee-growing highlands, mestizo women found economic opportunities to become more autonomous and less subject to the control of mestizo men of the same class. But in so doing, they found themselves the object of more sexual advances by elite men. They might accept such advances, perhaps with material benefits in mind, but they faced risks of sexual predation and loss of honor. For these women, maintaining honor could mean accepting a greater degree of subordination in a household with a man of her own class (Smith 1997). In sum, sexual exchanges between men and women continued to be powerfully structured by hierarchies of race and class, which were simultaneously structured by those same exchanges.

Male Sexual Agency

In the interplay of race, class, and gender, the operation of male sexual agency is key. Sexual double standards, combined with class and racial privilege, gave whiter, wealthier men the opportunity to form relationships with women of their own and lower classes; less wealthy men, often also darker skinned, had a more limited range of action. Lighter-skinned elite men had greater sexual agency, which could enhance their social capital (children, reputation).

Sexual agency of a different kind was attributed to indigenous, black, and mestizo men in varying ways. In the colonial period, indigenous men were often seen as sodomites and effeminate; African and black men (and women) tended to be seen as sexually excessive and threatening (Behar 1989; Wade 2009). In the republican period, similar images of sexual excess and perversion continued. For example, in the Brazilian army in the late nineteenth and early twentieth centuries, the lower ranks, made up mostly of nonwhite men, were seen by the officers as a hotbed of sexual degeneracy and sodomy: the men were lacking in the qualities of honorable masculinity needed for the nation (Beattie 2001). In other contexts, black men (and women) were seen as heterosexually excessive—images familiar from U.S. and European contexts (Fanon 1986 [1952]; Nagel 2003). The black boatmen of the Magdalena river (see the introduction) were described by travel writers as having "libertine" ways and a "shameless lubricity" (Villegas 2014: 156; Wade 1999: 177). In the 1920s and 1930s, Colombian novelists such as Tomás Carrasquilla and Bernardo Arias Trujillo gave highly eroticized descriptions of Afro-Colombian dances (Hincapié García 2010; Wade 1993: 90), reiterating the common associations made, in Latin America and elsewhere, between black music and dance, and sexual license or liberation (Chasteen 2004; Wade 2000). Homosexual or heterosexual, the common theme was the sexual excess of nonwhite men, especially black men.

Into the twentieth century and beyond, these questions of male sexual agency and race become more complex. In Mexico, for example, after the Revolution, the virility of upper-class men came under suspicion because of their tendency to adopt European fashions seen by some as pretentious and unmanly; there was a fear that effeminacy and homosexuality were undermining Mexican society. Against this, postrevolutionary literature began to vindicate a mestizo virility, recasting earlier images that depicted lower-class mestizo masculinity as barbarous and untamed (Irwin 2003). As the mestizo became a national icon, so the bounds of proper masculinity widened to include darker-skinned men in the embrace of racial fraternity. In Brazil, from the 1930s, the

sexual agency of white men—the ones who had laid the foundations of the nation's population by impregnating lots of dark-skinned women—was diluted
as working-class men—who would often be dark-skinned—were implicitly
included in a racially mixed fraternity of men who headed the honorable patriarchal households being promoted by Getúlio Vargas's support for traditional
family values (Caulfield 2000: 183–94).

By the late twentieth century, the way people in Rio de Janeiro talked about
white men's sexuality rendered it "opaque"—a bit lifeless, not worthy of much
comment—compared to the sexuality of brown and black men, which people
described with a wealth of adjectives, mostly aligned to predictable stereotypes about sexual desirability and physical prowess (Moutinho 2004). Some
Brazilian black and brown men were not averse to encouraging these images,
despite their stereotypical nature, and even actively promoted an image of
themselves as hypersexual (Pinho 2005). Some Afro-Colombian men accepted
stereotypical images of themselves as "Dionysian"—sensual, sexy, good danc-
ers, etc.—although others rejected these portrayals (Viveros Vigoya 2002).

This assertion of black male sexual agency, and its challenge to white men,
has been strengthened by the increasing educational and occupational upward mobility of some black men (and women), and the growing black social
movements that have given some men (and women) public and political visibility. Traditionally, it has been thought that black and brown men, if they had
valuable assets in economic, sexual, or other terms, have sought to "marry
up" and find a lighter-skinned partner, a tactic that implicitly challenges white
male superiority, even though in the long term it reproduces the underlying
value and position of lightness (Sue 2013: ch. 5; Telles 2004: 176; Wade 2009:
168–75). The marriage motives of successful dark-skinned men may not be
driven by a desire for upward mobility and whitening. There are affective motives as well, and structural contexts need to be taken into account: because of
their economic position, such men are likely to be moving in circles where the
women they meet will be lighter than they are. However, it is very common for
others to *assume* that upward mobility and whitening drive them—that is, their
challenge to the racial-class status quo is belittled by imputing base motives
of undignified and materialistic social climbing (Moutinho 2004: 320–43;
Wade 1993: 296).

Images of indigenous men's sexuality are not well documented in Latin
America, and show different tendencies. In Bolivia, for example, indigenous
men are generally seen as virtually asexual, which is perhaps why the indigenous president Evo Morales has made a point of humorously asserting his

sexual masculinity (Canessa 2008: 53, 55). Hale and Nelson both note that, in Guatemala, nonindigenous people may see some indigenous men, especially those empowered by education and/or indigenous social movements, as bent on a kind of sexual revenge, attempting to reassert their masculinity by dating or having sex with white women (Hale 2006: 159; Nelson 1999: 219). This perception is related to assumptions about social climbing, as just noted. Overall, however, the sexual images of indigenous men in Latin America are less erotically charged than those of black men.

In sum, the image of the mestizo nation is built on the idea of white male sexual agency, which created the foundations of the population through sexual relations with indigenous and black women. This agency has always been unsettled by the sexuality of subordinate black, indigenous, and mestizo men, which has been labeled as excessive, degenerate, and perverted, and not suitably productive for the colony or the nation, but which, especially for black men, always implied the possibility that it might be more powerful and erotically charged than white male sexuality. As the construction of the nation veered more toward the mestizo—a tendency particularly evident in Mexico and Brazil—and, more recently, toward multiculturalism and the empowerment of (some) black and indigenous people, the security of white male sexual agency has become, if anything, more unsettled: white men may feel threatened by indigenous or black men dating white or mestizo women; and some black and to a lesser extent indigenous men directly challenge white male sexuality.

Female Sexual Agency

In Cuba and Brazil, in the early decades of the twentieth century, the mulata (woman defined as of black–white ancestry) became a commodified symbol of national culture (Kutzinski 1993; Lopes 1996). In Cuba, the mulata became "the site where men of European and of African ancestry rhetorically reconcile their differences and, in the process, give birth to the paternalistic political fiction of a national multiculture in the face of a social system that resisted any real structural pluralism" (Kutzinski 1993: 12–13). In Brazil, the mulata continues to be a central figure in samba, carnival, sex tourism, and global representations of the nation, as well as a role that some women perform as a professional act (Gilliam 1998; Pravaz 2003). In Andean countries, a similar role is played by the chola—the mixed-race woman or the semiurbanized indigenous woman (De la Cadena 2000; Weismantel 2001)—although arguably, the sexualization of the chola is not as intense as that of the mulata.

Not surprisingly, these nationalist icons conceal powerful hierarchies of race, class, and gender, which depend on the sexualization of nonwhite women.

I have already suggested that nonwhite women were often seen by elites, from colonial times onward, as lacking in honor, with all the sexual connotations this implied. If common images of women in Latin America often play with a binary opposition between Madonna and whore, or between mother and mistress (Pescatello 1973), it is important to see that these stereotypes are also racialized by the processes described above, in which indigenous, black, and mestizo women could find themselves open to sexual predation by higher-status men, while some of them might also be willing to engage in relationships with these men as a means of improving their life chances and whitening their offspring. Maintaining an honorable reputation could be an uphill struggle for lower-class women, usually also black, indigenous, and mestizo, who often had to work on the streets, selling food, for example, or in domestic service in other people's houses. These locations put their honor at risk by exposing them directly to sexual predation by men—la calle or a rua (the street) in Latin America is seen as a mainly male space, where women's reputations are easily tarnished (Guy 2000: 15).

Domestic service was, and still is, an area where race, class, gender, and sexuality articulate together to form a powerful network of meanings and practices. In countries like Brazil, Colombia, and Mexico, domestic servants are commonly nonwhite, lower-class women working for families who are always wealthier and usually lighter-skinned than they are, although this is not always the case, especially among the middle classes, who can afford the cheap wages domestic workers are paid, but may not be much lighter-skinned. Domestic service is a means by which young, poorly educated, nonwhite women, especially those leaving rural or small-town backgrounds for more urban locations, start in the job market—although there is no guarantee they will be able to progress beyond this type of work. Domestic workers, above all younger ones, are at risk of sexual harassment: in someone else's private domestic environment, they are quite isolated and thus vulnerable. But this is not the only factor. The ideology of mestizaje depicts nonwhite women, especially those who occupy junior positions, as females who historically have been "available" to socially dominant men for sexual purposes, and who are seen as potentially "willing" to engage in intimate relationships because they think this—like domestic service itself—could be a route to social mobility. Interestingly, it is often the mixed-race woman—the mulata and the chola, the symbolic products of this sexual "availability"—who is seen by men as the most sexually attractive and the most available.

Domestic service is a practice in which the ideologies of white male sexual agency and nonwhite female sexual availability still exercise a powerful influence (Saldaña-Tejeda 2012; Wade 2013a). White middle-class men in Rio de Janeiro today, when asked about their teenage sexual experiences with the *empregada* (the maid), easily drew parallels between their personal histories and Freyre's description in his 1933 *Casa-grande e senzala* about young white men having sex with mulata girls (servants, slaves) in the household. Interestingly, however, the men preferred to evade the issue of the maid's color in their personal stories, thus subordinating racial hierarchies to class difference (Ribeiro Corossacz 2015).

For domestic workers, having sex with the men of the employing household may be a long way from any real prospect of upward mobility; it is more likely to be associated with sexual exploitation and perhaps an unwanted pregnancy, followed by the sack and a sideways move into selling food on the street. But sex can still figure in strategies or aspirations of upward mobility for dark-skinned women. Some women favela dwellers in Rio de Janeiro dream about finding a rich man, usually white, who will help them out materially in exchange for sex, and ideally would set them up in a nice apartment. Like the middle-class men described above, these women generally evade direct reference to racial difference, but this remains implicit in the class differences that separate the women from their hoped-for *coroas* (crowns, or knights in shining armor): the men's wealth is linked to whiteness, while the sexual availability of the women is linked to their nonwhiteness. Dark-skinned women in relationships with white men may have children who are much lighter-skinned than themselves: from their perspective, this may be a form of whitening that has value; it may also cause upset (or humor) when the mother is taken by observers to be the child's nanny—precisely because of the color difference (Goldstein 2003: 102, 108–11).

The key point is that mestizaje and the image of the mestizo nation depend on the idea of the sexual availability of black, indigenous, and mestizo women. This concept finds its most powerful expression in the sexualization and sometimes the glorification of the mulata, the chola, and the mestiza. Rather than those seen as fully black and indigenous, it is the women seen as mixed—that is, those who are the products of sexual availability and conquest—who are the most strongly sexualized. The sexualization of black women lies alongside the widespread association of blackness with ugliness in Latin America, so this qualifies their sexualization, compared to the mulata or the *morena* (brown woman). Likewise, the sexualization of indigenous women is uneven. In Guatemala, nonindigenous men express "a sexual fascination with Indian women" (Hale 2006: 159), and in Brazil, nineteenth-century romantic depictions of indigenous women could also be eroticized, as in Alencar's description of his novel's heroine, Iracema, as a "honey-lipped virgin," or in Victor Meirelles's 1866 oil painting of the naked Moema, killed by colonial violence. However, in other countries, indigenous women—rather like indigenous men—are not seen in particularly sexualized ways: in Ecuador, for example, indigenous women often "appear as nonsexual beings . . . [whose] bodies are represented as unattractively small and deprived of the curves that characterize black women's bodies in the popular imaginary" (Rahier 2003: 301). While radical otherness can certainly generate a powerful erotic charge, I argue that a more "available" and intimate form of otherness actually produces a more pervasive and everyday sexualization, which helps explain the particular eroticization of the mulata and the chola or mestiza, and also the greater sexualization of blackness compared to indigenousness (Wade 2009).

White femininity usually figures in the mestizo assemblage as something to be controlled and protected, by white men and women, and as a dominant aesthetic value (Nichols 2013; Simpson 1993). Although the sexual agency of white women in Latin America has generally been located in this frame, it is more complex. Historically, white women also exerted sexual agency by crossing racial and gender boundaries, creating links with nonwhite women and men (for examples, see Wade 2009: chs. 3, 4). Nowadays, too, being very white is not an unalloyed good for a woman in a mestizo society, despite the apparently high value attached to whiteness (Candelario 2007). In the south of Brazil, white middle-class women have to contend with the image of the "typical" Brazilian woman as a sexy mulata. Educated white women in Florianópolis assert themselves as legitimate Brazilians, despite their whiteness, by carefully combining sexual openness and love of sexual pleasure (associated with the mulata), with an assertion of modern sexual autonomy (associated with white masculinity), while also distancing themselves from working-class Portuguese immigrant women, seen as old-fashioned in their sexual morality and vulgar in their tastes (Turner 2013, 2014). The women verge on weakening the dominant value accorded to whiteness by adopting certain behaviors associated with nonwhiteness, while also trying to construct this as a modern feminist sensibility.

Genomics and Gendered Narratives of Mixture in Brazil, Colombia, and Mexico

This detailed account of sex, gender, and race in Latin America has apparently taken us far from mtDNA and Y-DNA, but my argument is that the apparently innocent mention of genetic data about Amerindian (and African) markers in the former and European in the latter in fact tacitly evokes the entire history and sociology of race, class, and sex/gender that I have outlined above—a history and sociology that is not just the purview of specialized academics, but has common currency as well, albeit reduced to some simple stereotypes. The DNA data evoke this social knowledge in a quite specific way. In the previous chapters, I have used the concept of topological relations as a way of thinking about how diverse nodes of meaning can be brought into and out of proximity, remaining always connected, but with some elements receding into the background in certain contexts, as the topological network linking them is twisted and bent into different shapes, producing morphed materializations of figures such as the mestizo, and connecting it to nodes apparently very distant from each other (e.g., racial difference and racelessness). In the same way, I suggest that data about biogeographical ancestries in mtDNA and Y-DNA become new nodes in a topological network that already connects multiple other nodes, which include not just "indigenous mothers" and "European fathers," but also "La Malinche," "sexual predation," "social climbing," "whitening," "domestic service," and the varied sexual imagery surrounding racialized categories of men and women. However, the genomic narratives, whether in scientific or popular outlets, gray out, deactivate, or push into the background all these complex and ambivalent nodes. For example, the distinct meanings of La Malinche, as both mother of the mestizo nation and traitorous whore, are simplified into a generic "indigenous mother." The apparently technical data about mtDNA and Y-DNA, especially when personified into indigenous/African women and European men, fit very easily with standard narratives about the origins of the nation's population by topologically entraining, as an absent presence, a whole network of meanings about race, gender, and sex, which are rooted in complex histories and still have resonant currency today. However, the only way gender figures in the genomic research itself is via the data on Amerindian and African markers in mtDNA and European markers in Y-DNA (plus some data on markers on the X-chromosomes), so we need to start there.

The analyses of mtDNA and Y-DNA show a common pattern: high frequencies of Amerindian haplogroups in the mtDNA, with lower frequencies of European and African ancestry; high levels of European haplogroups and lower levels of Amerindian and African ones in the Y-DNA. Specific results vary a good deal by sample. Thus a study of thirteen locations in Mexico, Guatemala, Colombia, Chile, Argentina, and Brazil, using samples classified as mestizo, showed the following broad patterns for the mtDNA (Ruiz Linares 2014; Wang et al. 2008):[4]

1. Amerindian ancestry was 70–90 percent for most samples. This varied from over 90 percent for samples from Medellín (the paisas) and another Andean highland area near Bogotá, to 77 percent for a Mexico City sample, and going down to an unusually low 37 percent for a sample from Rio Grande do Sul in southern Brazil.

2. African ancestry in the mtDNA was highest in the southern Brazil sample (37 percent), also high in a northwest Argentinean sample (Tucumán, 27 percent), but usually lower at 10–20 percent in six cases and below 5 percent in the other five.

3. European ancestry was highest in Rio Grande do Sul (26 percent), around 20 percent in the samples from Costa Rica and Guatemala, and under 12 percent everywhere else (being nonexistent in three cases).

In contrast, in the Y-DNA European ancestry was mainly dominant:

1. Nine samples (including Mexico City and Andean locations in Colombia) had levels of over 78 percent European ancestry.

2. Four samples (all Andean locations) showed large proportions (40–60 percent) Amerindian ancestry.

3. African ancestry was not present at all.

Researchers describe these patterns in terms of the "sexual asymmetry" of early colonial mating patterns in Latin America (Salzano and Bortolini 2002: 309). This feature had been noted by historians, but it was only with recent genomic studies that its "full genetic impact" has become apparent (Ruiz Linares 2014: 90). Scientists say that "the mixture at the origin of these populations [of mestizos sampled from all over Latin America] involved mainly immigrant European men and Native and African women" (Wang et al. 2008: 2), and that "strong sex-biased genetic blending" may be "a universal characteristic of the Iberian colonization of the Americas" (Gonçalves et al. 2007: 257). For Spanish colonies, they refer to "asymmetric mating" and the "introgression of [European] genes through native women" (Bortolini et al. 2004: 1–2), while for

Antioquia, Colombia, they say the data show "a biased pattern of mating at the foundation of Antioquia, admixture involving mostly immigrant men and native women" (Bedoya et al. 2006: 7234). Brazilian researchers note that the "first Brazilians were born mostly from the union between European males and Amerindian or African females" (Marrero et al. 2007: 168), that "European men preferentially mated with African and Amerindian women" (Palha et al. 2011: 477), and that there was "directional mating between European males and African females" (Ribeiro et al. 2009: 355). For Mexico, the data "show . . . directional mating, the asymmetric gene contribution of maternal or paternal lineages in cases of ethnic gene admixture" (Campos-Sánchez et al. 2006: 560) and a "strong gender-biased admixture history between European males and Native American females" (Martinez-Cortes et al. 2012).

Popular Science: Mothers and Fathers

These findings were reported in more popular publications, in slightly less technical language, and with more frequent use of kinship terms. Emilio Yunis, for example, in his popular book on Colombian history and identity, describes research revealing that a sample population from Antioquia had "Amerindian mothers [and] European fathers" (Yunis Turbay 2009: 117). A U.S.-based online journal, reporting on research by Yunis, referred to the "indigenous founding mothers of the Americas" (Kearns 2007) and commented: "The indigenous roots of Colombia are coming into focus, as it is yet another Latin American nation learning about its true history: the founding mothers of Colombia were indigenous." The national daily El Tiempo, in an article about El Día de la Raza (the day of the race, October 12, commemorating the arrival of Columbus in the Americas), said Yunis was "concerned exclusively with the genetic load transmitted by Colombian women," and that his data showed that "85.5 percent of Colombian mothers are of indigenous origin"—a misleading rendering of data showing that 85 percent of the haplogroups found in the mtDNA of the men and women in the sample had Amerindian origins. Referring briefly to Y-DNA data that Yunis had not yet analyzed, the reporter made a nod toward the "16 million" Asian men who shared the "same Y-chromosome, probably transmitted by the emperor Genghis Khan," thus invoking the image of the conquering male, even without the Colombian data to hand (Bejarano 2006). (The writer concluded that, while it might now be politically incorrect to use the word race, "it is clear that every pueblo (people) has a characteristic biological composition and the Colombians are no exception": apparently the presence of Amerindian markers in the mtDNA was enough to make them distinctive.) The *New Scientist*, reporting on research by Bedoya and colleagues (2006), remarked that the genetic data had borne out the story according to which "male European colonists arrived and married Colombian Indian women" (New Scientist 2006); similar language about "European fathers and indigenous or African women" or "Spanish men and indigenous women" was used in Spanish-language media reports on this research (Miraval 2008; Velásquez Gómez 2006).

A report on research of Pena (Pena et al. 2000) and Bortolini (Hünemeier et al. 2007) described how "the first groups of European colonists . . . were almost exclusively men [who] had children with the Indian women. Later, with the arrival of slaves . . . they went on to impregnate African women too." Obligatory reference was made to Freyre's *Casa-grande e senzala*, noting his view that African women "exercised a special enchantment, of a sexual kind, over the masters of the [sugar] mills of European origin," and the piece ended by citing Freyre's observation that "all Brazilians, even white ones with blond hair, carry in their soul, if not in the soul and the body . . . the shadow or at least a mark [*pinta*] of the indigenous or the black [person]" (Zorzett and Guimarães 2007). A Portuguese newspaper reported that Pena's research showed "the white population of Brazil is the result of mixture between mostly Portuguese European fathers and Amerindian or African mothers" (Nadais 2000).

Telescoping Time

The way time is configured in these accounts plays an interesting role in the meanings that can attach to them. The data refer to Amerindian, African, and European ancestry—that is, molecular lineages—but the ancestry is taken to indicate matings between kinds of people long ago. It is clear that the use of uniparental analysis allows geneticists to reach back in time and make inferences about the early colonial period, when Europeans, Amerindians, and Africans can easily be seen as apparently separate populations, meeting each other in an intercontinental encounter. Yet the data themselves are drawn from the DNA of living people, showing these sexual exchanges are still detectable in the infrastructure of their bodies.

This creates a classic mythical effect: it refers to the foundational past and the living present at the same time, bringing them into a close proximity that explains one in terms of the other, but also elides intervening histories. The apparent purities of the distant past are juxtaposed to the mestizo of the immediate present. DNA data of this kind are able to foreground foundational acts of mixture between clearly distinct populations: the roots of today's national populations are located in these quintessential moments of mestizaje. Each mestizo person, more than just a combination of abstract percentages of two or three original ingredients, is portrayed as bearing in his or her own DNA the traces of embodied acts of sex between two persons of clearly different racial categories. These unilineal genetic genealogies telescope the fact that people straightforwardly classified or perceived as European, indigenous, or African would quite soon have been outnumbered by mestizos of one kind or another, and that most mestizos today are more likely the product of a long series of sexual exchanges between mestizo ancestors, rather than between European men and African or indigenous women. The tension between purity and mixture is particularly evident here: the narrative is all about mixture, but the old original populations—which necessarily appear as relatively pure compared to their mixed products—are foregrounded in this configuration of the mestizo assemblage; they are brought onto the stage to make the narrative work. Its persuasiveness is helped by the dislocation in time: it all happened several centuries ago.

Eliding Hierarchy and Violence

The next thing to note about these depictions is that, the scientific papers use a technical language of "asymmetry" and "sex-biased genetic blending" between men and women, while the popular writing uses a kinship idiom of mothers and fathers; in both cases, hierarchies of class, race, and gender are left unsaid. Although the telescoping of time could elicit in quite a direct fashion the context of conquest, there is virtually no mention of coercion and rape, nor even of sexual exploitation; instead, there is mention of men "preferentially mating with African and Amerindian women." The genetic narratives often refer to the gender imbalance of the early colonial European population, which had more men than women, suggesting that sexual relations between the men and indigenous and African women were just a natural, consensual outcome. There is little hint that such relations would also have been located within highly skewed power relations and involved direct violence and coercion as well as structural processes producing very constrained "consent" for indigenous and African women. All the complex dynamics of sexual exchanges between men and women that cross boundaries of race and class—which I described earlier, and which involve calculations about instrumental value, social climbing, sexual predation, and reckonings of honor and reputation, as well as the recognition of erotic charge and emotion—are grayed out and deactivated. But I argue they remain as an absent presence, as nodes in the topological map that are elided, but not erased, when the technical papers bring genetic data (e.g., haplogroup frequencies) into close proximity with inferences about "directional mating" or the popular writings bring "asymmetry" into close relation with "indigenous mothers."

In the case of one popular publication, some space was made for social differences. Pena and colleagues, in their "Molecular Portrait of Brazil," say, as usual, that "the European contribution [to Brazil's trihybrid population] was basically through men and the Amerindian and African [contributions] were mainly through women" (Pena et al. 2000: 25). Unusually, they refer not only to early colonial processes, but also to late nineteenth-century European immigration, noting that many immigrants were poor men who "married poor women, which in Brazil meant women with dark skin (because of the correlation between skin color and social class)." This nod toward social difference is muted by the reference to marriage, which glosses over other more coercive, predatory practices and elides the complex processes of sexual exchange across racial and class hierarchies. (It is worth noting that one of the very few explicit references that I found to power difference in this context was made by Pena in an interview, when he referred to "the history of sexual exploitation of slave women by white men . . . an unpleasant history because it was based on relations of power" [Zorzett and Guimarães 2007].)[5]

The presence of these processes of sexual exchange is hinted at in a more explicit way, however, because in the "Molecular Portrait," Pena et al. (2000: 25) chose to illustrate their point about European immigration with a painting called A redencão de Can (The redemption of Ham, 1895, by Modesto Brocos y Gómez; see figure 8.1). The caption of the illustration explains that the painting shows a "black grandmother giving thanks to Heaven for her white grandson (in the lap of his mother, a mulata). The father is white and appears to be an immigrant of Iberian or Mediterranean origin." For the painter, this intergenerational process of whitening has removed the "curse of Ham," mythically borne by black people.[6] The painting illustrates a late nineteenth-century idea of whitening as an easygoing, untraumatic, and self-evidently positive process supposedly leading to a superior national population. It seems anachronistic when published in the context of multiculturalist reforms and debates about racism. On the one hand, it dramatizes the process of whitening and highlights the differential values attached to blackness and whiteness in a way that could elicit critical reflection by some of today's readers. On the other, it elides hierarchy with its cozy family scene and the positive connotations attached to whitening.

FIGURE 8.1 *A redenção de Can* (The redemption of Ham) by Modesto Brocos y Gómez, 1895. National Fine Arts Museum, Rio de Janeiro.

These muted references to hierarchy can elicit responses that refer to it more directly, bringing grayed-out nodes into action. One journalist, Elio Gaspari, commented that the "Molecular Portrait" showed that "there are more people [in Brazil] with one foot in the kitchen than with both in the drawing room" (Gaspari 2000), an expression that was also "used by former president Fernando Henrique Cardoso during his mid-1990s campaign"

(Santos and Maio 2005: 3). The well-known phrase "to have one foot in the kitchen" is a reference to sexual relations between black slaves/servants and their white masters/employers, and therefore evokes hierarchy in quite a direct way. This is evident from the row that broke out around Cardoso's use of the phrase to refer to himself: black movement activists protested that the phrase was "prejudiced," and Cardoso denied having said it (Folha de São Paulo 1994).

Overall, the "Molecular Portrait," like other accounts of these sexual exchanges, backgrounds hierarchy, power difference, and conflict. Topologically speaking, racial difference (parsed as continental origins) is brought into close proximity with sexual exchange between men and women, or between mothers and fathers, seen as an obvious and natural phenomenon. All the connecting points in the network—coercion, conquest, hierarchy, predation, exploitation—are usually grayed out as irrelevant or inaccessible. Yet they are still there, potentially active and able to resonate with today's racial/gender politics, which are still shaped by hierarchy and power differences.

Distributing Sexual Agency

The grayed-out but still potentially active presence of hierarchy is made evident by another key feature of the scientific and popular descriptions outlined above. This is the way sexual agency is distributed across the spectrum of gender, race, and class difference so as to imply white men's dominant position. The telescoping effect of these unilineal genetic genealogies preferentially reveals the contributions made by early colonial people whose sexual activities led to many subsequent sexually reproductive generations. This DNA analysis does not pick up maternal and paternal lineages that petered out before the late twentieth century—whether by chance or because of structural disadvantage affecting the reproductive chances of certain segments of the population. Nor does it pick up the contributions made to the autosomal DNA—the general genetic contributions made by all ancestors of living populations. It only picks up contributions made via unilineal descent. This means it is possible to focus on European men and indigenous and African women, with little or no reference to indigenous and African/black men or to European women, or indeed to actual mestizos of any kind, even as the foundational act of mixture is foregrounded. The postconquest context, in which different categories of people were exercising sexual agency of varying sorts, is flattened in the focus on early encounters. This focus reinforces some familiar images of race, sex, and gender, but also evokes elided topological relations, in quite particular ways.

EUROPEAN MEN · It is immediately clear that primary sexual agency is attributed to European men. Just as Y-DNA analysis is used in other contexts to talk about the sexual and military conquests of Genghis Khan or Niall of the Nine Hostages, or about the evolutionary success of dominant men in general, so here Y-DNA data attest to the Spanish and Portuguese conquerors, whose dominance allowed them to literally colonize the Y-chromosomes of what would become the national populations of the region. It is European men who were apparently having all the sex—or at least the sex that mattered for posterity. They were the ones busy making mestizos and making themselves into ancestral fathers. The history of white male sexual predation and the complex relationships between lighter-skinned men and darker-skinned women, mediated by whitening, money, sex, and desire, is grayed out by the neutral or kinship language, but it is simultaneously and insistently—but still tacitly—made present by the attribution of sexual agency to European men.

INDIGENOUS AND AFRICAN FEMALES · It is apparent that indigenous and African women are cast as relatively passive and accepting figures—in popular accounts they are "mothers," just as the European men are "fathers." These women seem to make themselves "available" in ways that easily evoke ideas of (domestic) service and care; of course, the service class of the early colonial period was largely made up of black and indigenous women. As time went on, mestizo women were increasingly important, but their presence is sidelined by the focus on early encounters. European men appear as the principal sexual partners of indigenous and African women; little mention is made of the women's relationships with indigenous and black men. Nor is there any hint of resistance, tactical accommodation, or even active engagement by these women—for example, by the use of sexual and love magic. The alleged practitioners of this magic, among them many indigenous, African, and mestizo women, were regularly persecuted by inquisitorial and other ecclesiastical authorities (Behar 1989; Wade 2009: 83–88). As with European sexual agency, the genetic accounts evoke familiar images of the sexual availability of nonwhite women, topologically backgrounding, without erasing, the complex race–gender politics surrounding such apparent "availability." The classic sexualized figures of the mulata and the chola are also grayed out—too sexually charged for these technical accounts or the discourse of mothers and fathers—yet they are topologically entrained, especially by the suggestion of availability.

It is worth noting that the genetic accounts establish a difference between indigenous and African women: in most samples classed as mestizo, Amerindian ancestry outweighed African ancestry in the mtDNA. This is not surprising for Mexico, where, as we have seen, the foundational conceptual distinction in history and genetics is between mestizos and indígenas, and African origins occupy a marginal role. Studies of mestizos show very low frequencies of African-origin haplogroups in the mtDNA, but sampling does not focus on areas where such haplogroups might perhaps be most frequent, such as the south coast of Guerrero state or the city of Veracruz (Bonilla et al. 2005; Campos-Sánchez et al. 2006; Green, Derr, and Knight 2000). In Brazil, geneticists included black people much more, whether in rural quilombos or in urban settings (Bortolini et al. 1995, 1999; Gonçalves et al. 2008; Palha et al. 2011). Colombian geneticists were located between Mexico and Brazil in this sense: the main focus was on mestizos, but there was some specific sampling of "African-descent" or "Afro-Colombian" people (Rojas et al. 2010; Yunis et al. 2013). Yet even in Brazil and Colombia—as well as in other countries with a history of significant black slavery, such as Puerto Rico (Martínez-Cruzado et al. 2005)—Amerindian ancestry was often reported to outweigh African ancestry in the mtDNA of mestizos (Rojas et al. 2010; Ruiz Linares 2014; Wang et al. 2008).

Exceptions existed: for example, in a sample of "whites" from the northeast region of Brazil (a historically black area) African-origin matrilineages outweighed Amerindian ones by 44 percent to 22 percent. Other samples classified by researchers as "black" and "mulatto" in Brazil or as Afro-descent in Colombia also showed higher levels of African than Amerindian ancestry in the mtDNA: in a sample of black Brazilians from Ribeirão Preto, the African contribution was as high as 82 percent (Bortolini et al. 1999; Gonçalves et al. 2008; Rojas et al. 2010). However, these exceptions and variations were dwarfed by the main message emerging from the genetic data, which focused on those classified as "mestizos" (or whites in Brazil), whose predominant maternal ancestry was usually Amerindian. The use of mtDNA allowed inferences about the earliest sexual encounters, which foregrounded the Amerindian contribution, even in countries like Brazil, where the African genetic contribution was much higher overall (i.e., in the autosomal DNA). The main pattern of indigenous matrilineages revealed by the genetic data, and highlighted in both technical and popular accounts of the studies, made resonant connections with nodes of indigenismo in the mestizo assemblage, in which ancient indigenous roots are venerated (rather than African ones).

BLACK/AFRICAN AND INDIGENOUS MALES · On the other side of the coin, the sexual agency of black/African and indigenous men tended to disappear from the network as configured by these genomic studies. In samples classified as mestizo (or white in Brazil), haplogroups identified as of Amerindian and African origin were generally heavily outweighed by European ones in the Y-DNA. This was true for Mexican samples, for which one study concluded 65 percent of paternal haplogroups were of European origin (Martinez-Cortes et al. 2012); for the paisa population of Antioquia in Colombia, with 94 percent European-origin paternal haplogroups (Bedoya et al. 2006); and for other Colombian samples drawn from various regions, which showed nearly 80 percent European ancestry for Y-DNA (Rojas et al. 2010). In Brazil too, samples of self-identified whites from various regions had 98 percent European haplogroups in the Y-DNA (Carvalho-Silva et al. 2001). Indigenous and African "fathers" rarely figured, compared to the way European men were routinely named in this role.

However, closer examination revealed that Y-DNA haplogroups identified as of Amerindian or African origin were frequent or even predominant in certain mestizo samples. The same study of Mexican mestizos that gave an average figure of 65 percent European haplogroups included data from samples from Oaxaca and Guerrero, in which haplogroups of Amerindian origin rose to nearly 50 percent (Martinez-Cortes et al. 2012: table 2). This pattern was also found in mestizo samples from areas of southern and northern Chile, historically linked to indigenous peoples, which showed proportions of over 50 percent (Ruiz Linares 2014: 93). Among the paisas, Amerindian and African haplogroups were a mere 2 percent and 4 percent, respectively, but in the province of Magdalena in the Caribbean coastal region of Colombia, Amerindian haplogroups were 33 percent of the total, while in Valle del Cauca, a previous slaveholding stronghold, African-origin haplogroups were likewise a third of the total (Rojas et al. 2010: table 3).

For Brazil, the samples with data on Y-DNA tended to focus either on self-identified whites or on "African-derived"/"Afro-Brazilian" populations, with the latter often not clearly defined: sometimes they referred to quilombo dwellers, sometimes to "black" people, and at other times to black and "mulatto" people (Abe-Sandes, Silva, and Zago 2004; Bortolini et al. 1999; Hünemeier et al. 2007). If the focus was on African-derived populations, the Y-DNA showed very varied patterns. One sample from Brazilian quilombos showed 54 percent African-origin haplogroups, while another study revealed proportions of such haplogroups that ranged from 5 to 38 percent (Palha et al. 2011; Ribeiro et al. 2009). Another study that included urban black people judged to show "no [morphological] indications of admixture [with non-African ancestry]," along with others "classified as admixed (Mulatto)," found that African-origin haplogroups were dominant (96 percent) in one sample of Ribeirão Preto black people deemed to show no admixture, and a majority (55 percent) in another sample from Salvador, which included admixed people (Bortolini et al. 1999).

These cases suggest that other patterns of mixture must have been going on even in the early history of these countries, let alone during the later colonial and republican periods. But the main message from all these studies was the same. The quilombo studies, just cited, concluded that "European men preferentially mated with African and Amerindian women," and highlighted "the directional mating between European males and African females" (Palha et al. 2011: 477; Ribeiro et al. 2009: 355). For the study that covered both quilombos and city samples, the authors said that, in the cases where there were low levels of European-origin haplogroups in the Y-DNA, "no evidence for asymmetrical matings in relation to sex and ethnic groups could be found." These cases merely departed from the "most consistent finding," which was "the introduction of European genes through males." The variety among the samples was certainly recognized, but the take-home message was about European men and African and indigenous women (Bortolini et al. 1999: 558–60).

Something similar, in terms of what is said and what is not, can be seen in a Colombian study that compared "Caucasian-mestizos" to "African-descent" individuals, using Y-DNA data. The study set out to correct the relative paucity of data on Afro-Colombians compared to mestizos, and presented data on haplotype frequencies for both categories; for Afro-Colombians they used samples from the Chocó province of the northern Pacific coast region.[7] The authors showed that rather few haplotypes are shared by the two sets of samples, suggesting that they have fairly separate demographic histories. The issue of "Caucasian/Amerindian sex bias" was raised for the mestizo population, in the standard terms, but interestingly no mention was made of sex bias or its absence for the African-descent samples: the issue was simply not discussed. We are thus left with an account of "limited female immigration from Spain during the conquest and colony periods," which meant "the genetic pool was limited to male European Caucasians and Amerindian mtDNA" (Yunis et al. 2013: 464). (Note how the European contribution is personified and given agency, while the

Amerindian component remains abstract and passive.) As usual, the possibility of sexual agency for African/black men is left in the shadows.

Topologically entrained as an absent presence in the network are the familiar figures—not grayed out in other configurations of the assemblage, described earlier—of black and indigenous men as sexual agents who are either excessive and/or driven by base motivations of self-interest. The explicit presence of European fathers in these genetic accounts, who figure as responsible family men who are founding the nation, is brought into topological proximity with the silence about black and indigenous men's fathering: the connections with other nodes, relating to sexual excess and materialistic social climbing, are grayed out, but not erased.

EUROPEAN WOMEN · The final category that gets little or no attention in the genetic accounts is European women, who generally only appear when their relative scarcity in the early colonies is noted. European ancestral markers are relatively infrequent in the mtDNA data—except in Brazil, where they account for about a third of the lineages in most regions and between 66 and 85 percent in some areas in the south of the country, which received large numbers of European migrants in the nineteenth century (Marrero et al. 2007: table 2). Nevertheless, the research papers hardly mention these lineages or the European women associated with them. They barely appear as mothers or sexual partners.[8] The silence about white women implicitly focuses attention on the main players in the mestizo assemblage—active white men and passive black/indigenous women—but it also entrains grayed-out meanings about white women who find it hard to establish legitimate national identities and, to do so, must find their own ways to hybridize or creolize their whiteness (cf. Tate and Law 2015: 106).

Race–Gender Politics Today

If the genetic data on unilineal ancestries focuses on early historical encounters and distributes sexual agency in very uneven ways, how does this square with race–gender politics in the era of multiculturalism? Most obviously, alongside the assertion of ethnic and racial identities and rights by indigenous and black social movements, and the increased educational and occupational upward mobility of some black and indigenous men (and women), there is also an affirmation of black and indigenous male sexual agency, as described earlier; for black men in particular, this builds in part on widely available images of the black male as a hypersexual being, who may be seen by others as a threat to be controlled, but also as a powerful attraction. White or light-skinned men arguably find themselves on the defensive, sexually speaking. As noted earlier, in Brazil their sexuality is "opaque" and nondescript compared to that of black and brown men (Moutinho 2004: 345); in Guatemala, it is light-skinned ladino men who insistently see upwardly mobile indigenous males as intent on dating white women (Hale 2006: 159; Nelson 1999: 219). The reinstatement of European men as the founding fathers of the nation, who apparently had easy access to amenable indigenous and African women—especially when this image is combined with the marginalization of the sexual agency of African and indigenous men—is an interesting counterbalance to this trend, conjured up easily by the commonsense reference to "European fathers." European men appear as dominant males, who were very sexually active, but in responsible ways that led to socially productive outcomes.

In indigenous and black social movements, many women have also attempted to construct a feminist project that conjoins women's rights with cultural rights—with mixed success, as they sometimes find themselves battling sexism within the movements (Caldwell 2007; Curiel 2008; Radcliffe and Pequeño 2010; Wade 2009: 218). Part of this struggle is to contest images of black and indigenous women as sexually available and as suited particularly to domestic service and other low-status occupations (McCallum 2007). It is notable, then, that an image of the indigenous and African woman as "mother" and as passive and accepting vehicle for the "introgression of European genes" comes out of the genetic accounts, both popular and technical. The image of mother downplays the sexualization associated with the mulata and the chola—these figures are grayed out, but not erased, in these family-based scenarios, where European men "married" indigenous women—but it also depoliticizes indigenous and black women by casting them as passive and available.

White women are, by their absence in the genomic accounts, cast as passive and under white male control, which hardly fits with the feminist currents in which white women have been active leaders. However, their absence specifically as mothers and their absent presence as sexual agents crossing boundaries to establish a sense of national belonging bring other possibilities, full of ambivalence.

Conclusion

An important component of the use of data about mtDNA and Y-DNA ancestry is antiracism and prodemocracy. In chapter 5, I quoted Pena: "if the many white Brazilians who have Amerindian or African mitochondrial DNA were to become aware of this, they would value more highly the exuberant genetic diversity of our people and, perhaps, would construct in the twenty-first century a more just and harmonious society" (Pena et al. 2000: 25). It is one element in the general contention that all Brazilians—and Colombians and Mexicans—are mixed. Yunis uses data of this kind as part of his overall critique of the exclusive and oppressive way mestizaje has operated in Colombia to produce a regional-racial hierarchy, with the most "whitened" regions lording it over others. He is insistent that even the Antioqueños—who practice "one of the strongest and most rigid cultural endogamies in the nation," and some of whom promote the notion of a whitened raza antioqueña—carry Amerindian ancestry in their mtDNA (Yunis Turbay 2009: 119–20).[9] In his view, a more complete mestizaje would produce a more democratic society.

Yet the way the data are deployed and popularized has other effects. There may be further proof that "we are all mestizos"—even those who consider themselves white—but the picture painted of the way mestizaje worked in the past reinforces a dominant and taken-for-granted version of the national origin narrative, and thus sustains an image of the social order structured in familiar and traditional ways by hierarchies of race, class, and gender, which put white men in control, cast black and indigenous women as passive recipients, and deny sexual agency to black and indigenous men and white women. Sexual exchanges traverse these hierarchies, but are strongly structured by them.

Gender and sex have always been central to ideologies and practices of mestizaje. One of the ways these ideas gain traction in Latin American societies—especially countries such as Brazil, Colombia, and Mexico, where the mestizo is so central to national identity—is that the enactment of racial difference and similarity, and of racialized inclusion and exclusion, operate as much through kinship and the family as they do through public politics and economic relations. The domains of kinship and family are always important in contexts of racial hierarchy, but they are particularly so when ideologies of mestizaje are at work, because the whole process operates through practices and ideas of gendered sexual relations and the production of offspring. If social orders structured by a mestizo assemblage depend in large part on the simultaneous existence of racialized inclusion and exclusion, which softens the edges of racial categories and racialized inequalities, then this simultaneity gains persuasive power from the fact that the assemblage embraces practices and relations of sex and family kinship, where people experience it as part of an everyday life that is both personal and public (Wade 2009: 158, 178). It is no surprise, then, that gender and sex are part of the story that genomics tells about the mestizo, reinforcing their centrality to a concept of the mestizo nation.

In terms of how this narrative impacts on race–gender politics today, there is little evidence that genetic data are being explicitly deployed by social movements or other commentators in the public sphere in ways that speak directly to issues of sexualized stereotypes. There is nothing to match the way genetic data have been used in the debates about affirmative action in Brazil. But the simple mention of "European fathers" and "indigenous or African mothers" in the press is enough to bring into play the whole entangled network of meanings around race, sex, and gender, in part because the basic narrative is so familiar and commonsense. As such, it goes against the grain of multiculturalist agendas (not to mention feminist ones) that seek to challenge the dominance of (masculine) lightness and promote the cultural and political—and, implicitly or explicitly, the sexual—agency of black and indigenous minorities. As usual, the genetic accounts both highlight difference in the form of ancestral populations and at once subsume it in a generalized mixedness, which takes center stage.

The reiteration of the story in genetic idiom has certain specific effects: the mythical telescoping of time, which reveals the traces of foundational encounters in the DNA infrastructure of individual bodies is one such effect; related to this is the focus on ancestral populations, not as abstract concepts that generate percentages of biogeographical ancestry, but as groups of gendered persons whose long-past sexual encounters remain of immediate relevance; and, of course, the familiar story, along with its particular distributions of sexual agency, is underwritten by the authority of science.

9

....

The Geneticization of Race and

Diversity in Everyday Life

This chapter explores data of a different kind from those in previous chapters. Until now, I have looked at the way genomic data about ancestry have worked in networks that also connect people, institutions, and objects that enact diversity in the nation, especially via multiculturalist agendas and policies. The actors in this assemblage have been the scientists themselves and their publications, and various people working or intervening in the public political arena—government officials, journalists, policymakers, and academics. For Colombia, I briefly presented some data from interviews and/or focus groups with forensic technicians and participants in courtroom processes (attorneys, investigators), while for Brazil I used material from interviews with black activists involved in the debates about race-based university quotas and health policies.[1] In this chapter, I look at data from focus groups and interviews with "members of the public"—in fact mainly, but not exclusively, university students. While many of these people had training in the life sciences, and thus had some acquaintance with technical information about genetics, very few were specialists in genetics, and most had little personal stake in human population genetics and genetic ancestry testing. This was less true of people who had volunteered to participate in an international genomics research project and had been promised the results of their personal DNA ancestry test; these people were often motivated by "curiosity" about their ancestry.

I also address the question of how genetic idioms and data appear in the way members of the "public"—in the selective form outlined above—talk about race and diversity in the nation, and in their own lives and bodies. We have seen in previous chapters that the impact of recent genomic science, with its depictions of ancestral populations, genetic ancestry percentages, and distant maternal and paternal ancestors, is quite uneven. If the language of transformation—the claim that identity and race, when "rewritten at the genomic level, visualized through a molecular optic," are "both transformed" (Rose 2007: 179)—needs to be tempered with an emphasis on continuity when we examine the way genetic data have been deployed in the national political arena, this conclusion is reinforced when we look at how "ordinary people" talk about these issues.

In simple terms, while genomic data about ancestry and diversity provide an additional idiom to talk about these things, there is not much of a transformative effect to be observed. People not only assimilate new data about genetic ancestry to existing ideas about genetics, which have long formed part of the basic conceptual toolkit of many people (including university students), but there is also a strong tendency for them to see the data as confirming scientifically things they already knew or thought about human diversity, regional differences in the nation, mestizos, bodies, heredity, disease, and so on. In particular, in relation to race, we see neither a simple "molecular reinscription of race" by genomics (Duster 2006), which reinforces the concept, nor its simple dismantling: instead, the uncertain status of race in daily life is not resolved in any one definite direction by genomic data. Genomic data provide additional idioms and concepts to talk about these matters—for example, percentages of genetic ancestry—and these certainly potentiate biologizing effects, but these were already present anyway, in uneven form, and the traction these effects have continues to be very uneven as well.

The effect of (uneven) continuity or confirmation is not only a matter of the way in which "laypeople" assimilate scientific information that is presented to them via various channels, such as the media and education. It is also because the concepts at stake—mestizo, black, indigenous, white, European, African, race, nation, population, ancestry, heredity, and so on—are all resilient categories that have circulated around science, politics, education, and everyday knowledge for a long time (see chapter 1). They can be seen as boundary objects in both social and scientific classifications; that is, they are objects that "inhabit several communities of practice and satisfy the informational requirements of each of them" (Bowker and Star 1999: 297). "Mestizo" might be defined differently by population geneticists and humanities undergraduates, but it has some common features in each case and is "plastic enough to adapt to local needs and constraints" of the two sets of people (Bowker and Star 1999: 297). As we have seen, social constructs such as mestizo and indigenous are key organizing categories for genomic science in the first place, so it is not realistic in this context to think in terms of brand new concepts emerging from the labs and "impacting" the public. Instead, we could think of a process of coproduction in which natural and social orderings are integrally linked in a process of mutual accommodation (Jasanoff 2004b), which needs to be understood in a temporal frame: over long periods of time, categories circulate through labs and field sites, classrooms, libraries, academic papers, media outlets, websites, and government offices, accruing and losing meanings and being reconfigured in the process. Or, as I argued in chapter 1, we can better envisage this as an assemblage, structured by certain tendential lines of force, with new components being added and organized according to these existing structures, which are flexible enough to adapt and be reconfigured without losing their basic shape.

In this assemblage, "mestizo" (and other related categories) is a mutable mobile, morphing into various materializations; it has been configured in diverse ways in politics and/or governance from colonial times through to the present. It was given a particular biological meaning at the population level by measurements of "racial mixture" based on blood type, dating back to the 1940s. Further biological meanings accrued with recent genomic measurements that allow the mestizo to be genetically individualized, while also allowing claims about the particularity of national populations to circulate through the political domain in discourses of "genomic sovereignty." The mestizo, construed in terms of abstract molecular calculus, is domesticated, or rather redomesticated, by laypeople in terms of a familiar genealogical reckoning of halves and quarters, based on actual relatives, and this practice is deployed by geneticists themselves when they popularize their findings in terms of "indigenous mothers" and "European fathers." The mestizo figure circulates through different realms of practice, accreting new connections and meanings that articulate with long-standing ones.

Publics

In collecting data on how "the public" thought about genetics, race, human diversity, and so on, our research team aimed to follow researchers such as Condit and colleagues, among others, who have focused on "ordinary people" who have no particular commitment to or involvement with genetics (Condit et al. 2004; Condit 1999a; Condit, Parrott, and Harris 2002; Jacob 2012). We took this approach because some of the ideas about the transformative impact of genetics on society are based on studies of people who do have a special relationship to genetics, such as associations of patients who suffer from genetic disorders, or people undergoing genetic tests and counseling, or people with a specific involvement with genetic disorders, such as community health outreach workers (Heath, Rapp, and Taussig 2004; Kohli-Laven 2012; Lippman 1991; Rapp 1999; Rose 2007; Rose and Novas 2005; Taussig 2009). Such publics are liable to highlight the transformative potential of genetics. Even studies of people who have chosen to take a DNA ancestry test indicate that genetic knowledge has an uneven effect (Nelson 2008).

Transformation is also privileged in accounts that trace how genetic data and arguments are deployed in the public arena of policy, politics, and biomedical business (Duster 2006; Kahn 2013; Roberts 2011). This approach is naturally selective, because by definition it focuses on sites where genetics has some notable impact: INMEGEN in Mexico and Pena in Brazil are obvious lodestones, because they involve overt entanglements with policy and politics. This is the approach I have taken in previous chapters, although I have taken care to suggest that the impact of genetics is rather disparate, even when viewed from this angle. Genetics in Colombia, for example, has had a lower political profile, despite its importance for forensic work linked to violence, so arguments about the transformative impact of genetics are harder to make using that country.

To counterbalance these biases toward transformative impacts, our research cast the net wider by recruiting a variety of focus groups and interviewees. The data presented here relate to the research conducted in Mexico and Colombia. Work in Brazil concentrated more narrowly on focus groups with black activists, the results of which I touched on in chapter 5 (see also Kent and Wade 2015), so Brazil is not considered. We worked with various publics, as follows:

· IN COLOMBIA, focus groups with groups of university students were organized by Ernesto Schwartz-Marín and Roosbelinda Cárdenas. The groups were divided by disciplinary background: five groups were from a life sciences background (medicine, biotechnology, genetics), and three had a humanities background, including one group of black activists from the Collective of Afro-Colombian University Students (CEUNA). These events were held in public and private universities in Bogotá.

· IN MEXICO, Vivette García Deister and Abigail Nieves Delgado organized focus groups in two prestigious public universities in Mexico City (biology students) and Puebla (social anthropology students).

- IN MEXICO, too, Sandra González Santos, Carlos López Beltrán, and Abigail Nieves Delgado ran a series of focus groups in two small, recently formed provincial public universities, in the states of Oaxaca and Michoacán, where the students were generally of a lower social class and a bit darker-skinned than in the other two Mexican universities. In the Oaxaca university group, for example, three students spoke an indigenous language as well as Spanish. These groups were organized by disciplinary background and included students with training in life sciences (biotechnology, nutritional genomics, nursing), mechatronics, and the humanities (governance and citizenship studies, and multicultural studies).[2]

- IN COLOMBIA AND MEXICO, the research teams worked with volunteers who had participated in a genomics research project, LATINA (pseudonym), being run in several Latin American countries, which aimed to explore the relation between genetic ancestry, phenotype, and certain social characteristics and attitudes.

- IN MEXICO, 120 short interviews (mostly 5–10 minutes) were done by Abigail Nieves Delgado with people immediately after they had been through the LATINA protocols, which involved an explanation of the project and of concepts such as genetic ancestry, followed by giving blood and filling in a questionnaire, which included questions asking people about their own racial/color identification and asking them to estimate their own ancestry as percentages of European, indigenous, and black contributions (these were the categories used in the question). These short exit interviews asked people about their reasons for participating in LATINA, their reactions to some parts of the LATINA questionnaire, their views on what a mestizo is, and on the relation between health and ancestry. All this took place in two public universities in Mexico City, and the volunteers were mainly university students, their relatives, university support staff, and people related to the LATINA researchers. Their backgrounds were varied: many were students of biology, physical anthropology, or genetics, but others had a background in the humanities or other sciences (geophysics, engineering, etc.).

- IN COLOMBIA, about a dozen interviews (about 30–90 minutes) with 1–3 people each were run by Ernesto Schwartz-Marín and Roosbelinda Cárdenas with just over thirty volunteers who had been through the LATINA process in a public university in the city of Medellín; the majority of these were students who had a background in life sciences, but others included an amateur genealogist, a historian, a psychologist, and an accountant. Some more informal discussions took place with a group of high school students in the same location. The interviews followed much the same format as the Colombian focus groups, but with a tighter focus on the interviewees' participation in LATINA.

I cite from recordings and transcriptions made by the researchers of the focus group conversations and interviews they organized (I also draw on López Beltrán et al. 2014; Schwartz-Marín and Wade 2015).

Race and Color in Everyday Discourse

Before looking at how ideas about genetics, and specifically recent data on genetic ancestry, articulate with ideas about race and racial categories in everyday thinking, it is useful to get some sense of how the latter set of ideas appear in everyday discourse in Mexico and Colombia. A key theme that emerges here is uncertainty and ambiguity: the term *raza* and racial categories are both normal and unexceptional, and at the same time awkward and thorny.

The first thing to note is that in Mexico and Colombia, the word *raza* is a completely normal term used to talk about breeds of animals and plants (Hartigan 2013a). It is commonplace to hear phrases such as: "*¿De qué raza es tu perro?*" (what breed is your dog?) or "*Los aztecas tenían varias razas de maíz que ya no existen*" (the Aztecs had various strains of maize that no longer exist). In more technical circles, the term is used by Mexico's National Commission for the Understanding and Use of Biodiversity, which says, "The concept and category of race is very useful as a rapid system of reference for understanding the variation of maize" (Biodiversidad Mexicana 2012). The Federation Cynologique Internationale, a dog-breeding organization, lists "razas" of dogs on its Spanish-language website (FCI n.d.). (The same is true for *race* in French, *razza* in Italian, *raça* in Portuguese, and *rasse* in German.) When it comes to talking about people, the word *raza* becomes more complex and potentially difficult.

Race and Color as Neutral Terms

On the one hand, raza is used to talk about a people who share history and origins, both cultural and biological (Hartigan 2013b), as I have noted previously. Thus a famous monument in Mexico City is called La Raza and commemorates the ancient indigenous peoples of Mexico, ancestors of the present-day population; a nearby metro stop is named after the monument. Many countries in Latin America started in the 1920s to celebrate El Día de la Raza on October 12, nominally to commemorate the arrival of Columbus in the Americas, but more widely to celebrate mestizo nationhood and pan-national Latin American identity (Rodríguez 2004)—although in some more critical perspectives, it may also symbolize indigenous resistance to conquest. The day is also celebrated by many Latinos in the United States, and the term la raza may be used to refer collectively to Latinos, as in the National Council of La Raza, a Latino advocacy organization. In this usage, the term has extended its reference from indigenous ancestors to their mestizo descendants. A related usage is seen in the way some Latinos, when responding to the U.S. census question on race, avoid the standard categories on offer, tick the "some other race," box and then, following the accompanying instruction to "write in race," add something like la raza dominicana (Rodríguez 2000: 132). Although this use of the term may be prompted in part by the instruction to specify a race, it also obeys a tendency for raza to refer to communities of people, often grouped by nation, but also by other criteria, as in the concept of la raza antioqueña in Colombia, a regional breed of people who share origins, descent, biology, history, place, and culture (see chapter 4). As we saw in chapter 6, one newspaper reported INMEGEN's genomic studies as showing that Mexicans were a mix of "35 races," which appeared to mean indigenous groups (Alcántara 2007).

It is also quite possible to hear the term raza used in phrases such as la raza negra or la raza indígena. For example, the Colombian salsa songwriter and performer Jairo Varela, in his song "Cicatrices" (Scars),[3] says that all the people who came to Colombia from Africa are de raza negra (of black race). Recently in Colombia, there was a controversy because the two candidates elected to Congress as special representatives of "black communities"—as allowed by Law 70 of 1993—were not apparently black. A national newspaper reported that they were not "de raza negra" (El Espectador 2014). A Constitutional Court judgment on the legislation that created the electoral mechanisms for these special representatives quoted the then minister of the interior as saying that the measures were intended to protect the interests of "la raza negra" (Gaviria Díaz 2001). The Ministry of Education's website Colombia aprende (Colombia learns), directed at children, makes several references to la raza indígena and la raza negra, some of them in questions posted by users—for example, one seventeen-year-old girl who says she is of "la raza negra" (Colombia aprende 2008). A website promoting the "friendly face" of Colombia, in describing "the ethnic groups of Colombia," remarks that the obvious presence of "ne-gros" in Colombia shows that "the Spanish and indigenous races were not the only ethnic components of Colombia's mestizaje" (Todo Colombia 2005).

On February 14, 2011, a Colombian state TV channel aired a program about race and racism in the country, and included a short video in which people on the streets of Bogotá were asked if they thought races existed. Many people said they did; one man said, "Yes, various races exist, like the indigenous [one], the Afros, the mestizos"; another said, "Yes, races exist as distinct human groups, with different skin, different hair color, different cultures"; a woman concurred, saying, "I think that races do exist. Human beings are different, both physi-cally and culturally." Others struck a different note, however. One man said, "I know that biologically races exist, but socially I don't accept [that]. It doesn't seem right to me to classify races, because it generates differences and dif-ferences separate people"; another said there was only one race, "the human race." When asked to which race they belonged, one woman said, "I am white, normal—but I am not racist." A Spanish visitor said, "I am white Caucasian, but I am Basque: I don't know if that is a separate race or not." Others iden-tified themselves as "Caucasian white," "white race," "afroamericano," "afrode-scendiente," and "raza mexicana" (Canal Capital 2011).

In Mexico, the comic book character Memín Pinguín—a caricatured black boy (see chapter 6)—is quite often described as being "de raza negra" (El País 2008; El Universo 2015; Las Mañanitas Show 2015; Memín Pinguín 2015). Newspaper reports will sometimes refer to a person as "de raza negra," often in relation to non-Mexicans, such as U.S. president Barack Obama or a black human rights activist from Honduras, who was the subject of various news re-ports in 2014 (El Universal 2014). There is also an occasional use of the term in relation to indigenous people, for example, in a newspaper report on students from "the original peoples" of Mexico, attending university in the capital, who "take pride in their race" (El Universal 2006). Use of the term to describe in-digenous people is also quite common in online comments from the general public on blogs and YouTube videos.

Race and Color as Morally Charged Terms

On the other hand, alongside the apparently unproblematic use of the term *race* and associated color terms, there are areas of doubt and uncertainty, which are hinted at by the response of the woman above, who immediately qualified her self-identification as white by saying "but I am not racist," as if saying she was white might lead others to suspect that she was a racist. Sue, in her study of Veracruz, Mexico, noted a marked difference between "race talk" and "color discourse." People would easily identify themselves and others by a series of color terms—such as negro, moreno (brown), güero (literally, blond; meaning light-skinned), blanco—but when they were asked about race, they "exhibited reservation, uncertainty, confusion, or became noticeably uncomfortable." This was because the "mention of race oftentimes connotes discrimination and hierarchical relationships . . . talking about race or classifying someone racially is perceived as racist" (Sue 2013: 30). Color talk used simple descriptors to identify individuals; race talk classified people into hierarchical groups. Color terms were not apt for classifying purposes because color was always judged in relational terms: the darkest-skinned, darkest-haired person in the family could be nicknamed el negro, while being deemed moreno claro (light brown) by work colleagues. More uncertainty was introduced by the fact that some words—negro, moreno, and blanco—could function in both race talk and color discourse; this depended on the context and whether a classificatory intention was at work. These terms could be a description of an individual's (relative) skin color, but they could also work to indicate an entire category of people—los negros, los blancos, and so on—in ways that evoked the possibility of seeing these categories in a hierarchical order (Sue 2013: 31–37).

There is some inconsistency in Sue's account, because she says that mestizo and indígena/indio are both racial terms, which should, according to her, be subject to the "social taboo against race discourse." While it may be true that mestizo is a term that local people recognize from school lessons but do not spontaneously use about themselves, and while it may be true that indígena (and more so, indio) can evoke connotations of hierarchy, it seems odd to see either term as subject to social taboo in Mexico, when they are both part of long-standing public political discourses, from both the state and social movements, and when mestizo has been used in nation-building projects precisely to blur racial distinctions. In this sense, it may be that a clear distinction between race talk and color talk is not so easy to draw. As Moreno Figueroa shows, the term güero, which Sue says is nothing but a color term, is also readily deployed in Mexico, often alongside the contrastive term moreno, to denote hierarchies of beauty and personal value—even within the family (Moreno Figueroa 2008, 2012).

This is also my experience from fieldwork in Colombia (Wade 1993: 259–60). I found that people were more likely to deploy color terms, both individually and categorically, than they were to use the word raza to talk about people—which doesn't mean the word was taboo, as indicated by the examples above. But it was not possible to see a clear difference between race talk and color talk, because (as Sue herself suggests) key color terms were always potentially loaded with connotations of hierarchy and status, and thus could also cause "reservation, uncertainty," and discomfort. For example, a friend in Colombia told me about an incident in a rural area of the Caribbean coastal region, where she was working with an archaeological team. Local people told her that a logistical problem with a vehicle that the team had encountered could be resolved by el blanco, who was the local landowner and big shot, and had a tractor. When he arrived, he looked to my friend and her colleagues like a dark-skinned negro or moreno. He was nicknamed el blanco because he had money, land, and status in the local context: this was one facet of the complex trope found in many Latin American countries, which says that "money whitens."

On the other side of the coin, the phrase él me trató de negro means "he called me negro" (i.e., used the color term to address me) and "he treated me like a black" (i.e., like a person of low status, like a servant, or with little respect), which also implies "he discriminated against me because of my color." As with being the local blanco, this phrase is highly context-dependent: the people who find themselves suddenly addressed/treated as negro might be a variety of skin tones; in a given context, they are classed as black as a marker of low status. The term mestizo was also subject to this kind of ambiguity. As in Mexico—although with less of an explicit state-driven, nation-building history—it could act as a neutral term, blurring difference: "we are all mestizos." But when counterposed to indígenas or negros, it could carry much more hierarchical connotations of superiority (not to mention the "Caucasian mestizo" deployed by some Colombian geneticists).

These examples show that color terms are not very good for denoting a coherent category of people, identified by phenotype and/or ancestry, but that they always have the potential to refer to hierarchy and power, even when used within the family (on Brazil, see also Hordge-Freeman 2015). The point is that any talk about race or color can be relatively neutral, but can also potentially evoke ideas of racism and hierarchy, depending on the context; use of the actual term raza may well intensify that potential, although the term can be used neutrally. "Context" here includes scenarios in which people in the same social interaction interpret the use of a word in very different ways, such that one person's "neutral" use of the term moreno sounds charged with meanings of hierarchy and even racism to someone else.

The fact that terms and ideas relating to color and race are both very unexceptional and routine, and also charged with the awkwardness of hierarchy and discrimination, is an expression of the inherent duality of mestizaje: it can connote sameness and democracy, where diverse skin tones and other racial markers are just part of an endless proliferation of difference; and simultaneously it can evoke hierarchy where differences are organized by nodal categories such as white, black, and indigenous. The ambiguity of race and color is important to bear in mind when considering the way genomic research does or does not alter the meanings and potentialities of race and color. For example, might genomics provide an apparently neutral, technical, and even apparently precise language for talking about potentially awkward issues? Or might it give added biological weight to racial/color differences?

Ancestry and Appearances

An important feature of the everyday use of race and color terms in Mexico and Colombia is the way they deploy notions of physical appearance, and of ancestry and genealogy. Appearance and ancestry are sometimes opposed in the literature and linked to "color" and "race," respectively (Sue 2013: 36–38), and the distinction has been taken further by some to suggest that, particularly in Brazil, people discriminate on the basis of color, whereas in the United States they do so on the basis of origin or ancestry (Nogueira 2008 [1959]). The U.S. "one-drop rule," which defines as black anyone presumed to have inherited "one drop" of "black blood," is contrasted with the Brazilian attention to physical appearance rather than origins (Twine 1998), although there are suggestions that the United States is becoming more color-based (Bonilla-Silva 2004) and thus closer to the "pigmentocracies" of Latin America (Telles and Project on Ethnicity and Race in Latin America 2014).

A related issue is the important role "culture" is said to play in defining race/color identifications in Latin America—again often making a contrast with the United States, where the emphasis placed on the ancestry-based one-drop rule can lead to the important role of culture in defining race being overlooked (Hartigan 2010). This emerges above all from countries where a key racial distinction is between indígena and mestizo (or white): this distinction operates to a large extent with a vocabulary of language, dress, place of residence, and occupation—what one might call behavioral appearances—rather than just phenotypical appearances such as color, hair type, body shape, and facial features (Wade 2010: 38). In Mexico and Colombia, the physical difference between many indígenas and many mestizos is not great—skin color in particular is not a reliable indicator at all. Different people with the same medium-brown skin tone self-identify as white, mestizo, and indigenous—and indeed black (Telles and Flores 2013).

The emphasis on culture in Latin American discourses about human diversity is slightly different from the widely noted trends in the United States and Europe toward "cultural racism," "raceless racism," or "cultural fundamentalism," in which, post–World War II, reference to biology became tainted with implications of racism and was replaced, at least in public discourse, by reference to ingrained cultural difference (see chapter 2 and also Goldberg 2008; Stolcke 1995; Taguieff 1990). The emphasis on culture in Latin America is historically more deeply rooted in distinctions between mestizos and indígenas, categories not easily separated by phenotype. In Europe and the United States, appearance can still operate as a pretty reliable cue for racial categorization; it is just that it can be too awkward to refer to it publicly. However, the Latin American emphasis on culture does converge conveniently with a more widespread postwar allergy to talking about differences in terms of bodies and biology.

My view is that it is important to understand that behavioral appearances, physical appearance, and ancestry are all important as ways of reckoning both race and color identifications in Latin America—a view that qualifies any assumed contrast between Latin America and the United States in terms of a singular or even dominant role for appearance and ancestry, respectively. Against the idea that "culture" is the only thing that matters in distinguishing between indígena and mestizo, there is plenty of evidence indicating an enduring and indeed obsessive concern with the body and its ancestrally inherited features, such as skin color, despite their indeterminacy in processes of racial identification. People in Mexico and Colombia, and elsewhere in Latin America, are very concerned with darkness and lightness of skin, the shape of the nose, the texture of the hair, and other bodily markers perceived as linked to race/color classifications. This is evident from research that looks at people's judgments about beauty, at their concern with how light or dark babies are at birth, at what they think needs to be "improved" with plastic surgery, at attempts to avoid dark-skinned egg donors for IVF treatments for infertile white women, and at ideas that indigenous or black ancestry is often perceptible in specific and often very slight physical characteristics, such as the shape of the hips and thighs, the shade of the fingernails, or vestiges of a "Mongolian spot"[4] (Edmonds 2010; Hale 2006: 25; Hordge-Freeman 2015; Moreno Figueroa 2012, 2013; Nelson 1999: 231; Roberts 2012; Wade 2015: 126–30).

These studies show that concern with the body frequently involves matters of parentage and ancestry. Decisions about IVF and concern with the appearance of babies are by definition bound up with parentage, the hereditary transmission of traits, and, possibly, a desire to *mejorar la raza*, improve the race or pedigree (of the family or the nation), by producing lighter-skinned offspring, often considered better-looking and better-equipped to face the challenges of a pigmentocratic society. In addition, mestizo people may well perceive their bodies, inside and out, as a mosaic of elements inherited in quasi-Mendelian fashion from ancestors, real or supposed (Wade 2005b). In Brazil, the saying "preto is a color, negro is a race" (Santos et al. 2009: 794) also indicates the coexisting roles of appearance and ancestry. Preto (black) is a census color term and a relatively little-used everyday color term; in both cases the focus is on skin color. Negro is in part a recent political category, as we saw in chapter 5, which embraces all pretos and pardos (browns), but it is also a term that captures people perceived to have African ancestry, which shows not only in skin color, but also in inherited facial features, hair type, and body shape (Cicalo 2012: 119). Rio favela dwellers, for example, while using a variety of color terms, also insist that all Afro-Brazilians are part of the "negra" (Sheriff 2003).

In short, ideas about ancestry are central to the constitution of racialized identities in Latin America, and, insofar as genomic research in the region has highlighted the issue of the genetic ancestry of mestizo and other populations, it is interesting to explore how a genetic idiom operates in this realm. Might genetics in one respect rebiologize race by highlighting ancestry, while also unsettling easy associations between color and genetics?

Race and Color in Focus Group Conversations

All the features noted above can be discerned in the data from the focus groups. The term *race* was introduced to the focus groups in an explicit fashion, so avoidance was not always obvious. But the characteristic ambiguous duality of race as both unexceptional and awkward was easily apparent.

Race as Neutral Classification

In Mexico and Colombia, among people with training in life sciences and natural sciences (LS people), some saw race as a simple device to classify people according to inherited phenotype—color was typically mentioned for humans. This view was held by some non-LS people too. Several LS people mentioned that race applied to animals as well: as one nutritional genomics student said, "To me, race seems to be for animals."

As kids we are taught that race in humans is about some people being güeri-tos, others are negritos, we are a mixture between those two and the Asians are amarillitos [yellow].[5] But race is not just among people, but also among animals. . . . For example, among cattle, there are differences in physique, in size, and genetically too. . . . They are mostly physical differences. (Bio-technology, Oaxaca)[6]

The concept of race is used to separate, to differentiate individuals who . . . are of the same species. It is based on appearance—the phenotype, as you'd say in biological terms. (Biotechnology, Oaxaca)

Race is to differentiate some people from others by color. (Biotechnology, Oaxaca)

Our parents tell us: if they see a güero they say s/he is de raza blanca and a moreno is de raza negra. (Nursing, Oaxaca)

[Race] is a word to catalogue the populations of the world by their physical characteristics, like skin color, visible [things]. Because ideology doesn't come into it, nor culture—well, a bit, yes, it depends on the region, [but] above all they are anatomical [characteristics]. (Mechatronics, Oaxaca)

Among Colombian medical students, race could also be a fairly obvious and unproblematic way of talking about difference and, true to the importance of region in perceptions of diversity in the country, race was often discussed in these terms. One student said, "Race is specific characteristics that dif-ferentiate one region from another"; another said the term meant "physical characteristics that come from environmental and genetic factors and that are different in each place, each geographical location"; a third, linking race to a more global geography, said, "I relate the white race with cold geographies, you know, in the north and all those places."

In these ideas about race, the categories generally mentioned were the predictable ones—negros/morenos, blancos, indígenas/indios—but people also referred to Spaniards, Mexicans, and Latinos as razas. Mestizos were a persistent referent in all this talk of race, but it was not clear that they fig-ured as a raza themselves. Occasionally, people would refer to the raza mes-tiza; moreno (which often implies mixture, as well as being a euphemism for negro) also sometimes appeared as a raza. But more commonly it was pre-cisely because mestizos were a mixture of razas that they did not constitute one themselves. As one biotechnology student said, "They say that dogs are mestizo when they are ordinary, but how do I define an ordinary dog? He simply has no race." That is, raza was often associated with some degree of "purity" (see below).

Race as Hierarchy and Discrimination

The use of race as a simple term of description and classification was by no means straightforward among these students. First, the word was frequently seen as linked to hierarchy and racism, often understood as an improper or misinformed use of the concept and relating to an old-fashioned ignorance that science, seen as a democratic force, could help banish by teaching that we are all mixed. In a focus group held in a different context—among forensic technicians in Colombia (see chapter 4)—there was discomfort with the very word *race*: one technician who let the word slip out immediately said, "you see, you made me say race . . . it is just that this word has been used as a jus- tification for terrible things in the past . . . we know there are no pure races" (Schwartz-Marín et al. 2015: 873). The nursing student above who said "our parents tell us" was referring to understandings of race in an older generation who "from our youth have inculcated us incorrectly"; she went on to say that "just because we were conquered by the Spanish, we should not feel any less [i.e., feel inferior]," thus bringing ideas of hierarchy into the picture. Others said similar things:

> When we are kids in primary school they teach us that the Spanish race came and conquered the indigenous race and gave rise to the mestizos. So as kids we play with those words and it is a word that I think is used as a denigrating word for other people . . . it can't be a good word. (Biotech- nology, Oaxaca)

> These concepts are badly used by teachers and parents themselves because they don't know the proper definition of the word and they are preoccu- pied with making social distinctions, with racism . . . [this] causes certain problems. (Biotechnology, Oaxaca)

Contesting the opinion of the mechatronics student, cited above, that race was not about ideology, others in the group said, "I think it does involve ideology: the Nazis . . ."; and, "Unfortunately, race does have a lot to do with ideology. . . . In the end it is a type of discrimination." Hierarchy was also apparent in the concept that it was worth trying to mejorar la raza (improve the race), an idea which was seen as racist and the product of ignorance: "In my family, they say it's necessary to improve the race. If you're a man, you should get a pretty, tall, *güera* woman so your kids come out pretty" (Mechatronics, Oaxaca).

For many humanities and social science students (HSS people), "ideology" played a much greater role, undermining the idea that there was a simple, neutral definition of race and challenging simple associations between color and race, by questioning the very notion of race. Some of these students took the classic social science line that race was a social construction that used a naturalizing discourse of biology and bodies to create systems of domination, often linked to colonial oppression.

> From my humanist perspective, words like race mark differences between humans but for [the purpose of] discrimination and to impose some people as superior and others as inferior, some as masters and lords, and others as slaves. (Governance, Michoacán)

> Race is violent and discriminatory concepts. (Governance, Michoacán)

> [Race] is a social construction used for political ends basically to discriminate between people. . . . [It is] a cultural classification that passes for biological, that is, it is inscribed in nature. (Humanities, Bogotá)

Racist claims to superiority were often associated with claims to racial purity, and, challenging this, it was quite common to assert that there are no pure races. One Colombian medical student said, "There are none [pure races] and there never have been." But this was qualified by a colleague who said:

> I say that there is no pure race because of the moral and social problem. There is nothing that separates you, that opens a gulf between the black and the white—there is no pure race. But in terms of [physical] characteristics, there is.

Purity could also be judged in relative terms: in Colombia, certain regions were seen as relatively pure, because they had been isolated and/or endogamous: the Pacific coastal region, certain indigenous groups and reservations, and certain regions of Antioquia (associated with the founding lineages of the paisas) were seen as relatively pure compared to a city such as Bogotá (Schwartz-Marín and Wade 2015: 893). In Mexico, "indigenous people could be seen as a purer race than those of us who are mestizos" (Multicultural Studies, Michoacán). As a hybrid, the mestizo was a product of procreation between "a pure race from here with another from Spain" (Biotechnology, Oaxaca). Mestizos were seen as the opposite of purity, which meant they were not easily conceived as a raza, even if they were the product of an encounter between razas. Insofar as racism was linked to ideas about purity, the mestizo could also figure as an antidote to racism.

The tension between a neutral biology and a hierarchy of value can be seen in these ideas about purity. On the one hand, purity was simply a relative descriptive term, designating certain historically original or geographically demarcated populations, who were less mixed than the mestizos they had produced by mixing. On the other hand, purity was associated with hierarchy and racist exclusions, and with claims to relative whiteness and superiority, alongside the relegation of relatively pure indigeneity or blackness to a low position on the scale of national value.

In sum, for some people, especially those from an LS background, there might be a simple biological definition of race, which was a neutral, acceptable one, and which could possibly encompass descriptive notions of relative biological purity, compared to Latin American mestizos. On the other hand, "ideology"—of which teachers and parents of an older generation were less aware—had unfortunately tainted this neutral usage with racist beliefs. For many HSS people, ideology was a whole system of colonially based classification, oppression, and racist discrimination, in which there was no neutral, biological reality to race. This distinction between LS and HSS people reflects the difference between some biologists who, after World War II, continued to seek a purely genetic definition of race, as a neutral descriptor, and most social scientists, who reconceived race as a "social construction," linked to a colonial history of racial oppression (Reardon 2005).

Race as Biology and Culture

A second key feature of ideas about race and racial categories was a notable degree of ambiguity about what the defining criteria of a racial classification were. Whether seen as a neutral description of diversity or linked to oppression, race was often defined in terms of its reference to biology. But for many, race also suggested a variety of nonbiological traits. For example, one student of nutritional genomics said race was "a way of grouping people by classes, following economic and cultural criteria"; groups could be "the rich and the poor," because "if a moreno is rich, people won't label him as raza indígena so much; but if he is poor, they will"; physical traits were in "third place" compared to economic and cultural ones in defining race. The mechatronics student who said race did have a lot to do with ideology went on to give the example of the Mennonites, who he said were very closed. The role of physical appearance here was vague, to say the least: even if Mennonites are whites in Mexican terms, religion and lifestyle are what define them as a community. One of his colleagues said, "I see race like this: people are cataloguing different ways of thinking, acting, and dressing. You could catalogue emos[7] and hippies as races."

Hippies as a race was an extreme example—which incidentally recalls some eighteenth-century usages, such as David Hume's references to a race of princes and even financiers (see Wade 2015: 65). But it was common in the Mexican groups to hear that the reason indigenous people were discriminated against was not mainly because of their dark skin or their features, but because they dressed and spoke differently, and were poor. Another mechatronics student said: "I think that the physical [aspect] has nothing to do with it—although some characteristics do. In general we Mexicans all have quite similar physical characteristics." A colleague recounted that in his village a tall, light-skinned youth, who looked "very good at first sight," gave a different impression when he opened his mouth, as his first language was an indigenous one and he spoke Spanish poorly. Ideas about the importance of language stood out in the Mexican focus groups, in part because of the provincial locations, which meant that many students had recent indigenous parentage and came from places where the mestizo–indígena categorical boundary was a present reality—three students in the Oaxaca groups were native speakers of an indigenous language. In Colombia, the role of culture in ideas about race was emphasized less by focus groups made up mainly of light-skinned, middle-class city dwellers; among these there was greater agreement that race was about physical appearance, while cultural diversity led to "ethnic" difference, envisaged typically as named indigenous groups.

In short, people were unsure and argued about the relative importance of inherited physical appearance and social traits. Color and appearance, seen as traits ancestrally inherited from parental "races" (not always named as razas), were a recurrent referent, but behavioral appearance was important too, especially in the Mexican groups.

Race and Genetics in Focus Group Conversations

On the very uneven terrain of racial and color discourse, fractured by uncertain tensions between routine usages and fears of racism, and between biology and culture, how did ideas about genetics and genetic ancestry fit in? The answer in simple terms is that genetic idioms reproduced the existing uneven terrain, being uncertain and uneven themselves in the way many people used them, and they did not seem to have transformed people's thinking about race and diversity in a major way.

For most focus group participants, information about genetics did not come principally from recent genomic science projects; instead, it was part of their general knowledge and education; many of the life sciences students had some basic training in biology, though very few of them had specialized training in genetics. Most of the LATINA project participants had received an introductory talk, outlining some elements of population genetics and ancestry testing.

The links between physical appearance and race, noted above, were reflected in ideas that genetics and race were also linked: it was relatively easy for many participants—usually those of a non-HSS background—to use a genetic idiom to talk about racial differences. This happened in two ways: with reference to evolutionary adaptation to an environmental niche, and with reference to propensities to disease. In both cases, focus groups were being prompted to talk about connections between race, genetics, disease, and so on, so these were not spontaneous associations.

Race and Genetics, via Geography: Uncertain Connections

In relation to the first tendency, many people made links between geography and genetics, using ideas of evolutionary natural selection, and this allowed a further connection to race or to a racialized category. In Colombia in particular, the association between race and region was strong for all respondents, as we have seen above and in chapter 4, and some people did not hesitate to make a further link to genetics. In Mexico, the regional aspect was less pronounced, but place was still important.

> Of course race and region coincide, because regions are different; if one region is hotter, then this will come out in the genes, genes will be of different color. (Medicine, Bogotá)

> We change genetically to adapt to the place where we are, so race and genetics are intimately related. (Medicine, Bogotá)

> Clearly there is a relation [between geography, race, and genetics]; if it was not the case there would be no heredity. Black parents could have a son with the phenotypical characteristics of a Chinese person. For me there is a clear relation, which is highly influenced by environmental and geographic

factors that influence the appearance of a certain phenotype. (Medicine, Bogotá)

In each continent, genetics did its work to adapt them [human beings] to the environment. (Mechatronics, Oaxaca)

Certain places have people with certain genes, which is what gives them their physical traits. (Mechatronics, Oaxaca)

I'd say race is directly related to genetics, because by means of the genetic code one can find out where one came from. (Biotechnology, Oaxaca)

Race is something genotypically speaking. (Nursing, Oaxaca)

[Indigenous people who live in isolated areas] make their population among themselves, conserve their genetics; that is, they carry on being the same color . . . one could say the same race, and they [carry on] speaking their same language. (Biotechnology, Oaxaca)

In Mexico there are certain zones, mostly in Oaxaca and Chiapas, that still preserve certain traits among people [i.e., indigenous people] who have lived in the mountains. And if we were to do a genetic analysis of them, it would show that they are similar [to each other], and if they were compared to us, well, there would certainly be some differences. (Biotechnology, Oaxaca)

These quotations show the possibility of linking race to genetics, but the tendency is uneven: it is one thing to see an association between geography, appearance, and genetics; it is another to use the idiom of race and racial categories, such as indígena, to talk about it, and not everyone did this. One student of nutritional genomics in Michoacán said, "I don't know if genetics has anything to do with race." Even when Mexican participants did refer to indigenous people, they often talked about a subcategory of isolated groups or mountain dwellers, rather than a racialized category as a whole.

People with an HSS background recognized links between geography and appearance, but they tended to avoid a reference to race, seen as a dangerous concept, and also avoided linking this directly to genetics. In Colombia, for example, HSS students readily recognized the regional diversity of the country and its links with human diversity—for example, easily associating blackness with the Pacific coastal region—but this was talked about in terms of culture, rather than race or genetics (Schwartz-Marín and Wade 2015). In Mexico, among the group of social anthropology students in Puebla, some considered that "genetic load" was a way of understanding the presence of Africanness in certain areas, such as Veracruz, or more European appearances in Sonora, and one even thought that an "African genetic load" explained why people in Veracruz were *animados* (lively). But these views were contested in the group by others who questioned the idea of linking specific genetic profiles to specific regions of the world: "One person may physically appear African, but genetically I do not know." In Michoacán, one governance studies student also challenged the link between genetics and racialized appearance: "Genetically, as mestizos, we all have a bit of everything. Even though a person may be darker [*más moreno*] than another, in the genes s/he might be closer to a white person." As noted before, questions of racism tended to emerge strongly in these HSS groups: in the Puebla social anthropology group, one student saw it as "risky to tell someone, 'you have European genes'": this could lead to discrimination.

Race and Genetics, via Disease: Uncertain Connections

With regard to the second pattern of talking about propensities to certain disorders, some people linked race and genetics via disorders that were seen to have some hereditary component—albeit uncertain—such as skin cancer, diabetes, and obesity. Talking about disease as simple biology could also be a way to skirt issues of hierarchy and racism:

> I agree with some [genetic] studies that . . . do not represent a conflict for us [in relation to awkward questions of race and intelligence] . . . studies that I've heard about in the news that dark people [*personas morenas*] are more likely to suffer one disease or another, or that white people are more likely to have skin cancer. . . . Genetic research is useful for showing us that we need to take care of ourselves according to skin color or the kind of race we belong to. (Mechatronics, Oaxaca)

> Depending on race and genetics, there is an increase in certain diseases. There are diseases that are more characteristic of one place than another. (Nursing, Oaxaca)

> I think that black race genes [*genes de raza negra*] . . . there are more diseases [related to them] that do not so easily affect the light-skinned race, such as disorders of the blood. And people of white race—skin diseases, skin cancer. (Nursing, Oaxaca)

Because we are mestizos—as many people say—so we find white race and black race.[8] If you are from the north [of Mexico] where there is more white race, then you are more liable to have a skin disorder. (Nursing, Oaxaca)

Health is also important [to take into account when relating race and genetics]. The genetic inheritance you're going to have depends on race. (Multicultural Studies, Michoacán)

But as with the linking of race and genetics via geography, the connection via disease was unevenly made, in two senses. First, while lots of people made a connection between genetics and disease, fewer made direct mention of race or racial categories in this regard, despite the fact that the focus group themes would allow such a mention. Sometimes the connection was simply not made; at others it was rejected: "It is not so much European or African origins, but rather, in relation to that [inherited] aspect of a disease, if your parents have it, you might have a predisposition" (Governance, Michoacán). Immediate parentage was often seen as more significant than a racialized ancestry.

This was reinforced by the exit interviews carried out with LATINA participants in Mexico. All these people had just come out of a test process that included being instructed to estimate their own ancestry using the categories of European, indigenous, and black. When asked in the exit interview if they thought there was a relation between health and ancestry, people had varied views of how strong the relationship was and whether doctors should ask about ancestry when assessing a person's health, but almost no one responded in terms of racial ancestry or racial categories. One person mentioned that "la raza indígena is very strong, right? in terms of certain diseases; it is longer lived than other races," while another said, more vaguely, that belonging to "distinct groups"—a likely euphemism for racial categories—was associated with a "heritage" and thus with certain characteristics that would "make you more resistant to some diseases." But these were rare exceptions. In general, race and color categories were not spontaneous associations made when thinking about genetic predisposition and resistance to disease.

Second, everyone thought that environmental influences and lifestyle made a huge difference to the incidence of disorders, and this line of reasoning broke any simple connection between genetics, race, and health.

Diabetes is not just about heredity . . . a person can get diabetes by saturating him/herself with sweets, his/her body will fill up with a lot of glucose and s/he doesn't have enough insulin for the glucose and that can cause diabetes. (Biotechnology, Oaxaca)

If a child has diabetic parents, the child might be predisposed, but if s/he takes care of him/herself, s/he may not inherit it. (Biotechnology, Oaxaca)

Genetics is something that can determine your physical characteristics and the type of diseases you might have. . . . But I'd say we can change that by changing our lifestyle. (Nursing, Oaxaca)

I think genetics is a factor which predisposes us to develop a disease, but . . . that depends on lifestyle, habits, environment. (Nursing, Oaxaca)

A part of our physique may well be genetic, but it is mixed up with our habits. (Nutritional Genomics, Michoacán)

A lot depends on our habits. If we smoke and drink, if we are in contact with chemical substances, we may have mutations in our genes and become predisposed to a disease. (Nutritional Genomics, Michoacán)

In the last quotation, a person's genome is seen as changeable within their lifetime, due to mutations caused by environmental impacts.

There was discussion and disagreement about this. People in the multicultural studies group in Michoacán debated at length the relations between race, genetics, and disease, and the person cited above, who causally linked the three, was contested by another who said, "Obesity is not inherited, you create it for yourself." Another person changed his tune within the same intervention. He started with an emphasis on genetics as the link between race and health: "Health and race are two related aspects: it is necessary to find a gene that is the key for a country and find its weaknesses and strengths." But he ended by relating health and race via patterns of consumption: "if a certain group consumes such and such foods which might be harmful to the health, well, if these foods are consumed there and not elsewhere then they [race and health] are related" (Governance, Michoacán). In this account, "race" was a biocultural construct, in which culture and biology (here, however, unrelated to genetics) went hand in hand: a raza might have certain habits that affected the health of its members (cf. Kuzawa and Thayer 2013).

In general, the HSS people were less likely to connect race and disease via genetics, because of their view of race as a concept connected to oppression and their reluctance to relate race to genetics in any way. But very few people adopted a strong genetic determinism of any kind. It was exceptional, for example, for one person to say:

> It is right that [DNA] is determinant: the problem is that we won't accept it. There are some races that perhaps tend to be more intelligent than others, or something like that. But it is accepted, I think, that people of Afro-American race have a muscular constitution that makes them in certain ways superior, resilient in everything physical and to do with sports . . . but no one takes that as a negative comment. But when you say they also have a certain deficiency [this is seen as discriminatory]. (Mechatronics, Oaxaca)

A link between race and intelligence was only discussed in this one focus group in Mexico, and was denied by other participants there: "I think race, genetics, and skin color are independent of whether someone is more intelligent than someone else."

The Collective and the Individual

Connections between race and genetics were subject to uncertainty in relation to both geography and disease, but it is important to note that these two domains had rather different affordances. Talking in terms of geographies, whether global or national, encouraged participants to generalize about populations and make statements at a collective level about genetics as a basis for racial categories, especially in Colombia, where region is such a powerful trope for talking about race (particularly blackness). As we saw, it was also at the collective level that people were likely to make statements about the relative purity of certain populations, while still holding on to the idea that "there are no pure races" (especially in Latin America) as a counter to racist claims of superiority. When LS people in Colombia were asked how they thought geneticists produced estimations of biogeographical genetic ancestry, they usually talked in terms of some notionally pure populations that could act as reference points. For African and European ancestry, such populations were usually seen as distant—although the Pacific coast could be seen as a location of relatively pure blackness—while local indigenous groups were the source of relatively pure Amerindian ancestry (Schwartz-Marín and Wade 2015: 893). The collective level of resolution can also be linked to a long-term and distant time frame in which such collectives and lineages could acquire their shape (López Beltrán et al. 2014).

On the other hand, when people talked about disorders, although it was certainly possible to make statements about the propensities of racialized populations, and link these to genetic profiles, they were more inclined to think about individuals as bearers of particular disorders or physical conditions, which might run in the family but were also strongly affected by lifestyle. This implied a proximate time frame of personal and family narratives. At the level of the individual body, the uncertainty and flexibility of links between racial ancestry, genetics, and person became even more marked, and the person was seen as a product of multiple influences. This flexibility meant that a genetic idiom did not possess the necessary affordances for it to thoroughly colonize or transform people's thinking about race and person. Flexibility operated at two overlapping levels.

First, as we have seen, if asked specifically about genetics, people always saw genetic inheritance as just one factor shaping the physical individual. This was even more pronounced when accounting for the psychological person. Some people did use ancestry, and specifically genetics, to explain cultural traits: "I think that likes and cultural traits are also hereditary, and I guess you could say genetic as well. . . . It has happened to me that you like something, and you don't know why, and then you look and you find that someone else in the family liked that" (Medicine, Bogotá, cited in Schwartz-Marín and Wade 2015: 895). But most people thought upbringing and environment were greater influences in this respect.

This was also true in relation to the more amorphous concept of identity. Some people among the social anthropology students in Puebla thought the knowledge that people from Sonora, in the north of Mexico, had higher levels of European genetic ancestry than people from the south might induce Sonoran individuals to identify with Europeanness; and one nutritional genomics student in Michoacán thought that "maybe genetics, a bit, would be a basis for constructing your identity." But most people thought genetic ancestry would have little or no influence on personal identity, compared to history and upbringing (Schwartz-Marín and Wade 2015). The geneticization of racial thinking was tempered by the indeterminacy of genetics itself.

Second, when asked what factors shaped a person's physical appearance, people in Mexico recognized that the raza of their immediate ancestors was an important factor, but they gave equal or even greater importance to lifestyle, as they did when assessing disease risk. The way you lived, and especially what you ate, were important influences on the way you looked. Even though appearance was central to racial categorization, ancestry was only one factor shaping it: this again constrained the way genetics could enter ways of thinking about race.

If we look at a couple of areas that were arguably the most fertile territory for the use of a genetic idiom in talking about race, we can see this flexibility at work. The first concerns a phenomenon well known in Latin America, in which a wide variety of race/color phenotypes can be found within families (Hordge-Freeman 2015; Moreno Figueroa 2012; Wade 1993). People were fully aware that the way physical appearance was inherited was subject to vagaries, and genetics was an easy idiom to use to explain this: "My grandfather has a light complexion and green eyes . . . and my uncles did not turn out like that and nor did I [but] genetics can persist so that my children turn out to be güeros and with light-colored eyes" (Mechatronics, Oaxaca). Others also spoke about this in terms of gene expression, recessive and dominant alleles, and so on:

> Genetics is expressed with the relation between the phenotype and the environment; just because I have something in my genes, doesn't mean it will be expressed. (Biotechnology, Oaxaca)

> Probably being blond-haired and blue-eyed is a recessive trait that jumps the first generation. (Medicine, Bogotá)

> I express different genes from those expressed by another person; this is what makes us different. (Biotechnology, Oaxaca)

These ideas broke a simple relation between an underlying genetic code and the physical appearances that people saw as central to racial categories, but they deployed a clearly genetic idiom to talk about these well-known vagaries of racial appearance:

> It is just that skin color is affected by many factors: what I see is only a small reflection of what I have inside. In a way it is cultural, the black skin color and broad nose are very suggestive of someone having black ancestry. But it is just that, suggestive: it does not mean that his/her genetic composition is always that. For example, I have a brother with a very different skin color, but I would not say we come from different places. Instead, I have to differentiate that one thing is what I am phenotypically, and another thing is what I am in my ancestry, where I come from. (Medicine, Bogotá, cited in Schwartz-Marín and Wade 2015: 899)

One person made a more ambiguous comment that did not explicitly make recourse to genetic heredity, but did so implicitly by mentioning phenotype: "I heard it is common for phenotypic traits to remain dormant, and then appear again in the third generation" (Humanities, Bogotá, cited in Schwartz-Marín and Wade 2015: 898). This ambiguity can be explained by the fact that ideas about traits jumping generations, atavism, and "throwbacks" are old and commonplace (Seitler 2008; Tyler 2007). People have often sought explanations for the presence of a "color outlier" in the family: in Veracruz, when a woman wondered about the presence of a very dark-skinned individual in the family, her grandmother explained that her great-grandfather was "one of those Cubans they call negros" (Sue 2013: 111). In this sense, while ideas about heredity were a resource to explain anomalies, the colonization of these ideas by a genetic idiom was uneven.

Ancestry Testing

The second example where a genetic idiom might be expected to appear strongly when talking about race was in people's ideas about taking a DNA ancestry test and the information it could give them. But the interest in genetic information and the use of a genetic idiom turned out to be very variable.

First, there was wide variation in how interested people were to learn about genetic ancestry at all. Those who participated in the LATINA project were obviously interested.[9] When asked why they had volunteered, they cited curiosity about what DNA might tell them about their past and their origins, often linking this explicitly to race and their own racialized appearance:

> I know nothing about my ancestors. Well, I know about my family, but I don't know what part is indigenous or what part is European or African. (LATINA interviews, Mexico City)

> I'd like to know what race I belong to. (LATINA focus group, Medellín)

> [I'd like to know] why I am so white when in my home there are so many morenitos. (LATINA focus group, Medellín)

> [I wanted to know] why we are physically like we are. And apart from that, where we came from, what was our racial mix, if I have more of an indigenous part, or a bit more mestizo, or a bit more mulatto. (LATINA focus group, Medellín)

One Mexican man had antiracist motives: "I come from a very racist family: they are all güeritos on my mum's side, and they all think they are the best, and the truth is I don't agree with that. So I was interested in knowing the percentages we have from certain places, just for personal satisfaction."

But people who had not volunteered for the LATINA project had less interest in knowing about their genetic ancestry (unless this gave them specific information about health) and did not link this obviously to race.

> In relation to health, I think I would like [to know]. . . . In relation to where I'm from and my heritage, knowing or not makes no difference to me. (Mechatronics, Oaxaca)

> I think the matter of one's ancestors is not important, maybe as a curious fact, but not very. The matter of health [having genetic information about disease propensity], I would think about. (Mechatronics, Oaxaca)

> Maybe I would do a test, but only to know [out of curiosity]. (Biotechnology, Oaxaca)

> I'd be interested to know culturally [my antecedents]. I don't know if a genetic test would help; it doesn't interest me. (Nutritional Genomics, Michoacán)

> It doesn't interest me and I wouldn't do a test. (Nutritional Genomics, Michoacán)

> My identity, my nationality, I define with my lifestyle and my beliefs, and whatever a test tells me is not going to alter my ideas. (Governance, Michoacán)

Second, the LATINA project participants, as part of the questionnaire they filled in after they had been given basic information about the genetics of ancestry testing and had given a blood sample, were asked to estimate their own genetic makeup in terms of proportions of European, indigenous, or black ancestry. We replicated this question in the focus groups, using the same basic format as the LATINA questionnaire. People's reactions to this question indicate that genetic idioms and information tended to be retranslated back to familiar tropes—literally to do with family. Some HSS students in Colombia were severely critical of the question itself, rejecting both its racial connotations and its genetic idiom of quantification:

> I felt very uncomfortable [with this question]—very, very. I don't like to categorize myself in this way and I don't know how to do it.

> None of the three [ancestry categories] meant anything to me; it's like Martian.

Quantifying how much I am indigenous is difficult. It may be that I identify with indigenousness [lo indígena] for one reason or another, but in quantitative terms it is not easy. (Humanities, Bogotá)

One source of discomfort—the overt use of racialized categories—was identified explicitly by one Afro-Colombian activist student in Bogotá who said that the categories looked similar to those he had seen in an anthropology class: "like Negroid, and Caucasoid. They just changed [the category] 'indigenous' because we are in America . . . these categories come from a very specific way of thinking" (Schwartz-Marín and Wade 2015).

More commonly, in Colombia and Mexico, people ran with the question, but also found it quite hard to answer: they were often not sure about what proportions to assign. When LATINA participants were asked if they thought ancestry could be measured, some of them responded with an unequivocal yes: they replied that measuring could be done using precisely the techniques of DNA ancestry testing on which they had been instructed. Some of the biology students in Mexico City agreed; family history would not be enough, said one: "I think you'd need precisely the kind of genetic research that they [the geneticists] are doing." However, other people were less sure and talked about origins and parents, rather than genetics.

Critical, puzzled, or otherwise, people answered the question, coming up with specific percentages of ancestral contributions, even if some felt this was a shot in the dark. When they discussed their answers, a widespread pattern was that, in attempting an answer, people made use of familiar sets of information, centered around their own persons and their families; in fact, in Mexico, ethnographic observations of people tackling the actual LATINA questionnaire found some of them phoning their relatives to make inquiries about their genealogy.[10] First, people thought about their own bodies and the racialized rasgos (traits) that they linked to the black, European, or indigenous categories offered by the question. Skin color, hair type, eye color, nose shape, some aspects of body shape (e.g., large or prominent behind), and height were all useful cues. Second, they also thought about their own parents and grandparents and what they looked like, and whether they spoke an indigenous language. Third, they adduced information about where they or their parents came from and whether these were regions known to have substantial black, white/light, or indigenous populations. Fourth, they made reference to surnames and their putative origin— which in many cases was, of course, Europe. In short, family history was the key theme, which could also involve ideas about class status and interracial unions:

> Well, I consider myself to be 40 percent indigenous, 40 percent European, and 20 percent black. I know that I don't look black, but where I come from 60 percent of the population is black, and in my family my grandmother is not white. I don't even know why I was born so white. (Medicine, Bogotá)

> I'd put 40 to 60 [percent] indigenous ancestry and the other two [ancestries] 0 to 20, and I'd base this on my family history, because I am from the Sierra Norte de Puebla and both my parents are from there and their parents too, and if we go further and further back, well, there will be some mestizaje, but I feel I am more indigenous than I am European. (Biology, Mexico City)

> My family is from Puebla. They were rich, owners of haciendas, so I probably have European ancestry. (Social Anthropology, Puebla)

> I am like a salad, physically white but mestizo [because of the relationship between a Spanish great-grandfather and a morena great-grandmother]. (Social Anthropology, Puebla)

These people, like Nelson's DNA ancestry test consumers, wanted to "align bios (life) and bios (life narratives, life histories) in ways that are meaningful to them" (Nelson 2008: 761).

A third indication of the diluted nature of genomic knowledge was the way people responded to the hypothetical suggestion that their DNA test results might be wildly at variance with their own estimations of their ancestral origins. For some people who knew about DNA ancestry testing and the relation between genotype and phenotype, this was not a particularly taxing scenario: they were aware that a "black" person could have high levels of European genetic ancestry (e.g., the case of Neguinho da Beija Flor; see chapter 5). But the question was not particularly troublesome for others either. Nearly everyone ceded authority to the DNA—mistakes were possible, but a retest would deal with that—but they did not attribute much importance to a counterintuitive result. A few said they would feel disturbed by an unexpected result: "It would cause conflict in me to have a lot of African ancestry because of what I know, that this group has been attacked and there is a [negative] religious concept of them" (Social Anthropology, Puebla). But for most, the scenario was not troubling. The nature of mestizaje and the unpredictability of inheritance—recognized to give rise to families consisting of individuals of very varied skin color, eye color, and so on—meant that it was always possible for varied results to emerge. People responded that they might go back over their family history as a matter of curiosity, but they also mostly said it would make little difference, especially in relation to one's identity. One black woman said:

> It would give me a shock. I don't see myself as within [sic] European ancestry. But if that is the way it was, I wouldn't feel proud of having European ancestry. It wouldn't change me at all. Genetically, what could be done— nothing! Culturally I consider myself an *afro*[11] woman, so that would be my stance. (Humanities, Bogotá)

In short, the introduction of an explicitly genomic way of talking about race and racial categories produced some rejection and some perplexity, but mostly a reliance on familiar ways of thinking: a question posed in terms of a molecular calculus of percentages was answered in those terms, because people felt they should comply with the exercise, but to generate the necessary data they resorted to a kinship reckoning of persons, based on racialized notions of genealogy, place, and even class. This supports Nelson's finding from interviews with DNA roots-seekers that "while the geneticization of 'race' and ethnicity may be the basic logic of genetic genealogy testing, it is not necessarily its inexorable outcome" (Nelson 2008: 761).

The Mexican Genome Project and Genetic Discrimination

A final area where one might expect a genetic idiom to gain significant traction in people's thinking about diversity is in reactions to the Mexican Genome Diversity Project, which was introduced as a specific topic in the Mexican focus groups. Most people had heard of this project from media reports of the results in 2009, and many said they had not paid it much attention at the time. On thinking about it again, reactions were varied and even contradictory. On the one hand, biology students in Mexico City said the MGDP simply confirmed things they already knew about their country—for example, that people in Sonora were often quite light-skinned and European-looking.

Aside from that, however, these students saw a double potential in the MGDP: on the one hand, it could be an objective biological study giving information about the Mexican population and its history, and perhaps some data about propensity to diseases; on the other hand, it could impact existing ideas about racial difference, but in contradictory ways. While one student thought (like Pena and colleagues: see chapter 5) that people who considered themselves white, on learning about the indigenous ancestry in their DNA, might become less racist, more of his colleagues thought lighter-skinned people in Mexico would use the genetic data to support a sense of superiority: "The study does not have these ends in mind, but people do: the people who have European genes feel superior"; as mentioned above, a social anthropology student in Puebla said it was "risky to tell someone, 'you have European genes,'" as this could encourage racism.

This reaction was not uncommon. Given the links many people made between race and racism—the idea that classifying people by ancestry or ancestrally inherited racial traits could imply racist discriminations—it is not surprising that people might also make some links between sorting people in terms of their genetic ancestry and possible discrimination against them, especially where genetic and perceived racial ancestries were closely connected. Commenting on the MGDP, one Puebla social anthropology student said, "In every genomic investigation, isn't the goal to know that racial categories [exist]? . . . When you make a classification, you give a category [12] to X race and therefore you are going to discriminate against another X race." A colleague responded: "So it's no longer 'I'm Mexican,' [instead] it's 'I'm more European,' 'I'm more African.'" One mechatronics student in Oaxaca went so far as to say that a genetic ancestry study like the MGDP "is practically the same as the racial selection of the Nazis; whether you like it or not, it's going that way," although others contested this, saying it was just a medical contribution that did not discriminate.

Others were critical of the implications of homogeneity they saw in the project, which seemed to them to overgeneralize about Mexicans, perhaps for nationalist purposes. And a few mentioned the possibilities of genetic discrimination by the private sector (a couple of people drew parallels with the 1997 film *Gattaca*, which portrays a dystopian future based on eugenicist uses of DNA testing).

> The Mexican Genome [project] fulfills a political and legal goal more than anything else. Which Mexican [are they talking about]? Genetically I think the most traceable gene is the Spanish one, but then again, which Spaniard if they already had 500 years of mestizaje [before coming to the Americas]? (Nutritional Genomics, Michoacán)

> I don't like the idea [of wanting to find the genome of the Mexicans] because it is another way of wanting to categorize us: the Mexicans are like

this and the Europeans are like that, but I think it is impossible because every person is supposed to have different DNA . . . and we share characteristics of diet with the Europeans and the Americans, so I think because of that, it is impossible (Governance, Michoacán)

[The MGDP] could be monopolized by companies to do business, for example, the insurance companies. If it comes out in the Mexican genome that Mexicans might develop a fatal disease like diabetes at 30 or 40 years old, then if I, at 25, want to buy life insurance, then [they'll say] no, you'll die young for certain or, OK, but we won't cover diabetes. (Biotechnology, Oaxaca)

The MGDP, then, was probably the area in which genetic idioms and ways of thinking through diversity had the most impact: people thought it could provide useful information about disease, and that it might encourage existing racism and even create new forms of genetic discrimination (which nevertheless harked back to familiar eugenic tendencies).

Conclusion

The data presented here show that the geneticization of racial thinking in Mexico and Colombia—among the particular publics we worked with—was highly uneven. Language highlighting the transformative power of genetics and the new genomics represented by the MGDP and projects such as LATINA can look overblown, in light of the reactions of people who have little in the way of a vested interest in genetics, even though many of them have university-level training in the life sciences and some of them had also volunteered to donate samples for a project about genetic ancestry.

Within this unevenness, two important things are noteworthy (Schwartz-Marín and Wade 2015). First, a person's location in the overall assemblage makes a significant difference to how s/he reacts to genetic idioms and information. Although there was overlap between the HSS and the LS people in terms of how they are connected to various nodes of knowledge-making practices, HSS people were very reluctant to activate connections that would link race and genetics; they preferred to maintain a good topographical distance because they were very aware of the possibility of creating topological proximity. This may seem unsurprising given what we know about the training HSS people are likely to receive in relation to race, and the stance most natural and life scientists are likely to adopt toward information they perceive as stemming from science. In some respects, our LS people fell into the "trough of certainty" (Mackenzie 1999), a location occupied by people intermediate between those fully plugged into the networks of a specific science subfield (who tend to be cautious about the certainty of their field's knowledge, as they know its complexities) and those who are rather disconnected from it (who tend to be skeptical of its claims). Those in the trough know enough about science to feel confident in its power, but not enough about the specific field to be aware of the provisional nature of some of its knowledge. As unsurprising as it may seem, however, it is important to keep this finding in mind when we consider the geneticization of racial thinking. It is tempting to conclude or fear that popular notions of genetics have the power to colonize ideas about race, making connections and creating topological proximities, because race seems like a discursive field particularly ripe for such colonization, given its history, and because genetics is widely seen as a truth machine in matters such as DNA identification (Lynch et al. 2008). In fact, not only does genetics gain very uneven traction in people's thinking about race, but HSS training acts as a powerful resource for resisting this traction and blocking connections.

Second, a significant difference is made by the level of resolution at which—or the type of assemblage within which—people are conceiving possible links between race, genetics, and ancestry. When thinking of regions or continents, and of whole populations or collective categories of people, it was easier to link geography, genes, and race via ancestry; disease could be added to this network. Even then, we found no single tendency here: people also unsettled such linkages. When thinking about the individual body and its family relations, the linkages became more entangled and complicated, and tracing connections tended to revert to familiar pathways of kinship and place. This is another dimension to which we need be attentive in understanding how genetics does and does not shape racial thinking.

The central message is that genetic knowledge seems to follow pathways already in place, while adding some new connections and imaginative possibilities. Race and color evoke divergent but simultaneous options in Latin America—neutral, egalitarian description and racist hierarchy, and categorizations based on both biological and cultural criteria—and genomic versions of racialized diversity end up reiterating these tensions and divergences. This reiterative tension is facilitated by the disagreements within genomic science itself on the status of race, and by the consensus within genomics that genetics and culture are involved in complex recursive relations. Thus genetic information tends to be persistently redomesticated into the family of existing concepts as they all circulate through different public domains, participating together in multiple assemblages.

Still, there is no doubt that genomics does provide some new affordances. First, if race and color reckonings in Latin America are always shuffling criteria of physical appearance, ancestry, and behavior, then data on genetic ancestry clearly privilege one set of connections in that multiplex braid. Yet not only are genomic versions of ancestry (divorced from family and subject to molecular calculus) persistently rearticulated to genealogical reckonings, but physical appearance and lifestyle are always brought back into the picture when thinking about racial and color categories. The topological network that connects nodes such as race, color, ancestry, mestizos, negros, blancos, indígenas, diseases, habits, predilections, and culture thus acquires some new nodes— genetic ancestry, percentage reckoning, the Mexican genome, the molecular portrait, a populational (rather than family) propensity to disease—but these are closely tied to existing nodes and do not transform them or their relationships. Rather, they add some new tropes to talk about the same things in familiar ways.

Second, if race and color can appear as neutral descriptors—always, however, redolent of hierarchy—then talk of genetic ancestry, in an apparently neutral, technical language of genetic markers and percentages, does provide a particular idiom for neutrality and associated ideas of equality and democracy. It is easy to see how a genetic language of ancestry can add a new wrinkle to the decades-old project of separating the "biological fact" from the "social myth" of race, as UNESCO put it in 1950, while the very neutrality of the science lends authority to the biological facts. As we have seen, however, people easily perceive the potential for racist discrimination behind that idiom. For our respondents, such racism was often linked to the concept of purity, seen as wrongheaded and out of date in view of genetic data showing everyone is mixed and "we are all the same"; this was despite the fact that the same respondents often implicitly used a concept of relative purity when discussing human diversity, globally and nationally. The relational dynamic between mixture and purity is once again made evident.

CONCLUSION

....

In considering the question of the socially transformative potential of genomic knowledge and technology, I have argued that caution is advisable. Transformation may occur, but very unevenly: it depends on how much you have invested in genomics and how engaged with it you are. For associations of patients affected by genetic disorders, or even diseases said to have a significant but as yet indeterminate genetic component, genomics may have significant effects on perceptions of belonging, relatedness, family, citizenship, risk, the future, and self. Notions of identity, and indeed of what it means to be human, may be subject to important changes. But change is not in a zero-sum relationship with continuity: more of the first does not necessarily mean less of the second.

The concept of race illustrates this very well. Genetics has both altered and reinforced this concept in different ways, from the moment the science emerged as a named specialism in the early twentieth century. At first, genetic data were drawn into "racial studies" and were used in an attempt to describe "races," now defined in terms of the frequency distribution of specific traits. This was not a new endeavor: as I pointed out in chapter 1, the sociologist William Z. Ripley was already talking in terms of frequency distributions of physical traits in his 1899 book, *Races of Europe*. But he was attempting to infer underlying racial types or essences, a task which became increasingly fruitless as genetic data on human diversity multiplied. Genetics thus refuted the possibility of distinct racial types—already seen by Ripley as an "unattainable" abstraction (cited by Stepan 1982: 94)—but retained the idea expressed by Dobzhansky that "race differences are objectively ascertainable biological phenomena" (Livingstone and Dobzhansky 1962), although some scientists rejected the idea that "race" expressed an objective biological reality (Lewontin 1972). In this century, the much-cited datum that all humans are "99.9 percent identical" in genetic terms has been widely used to refute the concept of race as a biological reality and attack it as a social categorization. However, other genomic data, focusing on the 0.1 percent of difference—which includes the more than 10 million SNPs currently identified for humans—have been used by some geneticists (Burchard et al. 2003; Risch et al. 2002) to reassert the biological meaningfulness of race for medical purposes (see Bliss 2012: ch. 4). The famous 99.9 percent figure has recently been downsized to 99.5 percent, giving added room for identifying structured differences (Levy et al. 2007).

Genetics has transformed race in some ways: (1) the concept of "racial type" has long been refuted and replaced by frequency distributions of genetic variants; (2) scientists may now prefer to use the language of "continental biogeographical ancestry" rather than race; (3) ancestry informative genetic markers are often not linked to racialized phenotypical traits such as skin color; (4) ancestry can be traced using autosomal, mitochondrial, or Y-chromosome DNA, which may give very different results, thus fragmenting the idea of a single "racial" origin; (5) genetics is rarely seen as determinist, but instead is understood to confer a risk factor (Abu El-Haj 2007, 2012; Wade 2014). Yet many argue that it reiterates race as well, and for a number of reasons: (1) some geneticists continue to argue for the biological reality of race as a relevant medical fact; (2) some drug companies market their products to racialized groups; (3) DNA data are used in forensic work to racially profile suspects; (4) social categories of race are deployed in medical research and practice (albeit often with the antiracist aim of monitoring racial disparities in health), and in genomic project sampling strategies, which encourages the genetic reification of these categories (as I have shown in this book); and (5) continental biogeographic ancestries continue to look very much like familiar racial categories (Bliss 2012; Duster 2015; Fujimura and Rajagopalan 2011; Fullwiley 2007; Kahn 2013; Koenig, Lee, and Richardson 2008; M'charek 2008, 2013; Weiss and Lambert 2014). Claims about the transformative potential of genomics need to be seen in context and taken with a sizable pinch of salt. Purity might appear an anachronistic concept, but insofar as it stands in for "racial difference," one can still detect its magnetic field in constant tension with "mixture."

In assessing the potential of these technologies for generating social change, genomics may be associated with neo-eugenic sci-fi dystopias of genetic discrimination and stratification, but they are more commonly linked to modernist narratives that cast science as promoting democratic progress and social justice. Genomics has been heralded as ushering in an era of personalized medicine and improved health, reducing costs so that access to health is increasingly democratic. As a forensic technology, it is a tool for justice and the resolution of conflict, bringing incontrovertible evidence to bear on wrongdoers, whether these are delinquent criminals or state officials abusing human rights while assuming impunity; it helps restore the remains of loved ones to bereaved families, and reconnects long-lost children to the birth parents from whom they were illegally abducted (García Deister and López-Beltrán 2015; Smith 2013). And it is often heralded as being a final nail in the coffin of racism, guiding the world toward a postracial social condition by virtue of its affirmation of genetic postraciality and/or the explicit adherence of many of its practitioners to an antiracist stance (Bliss 2012).

Here genomics joins forces—in an uneven fashion—with a wide array of antiracist political positions, whose advocates in different ways look forward to a postracial condition in which the world is free from the scourge of racism. These advocates include those on the left, who see racial division as false consciousness; those on the right, who decry what they see as the absolutist divisiveness of multiculturalism and multiracialism; those who support multiculturalism, but see it as a temporary affirmative action preparatory to a color-blind society that is truly racially democratic; and those who criticize multiculturalism as a token and inadequate response to deeply rooted structures of racialized coloniality, which need to be dismantled. Among the latter group, there are those who envisage the possibility of a society in which racialized difference is recognized as a positive and irreducible feature of human conviviality and cultural diversity, but these people are also vehemently antiracist (Bonnett 2000; Lentin 2004, 2011). Everyone agrees on the ethical stance of antiracism, even if they disagree on what its practice entails, so when geneticists set their faces against racism, they align themselves and their science with a multifaceted consensus.

Latin American Racial Exceptionalism

In the scenario just outlined, Latin America often figures as something of a leader, working from the global periphery. As we saw in the introduction, at a time when European and American thinkers were elaborating scientific racism, some Latin American thinkers were developing theories about the connections between racial mixture and social democracy, often reacting to Northern imperialist views of their region as uncivilized and racially degenerate, and criticizing the undemocratic racism that pervaded Northern nations, especially the United States (Hatfield 2010; Hooker 2014; Seigel 2009). This racially exceptionalist image of Latin America has continued until today, despite the accumulation of evidence from numerous studies demonstrating the presence of massive racial inequality and active racism. The apparent fact of pervasive mixture, self-evident and easily adduced, still occupies a central organizing role in Latin American assemblages—sometimes taken for granted and hidden, sometimes materializing in the background, sometimes fully foregrounded—and it works to push this weight of evidence to the margins, graying out the connections it establishes.

Something of this can be glimpsed in the idea that the increasing presence of Latinos is unhinging the racial binaries of the United States and leading to a less racially divided society. As noted in the introduction, a number of commentators have remarked on the "browning" of the country, which supposedly brings it into closer alignment with Brazil, as race there also becomes increasingly politicized. Others have challenged this, noting that existing U.S. racial binaries structure Latinos' experience of race and stratify Latinos by skin color (for a discussion and references, see Wade 2009: 232–39), but many have attached importance to the fact that in the censuses of 2000 and 2010, about 40 percent of people identifying as Hispanic or Latino ticked the box "some other race" when presented with the standard options (compared to 0.2 percent of the non-Latino population) (Humes, Jones, and Ramirez 2010; Rodríguez 2000). This is thought to have the potential to transform the racial formation of the United States.

Related to this is the frequent association of latinidad with cosmopolitanism, often assumed to be antithetical to racial absolutism and racism, although it can also be elitist and thus racially marked as "white" (Friedman 1997; Ribeiro 2005). Latinidad—a term used to refer to the cultural commonality of Latin Americans and Latinos—could be perceived as a somewhat parochial trait, rooted in a specific language, history, and regional origin. But its inherently transnational character has made it fertile ground for ideas about cosmopolitanism. A study based in New York noted that "the hallmark of Puerto Rican latinidad in multi-ethnic Lower East Side has been its cosmopolitanism . . . latinidad is invoked not in a defensive sense, but in a cosmopolitan sense, as a cultural style that allowed for greater sharing and enjoyment of the city, especially with other minority groups." The study cited a Puerto Rican woman who, remarking that the area had recently become less diverse and more white, said "they [the whites] don't understand your background. . . . I feel like Spanish people—we're more likely to try new stuff and do things" (Martinez 2010: 131–32). Whiteness is associated with narrow-mindedness, while Latinos are more open to change.

This study focused on what might be called vernacular cosmopolitanism (Werbner 2006), while a study of queer public culture among Latinos in Phoenix, Arizona, noted that class status inflected the possibility of associating latinidad with cosmopolitanism. Increasing Mexican immigration had attracted some resentment, targeted at lower-class Mexicans, while middle-class Latinos were achieving more public visibility and acceptance. In this context, "to be lower class and *mexicano* was to spoil the party of affluence. To be Mexican and chic, on the other hand, became an easy sign of Phoenix's newly achieved cosmopolitanism" (Rivera-Servera 2012: 187). In Charlotte, North Carolina, Latino musicians claim a sense of cosmopolitanism for themselves, partly in reaction to the racialized cultural hierarchies, dominated by the city's white elites, that relegate them to a secondary status as purveyors of immigrant working-class global culture. Resisting this, "they take pride in what they see as their markedly greater sense of cosmopolitanism and connection to global cultural trends." The author of the study concurs: "If Charlotte is a 'globalizing city' . . . then Charlotte's Latino immigrants are its most vital link to a transnational cosmopolitanism." An integral aspect of that cosmopolitanism is antiracism: "Music is part of a larger dream they share with their audience of interracial harmony and opportunity for aspiring immigrants like themselves" (Byrd 2015: 10, 187–88, 237). Key characteristics of cosmopolitanism are open-mindedness and tolerance, and these are often seen to result from processes of mixture and hybridity (see introduction): latinidad is well placed to capitalize on this, as the concept can draw—necessarily in a very selective and one-sided way—on a narrative of mestizaje.

Another dimension of tolerance, conviviality, and cosmopolitanism is multiculturalism. Despite allegations that multiculturalist policies exacerbate divisiveness and mistrust, the intent behind such approaches is certainly to enhance equality and democratic inclusion. Latin American countries may have come a bit late to the table of multiculturalism, compared to Canada, Australia, and the U.K., which introduced multiculturalist policies in the 1970s. But once they got started, after 1990, several countries in the region now compete globally in terms of formal recognition of and rights for indigenous minorities and, in some cases, Afro-descendants: Colombia, Brazil, and Mexico are good examples, alongside Ecuador and Bolivia (Van Cott 2006). Without arguing that these countries are seen to set an multiculturalist example to the rest of the world, given that Latin America and Latinos are sometimes cast—or cast themselves—as a model for racial tolerance and cosmopolitan conviviality, one may nevertheless wonder how nations previously wedded to ideologies of mestizaje and the apparent submersion of racial difference in a mestizo identity could, in the space of a decade, become part of the global vanguard of multiculturalist governance. Part of the answer lies in the possibility of seeing both in mestizaje and in multiculturalism pathways to ideals of democracy and, especially, racial democracy. Whatever their differences—and I think that these tend to be overstated by those who see in the rise of multiculturalism a radical break with ideologies of mestizaje, in terms of the recognition of difference—both stances converge on the same goal: racial democracy. Because Latin American states tended to see themselves as torchbearers in relation to that goal, they had little difficulty in adopting a different means to the desired end, when the transnational consensus increasingly defined a democracy as a system in which respect for minority rights was translated into legislation.

Latin American Genomics

How does Latin American genomics work in an assemblage in which the region's mestizaje is configured in global networks as a lead worth following in the search for racial tolerance? It is worth bearing mind that Latin American genomics occupies the vanguard in two other respects, in which genomics in general is related to ideas of progress and democratic inclusion. First, in the field of forensics, genetics has been deployed as a technology to address the trauma caused by political violence and state impunity. By "linking objectivity, rigorous methods, and technological determinism with a politics of human dignity and rights, Latin American scientists emerged as world experts in a forensics centered in identifying, burying, and mourning the disappeared" (Smith 2013). For example, the Equipo Argentino de Antropología Forense (EAAF), founded in 1984, has trained experts in Asia and Africa, and sent missions to these regions (EAAF 2003). In Mexico, the NGO Gobernanza Forense Ciudadana is pioneering citizen-led forensics as an innovative way to enhance democratic governance (GFC 2014). Second, Latin American geneticists—mostly based in U.S. universities—have been leading the way in the call for a more inclusive global genomics, with databases less biased toward Euro-American samples and thus better able to address an agenda of "health for all." They have also pointed out the usefulness for medical genomics of Latin American and Latino mestizo populations (Burchard et al. 2005; Bustamante, De La Vega, and Burchard 2011).

It would be quite logical, then, for Latin American geneticists to be vigorous flag-wavers for antiracism too. And in the figure of Sérgio Pena, they have a standard-bearer: he has insisted on the invalidity of race as a biological concept, sees this as a good reason for banishing the social category of race from public policy, and has initiated a media campaign called "We R No Race" (Pena 2012). Even if one might forcefully object that antiracialism (as a critique of the concept of biological race) is very different from antiracism (which entails recognizing the force of the social category of race, independent of its biological nonexistence), there is no doubt that Pena espouses antiracist values. In Colombia and Mexico, we saw that some geneticists produced more pessimistic versions of the mestizo—as a person obsessed with racial hierarchy, or a person burdened with high-risk indigenous-origin alleles—but even Yunis had faith that more mestizaje would bring greater democracy, and the Mexican mestizo, although predisposed to obesity and diabetes, was not seen as a racist.

And yet, despite the democratic and progressive credentials of genomics, the science is providing knowledge that reinforces aspects of the status quo in Latin America. This goes beyond a direct engagement with race and antiracism—which are, after all, words and topics that geneticists only occasionally deploy, and almost never in their scientific publications. I am referring here to the way genetic data and practice colonize certain pathways in the assemblage of configurations of diversity in the nation and the world. At a basic level, genomic practice takes social categories and differentiates them in genetic terms, with a predominant emphasis on difference, rather than similarity. This is an inevitable emphasis, because it is clearly the differences among humans that apparently contain everything that is of interest for human population genetics—in terms of tracing genetic variants related to diseases, tracking population migrations in the peopling of the world, being able to make individual identifications, and so on. An emphasis on these differences, however, masks the similarity shared by all humans—the famous 99.9 percent (or now 99.5 percent) gets grayed out in the assemblage.

The fact that familiar social categories are used to label the entities used by geneticists, such as ancestries or populations, also inevitably results in a process of genetic reification. This labeling makes sense for the geneticists, because social categories reflect and indeed shape evolutionary history to some extent. Social categories reflect the geographical niches in which processes of evolutionary specialization tend to take place, while also shaping the mating behaviors that form part of those same processes (e.g., through endogamous practices). But, as discussed in chapter 1, these processes, which are held to constitute breeding "populations," seen as relatively bounded, are in permanent tension with other processes that move people around, mix populations together, and distribute genetic material in clinal fashion. Therefore, there is only an approximate correlation between social identity and genetic profiles—always bearing in mind that the vast majority of people share over 99 percent of their genetic material and that differences are nearly always in terms of frequencies of genetic variants. This approximate aspect gets hidden by the very common practice of starting with social categories to define samples.

These well-known points apply to human population genetics in general. In relation to Latin America, these tendencies are manifested in the constant reiteration of Africans, Europeans, and Amerindians as the three root stocks of Latin American mestizo nations. This is evident in the way continental biogeographical genetic ancestry is depicted in graphs and plots, using standard parental population samples: difference is maximized by showing the Yoruba, Utah (European ancestry), and Beijing/Tokyo samples as widely separated and tightly bounded clusters (Silva-Zolezzi et al. 2009); or showing "America," "Europe," and "Africa" as distinct vertices of a triangle, inside which mestizo samples are placed according to their percentage share of each type of ancestry (Pena et al. 2011); or simply disaggregating European, African, and Amerindian ancestries for a mestizo person or population. While this is unexceptional from a genomic science point of view, it powerfully reinforces and genetically reifies standard images of the nation, lending the authority of the latest science to well-established historical, cultural, and to preexisting scientific narratives. The same is true of genomic accounts of the mixture between European men and Amerindian and African women: this story is already well known and subject to different readings (e.g., La Malinche as traitorous whore or as mother of the Mexican nation). The way this particular scientific account is narrated, using technical language and/or kinship terminology, produces an image of consensual racial democracy, while also forcefully reinscribing traditional hierarchies of sex and race.

Overall, there is a double emphasis on diversity and mixture, which complements the coexistence of mestizaje and multiculturalism as organizing frames for the nation. The major emphasis is on mixture: Latin Americans are, above all, mestizos. The mestizo category—left silent and unmarked in multiculturalism, which focuses on racial minorities—is made explicit and marked out as constituting the specificity of Latin American nations. This reinscribes the particular pathways of the mestizo assemblage that highlight its inclusiveness. At the same time, genomic studies separate out Afro-descendants, indigenous peoples, and mestizos (and, in Brazil, whites): they are sampled separately and presented as separate populations in the genetic results. This underwrites multiculturalist versions of the mestizo assemblage. Multiculturalism has suffered many critiques—as tokenistic, as divisive—but it can encompass the potential for democratic change: it can open up spaces for claims for social justice, which outstrip whatever controls the state imposes through tokenism and divide-and-rule (Wade 2011). But genomic versions of the multiculturalist nation effectively neutralize this potential by reifying social categories and lending them a genetic dimension. Like the social orders in which it operates, genomics is riven by a tension between democracy and hierarchy, and between mixture and purification. These are not opposed poles, pulling against each other; each inhabits the other. Genomics has great potential to contribute to democratization, but at the very moment in which it emphasizes mixture as conducive to democracy, it reestablishes the relative purifications, boundaries, and separations that enable hierarchy.

NOTES

1 In this book, I will only use *mestiçagem* when referring specifically to Brazil.
2 *La raza* in Latin America can refer to "a people" conceived as a biocultural unity; for example, *la raza colombiana* means "the Colombian people," understood to share biology, history, and culture. This book title therefore can mean "the problems of race in Colombia" but also "the problems facing *la raza colombiana*."
3 See Wade (2010, 2015:ch. 6), Sanchez and Bryan (2003), Psacharopoulos and Patrinos (1994), Telles and Project on Ethnicity and Race in Latin America (2014). On Mexico specifically, see also Moreno Figueroa (2010, 2012), and Sue (2013).
4 For details about RGMLA, see the preface.

CHAPTER 1 · Purity and Mixture in Human Population Genetics

1 Lateral gene transfer occurs when genetic variants are transferred horizontally between genealogically distinct lineages (common among microbes); hybrid species are created when two different species breed to produce a new fertile species (which contradicts the standard definition of a species); a polygenomic organism is one that hosts different genomes, whether from the same species (e.g., a chimera) or different species (e.g., the ratio of microbial to human cells in a human body was widely reported to be 10:1, although this figure has recently been revised down to 1:1 [Campbell 2016]).
2 In GWAS, it is important to make sure that cases and controls are matched for BGA (i.e., population stratification is controlled for). If people with a high proportion of a given BGA are overrepresented among cases, genetic variants that are associated with that BGA will show up as candidate genes, even if they have no influence on the disease.
3 See Paz's analysis of this well-known Mexican phrase, which is usually translated as "son of a bitch/whore," but really means "son of the act of fucking up/over" (Paz 1950).
4 In 2009, I participated with colleagues in a research group in the ESRC Centre for the Research on Socio-Cultural Change (CRESC), hosted by the University of Manchester and the Open University. We discussed the concept of topology at some length, and I am indebted to these discussions.

CHAPTER 2 · From Eugenics to Blood Types

1 The committee was the initiative of U.S. anthropologist Otto Klineberg, head of UNESCO's social science division, and was put into practice by his successor, Brazilian cultural anthropologist Arturo Ramos. When Ramos died, he was replaced by physical anthropologist Ashley Montagu. A Mexican physical anthropologist, Juan Comas, and a Brazilian sociologist, Luiz de Aguiar Costa Pinto, sat on the committee, the rest of which, apart from an Indian social scientist, was composed of people from Europe, the United States, and New Zealand. The presence of two Latin Americans may have been due to UNESCO's sense that Latin American countries had solved the problem of racism, which was reflected in UNESCO's sponsorship of research on race in Brazil (Maio 2001).

2 I am grateful to Eduardo Restrepo for supplying me with a draft of his paper on this topic and for bringing to my attention the various studies which I explore here.

3 Glucose-6-phosphate dehydrogenase deficiency.

4 For example, the work of the French Commission Scientifique du Mexique (1864–67), Colombia's Chorographic Commission (1850), Mexico's Sociedad Mexicana de Geografía y Estadística (founded 1833), the Instituto Histórico e Geográfico Brasileiro (founded 1838), and publications such as *Manual de geografía y estadística de la República Mexicana* by Jesús Hermosa (1857) and *Nueva geografía de Colombia* by Francisco Vergara y Vergara (1901). For details, see Appelbaum (2013), Edison (2003), and Schwarcz (1999).

CHAPTER 3 · Changing Practices

1 A polymorphic locus is a place on the DNA chain where different individuals may display genetic variation.

2 *Raizal* refers to people from Colombia's Caribbean islands of San Andrés and Providencia. *Palenquero* refers to people from the town of San Basilio de Palenque, a former maroon settlement, which has retained a distinct cultural identity.

CHAPTER 4 · Colombia, Country of Regions

1 This chapter draws on research carried out under the aegis of the RGMLA project by María Fernanda Olarte, Adriana Díaz del Castillo, Eduardo Restrepo, Ernesto Schwartz-Marín, and Roosbelinda Cárdenas, and reported in a number of articles, which are cited in the relevant places.

2 See http://www.javeriana.edu.co/Humana/publicaciones.html, accessed February 23, 2016.

3 See http://www.javeriana.edu.co/Humana/humana.html, accessed February 23, 2016.

4 See http://www.javeriana.edu.co/Humana/terrenos6.html, accessed February 23, 2016.

5 Interview carried out by María Fernanda Olarte Sierra and Adriana Díaz del Castillo, 2010.

6 Because indigenous communities were seen as containing valuable data, the EH became involved in a scandal about the collection and supposed export and commercialization of indigenous samples; they were accused of being "gene-hunters." Although the accusations were refuted, the scandal caused the project some problems. See Barragán (2011).

7 Interview with same senior researcher, carried out by Olarte Sierra and Díaz del Castillo, 2010.

8 For details of his company and his books, see http://www.serviciosmedicosyunis turbay.com/, accessed February 23, 2016.

9 Colombia is often described as a "country of regions" (Centro de Investigación y Educación Popular 1998; Zambrano and Bernard 1993). The state's Instituto Geográfico Agustín Codazzi (IGAC) divides the country into five "natural regions" (see the map at http://geoportal.igac.gov.co/mapas_de_colombia/IGAC/Tematicos/34813 .jpg, accessed February 23, 2016). Such regions are used by scholars to describe the country's cultural zones (Abadía Morales 1983; Ocampo López 1988), and they are common in tourist descriptions (e.g., http://encolombia.about.com/od /ViajaraColombia/tp/Regiones-Colombianas.htm, accessed February 23, 2016).

10 See https://es.wikipedia.org/wiki/Discusi%C3%B3n:Antioquia/Archivo_1#Aislado _genetico, accessed August 28, 2016.

11 A haplogroup defines a set of genetic variants, all of which share a common ancestor who has bequeathed the same SNP to all of them. The presence of a particular SNP can be used to define a genetic population. (An SNP is a single nucleotide polymorphism, a DNA variation, found at a single location on the genome, in which a single nucleotide [A, T, C, or G] differs between members of a biological species. To count as an SNP, the variation must be present in at least 1 percent of the species.)

12 These 2009 figures are from Comisión de Seguimiento a la Política Pública Sobre Desplazamiento Forzado (2009: 145). Figures for 2008 estimated 23 percent of displaced people were Afro-Colombian (Rodríguez Garavito, Alfonso Sierra, and Cavelier Adarve 2009: 72). Figures for 2002 estimated displaced people were 33 percent Afro-Colombian and 5 percent indigenous: see CODHES Bulletin 44, *Destierro y repoblamiento*, April 2003, http://www.codhes.org/index.php?option =com_si&type=4, accessed February 23, 2016.

13 Interview with Manuel Paredes, director of the Forensic Genetics Group of the INMLYCF, by Ernesto Schwartz-Marín and Roosbelinda Cárdenas, December 7, 2011.

14 Data from focus groups with peritos organized by Ernesto Schwartz-Marín in Bogotá in 2012, reported in Schwartz-Marín et al. (2015).

CHAPTER 5 · Brazil, Race, and Affirmative Action

1 The chapter on Brazil draws on research carried out under the aegis of the RGMLA project by Michael Kent, with the support of Ricardo Ventura Santos, and reported in a number of papers in which Kent has been lead author, which are cited as appropriate. See also Santos, Kent, and Gaspar Neto (2014).

2 For details of him and his company, see http://www.laboratoriogene.com.br/; for details of his media profile, http://www.laboratoriogene.com.br/blog/gene-na -imprensa/, both accessed February 24, 2016.

3 See also Birchal and Pena (2011).

4 À flor da pele can mean skin deep, and Pena has used the phrase to mean color is only skin deep (Pena and Birchal 2006), but it can also mean something very apparent and intensely felt, which could refer both to the intense feelings skin color can evoke, and, in this book title, the idea that Pena feels strongly about genetics.

5 Interviews were conducted by Michael Kent in 2011–12, mostly in São Paulo, Porto Alegre, and Rio de Janeiro.

6 This balance is revealed in the terminology used: SCA can affect any "Afro-descendant" (i.e., a person with some African genetic ancestry), whatever their race-color identity; but the term Afro-descendant is generally also used as a synonym for "black population."

CHAPTER 6 · Mexico, Public Health, and State Genomics

1 The chapter on Mexico draws on research carried out under the aegis of the RGMLA project by Vivette García Deister and Carlos López-Beltrán (with additional input by Mariana Rios and Francisco Vergara Silva). Ernesto Schwartz-Marín's work on Mexico, carried out mainly before the RGMLA project, also contributed to some RGMLA publications (Kent et al. 2015; Schwartz-Marín and Restrepo 2013).

2 See note 2 in chapter 1.

3 A haplotype is a set of DNA variants that tend to be inherited together. Haplotypes that share a common ancestor form a haplogroup.

CHAPTER 7 · Genomics and Multiculturalism

1 The comments of Colombian geneticists are from interviews carried out by María Fernanda Olarte Sierra and Adriana Díaz del Castillo, 2010.

2 See note 2 in chapter 1.

3 Colombia's Caribbean island possessions of San Andrés and Providencia, off the coast of Nicaragua, were also strong locations of African ancestry, but their status is a little different: for reasons to do with their Anglo-colonial history, they are seen as rather peripheral to the nation.

4 See the project website at http://www.ucl.ac.uk/silva/candela, accessed February 25, 2016.

5 The Mongolian spot is a congenital birthmark, often found on the back or sides, which usually disappears by puberty and which is often taken as a sign of indigenous ancestry.

6 Vasconcelos's famous slogan, "For my race, the spirit will speak," was apparently originally "For my bronze race, the universal spirit will speak."

CHAPTER 8 · Gender, Genealogy, and Mestizaje

1 *Malinchismo* in Mexico today is a pejorative term referring to a preference for the foreign over the national.

2 Report available at Oxford Ancestors' website, http://www.oxfordancestors.com/content/view/80/125/, accessed March 1, 2016.

3 Some of the material in this section draws on Wade (2009).

4 I am grateful to Andrés Ruiz Linares for supplying me with a graphic that contained the percentage figures.

5 Yunis also refers to violence and the "vanquishing and humiliation" of indigenous women by Spanish men during the conquest period. However, he does not link this directly to the genetic data, and narrates it instead as part of a general history of conquest (Yunis Turbay 2009: 124).

6 The curse of Ham is a story, dating back many centuries, according to which Ham, whose father was cursed by Noah, was the ancestor of all black people, who therefore inherited the curse (Goldenberg 2009).

7 A haplotype is a set of DNA variants that tend to be inherited together.

8 An exception to this is a press report on a study done in Argentina. The study revealed that non-Amerindian haplogroups in the mtDNA were a majority (49–61 percent, depending on the region) (Corach, Marino, and Sala 2006). The report made explicit reference to "European mothers" (Heguy 2005).

9 Argentinean geneticists also used mtDNA data to challenge their country's claim "to be the most European country of Latin America" (Corach, Marino, and Sala 2006).

CHAPTER 9 · The Geneticization of Race and Diversity in Everyday Life

1 As noted previously, these data were collected by Ernesto Schwartz-Marín and Roosbelinda Cárdenas in Colombia, and by Michael Kent in Brazil.

2 The methodology of the various focus groups in Mexico and Colombia was not exactly the same in all cases, but they all involved an open discussion of key concepts, such as race, nation, mestizo, mestizaje, physical appearance, heredity, diseases (such as obesity and diabetes), medicine, genetics, and genomics; they also involved the use of some visual material (a video clip of a news report on the Mexican Genome Diversity Project, a video of a Mexican TV discussion about mestizaje and diversity, PR material about the Colombian 2005 census and its question designed to count Afro-Colombian and indigenous people, or PR

material for antiracist campaigns in Colombia); many groups also asked people to estimate their own percentages of biogeographical genetic ancestry, using the question that appeared in the LATINA project questionnaire.

3 On the LP *Triunfo* (Codiscos, Medellín, catalogue number 222 00490). See Wade (1993: 263).

4 See note 5 in chapter 7.

5 The diminutive form of race/color terms—the *-ito* suffix—is often interpreted as minimizing awkwardness: a power-evasive tactic.

6 Quotations are associated with focus groups identified by degree program and location.

7 People who dress in a quasi-Gothic, quasi-punk fashion and listen to rock music with "emotional," often confessional, lyrics.

8 This use of language is worth noting. The person says "*entonces encontramos raza blanca y raza negra,*" not "*la raza blanca y la raza negra*" (the white race and the black race). The latter formulation implies two social groups; the former implies two qualities, which in this case would be types of inheritance. It recalls concepts of race as lineage (Banton 1987), which were current in conquest-era Spain, where people could be accused of having *raza de judío,* Jewish blood.

9 The PR used to recruit people included a Facebook page and pages on the university website, reproduced in the local press, inviting volunteers who wanted to "find out their genetic composition and ancestral origins in order to find out how Amerindian, European, and African we are."

10 Observations by Vivette García Deister and Abigail Nieves Delgado.

11 The term *afro* has gained currency in Colombia as a politically correct way of referring to self and others, alongside *negro* or the full term *afrocolombiano.*

12 *De categoría* means of good quality, so giving someone a category can also imply giving them a high ranking.

REFERENCES

AAFESP. 2007. *O que é anemia falciforme*. Associação de Anemia Falciforme do Estado de São Paulo. Accessed February 26, 2015. http://www.aafesp.org.br/o-que -anemia-falciforme.shtml.

Abadía Morales, Guillermo. 1983. *Compendio general del folklore colombiano*. Bogotá: Fondo de Promoción de la Cultura del Banco Popular.

Abe-Sandes, Kiyoko, Wilson A. Silva Jr., and Marco A. Zago. 2004. "Heterogeneity of the Y Chromosome in Afro-Brazilian Populations." *Human Biology* 76 (1): 77–86.

Abu El-Haj, Nadia. 2007. "The Genetic Reinscription of Race." *Annual Review of Anthropology* 36 (1): 283–300.

———. 2012. *The Genealogical Science: The Search for Jewish Origins and the Politics of Epistemology*. Chicago: University of Chicago Press.

Acosta, María Amparo, Alejandro Blanco-Verea, María Victoria Lareu, et al. 2009. "The Genetic Male Component of Two South-Western Colombian Populations." *Forensic Science International: Genetics* 3 (2): e59–e61.

Acuña-Alonzo, Víctor, Teresa Flores-Dorantes, Janine K. Kruit, et al. 2010. "A Functional ABCA1 Gene Variant Is Associated with Low HDL-Cholesterol Levels and Shows Evidence of Positive Selection in Native Americans." *Human Molecular Genetics* 19 (14): 2877–85.

Aguirre Beltrán, Gonzalo. 1946. *La población negra de México, 1519–1810: Estudio etno-histórico*. Mexico City: Ediciones Fuente Cultural.

Alcántara, Liliana. 2007. "Genes mexicanos, mezcla de 35 razas." *El Universo*, March 9.

Ambrose, Stanley H. 1998. "Late Pleistocene Human Population Bottlenecks, Volcanic Winter, and Differentiation of Modern Humans." *Journal of Human Evolution* 34 (6): 623–51.

Anjos, José Carlos dos. 2005. "O tribunal dos tribunais: Onde se julgam aqueles que julgam raças." *Horizontes Antropológicos* 11:232–36.

Anzaldúa, Gloria. 1987. *Borderlands/La frontera: The New Mestiza*. San Francisco: Aunt Lute Books.

Appelbaum, Nancy P. 2013. "Envisioning the Nation: The Mid-Nineteenth-Century Colombian Chorographic Commission." In *State and Nation Making in Latin America and Spain: Republics of the Possible*, edited by Miguel A. Centeno and Agustin E. Ferraro, 375–98. Cambridge: Cambridge University Press.

Appelbaum, Nancy P., Anne S. Macpherson, and Karin A. Rosemblatt, eds. 2003. *Race and Nation in Modern Latin America*. Chapel Hill: University of North Carolina Press.

Arcila Vélez, Graciliano. 1943. "Grupos sanguíneos entre los indios páez." *Revista del Instituto Etnológico Nacional* 1 (1): 7–14.

Arnold, Michael L. 2008. *Reticulate Evolution and Humans: Origins and Ecology*. Oxford: Oxford University Press.

Arruti, José Mauricio Andion. 1997. "A emergência dos 'remanescentes': Notas para o diálogo entre indígenas e quilombolas." *Mana: Estudos de Antropología Social* 3 (2): 7–38.

Arteaga, C., M. Salazar-Mallén, E. L. Ugalde, et al. 1951. "Blood Agglutinogens of the Mexicans." *Annals of Eugenics* 16 (1): 351–58.

Ayala, Francisco J. 1970. "Teleological Explanations in Evolutionary Biology." *Philosophy of Science* 37 (1): 1–15.

Azevedo, Ana Lucia. 2000a. "Brasil ganha seu primeiro retrato genético." *O Globo*, April 2, 51.

———. 2000b. "El mosaico de DNA que compõe o povo brasileiro." *O Globo*, September 17, 43.

———. 2002. "Genética derruba conceito de raça." *O Globo*, December 17, 32.

Azevedo, Reinaldo. 2011. *Que Mama África que nada! É Mama Europa, mesmo!* Veja. Accessed February 22, 2015. http://veja.abril.com.br/blog/reinaldo/geral/que-mama-africa-que-nada-e-mama-europa-mesmo/.

Baker, Lee D. 1998. *From Savage to Negro: Anthropology and the Construction of Race, 1896–1954*. Berkeley: University of California Press.

Balibar, Etienne. 1991. "Racism and Nationalism." In *Race, Nation and Class: Ambiguous Identities*, edited by Etienne Balibar and Immanuel Wallerstein, 37–67. London: Verso.

Banton, Michael. 1987. *Racial Theories*. Cambridge: Cambridge University Press.

Barahona, Ana. 2010. *Historia de la genética humana en México, 1870–1970*. Mexico City: Universidad Nacional Autónoma de México.

Barbary, Olivier, and Fernando Urrea, eds. 2004. *Gente negra en Colombia, dinámicas sociopolíticas en Cali y el Pacífico*. Cali: CIDSE/Univalle, IRD, Colciencias.

Barkan, Elazar. 1992. *The Retreat of Scientific Racism: Changing Concepts of Race in Britain and the United States between the World Wars*. Cambridge: Cambridge University Press.

Barker, Martin. 1981. *The New Racism: Conservatives and the Ideology of the Tribe*. London: Junction Books.

Barnes, Barry, and John Dupré. 2008. *Genomes and What to Make of Them*. Chicago: University of Chicago Press.

Barragán, Carlos Andrés. 2011. "Molecular Vignettes of the Colombian Nation: The Place(s) of Race and Ethnicity in Networks of Biocapital." In *Racial Identities, Genetic Ancestry, and Health in South America: Argentina, Brazil, Colombia, and Uruguay*, edited by Sahra Gibbon, Ricardo Ventura Santos, and Mónica Sans, 41–68. New York: Palgrave Macmillan.

Barragán Duarte, José Luis. 2007. "Mapa genético de los colombianos." UN *Periódico* 105. Accessed March 27, 2015. http://historico.unperiodico.unal.edu.co /ediciones/105/15.html.

Barry, Brian. 2000. *Culture and Equality: An Egalitarian Critique of Multiculturalism*. Cambridge: Polity Press.

Basave Benítez, Agustín Francisco. 1992. *México mestizo: Análisis del nacionalismo mexicano en torno a la mestizofilia de Andrés Molina Enríquez*. Mexico City: Fondo de Cultura Económica.

Batista, Luís Eduardo, Rosana Batista Monteiro, and Rogério Araujo Medeiros. 2013. "Iniquidades raciais e saúde: O ciclo da política de saúde da população negra." *Saúde em Debate* 37 (99): 681–90.

Beattie, Peter. 2001. *Tribute of Blood: Army, Honor, Race and Nation in Brazil, 1864–1945*. Durham, NC: Duke University Press.

Bedoya, Gabriel, Patricia Montoya, Jenny García, et al. 2006. "Admixture Dynamics in Hispanics: A Shift in the Nuclear Genetic Ancestry of a South American Population Isolate." *Proceedings of the National Academy of Sciences of the United States of America* 103 (19): 7234–39.

Behar, Ruth. 1989. "Sexual Witchcraft, Colonialism and Women's Powers: Views from the Mexican Inquisition." In *Sexuality and Marriage in Colonial Latin America*, edited by Asunción Lavrin, 178–206. Lincoln: University of Nebraska Press.

Bejarano, Bernardo. 2006. "El 85,5 por ciento de las madres colombianas tiene origen indígena." *El Tiempo*, October 13.

Benjamin, Ruha. 2009. "A Lab of Their Own: Genomic Sovereignty as Postcolonial Science Policy." *Policy and Society* 28 (4): 341–55.

Bernal Villegas, Jaime. 2000. "Presentación." In *Variación biológica y cultural en Colombia*, edited by Adriana Ordóñez Vásquez, 9–21. Bogotá: Instituto Colombiano de Cultura Hispánica.

Bertoni, Bernardo. 2011. "Admixture Mapping and Genetic Technologies: Perspectives from Latin America." In *Racial Identities, Genetic Ancestry, and Health in South America: Argentina, Brazil, Colombia, and Uruguay*, edited by Sahra Gibbon, Ricardo Ventura Santos, and Mónica Sans, 103–20. New York: Palgrave Macmillan.

Biodiversidad Mexicana. 2012. *Razas de maíz en México*. Comisión Nacional para el Conocimiento y Uso de la Biodiversidad. Accessed May 19, 2015. http://www .biodiversidad.gob.mx/usos/maices/razas2012.html.

Birchal, Telma S., and Sérgio D. J. Pena. 2011. "The Biological Nonexistence versus the Social Existence of Human Races: Can Science Instruct the Social Ethos?" In *Racial Identities, Genetic Ancestry, and Health in South America: Argentina, Brazil, Colombia, and Uruguay*, edited by Sahra Gibbon, Ricardo Ventura Santos, and Mónica Sans, 69–99. New York: Palgrave Macmillan.

Blake, Stanley E. 2011. *The Vigorous Core of Our Nationality: Race and Regional Identity in Northeastern Brazil*. Pittsburgh, PA: University of Pittsburgh Press.

Bliss, Catherine. 2009. "Genome Sampling and the Biopolitics of Race." In *A Foucault for the 21st century: Governmentality, Biopolitics and Discipline in the New Millennium*, edited by Samuel Binkley and Jorge Capetillo, 320–37. Newcastle upon Tyne, UK: Cambridge Scholars Publishing.

———. 2012. *Race Decoded: The Genomic Fight for Social Justice*. Stanford, CA: Stanford University Press.

Bolnick, Deborah A. 2008. "Individual Ancestry Inference and the Reification of Race as a Biological Phenomenon." In *Revisiting Race in a Genomic Age*, edited by Barbara A. Koenig, Sandra Soo-Jin Lee, and Sarah S. Richardson, 70–85. New Brunswick: Rutgers University Press.

Bonfil Batalla, Guillermo. 1996. *México Profundo: Reclaiming a Civilization*. Translated by Philip A. Dennis. Austin: University of Texas Press.

Bonilla, Carolina, Gerardo Gutiérrez, Esteban J. Parra, et al. 2005. "Admixture Analysis of a Rural Population of the State of Guerrero, Mexico." *American Journal of Physical Anthropology* 128 (4): 861–69.

Bonilla-Silva, Eduardo. 2004. "From Bi-Racial to Tri-Racial: Towards a New System of Racial Stratification in the USA." *Ethnic and Racial Studies* 27 (6): 931–50.

Bonnett, Alistair. 2000. *Anti-Racism*. London: Routledge.

Bortolini, Maria Cátira, Wilson Araújo Da Silva, Dinorah Castro De Guerra, et al. 1999. "African-Derived South American Populations: A History of Symmetrical and Asymmetrical Matings according to Sex Revealed by Bi- and Uni-Parental Genetic Markers." *American Journal of Human Biology* 11 (4): 551–63.

Bortolini, Maria Cátira, Mark G. Thomas, Lourdes Chikhi, et al. 2004. "Ribeiro's Typology, Genomes, and Spanish Colonialism, as Viewed from Gran Canaria and Colombia." *Genetics and Molecular Biology* 27:1–8.

Bortolini, Maria Cátira, Tania De Azevedo Weimer, Francisco M. Salzano, et al. 1995. "Evolutionary Relationships between Black South American and African Populations." *Human Biology* 67:547.

Bouquet, Mary. 1996. "Family Trees and Their Affinities: The Visual Imperative of the Genealogical Diagram." *Journal of the Royal Anthropological Institute* 2 (1): 43–66.

Bowker, Geoffrey C., and Susan Leigh Star. 1999. *Sorting Things Out: Classification and Its Consequences*. Cambridge, MA: MIT Press.

Brading, David. 1988. "Manuel Gamio and Official Indigenismo." *Bulletin of Latin American Research* 7 (1): 75–90.

Brandtstädter, Susanne, Peter Wade, and Kath Woodward. 2011. "Introduction: Rights, Cultures, Subjects and Citizens." *Economy and Society* 40 (2): 167–83.

Brodwin, Paul. 2002. "Genetics, Identity and the Anthropology of Essentialism." *Anthropological Quarterly* 75 (2): 323–30.

Brown, Ryan A., and George J. Armelagos. 2001. "Apportionment of Racial Diversity: A Review." *Evolutionary Anthropology* 10:34–40.

Bryant, Levi R. 2009. *Deleuze on Assemblages*. Accessed July 28, 2015. https://larvalsubjects.wordpress.com/2009/10/08/deleuze-on-assemblages/.

Burchard, Esteban Gonzalez, Luisa N. Borrell, Shweta Choudhry, et al. 2005. "Latino Populations: A Unique Opportunity for the Study of Race, Genetics, and Social Environment in Epidemiological Research." *American Journal of Public Health* 95 (12): 2161–68.

Burchard, Esteban Gonzalez, Elad Ziv, Natasha Coyle, et al. 2003. "The Importance of Race and Ethnic Background in Biomedical Research and Clinical Practice." *New England Journal of Medicine* 348 (12): 1170–75.

Burke, Peter, and Maria Lúcia G. Pallares-Burke. 2008. *Gilberto Freyre: Social Theory in the Tropics.* Oxford: Peter Lang.

Bushnell, David. 1993. *The Making of Modern Colombia: A Nation in Spite of Itself.* Berkeley: University of California Press.

Bustamante, Carlos D., Francisco M. De La Vega, and Esteban G. Burchard. 2011. "Genomics for the World." *Nature* 475 (7355): 163–65.

Byrd, Samuel K. 2015. *The Sounds of Latinidad: Immigrants Making Music and Creating Culture in a Southern City.* New York: NYU Press.

Byrd, W. Carson, and Matthew W. Hughey. 2015. "Biological Determinism and Racial Essentialism: The Ideological Double Helix of Racial Inequality." *Annals of the American Academy of Political and Social Science* 661 (1): 8–22.

Caldwell, Kia Lilly. 2007. *Negras in Brazil: Re-Envisioning Black Women, Citizenship, and the Politics of Identity.* New Brunswick, NJ: Rutgers University Press.

Calvo-González, Elena, and Vera Rocha. 2010. " 'Está no sangue': A articulação de ideias sobre 'raça,' aparência e ancestralidade entre famílias de portadores de doença falciforme em Salvador, Bahia." *Revista de Antropologia* 53 (1): 276–320.

Camacho Servín, Fernando. 2014. "Incuestionable, el racismo en México." *La Jornada,* May 5.

Cámara de Diputados. 2008. *Decreto por el que se reforma . . . la Ley General de Salud.* Secretaría de Servicios Parlamentarios, Cámara de Diputados, July 14. Accessed March 13, 2015. http://www.diputados.gob.mx/LeyesBiblio/proceso/lx/101_DOF _14ju108.pdf.

Campbell, Kristina. 2016. "1:1 Is New Estimated Ratio of Bacterial to Human Cells." *Gut Microbiota for Health.* Accessed March 30, 2016. http://www .gutmicrobiotaforhealth.com/en/11-is-new-estimated-ratio-of-bacterial-to -human-cells/.

Campos-Sánchez, Rebeca, Ramiro Barrantes, Sandra Silva, et al. 2006. "Genetic Structure Analysis of Three Hispanic Populations from Costa Rica, Mexico, and the Southwestern United States Using Y-Chromosome STR Markers and MtDNA Sequences." *Human Biology* 78 (5): 551–63.

Canal Capital. 2011. *Raza y racismo en Colombia.* Accessed May 26, 2015. http://www .youtube.com/watch?v=LDHXls8wduo&p=292C776DB8B3121B.

Candelario, Ginetta E. B. 2007. *Black behind the Ears: Dominican Racial Identity from Museums to Beauty Shops.* Durham, NC: Duke University Press.

Canessa, Andrew. 2008. "Sex and the Citizen: Barbies and Beauty Queens in the Age of Evo Morales." *Journal of Latin American Cultural Studies* 17 (1): 41–64.

Caracol Radio. 2006. *Se confirma que Antioquia es lo que se llama un aislado genético: Los antioqueños son europeos en un 80%.* Accessed February 12, 2015. http://www.caracol

.com.co/audio_programas/archivo_de_audio/se-confirma-que-antioquia-es-lo
-que-se-llama-un-aislado-genetico-los-antioquenos-son-europeos-en-un-80
/20060425/0ir/279718.aspx.

Cardoso, Greice Lemos, and João Farias Guerreiro. 2006. "African Gene Flow to
North Brazil as Revealed by HBB*S Gene Haplotype Analysis." *American Journal of
Human Biology* 18:93–98.

Cartmill, Matt. 1998. "The Status of the Race Concept in Physical Anthropology."
American Anthropologist 100 (3): 651–60.

Carvajal-Carmona, Luis G., Roel Ophoff, Susan Service, et al. 2003. "Genetic
Demography of Antioquia (Colombia) and the Central Valley of Costa Rica."
Human Genetics 112 (5): 534–41.

Carvajal-Carmona, Luis G., Iván D. Soto, Nicolás Pineda, et al. 2000. "Strong Amer-
ind/White Sex Bias and a Possible Sephardic Contribution among the Founders
of a Population in Northwest Colombia." *American Journal of Human Genetics* 67 (5):
1287–95.

Carvalho, José Jorge de. 2003. "As ações afirmativas como resposta ao racismo
acadêmico e seu impacto nas ciências sociais brasileiras." *Teoria e Pesquisa*
42/43:303–40.

Carvalho-Silva, Denise R., Fabrício R. Santos, Jorge Rocha, et al. 2001. "The Phylogeography of Brazilian Y-Chromosome Lineages." *American Journal of Human
Genetics* 68 (1): 281–86.

Castro-Gómez, Santiago, and Eduardo Restrepo, eds. 2008. *Genealogías de la colombianidad: Formaciones discursivas y tecnologías de gobierno en los siglos XIX y XX.* Bogotá:
Pontificia Universidad Javeriana.

Caulfield, Sueann. 2000. *In Defense of Honor: Sexual Morality, Modernity, and Nation in
Early-Twentieth-Century Brazil.* Durham, NC: Duke University Press.

———. 2003. "Interracial Courtship in the Rio de Janeiro Courts, 1918–1940." In
Race and Nation in Modern Latin America, edited by Nancy P. Appelbaum, Anne S.
Macpherson, and Karin A. Rosemblatt, 163–86. Chapel Hill: University of North
Carolina Press.

Cavalcanti, Juliana Manzoni, and Marcos Chor Maio. 2011. "Between Black and Mis-
cegenated Population Groups: Sickle Cell Anemia and Sickle Cell Trait in Brazil
in the 1930s and 1940s." *História, Ciências, Saúde—Manguinhos* 18 (2): 377–406.

Centro de Investigación y Educación Popular. 1998. *Colombia, país de regiones.* 4 vols.
Bogotá: Cinep, Colciencias.

Chakravarti, Aravinda. 2014a. "Perspectives on Human Variation through the Lens
of Diversity and Race." In *Human Variation: A Genetic Perspective on Diversity, Race,
and Medicine*, edited by Aravinda Chakravarti, 1–14. Cold Spring Harbor, NY:
Cold Spring Harbor Laboratory Press.

———, ed. 2014b. *Human Variation: A Genetic Perspective on Diversity, Race, and Medicine.*
Cold Spring Harbor, NY: Cold Spring Harbor Laboratory Press.

Chasteen, John Charles. 2004. *National Rhythms, African Roots: The Deep History of Latin
American Popular Dance.* Albuquerque: University of New Mexico Press.

Cicalo, André. 2012. *Urban Encounters: Affirmative Action and Racial Identities in Brazil.* New York: Palgrave Macmillan.

CODHES. 2012. *Estadísticas históricas de desplazamiento.* Consultoría para los Derechos Humanos y el Desplazamiento. Accessed January 5, 2015. http://www.codhes .org/index.php?option=com_si&type=1.

Collier, Stephen J., and Aihwa Ong. 2008. "Global Assemblages, Anthropological Problems." In *Global Assemblages: Technology, Politics, and Ethics as Anthropological Problems,* edited by Aihwa Ong and Stephen J. Collier, 3–21. Oxford: Blackwell Publishing.

Colombia aprende. 2008. *Los resguardos fueron creados para conservar la raza indígena.* Ministerio de Educación Nacional. Accessed May 26, 2015. http://www .colombiaaprende.edu.co/html/productos/1685/article-226378.html.

Comas, Juan. 1941. "Aportación a la bibliografía y estadística serológica racial americana." *Boletín Bibliográfico de Antropología Americana (1937–1948)* 5 (1–3): 29–37.

———. 1942. "Los grupos sanguíneos y la raciología americana." *Revista Mexicana de Sociología* 4 (3): 69–73.

———. 1951. *Racial Myths.* Paris: UNESCO.

———. 1961. "Scientific" Racism Again? *Current Anthropology* 2 (4): 303–40.

Comisión de Seguimiento a la Política Pública Sobre Desplazamiento Forzado. 2009. *El reto ante la tragedia humanitaria del desplazamiento forzado, Vol. 3: Superar la exclusión social de la población desplazada.* Bogotá: Comisión de Seguimiento a la Política Pública Sobre Desplazamiento Forzado.

Conceição, Ísis. 2014. *Brazil's Laws on Quotas and the Road to Racial Equality.* OxHRH Blog. Accessed January 29, 2015. http://ohrh.law.ox.ac.uk/brazils-laws-on -quotas-and-the-road-to-racial-equality/.

Condit, Celeste Michelle. 1999a. "How the Public Understands Genetics: Non-Deterministic and Non-Discriminatory Interpretations of the 'Blueprint' Metaphor." *Public Understanding of Science* 8:169–80.

———. 1999b. *The Meanings of the Gene: Public Debates about Human Heredity.* Madison: University of Wisconsin Press.

Condit, Celeste Michelle, Roxanne Parrott, and Tina M. Harris. 2002. "Lay Understandings of the Relationship between Race and Genetics: Development of a Collectivized Knowledge through Shared Discourse." *Public Understanding of Science* 11:373–87.

Condit, Celeste M., Roxanne L. Parrott, Tina M. Harris, et al. 2004. "The Role of 'Genetics' in Popular Understandings of Race in the United States." *Public Understanding of Science* 13 (3): 249–72.

Conklin, Alice L. 2013. *In the Museum of Man: Race, Anthropology, and Empire in France, 1850–1950.* Ithaca, NY: Cornell University Press.

Coordinación de Medios de Comunicación Universidad Autónoma de Yucatán. 2015. "Combate a enfermedades crónico-degenerativas." *Boletín Informativo.* Accessed September 16, 2015. http://www.uady.mx/sitios/prensa/boletines/abr-15 /30-abr-15.html.

Cope, R. Douglas. 1994. *The Limits of Racial Domination: Plebeian Society in Colonial Mexico City, 1660–1720*. Madison: University of Wisconsin Press.

Corach, Daniel, Miguel Marino, and Andrea Sala. 2006. "Relevant Genetic Contribution of Amerindian to the Extant Population of Argentina." *International Congress Series: Progress in Forensic Genetics* 1288:397–99.

Cordova, Maria S., Ruben Lisker, and Alvar Loria. 1967. "Studies on Several Genetic Hematological Traits of the Mexican Population. XII. Distribution of Blood Group Antigens in Twelve Indian Tribes." *American Journal of Physical Anthropology* 26 (1): 55–65.

Cruz Martínez, Angeles. 2006. "Millones de mexicanos, con disposición genética a sufrir males cardiovasculares." *La Jornada*, September 13.

Cunin, Elisabeth, and Odile Hoffmann, eds. 2013. *Blackness and Mestizaje in Mexico and Central America*. Trenton, NJ: Africa World Press.

Curiel, Ochy. 2008. "Superando la interseccionalidad de categorías por la construcción de un proyecto político feminista radical: Reflexiones en torno a las estrategias políticas de las mujeres afrodescendientes." In *Raza, etnicidad y sexualidades: Ciudadanía y multiculturalismo en América Latina*, edited by Peter Wade, Fernando Urrea Giraldo, and Mara Viveros Vigoya, 461–84. Bogotá: Instituto CES, Facultad de Ciencias Humanas, Universidad Nacional de Colombia.

Daflon, Verônica Toste, João Feres Júnior, and Luiz Augusto Campos. 2013. "Race-Based Affirmative Actions in Brazilian Public Higher Education: An Analytical Overview." *Cadernos de Pesquisa* 43:302–27.

Daher, Adel, Adelaide Jóia, Adriana Atila, et al. 2008. *113 cidadãos anti-racistas contra as leis raciais*. Accessed October 3, 2014. http://revistaepoca.globo.com/Revista/Epoca/0,,EDR83466–6014,00.html.

DANE. 2006. *Colombia una nación multicultural: Su diversidad étnica*. Bogotá: Departamento Administrativo Nacional de Estadística.

Daniel, G. Reginald. 2006. *Race and Multiraciality in Brazil and the United States: Converging Paths?* University Park: Pennsylvania State University Press.

Deans-Smith, Susan. 2005. "Creating the Colonial Subject: Casta Paintings, Collectors, and Critics in Eighteenth-Century Mexico and Spain." *Colonial Latin American Review* 14 (2): 169–204.

de Assis Poiares, Lilian, Paulo de Sá Osorio, Fábio Alexandre Spanhol, et al. 2010. "Allele Frequencies of 15 STRs in a Representative Sample of the Brazilian Population." *Forensic Science International: Genetics* 4 (2): e61–e63.

De la Cadena, Marisol. 2000. *Indigenous Mestizos: The Politics of Race and Culture in Cuzco, 1919–1991*. Durham, NC: Duke University Press.

DeLanda, Manuel. 2006. *A New Philosophy of Society: Assemblage Theory and Social Complexity*. London: Bloomsbury Academic.

De la Peña, Guillermo. 2006. "A New Mexican Nationalism? Indigenous Rights, Constitutional Reform and the Conflicting Meanings of Multiculturalism." *Nations and Nationalism* 12 (2): 279–302.

Deleuze, Gilles. 2006. *Foucault*. Translated by Seán Hand. London: Continuum.

Deleuze, Gilles, and Félix Guattari. 1988. *A Thousand Plateaus: Capitalism and Schizophrenia*. Translated by Brian Massumi. Minneapolis: University of Minnesota Press.

Dellalibera, Edileine, Michele Lucy Bezerra Havro, Marcela Souza, et al. 2004. "Genetic Analysis of 13 STR Loci in the Population from the State of Pernambuco, Northeast Brazil." *Forensic Science International* 146 (1): 57–59.

Devine Guzmán, Tracy L. 2005. " 'Diacuí Killed Iracema': Indigenism, Nationalism and the Struggle for Brazilianness." *Bulletin of Latin American Research* 24 (1): 92–122.

Díaz del Castillo H., Adriana, María Fernanda Olarte Sierra, and Tania Pérez-Bustos. 2012. "Testigos modestos y poblaciones invisibles en la cobertura de la genética humana en los medios de comunicación colombianos." *Interface: Comunicação, Saúde, Educação* 16 (41): 451–67.

Diniz, Debora, and Cristiano Guedes. 2006. "Informação genética na mídia impressa: A anemia falciforme em questão." *Ciência & Saúde Coletiva* 11 (4): 1055–62.

Doolittle, W. Ford. 1999. "Phylogenetic Classification and the Universal Tree." *Science* 284 (5423): 2124–28.

Douglas, Mary. 1966. *Purity and Danger: An Analysis of Concepts of Pollution and Taboo*. London: Routledge and Kegan Paul.

Dumit, Joe. 2012. *Drugs for Life: How Pharmaceutical Companies Define Our Health*. Durham, NC: Duke University Press.

Dupré, John. 2015. "The Polygenomic Organism." In *Postgenomics: Perspectives on Biology after the Genome*, edited by Susan S. Richardson and Hallam Stevens, 56–72. Durham, NC: Duke University Press.

Duque Gómez, Luis. 1944. "Grupos sanguíneos entre los indígenas del departamento de Caldas." *Revista del Instituto Etnológico Nacional* 1 (2): 623–53.

———. 1961. "Los prejuicios raciales." *Revista Colombiana de Antropología* 10:357–60.

Duster, Troy. 2006. "The Molecular Reinscription of Race: Unanticipated Issues in Biotechnology and Forensic Science." *Patterns of Prejudice* 40 (4–5): 427–41.

———. 2011. "Ancestry Testing and DNA: Uses, Limits and *Caveat Emptor*." In *Race and the Genetic Revolution: Science, Myth, and Culture*, edited by Sheldon Krimsky and Kathleen Sloan, 99–115. New York: Columbia University Press.

———. 2015. "A Post-Genomic Surprise: The Molecular Reinscription of Race in Science, Law and Medicine." *British Journal of Sociology* 66 (1): 1–27.

Dziebel, German. 2015. *Amerindians Are Even More Genetically Diverse and Older Than You Thought*. Accessed February 15, 2016. http://anthropogenesis.kinshipstudies.org/2015/07/amerindians-are-even-more-genetically-diverse-and-older-than-we-thought/.

EAAF. 2003. *EAAF Annual Report*. Buenos Aires: Equipo Argentino de Antropología Forense.

Edison, Paul N. 2003. "Conquest Unrequited: French Expeditionary Science in Mexico, 1864–1867. *French Historical Studies* 26 (3): 459–95.

Edmonds, Alexander. 2010. *Pretty Modern: Beauty, Sex, and Plastic Surgery in Brazil*. Durham, NC: Duke University Press.

Edwards, Jeanette, and Carles Salazar, eds. 2009. *European Kinship in the Age of Biotechnology*. Oxford: Berghahn Books.

El Espectador. 2014. "Representante a la Cámara de Comunidades Negras No Es Afrodescendiente." *El Espectador*, March 10.

Ellison, George T. H., Andrew Smart, Richard Tutton, et al. 2007. "Racial Categories in Medicine: A Failure of Evidence-Based Practice?" *PLoS Medicine* 4 (9): e287.

El País. 2008. "El cómic Memín Pinguín vuelve a abrir la polémica por racismo en EE UU." *El País*, July 10.

El Universal. 2003. "Desmiente genética al racismo: Académica." *El Universal*, November 13.

———. 2006. "Pese a burlas, asumen sus raíces con orgullo." *El Universal*, October 12.

———. 2009. "Mapa genómico: una herramienta útil en investigaciones sociales." *El Universal*, May 19.

———. 2011. "Crean polémica por racismo y discriminación." *El Universal*, December 28.

———. 2014. "Amnistía denuncia aumento de torturas en México." *El Universal*, September 4.

El Universo. 2015. "Sixto Valencia, dibujante de Memín Pinguín, falleció a los 81 años." *El Universo*, April 23.

Engerman, Stanley L., and Kenneth L. Sokoloff. 2005. "The Evolution of Suffrage Institutions in the New World." *Journal of Economic History* 65 (4): 891–921.

Engle, Karen. 2010. *The Elusive Promise of Indigenous Development: Rights, Culture, Strategy*. Durham, NC: Duke University Press.

Epstein, Steven. 2007. *Inclusion: The Politics of Difference in Medical Research*. Chicago: University of Chicago Press.

Erickson, Jim. 2008. "Researchers Release Most Detailed Global Study of Genetic Variation." *Michigan News*, University of Michigan, February 20. Accessed February, 16, 2016. http://ns.umich.edu/new/releases/6357-u-m-researchers-release -most-detailed-global-study-of-genetic-variation.

Ettorre, Elizabeth. 2002. *Reproductive Genetics, Gender and the Body*. London: Routledge.

Fanon, Frantz. [1952] 1986. *Black Skin, White Masks*. London: Pluto Press.

Faria, Luís de Castro. 1952. "Pesquisas de antropologia física no Brasil." *Boletim do Museu Nacional, Nova Série, Antropologia* 13:1–106.

Fausto-Sterling, Anne. 2000. *Sexing the Body: Gender Politics and the Construction of Sexuality*. New York: Basic Books.

FCI. n.d. *Nomenclatura de las razas de la FCI*. Federation Cynologique Internationale. Accessed May 26, 2015. http://www.fci.be/es/Nomenclature/.

Fernandes, Sofia. 2009. "SUS fará teste de anemia falciforme em bebês." *Folha de São Paulo*, May 9.

Fernández, Bernardo. 2014. *Memín Pinguín y el desconocimiento del otro*. Milenio.com. Accessed March 12, 2015. http://www.milenio.com/tribunamilenio/que_tan

_racistas_somos_los_mexicanos/Memin_Pinguin-racismo-desconocimiento
_del_otro-caricatura_13_376892310.html.

Finkler, Kaja. 2001. "The Kin in the Gene: The Medicalization of Family and Kinship in American Society." Current Anthropology 42 (2): 235–63.

FitzGerald, David Scott, and David Cook-Martín. 2014. Culling the Masses: The Democratic Origins of Racist Immigration Policy in the Americas. Cambridge, MA: Harvard University Press.

Fog, Lisbeth. 2006. Emilio Yunis Turbay. Universia Colombia SAS. Accessed August 23, 2013. http://cienciagora.com.co/galeria_de_cientificos/ciencias-de-la-salud-150/emilio-yunis-turbay/65.html.

Folha de São Paulo. 1994. "FHC nega ter dito que tem um 'pé na cozinha.'" Folha de São Paulo, June 1.

Fontaine, Pierre-Michel, ed. 1985. Race, Class and Power in Brazil. Los Angeles: Center of Afro-American Studies, University of California.

Fortun, Michael. 2008. Promising Genomics: Iceland and deCODE Genetics in a World of Speculation. Berkeley: University of California Press.

Foucault, Michel. 1998. The Will to Knowledge. The History of Sexuality, Vol. 1. Translated by Robert Hurley. London: Penguin Books.

Francez, Pablo Abdon da Costa, Elzemar Martins Ribeiro Rodrigues, Gleycianne Furtado Frazão, et al. 2011. "Allelic Frequencies and Statistical Data Obtained from 12 Codis STR Loci in an Admixed Population of the Brazilian Amazon." Genetics and Molecular Biology 34:35–39.

Frank, Reanne. 2015. "Back to the Future? The Emergence of a Geneticized Conceptualization of Race in Sociology." Annals of the American Academy of Political and Social Science 661 (1): 51–64.

Fraser, Nancy, and Axel Honneth. 2003. Redistribution or Recognition? A Political-Philosophical Exchange. London: Verso.

Freire-Maia, Newton. 1973. Brasil: Laboratório racial. Petrópolis: Vozes.

French, Jan Hoffman. 2009. Legalizing Identities: Becoming Black or Indian in Brazil's Northeast. Chapel Hill: University of North Carolina Press.

Freyre, Gilberto. 1986. The Masters and the Slaves: A Study in the Development of Brazilian Civilization. Berkeley: University of California Press.

Friedman, Jonathan. 1997. "Global Crises, the Struggle for Cultural Identity and Intellectual Porkbarrelling: Cosmopolitans versus Locals, Ethnics and Nationals in an Era of De-Hegemonisation." In Debating Cultural Hybridity: Multi-Cultural Identities and the Politics of Anti-Racism, edited by Pnina Werbner and Tariq Modood, 70–89. London: Zed Books.

Fry, Peter H. 2005. "O significado da anemia falciforme no contexto da 'política racial' do governo brasileiro 1995–2004." História, Ciências, Saúde—Manguinhos 12 (2): 374–70.

Fry, Peter, Yvonne Maggie, Marcos Chor Maio, et al., eds. 2007. Divisões perigosas: Políticas raciais no Brasil contemporâneo. Rio de Janeiro: Civilização Brasileira.

Fuentes, Carlos. 1992. El espejo enterrado. Mexico City: Fondo de Cultura Económica.

Fujimura, Joan H., and Ramya Rajagopalan. 2011. "Different Differences: The Use of 'Genetic Ancestry' versus Race in Biomedical Human Genetic Research." *Social Studies of Science* 41 (1): 5–30.

Fullwiley, Duana. 2007. "The Molecularization of Race: Institutionalizing Human Difference in Pharmacogenetics Practice." *Science as Culture* 16 (1): 1–30.

———. 2008. "The Biologistical Construction of Race: 'Admixture' Technology and the New Genetic Medicine." *Social Studies of Science* 38 (5): 695–735.

———. 2011. "Can DNA 'Witness' Race? Forensic Uses of an Imperfect Ancestry Testing Technology." In *Race and the Genetic Revolution: Science, Myth, and Culture*, edited by Sheldon Krimsky and Kathleen Sloan, 116–26. New York: Columbia University Press.

Fundação Cultural Palmares. 2014. *Comunidades quilombolas.* Accessed January 29, 2015. http://www.palmares.gov.br/?page_id=88.

Galanter, Joshua Mark, Juan Carlos Fernandez-Lopez, Christopher R. Gignoux, et al. 2012. "Development of a Panel of Genome-Wide Ancestry Informative Markers to Study Admixture throughout the Americas." *PLoS Genetics* 8 (3): e1002554.

Gannett, Lisa. 2003. "Making Populations: Bounding Genes in Space and Time." *Philosophy of Science* 70:989–1001.

———. 2014. "Biogeographical Ancestry and Race." *Studies in History and Philosophy of Biological and Biomedical Sciences* 47 (Part A): 173–84.

García Deister, Vivette. 2011. "Mestizaje en el laboratorio, una toma instantánea." In *Genes (&) mestizos: Genómica y raza en la biomedicina mexicana*, edited by Carlos López Beltrán, 143–54. Mexico City: Ficticia Editorial.

———. 2014. "Laboratory Life of the Mexican Mestizo." In *Mestizo Genomics: Race Mixture, Nation, and Science in Latin America*, edited by Peter Wade, Carlos López Beltrán, Eduardo Restrepo, and Ricardo Ventura Santos, 161–82. Durham, NC: Duke University Press.

García Deister, Vivette, and Carlos López-Beltrán. 2015. "País de Gordos/País de Muertos: Obesity, Death and Nation in Biomedical and Forensic Genetics in Mexico." *Social Studies of Science* 45 (6):797–815.

Garrido, Margarita. 2005. " 'Free Men of All Colours' in New Granada: Identity and Obedience before Independence." In *Political Cultures in the Andes, 1750–1950*, edited by Cristóbal Aljovín de Losada and Nils Jacobsen, 165–83. Durham, NC: Duke University Press.

Gaspari, Elio. 2000. "O branco tem a marca de Naná." *Folha de São Paulo*, April 16, Caderno A, 14.

Gaviria Díaz, Carlos. 2001. "Sentencia C-169/01." Bogotá: Corte Constitucional.

GFC. 2014. *Gobernanza Forense Ciudadana.* Accessed November 10, 2015. http://gobernanzaforense.org/.

Gilliam, Angela. 1998. "The Brazilian Mulata: Images in the Global Economy." *Race and Class* 40 (1): 57–69.

Gilroy, Paul. 2000. *Between Camps: Nations, Cultures and the Allure of Race.* London: Penguin Books.

————. 2004. *Between Camps: Nations, Cultures and the Allure of Race.* 2nd ed. London: Routledge.

Glycerio, Carolina. 2007. *68% africano, ativista queria mais detalhes.* BBC Brasil.com. Accessed February 25, 2015. http://www.bbc.co.uk/portuguese/reporterbbc /story/2007/05/070507_dna_freidavid_cg.shtml.

Goldberg, David Theo. 2008. *The Threat of Race: Reflections on Racial Neoliberalism.* Malden, MA: Wiley-Blackwell.

Goldenberg, David M. 2009. *The Curse of Ham: Race and Slavery in Early Judaism, Christianity, and Islam.* Princeton, NJ: Princeton University Press.

Goldstein, Donna M. 2003. *Laughter out of Place: Race, Class, Violence and Sexuality in a Rio Shantytown.* Berkeley: University of California Press.

Gomes, Daniela. 2007. "Pesquisa genética divide opinião." *Revista Afirmativa Plural* (August–September): 70–72.

Gómez, Laureano. [1928] 1970. *Interrogantes sobre el progreso de Colombia.* 2nd ed. Bogotá: Colección Populibro.

Gómez Gutiérrez, Alberto, Ignacio Briceño Balcázar, and Jaime Eduardo Bernal Villegas. 2007. *Hereditas, diversitas et variatio: Aproximación a la historia de la genética humana en Colombia.* Bogotá: Pontificia Universidad Javeriana, Academia Nacional de Medicina.

Gómez Izquierdo, Jorge, and María Eugenia Sánchez Díaz. 2011. *La ideología mestizante, el guadalupanismo y sus repercusiones sociales: Una revisión crítica de la "identidad nacional."* Puebla: Universidad Iberoamericana de Puebla/Lupus Inquisitor.

Gonçalves, V. F., C. M. B. Carvalho, M. C. Bortolini, et al. 2008. "The Phylogeography of African Brazilians." *Human Heredity* 65 (1): 23–32.

Gonçalves, V. F., F. Prosdocimi, L. S. Santos, et al. 2007. "Sex-Biased Gene Flow in African Americans but Not in American Caucasians." *Genetics and Molecular Research* 6 (2): 256–61.

Goodman, Alan H., Yolanda T. Moses, and Joseph L. Jones, eds. 2012. *Race: Are We So Different?* Oxford: Wiley-Blackwell.

Granados Arriola, Julio, Alejandra Lara Mejía, Bernardo Moreno Peniche, et al. 2011. "El genoma del mexicano y sus enfermedades." *Mensaje Bioquímico (Depto de Bioquímica, Universidad Nacional Autónoma de México)* 35: 107–14.

Grattapaglia, D., A. B. Schmidt, C. Costa e Silva, et al. 2001. "Brazilian Population Database for the 13 STR Loci of the AmpFlSTR® Profiler Plus™ and Cofiler™ Multiplex Kits." *Forensic Science International* 118 (1): 91–94.

Green, Lance D., James N. Derr, and Alec Knight. 2000. "mtDNA Affinities of the Peoples of North-Central Mexico." *American Journal of Human Genetics* 66 (3): 989–98.

Greene, Shane. 2007. "Introduction: On Race, Roots/Routes, and Sovereignty in Latin America's Afro-Indigenous Multiculturalisms." *Journal of Latin American and Caribbean Anthropology* 12 (2): 441–74.

Grossberg, Lawrence. 1986. "On Postmodernism and Articulation: An Interview with Stuart Hall." *Journal of Communication Inquiry* 10 (2): 45–60.

Grosz, Elizabeth. 2004. *The Nick of Time: Politics, Evolution, and the Untimely.* Durham, NC: Duke University Press.

Guedes, Ciça. 2006. "Estudiosos discutem se genética poderia determinar acesso a cotas." *O Globo*, February 10, 4.

Guerrero Mothelet, Verónica. 2006. "¿Existe un genoma mestizo? Perspectiva del doctor León Olivé." *Andamios* 2:263–67.

Guerrero Mothelet, Verónica, and Stephan Herrera. 2005. "Mexico Launches Bold Genome Project." *Nature Biotechnology* 23 (9): 1030.

Guimarães, Antonio Sérgio. 2007. "Racial Democracy." In *Imagining Brazil*, edited by Jessé Souza and Valter Sinder, 119–40. Lanham, MD: Lexington Books.

Gurdasani, Deepti, Tommy Carstensen, Fasil Tekola-Ayele, et al. 2015. "The African Genome Variation Project Shapes Medical Genetics in Africa." *Nature* 517 (7534): 327–32.

Gutiérrez Torres, Carolina. 2012. "Emilio José Yunis, un genetista de mal humor." *El Espectador*, September 19.

Guy, Donna J. 2000. *White Slavery and Mothers Alive and Dead: The Troubled Meeting of Sex, Gender, Public Health, and Progress in Latin America.* Lincoln: University of Nebraska Press.

Hale, Charles R. 1996. "Mestizaje." Special journal issue. *Journal of Latin American Anthropology* 2 (1).

———. 2002. "Does Multiculturalism Menace? Governance, Cultural Rights and the Politics of Identity in Guatemala." *Journal of Latin American Studies* 34:485–524.

———. 2006. *Más Que un Indio (More Than an Indian): Racial Ambivalence and Neoliberal Multiculturalism in Guatemala.* Santa Fe, NM: School for Advanced Research Press.

Hannaford, Ivan. 1996. *Race: The History of an Idea in the West.* Washington, DC: Woodrow Wilson Center Press.

Haraway, Donna. 1989. *Primate Visions: Gender, Race and Nature in the World of Modern Science.* New York: Routledge.

———. 1991. *Simians, Cyborgs and Women: The Re-Invention of Nature.* London: Free Association Books.

———. 1997. *Modest_Witness@Second_Millenium.FemaleMan©_Meets_Oncomouse™.* London: Routledge.

Hartigan, John. 2010. *Race in the 21st Century: Ethnographic Approaches.* Oxford: Oxford University Press.

———. 2013a. "Looking for Race in the Mexican 'Book of Life': INMEGEN and the Mexican Genome Project." In *Anthropology of Race: Genes, Biology, and Culture*, edited by John Hartigan, 125–50. Santa Fe, NM: School for Advanced Research Press.

———. 2013b. "Mexican Genomics and the Roots of Racial Thinking." *Cultural Anthropology* 28 (3): 372–95.

———. 2013c. "Translating 'Race' and 'Raza' between the United States and Mexico." *North American Dialogue* 16 (1): 29–41.

————, ed. 2013d. *Anthropology of Race: Genes, Biology, and Culture*. Santa Fe, NM: School for Advanced Research Press.

Harvey, Penny, and Hannah Knox. 2012. "The Enchantments of Infrastructure." *Mobilities* 7 (4): 521–36.

Hasenbalg, Carlos. 1985. "Race and Socioeconomic Inequalities in Brazil." In *Race, Class and Power in Brazil*, edited by Pierre-Michel Fontaine, 25–41. Los Angeles: Center for Afro-American Studies, University of Califonia.

Hatfield, Charles. 2010. "The Limits of 'Nuestra América.'" *Revista Hispánica Moderna* 63 (2): 193–202.

Hawks, John. 2015. *What Is the "Braided Stream" Analogy for Human Evolution?* Accessed February 15, 2016. http://johnhawks.net/weblog/topics/news/finlayson-braided -stream-2013.html.

Heath, Deborah, Rayna Rapp, and Karen-Sue Taussig. 2004. "Genetic Citizenship." In *A Companion to the Anthropology of Politics*, edited by David Nugent and Joan Vincent, 152–67. New York: Blackwell.

Heguy, Silvina. 2005. "El 56% de los argentinos tiene antepasados indígenas." *El Clarín*, January 16.

Helg, Aline. 1989. "Los intelectuales frente a la cuestión racial en el decenio de 1920." *Estudios Sociales* (FAES) 4:36–53.

————. 1995. *Our Rightful Share: The Afro-Cuban Struggle for Equality, 1886–1912*. Chapel Hill: University of North Carolina Press.

Helmreich, Stefan. 2003. "Trees and Seas of Information: Alien Kinship and the Biopolitics of Gene Transfer in Marine Biology and Biotechnology." *American Ethnologist* 30 (3): 340–58.

Henare, Amiria, Martin Holbraad, and Sari Wastell. 2007. "Introduction." In *Thinking through Things: Theorising Artefacts Ethnographically*, edited by Amiria Henare, Martin Holbraad, and Sari Wastell, 1–32. London: Routledge.

Herbert, Siân. 2012. "As It Enters the Sporting Spotlight, Brazil Calls on the World to Rethink Race." *Guardian*, August 14. Accessed February 20, 2015. http://www .theguardian.com/commentisfree/2012/aug/14/brazil-free-dna-testing-rethink-race.

Hernández, Astrid, and David A. Pinilla. 2010. "Visibilización de la población étnica en el Censo general 2005: Análisis comparativo de los principales indicadores demográficos." *Ib Revista de la información básica* 4 (2). Accessed October 5, 2015. https://www.dane.gov.co/revista_ib/html_r8/articu105.html.

Hernández, Tanya Kateri. 2013. *Racial Subordination in Latin America: The Role of the State, Customary Law, and the New Civil Rights Response*. Cambridge: Cambridge University Press.

Hincapié García, Alexánder. 2010. "Raza, masculinidad y sexualidad: Una mirada a la novela *Risaralda* de Bernardo Arias Trujillo." *Nómadas* 32:235–46.

Hinterberger, Amy. 2012. "Investing in Life, Investing in Difference: Nations, Populations and Genomes." *Theory, Culture and Society* 29 (3): 72–93.

Hofbauer, Andreas. 2006. *Uma história do branqueamento ou o negro em questão*. São Paulo: Editora UNESP.

Hoffmann, Odile, and María Teresa Rodríguez, eds. 2007. *Los retos de la diferencia: Los actores de la multiculturalidad entre México y Colombia*. Mexico City: Centro de Estudios Mexicanos y Centroamericanos—CEMCA; Centro de Investigación y Estudios Superiores en Antropología Social—CIESAS; Institut de Recherche pour le Développement—IRD; Instituto Colombiano de Antropología e Historia; Publicaciones de la Casa Chata.

Hooker, Juliet. 2009. *Race and the Politics of Solidarity*. Oxford: Oxford University Press.

———. 2014. "Hybrid Subjectivities, Latin American Mestizaje, and Latino Political Thought on Race." *Politics, Groups, and Identities* 2 (2): 188–201.

Hordge-Freeman, Elizabeth. 2015. *The Color of Love: Racial Features, Stigma, and Socialization in Black Brazilian Families*. Austin: University of Texas Press.

Htun, Mala. 2004. "From 'Racial Democracy' to Affirmative Action: Changing State Policy on Race in Brazil." *Latin American Research Review* 39 (1): 60–89.

Humes, Karen R., Nicholas A. Jones, and Roberto R. Ramirez. 2010. "Overview of Race and Hispanic Origin: 2010." Washington, DC: U.S. Bureau of the Census.

Hünemeier, Tábita, Cláudia Carvalho, Andrea Rita Marrero, et al. 2007. "Niger-Congo Speaking Populations and the Formation of the Brazilian Gene Pool: mtDNA and Y-Chromosome Data." *American Journal of Physical Anthropology* 133 (2): 854–67.

Hunt, Linda M., and Nicole Truesdell. 2013. "Observations on the Tenacity of Racial Concepts In Genetics Research." In *Anthropology of Race: Genes, Biology, and Culture*, edited by John Hartigan, 83–108. Santa Fe, NM: School for Advanced Research Press.

INCRA. 2014. *Títulos expedidos às comunidades quilombolas*. Instituto Nacional de Colonização e Reforma Agrária. Accessed January 29, 2015. http://www.incra.gov.br/sites /default/files/uploads/estrutura-fundiaria/quilombolas/titulos_expedidos.pdf.

INMEGEN. 2009a. *Cronología del genoma humano al mapa del genoma de poblaciones Mexicanas*. INMEGEN. Accessed March 16, 2015. http://genomamexicanos.inmegen .gob.mx/material_grafico/poster_cronologico.jpg.

———. 2009b. *Mapa del genoma de poblaciones Mexicanas*. INMEGEN. Accessed March 13, 2015. http://genomamexicanos.inmegen.gob.mx/index.html.

———. 2014. "Diabetes." *Boletín Expresión Inmegen* 4 (19) (June–July). Accessed September 16, 2015. http://boletin.inmegen.gob.mx/boletin19/enaccion.html.

Instituto Socioambiental. 2015. *Povos indígenas no Brasil: Terras indígenas*. Accessed August 28, 2016. https://pib.socioambiental.org/en/c/terras-indigenas /demarcacoes/localizacao-e-extensao-das-tis.

Irwin, Robert McKee. 2003. *Mexican Masculinities*. Minneapolis: University of Minnesota Press.

Iverson, Margot Lynn. 2007. "Blood Types: A History of Genetic Studies of Native Americans, 1920–1955." PhD diss., University of Minnesota, Minneapolis.

Jacob, Michelle M. 2012. "Making Sense of Genetics, Culture, and History: A Case Study of a Native Youth Education Program." In *Genetics and the Unsettled Past: The Collision of DNA, Race, and History*, edited by Keith Wailoo, Alondra Nelson, and Catherine Lee, 279–94. New Brunswick, NJ: Rutgers University Press.

Jansen, Roberta. 2011. "Un Brasil europeu." *O Globo*, February 18, 36.

Jasanoff, Sheila. 2004a. "Ordering Knowledge, Ordering Society." In *States of Knowledge: The Co-Production of Science and Social Order*, edited by Sheila Jasanoff, 13–45. London: Routledge.

———, ed. 2004b. *States of Knowledge: The Co-Production of Science and Social Order*. London: Routledge.

Jiménez López, Miguel, Luis López de Mesa, Calixto Torres Umaña, et al. 1920. *Los problemas de la raza en Colombia*. Bogotá: El Espectador.

Jiménez Román, Miriam. 2007. "Looking at That Middle Ground: Racial Mixing as Panacea?" In *A Companion to Latina/o Studies*, edited by Juan Flores and Renato Rosaldo, 325–36. Oxford: Blackwell.

Jiménez Sánchez, Gerardo. 2003. "Developing a Platform for Genomic Medicine in Mexico." *Science* 300:295–96.

Jiménez Sánchez, Gerardo, Irma Silva-Zolezzi, Alfredo Hidalgo, et al. 2008. "Genomic Medicine in Mexico: Initial Steps and the Road Ahead." *Genome Research* 18 (8): 1191–98.

Johnson, Lyman L., and Sonya Lipsett-Rivera, eds. 1998. *The Faces of Honor: Sex, Shame, and Violence in Colonial Latin America*. Albuquerque: University of New Mexico Press.

Kahn, Jonathan. 2012. "Forensic DNA and the Inertial Power of Race in American Legal Practice." In *Genetics and the Unsettled Past: The Collision of DNA, Race, and History*, edited by Keith Wailoo, Alondra Nelson, and Catherine Lee, 114–42. New Brunswick, NJ: Rutgers University Press.

———. 2013. *Race in a Bottle: The Story of Bidil and Racialized Medicine in a Post-Genomic Age*. New York: Columbia University Press.

Kapchan, Deborah A., and Pauline Turner Strong. 1999. "Theorizing the Hybrid." *Journal of American Folklore* 112 (445): 239–53.

Kapila, Kriti. 2007. "On Global Measures of Culture: A View from India." In *Cultural Politics in a Global Age: Uncertainty, Solidarity and Innovation*, edited by David Held and Henrietta Moore, 242–49. Oxford: One Books.

Kaszycka, Katarzyna A., and Jan Strzałko. 2003. " 'Race': Still an Issue for Physical Anthropology? Results of Polish Studies Seen in the Light of the U.S. Findings." *American Anthropologist* 105 (1): 116–24.

Katzew, Ilona. 2004. *Casta Painting: Images of Race in Eighteenth-Century Mexico*. New Haven, CT: Yale University Press.

Kaufmann, Roberta Fragoso Menezes. 2007. *Ações afirmativas à brasileira: Necessidade ou mito? Uma análise histórico-jurídico-comparativo do negro nos Estados Unidos da América e no Brasil*. Porto Alegre: Livraria do Advogado.

———. 2009. "Arguição de descumprimento de preceito fundamental 186–2/800." Brasilia: Supremo Tribunal Federal.

———. 2010. "A desconstrução do mito da raça e a inconstitucionalidade de cotas raciais no Brasil." *Dereito Público* 36:18–54.

———. 2011. *Sobre cotas raciais e escravidão: Uma explicação necessária*. Accessed March 23, 2012. www.robertafragosokaufmann.com.

Kearns, Rick. 2007. *Indigenous Founding Mothers of the Americas*. The CAC Review. Accessed April 29, 2015. http://cacreview.blogspot.co.uk/2007/04/indigenous -founding-mothers-of-americas.html.

Kent, Michael, Vivette García Deister, Carlos López Beltrán, et al. 2015. "Building the Genomic Nation: 'Homo Brasilis' and the 'Genoma Mexicano' in Comparative Cultural Perspective." *Social Studies of Science* 45 (6): 839–61.

Kent, Michael, Ricardo Ventura Santos, and Peter Wade. 2014. "Negotiating Imagined Genetic Communities: Unity and Diversity in Brazilian Science and Society." *American Anthropologist* 116 (4): 1–13.

Kent, Michael, and Peter Wade. 2015. "Genetics against Race: Science, Politics and Affirmative Action in Brazil." *Social Studies of Science* 45 (6): 816–38.

Kevles, Daniel J. 1995. *In the Name of Eugenics: Genetics and the Uses of Human Heredity*. 2nd ed. Cambridge, MA: Harvard University Press.

Keyeux, Genoveve. 2000. "Poblaciones negras de Colombia: Una primera aproximación a su estructura molecular." In *Variación biológica y cultural en Colombia*, edited by Adriana Ordóñez Vásquez, 345–57. Bogotá: Instituto Colombiano de Cultura Hispánica.

Knight, Alan. 1990. "Racism, Revolution and Indigenismo in Mexico, 1910–1940." In *The Idea of Race in Latin America*, edited by Richard Graham, 71–113. Austin: University of Texas Press.

Kobayashi, Elisabete, Lina Faria, and Maria Conceição da Costa. 2009. "Eugenia e Fundação Rockefeller no Brasil: A saúde como proposta de regeneração nacional." *Sociologias* 22:314–51.

Koenig, Barbara A., Sandra Soo-Jin Lee, and Sarah S. Richardson, eds. 2008. *Revisiting Race in a Genomic Age*. New Brunswick, NJ: Rutgers University Press.

Kohli-Laven, Nina. 2012. "French Families, Paper Facts: Genetics, Nation, and Explanation." In *Genetics and the Unsettled Past: The Collision of DNA, Race, and History*, edited by Keith Wailoo, Alondra Nelson, and Catherine Lee, 183–203. New Brunswick, NJ: Rutgers University Press.

Krieger, H., N. E. Morton, M. P. Mi, et al. 1965. "Racial Admixture in North-Eastern Brazil." *Annals of Human Genetics* 29 (2): 113–25.

Krimsky, Sheldon, and Kathleen Sloan. 2011. *Race and the Genetic Revolution: Science, Myth, and Culture*. New York: Columbia University Press.

Kutzinski, Vera. 1993. *Sugar's Secrets: Race and the Erotics of Cuban Nationalism*. Charlottesville: University of Virginia Press.

Kuzawa, Christopher W., and Zaneta M. Thayer. 2013. "Toppling Typologies: Developmental Plasticity and the Environmental Origins of Human Biological Variation." In *Anthropology of Race: Genes, Biology, and Culture*, edited by John Hartigan, 43–56. Santa Fe, NM: School for Advanced Research Press.

Laguardia, Josué. 2006. "No fio da navalha: Anemia falciforme, raça e as implicações no cuidado à saúde." *Revista Estudos Feministas* 14 (1): 243–62.

Las Mañanitas Show. 2015. *Muere Sixto Valencia, dibujante de "Memín Pinguín."* Entravision. Accessed May 26, 2015. http://lasmananitas.entravision.com/2015/04/23 /muere-sixto-valencia-dibujante-de-memin-pinguin/.

Lasso, Marixa. 2007. *Myths of Harmony: Race and Republicanism during the Age of Revolution, Colombia 1795–1831*. Pittsburgh: University of Pittsburgh Press.

Latour, Bruno. 1987. *Science in Action: How to Follow Scientists and Engineers through Society*. Milton Keynes, UK: Open University Press.

———. 1990. "Visualisation and Cognition: Drawing Things Together." In *Representation in Scientific Practice*, edited by Michael Lynch and Steve Woolgar, 19–68. Cambridge, MA: MIT Press.

———. 1993. *We Have Never Been Modern*. Translated by Catherine Porter. London: Harvester Wheatsheaf.

———. 2005. *Reassembling the Social: An Introduction to Actor-Network-Theory*. Oxford: Oxford University Press.

Lee, Catherine. 2012. "The Unspoken Significance of Gender in Constructing Kinship, Race, and Nation." In *Genetics and the Unsettled Past: The Collision of DNA, Race, and History*, edited by Keith Wailoo, Alondra Nelson, and Catherine Lee, 32–40. New Brunswick, NJ: Rutgers University Press.

Lehmann, Henry, Luis Duque Gómez, and M. Fornaguera. 1944. "Grupos sanguíneos entre los indios guambiano-kokonuko." *Revista del Instituto Etnológico Nacional* 1:197–208.

Leite, Marcelo. 2000. "Retrato molecular do Brasil." *Folha de São Paulo*, March 26.

Lentin, Alana. 2004. *Racism and Anti-Racism in Europe*. London: Pluto.

———. 2011. "What Happens to Anti-Racism When We Are Post Race?" *Feminist Legal Studies* 19 (2): 159–68.

———. 2014. "Post-Race, Post Politics: The Paradoxical Rise of Culture after Multiculturalism." *Ethnic and Racial Studies* 37 (8): 1268–85.

Lentin, Alana, and Gavan Titley. 2011. *The Crises of Multiculturalism: Racism in a Neoliberal Age*. London: Zed Books.

Lervolino, Luciana Garcia, Paulo Eduardo Almeida Baldin, Silvia Miguéis Picado, et al. 2011. "Prevalence of Sickle Cell Disease and Sickle Cell Trait in National Neonatal Screening Studies." *Revista Brasileira de Hematologia e Hemoterapia* 33 (1): 49–54.

Levy, Samuel, Granger Sutton, Pauline C. Ng, et al. 2007. "The Diploid Genome Sequence of an Individual Human." *PLoS Biology* 5 (10): e254.

Lewandowski, Ricardo. 2012. "Arguição de descumprimento de preceito fundamental 186: Voto." Brasília: Supremo Tribunal Federal.

Lewontin, Richard C. 1972. "The Apportionment of Human Diversity." *Evolutionary Biology* 6:381–98.

Lieberman, Leonard, and Larry T. Reynolds. 1996. "Race: The Deconstruction of a Scientific Concept." In *Race and Other Misadventures: Essays in Honor of Ashley Montagu in His Ninetieth Year*, edited by Larry T. Reynolds and Leonard Lieberman, 142–73. Dix Hills, NY: General Hall Inc.

Lins, Tulio C., Rodrigo G. Vieira, Breno S. Abreu, et al. 2010. "Genetic Composition of Brazilian Population Samples Based on a Set of Twenty-Eight Ancestry Informative SNPs." *American Journal of Human Biology* 22 (2): 187–92.

Lipphardt, Veronika. 2012. "Isolates and Crosses in Human Population Genetics; or, a Contextualization of German Race Science." *Current Anthropology* 53 (S5): S69–S82.

———. 2013. "From 'Races' to 'Isolates' and 'Endogamous Communities.'" In *Human Heredity in the Twentieth Century*, edited by Bernd Gausemeier, Staffan Müller-Wille, and Edmund Ramsden, 55–68. London: Pickering and Chatto.

Lippman, Abby. 1991. "Prenatal Genetic Testing and Screening: Constructing Needs and Reinforcing Inequities." *American Journal of Law and Medicine* 17 (1–2): 15–50.

Lisker, Ruben, Alvar Loria, and M. Soledad Cordova. 1965. "Studies on Several Genetic Hematological Traits of the Mexican Population, VIII: Hemoglobin s, Glucose-6-Phosphate Dehydrogenase Deficiency and Other Characteristics in a Malarial Region." *American Journal of Human Genetics* 17 (2): 179–87.

Lisker, Ruben, Graciela Zarate, and Alvar Loria. 1966. "Studies on Several Genetic Hematologic Traits of Mexicans, IX: Abnormal Hemoglobins and Erythrocytic Glucose-6-Phosphate Dehydrogenase Deficiency in Several Indian Tribes." *Blood* 27 (6): 824–30.

Livingstone, Frank B., and Theodosius Dobzhansky. 1962. "On the Non-Existence of Human Races." *Current Anthropology* 3 (3): 279–81.

Lobato, Fátima, and Renato Emerson dos Santos, eds. 2003. *Ações afirmativas: Políticas públicas contra as desigualdades raciais*. Rio de Janeiro: Lamparina.

Long, Jeffrey C. 2013. "The Aimless Genome." In *Anthropology of Race: Genes, Biology, and Culture*, edited by John Hartigan, 169–86. Santa Fe, NM: School for Advanced Research Press.

Lopes, Antonio Herculano. 1996. "Vem cá, mulata!" *Tempo* 26:80–100.

López Beltrán, Carlos. 2007. "Hippocratic Bodies: Temperament and Castas in Spanish America (1570–1820)." *Journal of Spanish Cultural Studies* 8 (2): 253–89.

López Beltrán, Carlos, Vivette García Deister, and Mariana Rios Sandoval. 2014. "Negotiating the Mexican Mestizo: On the Possibility of a National Genomics." In *Mestizo Genomics: Race Mixture, Nation, and Science in Latin America*, edited by Peter Wade, Carlos López Beltrán, Eduardo Restrepo, and Ricardo Ventura Santos, 85–106. Durham NC: Duke University Press.

López Beltrán, Carlos, Sandra González Santos, Abigail Nieves Delgado, et al. 2014. "Ways of Inheriting: Genetic Narratives of Ancestry, Mestizaje, Disease and Nation in Mexico." Unpublished work. Mexico City.

López Beltrán, Carlos, and Francisco Vergara Silva. 2011. "Genómica Nacional: El INMEGEN y el Genoma del Mestizo." In *Genes (&) mestizos: Genómica y raza en la biomedicina mexicana*, edited by Carlos López Beltrán, 99–142. Mexico City: Ficticia Editorial.

López de Mesa, Luis. [1934] 1970. *De cómo se ha formado la nación colombiana*. Medellín: Editorial Bedout.

Loveman, Mara. 2014. *National Colors: Racial Classification and the State in Latin America*. New York: Oxford University Press.

Lury, Celia, Luciana Parisi, and Tiziana Terranova. 2012. "Introduction: The Becoming Topological of Culture." *Theory, Culture and Society* 29 (4–5): 3–35.

Lynch, Michael, Simon A. Cole, Ruth McNally, et al. 2008. *Truth Machine: The Contentious History of DNA Fingerprinting*. Chicago: University of Chicago Press.

Lynn, Richard. 2006. *Race Differences in Intelligence: An Evolutionary Analysis*. Augusta, GA: Washington Summit.

Mackenzie, Donald. 1999. "Nuclear Missile Testing and the Social Construction of Accuracy." In *The Science Studies Reader*, edited by Mario Biagioli, 342–57. Abingdon, UK: Psychology Press.

Maio, Marcos Chor. 2001. "UNESCO and the Study of Race Relations in Brazil: Regional or National Issue?" *Latin American Research Review* 36 (2): 118–36.

Maio, Marcos Chor, and Simone Monteiro. 2010. "Política social com recorte racial no Brasil: O caso da saúde da população negra." In *Raça como questão: História, ciência e identidades no Brasil*, edited by Marcos Chor Maio and Ricardo Ventura Santos, 285–314. Rio de Janeiro: Editora Fiocruz.

Maio, Marcos Chor, and Ricardo Ventura Santos. 2005. "Política de cotas raciais, os 'olhos da sociedade' e os usos da antropologia: O caso do vestibular da Universidade de Brasília (UnB)." *Horizontes Antropológicos* 11 (23): 181–214.

———. 2010. "Cientificismo e antirracismo no pós-Segunda Guerra Mundial: Una análise das primeiras Declaraçãoes sobre Raça da Unesco." In *Raça como questão: História, ciência e identidades no Brasil*, edited by Marcos Chor Maio and Ricardo Ventura Santos, 145–70. Rio de Janeiro: Editora Fiocruz.

Marcus, George E., and Erkan Saka. 2006. "Assemblage." *Theory, Culture and Society* 23 (2–3): 101–6.

Marks, Jonathan. 1996. "The Legacy of Serological Studies in American Physical Anthropology." *History and Philosophy of the Life Sciences* 18 (3): 345–62.

———. 2001. "We're Going to Tell These People Who They Really Are: Science and Relatedness." In *Relative Values: Reconfiguring Kinship Studies*, edited by Sarah Franklin and Susan McKinnon, 355–83. Durham, NC: Duke University Press.

———. 2010. "The Two 20th-Century Crises of Racial Anthropology." In *Histories of American Physical Anthropology in the Twentieth Century*, edited by Michael A. Little and Kenneth A. R. Kennedy, 187–206. Lanham, MD: Rowman and Littlefield.

Marques, Hugo. 2012. *Roberta Fragoso Kaufmann: "Cotas geram ódio racial."* Istoé Independente. Accessed February 22, 2015. http://www.terra.com.br/istoe-temp/edicoes/2012/artigo89658-1.htm.

Marrero, A. R., C. Bravi, S. Stuart, et al. 2007. "Pre- and Post-Columbian Gene and Cultural Continuity: The Case of the *Gaucho* from Southern Brazil." *Human Heredity* 64 (3): 160–71.

Marrero, Andrea Rita, Fábio Pereira Das Neves Leite, Bianca De Almeida Carvalho, et al. 2005. "Heterogeneity of the Genome Ancestry of Individuals Classified as

White in the State of Rio Grande do Sul, Brazil." *American Journal of Human Biology* 17 (4): 496–506.

Martínez, María Elena. 2008. *Genealogical Fictions: Limpieza de Sangre, Religion, and Gender in Colonial Mexico*. Stanford, CA: Stanford University Press.

Martinez, Miranda J. 2010. *Power at the Roots: Gentrification, Community Gardens, and the Puerto Ricans of the Lower East Side*. Lanham, MD: Lexington Books.

Martinez-Alier [Stolcke], Verena. [1974] 1989. *Marriage, Colour and Class in Nineteenth-Century Cuba: A Study of Racial Attitudes and Sexual Values in a Slave Society*. 2nd ed. Ann Arbor: University of Michigan Press.

Martinez-Cortes, Gabriela, Joel Salazar-Flores, Laura Gabriela Fernandez-Rodriguez, et al. 2012. "Admixture and Population Structure in Mexican-Mestizos Based on Paternal Lineages." *Journal of Human Genetics* 57 (9): 568–74.

Martínez-Cruzado, Juan C., Gladys Toro-Labrador, Jorge Viera-Vera, et al. 2005. "Reconstructing the Population History of Puerto Rico by Means of mtDNA Phylogeographic Analysis." *American Journal of Physical Anthropology* 128 (1): 131–55.

McCallum, Cecilia. 2007. "Women out of Place? A Micro-Historical Perspective on the Black Feminist Movement in Salvador da Bahia, Brazil." *Journal of Latin American Studies* 39 (1): 55–80.

M'charek, Amade. 2000. "Technologies of Population: Forensic DNA Testing Practices and the Making of Differences and Similarities. *Configurations* 8 (1): 121–58.

———. 2005. *The Human Genome Diversity Project: An Ethnography of Scientific Practice*. Cambridge: Cambridge University Press.

———. 2008. "Silent Witness, Articulate Collective: DNA Evidence and the Inference of Visible Traits." *Bioethics* 22 (9): 519–28.

———. 2013. "Beyond Fact or Fiction: On the Materiality of Race in Practice." *Cultural Anthropology* 28 (3): 420–42.

M'charek, Amade, Katharina Schramm, and David Skinner. 2014. "Topologies of Race: Doing Territory, Population and Identity in Europe." *Science, Technology and Human Values* 39 (4): 468–87.

McGraw, Jason. 2007. "Purificar la nación: Eugenesia, higiene y renovación moral-racial de la periferia del Caribe colombiano, 1900–1930." *Revista de Estudios Sociales* 27:62–75.

McKinnon, Susan. 2005. *Neo-Liberal Genetics: The Myths and Moral Tales of Evolutionary Psychology*. Chicago: Prickly Paradigm Press.

Mehta, Uday Singh. 1997. "Liberal Strategies of Exclusion." In *Tensions of Empire: Colonial Cultures in a Bourgeois World*, edited by Frederick Cooper and Ann L. Stoler, 59–86. Berkeley: University of California Press.

Memín Pinguín. 2015. *Quien es Memín?* Accessed May 26, 2015. http://meminpinguin.com/quien-es-memin/.

Mendoza Mendoza, Jesús. 2010. "La comunidad indígena en el contexto urbano: Desafíos de sobrevivencia." Mexico City: Centro de Estudios Sociales y de Opinión Pública.

Mikulak, Michael. 2007. "The Rhizomatics of Domination: From Darwin to Biotech-nology." *Rhizomes: Cultural Studies in Emerging Knowledge* 15. Accessed February 4, 2016. http://www.rhizomes.net/issue15/mikulak.html.

Mill, John Stuart. 1859. *On Liberty.* London: Walter Scott Publishing Co.

Ministério da Saúde. 2001. *Manual de doenças mais importantes, por razões étnicas, na população brasileira afro-descendente.* Brasília: Secretaria de Políticas de Saúde, Ministerio da Saúde.

———. 2010. *Política Nacional de Saúde Integral da População Negra: Uma política do SUS.* Brasília: Ministério da Saúde.

Miraval, Francisco. 2008. "Nuevo estudio genético confirma la 'hermandad' de los latinos." *La Voz Bilingüe,* March 31.

Modood, Tariq. 2007. *Multiculturalism: A Civic Idea.* Cambridge: Polity.

Modood, Tariq, and Pnina Werbner, eds. 1997. *The Politics of Multiculturalism in the New Europe: Racism, Identity and Community.* London: Zed Books.

Mol, Annemarie. 2002. *The Body Multiple: Ontology in Medical Practice.* Durham NC: Duke University Press.

Mol, Annemarie, and John Law. 1994. "Regions, Networks and Fluids: Anaemia and Social Topology." *Social Studies of Science* 24 (4): 641–71.

Molina Echeverri, Hernán. 2012. *La población indígena y las ciudades.* Centro de Coop-eración al Indígena. Accessed October 5, 2015. http://observatorioetnicocecoin .org.co/cecoin/index.php?option=com_content&view=category&layout =blog&id=45&Itemid=103.

Molina Enríquez, Andrés. [1909] 2004. "Los grandes problemas nacionales." Ali-cante: Biblioteca Virtual Miguel de Cervantes.

Monahan, Michael J. 2011. *The Creolizing Subject: Race, Reason, and the Politics of Purity.* New York: Fordham University Press.

Montagu, Ashley. 1942. *Man's Most Dangerous Myth: The Fallacy of Race.* New York: Columbia University Press.

Montoya, Michael J. 2011. *Making the Mexican Diabetic: Race, Science, and the Genetics of Inequality.* Berkeley: University of California Press.

Morales, Mary Luz, and Esperanza Niño Córdoba. 2009. *Identificación de cadáveres en la práctica forense.* Bogotá: Instituto Nacional de Medicina Legal y Ciencias Forenses.

Moreno, Andrés, and Karla Sandoval. 2013. "Diversidad genómica en México: Pasado indígena y mestizaje." *Cuicuilco* 20 (58): 249–75.

Moreno-Estrada, Andrés, Christopher R. Gignoux, Juan Carlos Fernández-López, et al. 2014. "The Genetics of Mexico Recapitulates Native American Substruc-ture and Affects Biomedical Traits." *Science* 344 (6189): 1280–85.

Moreno Figueroa, Mónica. 2008. "Historically-Rooted Transnationalism: Slighted-ness and the Experience of Racism in Mexican Families." *Journal of Intercultural Studies* 29 (3): 283–97.

———. 2010. "Distributed Intensities: Whiteness, Mestizaje and the Logics of Mexican Racism." *Ethnicities* 10 (3): 387–401.

————. 2012. " 'Linda Morenita': Skin Colour, Beauty and the Politics of Mestizaje in Mexico." In *Cultures of Colour: Visual, Material, Textual*, edited by Chris Horrocks, 167–80. Oxford: Berghahn Books.

————. 2013. "Displaced Looks: The Lived Experience of Beauty and Racism." *Feminist Theory* 14 (2): 137–51.

Moreno Figueroa, Mónica, and Emiko Saldívar. 2015. " 'We Are Not Racists, We Are Mexicans': Privilege, Nationalism and Post-Race Ideology in Mexico." *Critical Sociology*. Accessed June 18, 2015. http://crs.sagepub.com/content/early/2015/06/09/0896920515591296.abstract.

Mörner, Magnus. 1967. *Race Mixture in the History of Latin America*. Boston: Little, Brown.

Morning, Ann. 2008. "Ethnic Classification in Global Perspective: A Cross-National Survey of the 2000 Census Round." *Population Research and Policy Review* 27 (2): 239–72.

Mosquera Rosero-Labbé, Claudia, and Luiz Claudio Barcelos, eds. 2007. *Afro-reparaciones: Memorias de la esclavitud y justicia reparativa para negros, afrocolombianos y raizales*. Bogotá: Universidad Nacional de Colombia.

Mosquera Rosero-Labbé, Claudia, and Ruby Ester León Díaz, eds. 2010. *Acciones afirmativas y ciudadanía diferenciada étnico-racial negra, afrocolombiana, palenquera y raizal: Entre Bicentenarios de las Independencias y Constitución de 1991*. Bogotá: Universidad Nacional de Colombia.

Moutinho, Laura. 2004. *Razão, "cor" e desejo: Uma análise comparativa sobre relacionamentos afetivo-sexuais "inter-raciais" no Brasil e África do Sul*. São Paulo: Editora da UNESP.

Müller-Wille, Staffan. 2010. "Claude Lévi-Strauss on Race, History and Genetics." *BioSocieties* 5 (3): 330–47.

Munanga, Kabengele. 2004. "A difícil tarefa de definir quem é negro no Brasil." *Estudos Avançados* 18:51–66.

————. 2005. "Algumas considerações sobre 'raça,' ação afirmativa e identidade negra no Brasil: Fundamentos antropológicos." *Revista USP* 68:46–57.

Munguia, Damaris. 2009. *No heredes la diabetes*. Diabetes Bienestar y Salud. Accessed March 27, 2015. http://www.diabetesbienestarysalud.com/2009/09/no-heredes-la-diabetes/.

Muñoz Rojas, Catalina, ed. 2011. *Los problemas de la raza en Colombia: Más allá del problema racial: El determinismo geográfico y las "dolencias sociales."* Bogotá: Editorial Universidad del Rosario.

Murdoch, H. Adlai. 2013. "Édouard Glissant's Creolized World Vision: From Resistance and Relation to *Opacité*." *Callaloo* 36 (4): 875–90.

Nadais, Inês. 2000. "Os genes de Cabral." *Público*, March 21.

Nagel, Joane. 2003. *Race, Ethnicity, and Sexuality: Intimate Intersections, Forbidden Frontiers*. Oxford: Oxford University Press.

Nascimento, Alexandre do, Carla Patrícia Frade Nogueira Lopes, Carlos Alberto Medeiros, et al. 2008. *120 anos da luta pela igualdade racial no Brasil: Manifesto em defesa*

da justiça e constitucionalidade das cotas. Accessed September 25, 2014. http://media
.folha.uol.com.br/cotidiano/2008/05/13/stf_manifesto_13_maio_2008.pdf.

Nash, Catherine. 2004. "Genetic Kinship." *Cultural Studies* 18 (1): 1–33.

———. 2015. *Genetic Geographies: The Trouble with Ancestry.* Minneapolis: University of
Minnesota Press.

Nash, Gary. 1995. "The Hidden History of Mestizo America." *Journal of American History* 82 (3): 941–64.

National Academy of Sciences. 2005. *An International Perspective on Advancing Technologies and Strategies for Managing Dual-Use Risks: Report of a Workshop.* Washington,
DC: National Academies Press.

Nelkin, Dorothy, and Susan Lindee. 1995. *The DNA Mystique: The Gene as Cultural Icon.*
New York: W. H. Freeman.

Nelson, Alondra. 2008. "Bio Science: Genetic Genealogy Testing and the Pursuit of
African Ancestry." *Social Studies of Science* 38 (5): 759–83.

Nelson, Diane M. 1999. *A Finger in the Wound: Body Politics in Quincentennial Guatemala.*
Berkeley: University of California Press.

Nemogá S., Gabriel Ricardo. 2006. "Marco jurídico de la investigación científica y
tecnológica sobre genoma humano en Colombia." In *Panorama sobre la legislación
en materia de genoma humano en América Latina y el Caribe,* edited by Diego Valadés
and Alya Saada, 183–230. Mexico City: Universidad Nacional Autónoma de
México, Red Latinoamericana y del Caribe de Bioética de la UNESCO.

Newitz, Annalee. 2016. *The Caste System Has Left Its Mark on Indians' Genomes.* Ars Technica. Accessed February 23, 2016. http://arstechnica.com/science/2016/01/the
-caste-system-has-left-its-mark-on-indians-genomes/.

New Scientist. 2006. "Cracking Colombia's Genetic Mystery." *New Scientist,* April 29.

Nichols, Elizabeth Gackstetter. 2013. " 'Decent Girls with Good Hair': Beauty, Morality and Race in Venezuela." *Feminist Theory* 14 (2): 171–85.

Nissen, Lowell. 1997. *Teleological Language in the Life Sciences.* Lanham, MD: Rowman
and Littlefield Publishers.

Nogueira, Oracy. [1959] 2008. "Skin Color and Social Class." *Vibrant* 5 (1): xxix–li.

Noguera, Carlos Ernesto. 2003. *Medicina y política: Discurso médico y prácticas higiénicas
durante la primera mitad del siglo XX en Colombia.* Medellín: Fondo Editorial Universidad EAFIT.

Ocampo López, Javier. 1988. *Las fiestas y el folclor en Colombia.* Bogotá: El Ancora
Editores.

O Globo. 2011a. "Genética derruba teses racialistas." *O Globo,* February 19, 6.

———. 2011b. "Um país mais europeu: Genética de brasileiros revela menor ancestralidade negra e índia." *O Globo,* February 18, 1.

Olarte Sierra, María Fernanda, and Adriana Díaz del Castillo H. 2013. " 'We Are All
the Same, We All Are Mestizos': Imagined Populations and Nations in Genetic
Research in Colombia." *Science as Culture* 23 (2): 226–52.

Oppenheimer, Stephen. 2003. *Out of Eden: The Peopling of the World.* London:
Constable.

Ortega Guerrero, Marisol. 1993. "Humana expedición." *El Tiempo*, February 1.

Ottenberg, Ruben. 1925. "A Classification of Human Races Based on Geographic Distribution of the Blood Group." *Journal of the American Medical Association* 84 (19): 1393–95.

Ottensooser, Friedrich. 1944. "Cálculo do grau de mistura racial através dos grupos sangüíneos." *Revista Brasileira de Biologia* 4:531–37.

———. 1962. "Analysis of trihybrid populations." *American Journal of Human Genetics* 14:278–80.

Oxford Ancestors. 2015. *Tribes of Britain Service*. Accessed April 23, 2015. http://www .oxfordancestors.com/component/page,shop.product_details/flypage,flypage /product_id,40/category_id,7/option,com_virtuemart/Itemid,67/.

Páez Pérez, Carlos, and Kurt Freudenthal. 1944. "Grupos sanguíneos de los Indios Sibundoy, Santiagueños, Kuaiker e Indios y mestizos de los alrededores de Pasto." *Revista del Instituto Etnológico Nacional* 1:411–15.

Palha, Teresinha de Jesus Brabo Ferreira, Elzemar Martins Ribeiro-Rodrigues, Ândrea Ribeiro-dos-Santos, et al. 2011. "Male Ancestry Structure and Interethnic Admixture in African-Descent Communities from the Amazon as Revealed by Y-Chromosome STRs." *American Journal of Physical Anthropology* 144 (3): 471–78.

Palmié, Stephan. 2007. "Genomics, Divination and 'Racecraft.'" *American Ethnologist* 34 (2): 205–22.

Pálsson, Gísli. 2007. *Anthropology and the New Genetics*. Cambridge: Cambridge University Press.

Papastergiadis, Nikos. 1997. "Tracing Hybridity in Theory." In *Debating Cultural Hybridity: Multi-Cultural Identities and the Politics of Anti-Racism*, edited by Tariq Madood and Pnina Werbner, 257–81. London: Zed Books.

Paredes, Manuel, Aida Galindo, Margarita Bernal, et al. 2003. "Analysis of the CODIS Autosomal STR Loci in Four Main Colombian Regions." *Forensic Science International* 137 (1): 67–73.

Parra, Flavia C., Roberto C. Amado, José R. Lambertucci, et al. 2003. "Color and Genomic Ancestry in Brazilians." *Proceedings of the National Academy of Sciences of the United States of America* 100 (1): 177–82.

Patterson, Nick, Desiree C. Petersen, Richard E. van der Ross, et al. 2010. "Genetic Structure of a Unique Admixed Population: Implications for Medical Research." *Human Molecular Genetics* 19 (3): 411–19.

Paul, Diane B. 1995. *Controlling Human Heredity: 1865 to the Present*. Atlantic Highlands, NJ: Humanities Press.

Paz, Octavio. 1950. *El laberinto de la soledad*. Mexico City: Cuadernos Americanos.

Pena, Sérgio D. J. 2002a. "Há uma base objetiva para definir o conceito de raça?" *Folha de São Paulo*, December 21.

———, ed. 2002b. *Homo brasilis: Aspectos genéticos, lingüísticos, históricos e socioantropológicos da formação do povo brasileiro*. Ribeirão Preto: FUNPEC-RP.

———. 2005. "Razões para banir o conceito de raça da medicina brasileira." *História, Ciências, Saúde—Manguinhos* 12 (2): 321–46.

———. 2007. À flor da pele—reflexões de um geneticista. São Paulo: Vieira and Lent.

———. 2008. Humanidade sem raças? São Paulo: Publifolha.

———. 2012. We R No Race. YouTube. Accessed January 21, 2015. https://www.youtube.com/watch?v=XuEOXwW6K88.

Pena, Sérgio D. J., and Telma S. Birchal. 2006. "A inexistência biológica versus a existência social de raças humanas: pode a ciência instruir o etos social?" Revista USP 68:10–21.

Pena, Sérgio D. J., and Maria Cátira Bortolini. 2004. "Pode a genética definir quem deve se beneficiar das cotas universitárias e demais ações afirmativas?" Estudos Avanzados 18 (50): 31–50.

Pena, Sérgio D. J., Denise R. Carvalho-Silva, Juliana Alves-Silva, et al. 2000. "Retrato molecular do Brasil." Ciência Hoje 159:16–25.

Pena, Sérgio D. J., Giuliano Di Pietro, Mateus Fuchshuber-Moraes, et al. 2011. "The Genomic Ancestry of Individuals from Different Geographical Regions of Brazil Is More Uniform Than Expected." PLoS One 6 (2): e17063.

Pena, Sérgio D. J., Fabricio R. Santos, Nestor O. Bianchi, et al. 1995. "A Major Founder Y-Chromosome Haplotype in Amerindians." Nature Genetics 11 (1): 15–16.

Pescatello, Ann M., ed. 1973. Female and Male in Latin America. Pittsburgh: University of Pittsburgh Press.

Pinho, Osmundo de Araújo. 2005. "Etnografias do brau: Corpo, masculinidade e raça na reafricanização em Salvador." Revista Estudos Feministas 13 (1): 127–45.

Pinto, Elisabete Aparecida, and Fernando Luiz Lupinacci. 2008. "Programa de atenção integral às pessoas com doenças falciformes e outras hemoglobinopatias da cidade de São Paulo." São Paulo: Área Técnica de Saúde da População Negra, Coordenação de Desenvolvimento de Programas e Políticas de Saúde, Município de São Paulo.

Pinto, Laélia Maria, Cristiane Lommez de Oliveira, Luciana Lara dos Santos, et al. 2014. "Molecular Characterization and Population Genetics of Non-CODIS Microsatellites Used for Forensic Applications in Brazilian Populations." Forensic Science International: Genetics 9 (March): e16–e17.

Pohl-Valero, Stefan. 2014. " 'La Raza Entra por la Boca': Energy, Diet, and Eugenics in Colombia, 1890–1940." Hispanic American Historical Review 94 (3): 455–86.

Portal da Copa. 2012. Copa do Mundo impulsiona estudo de genética contra o racismo. Accessed February 20, 2015. http://www.copa2014.gov.br/pt-br/noticia/copa-do-mundo-impulsiona-estudo-de-genetica-contra-o-racismo.

Postero, Nancy Grey. 2007. Now We Are Citizens: Indigenous Politics in Postmulticultural Bolivia. Stanford, CA: Stanford University Press.

Powers, Karen Vieira. 2005. Women in the Crucible of Conquest: The Gendered Genesis of Spanish American Society, 1500–1600. Albuquerque: University of New Mexico Press.

Pravaz, Natasha. 2003. "Brazilian Mulatice: Performing Race, Gender, and the Nation." Journal of Latin American Anthropology 8 (1): 116–46.

Psacharopoulos, George, and Harry Anthony Patrinos. 1994. "Indigenous People and Poverty in Latin America." Washington, DC: World Bank.

Pujol, Nicole. 1970–71. "La Raza Negra en el Chocó: Antropología Física." *Revista Colombiana de Antropología* 15:256–92.

Quintero Restrepo, Mónica. 2013. "Antioqueños en plural." *El Colombiano*, August 9.

Radcliffe, Sarah. 1990. "Ethnicity, Patriarchy and Incorporation into the Nation: Female Migrants as Domestic Servants in Southern Peru." *Environment and Planning D: Society and Space* 8 (4): 379–93.

Radcliffe, Sarah, and Andrea Pequeño. 2010. "Ethnicity, Development and Gender: Tsáchila Indigenous Women in Ecuador." *Development and Change* 41 (6): 983–1016.

Raghavan, Maanasa, Pontus Skoglund, Kelly E. Graf, et al. 2014. "Upper Palaeolithic Siberian Genome Reveals Dual Ancestry of Native Americans." *Nature* 505 (7481): 87–91.

Rahier, Jean. 2003. "Racist Stereotypes and the Embodiment of Blackness: Some Narratives of Female Sexuality in Quito, Ecuador." In *Millennial Ecuador: Critical Essays on Cultural Transformations and Social Dynamics*, edited by Norman Whitten, 296–324. Iowa City: University of Iowa Press.

———, ed. 2012. *Black Social Movements in Latin America: From Monocultural Mestizaje to Multiculturalism*. New York: Palgrave Macmillan.

Ramos, Alcida. 1998. *Indigenism: Ethnic Politics in Brazil*. Madison: University of Wisconsin Press.

Raoult, Didier. 2010. "The Post-Darwinist Rhizome of Life." *The Lancet* 375 (9709): 104–5.

Rapp, Rayna. 1999. *Testing Women, Testing the Fetus: The Social Impact of Amniocentesis in America*. London: Routledge.

Rappaport, Joanne. 2014. *The Disappearing Mestizo: Configuring Difference in the Colonial New Kingdom of Granada*. Durham, NC: Duke University Press.

Reardon, Jenny. 2005. *Race to the Finish: Identity and Governance in an Age of Genomics*. Princeton, NJ: Princeton University Press.

———. 2007. "Democratic Mis-Haps: The Problem of Democratization in a Time of Biopolitics." *BioSocieties* 2 (2): 239–56.

———. 2008. "Race without Salvation: Beyond the Science/Society Divide in Genomic Studies of Human Diversity." In *Revisiting Race in a Genomic Age*, edited by Barbara A. Koenig, Sandra Soo-Jin Lee, and Sarah S. Richardson, 304–19. New Brunswick, NJ: Rutgers University Press.

Reich, David, Nick Patterson, Desmond Campbell, et al. 2012. "Reconstructing Native American Population History." *Nature* 488 (7411): 370–74.

Reichel-Dolmatoff, Gerardo, and Alicia Reichel-Dolmatoff. 1944. "Grupos sanguíneos entre los indios pijao de Tolima." *Revista del Instituto Etnológico Nacional* 1:507–20.

Restrepo, Eduardo. 2007. "Imágenes del 'negro' y nociones de raza en Colombia a principios del siglo XX." *Revista de Estudios Sociales* 27:46–61.

————. 2013a. *Etnización de la negridad: La invención de las "comunidades negras" como grupo étnico en Colombia*. Popayán: Universidad del Cauca.

————, ed. 2013b. *Estudios afrocolombianos hoy: Aportes a un campo transdisciplinario*. Popayán: Universidad del Cauca.

————. 2014. "La antropología física o biológica en Colombia: Trayectorias e imaginación de la diferencia." Unpublished manuscript, Bogotá.

Restrepo, Eduardo, Ernesto Schwartz-Marín, and Roosbelinda Cárdenas. 2014. "Nation and Difference in the Genetic Imagination of Colombia." In *Mestizo Genomics: Race Mixture, Nation, and Science in Latin America*, edited by Peter Wade, Carlos López Beltrán, Eduardo Restrepo, and Ricardo Ventura Santos, 55–84. Durham, NC: Duke University Press.

Restrepo, Luis Antonio. 1988. "El pensamiento social e histórico." In *Historia de Antioquia*, edited by Jorge Orlando Melo, 373–82. Medellín: Suramericana de Seguros.

Ribeiro, Guilherme Galvarros Bueno Lobo, Reginaldo Ramos De Lima, Cláudia Emília Vieira Wiezel, et al. 2009. "Afro-Derived Brazilian Populations: Male Genetic Constitution Estimated by Y-Chromosomes STRS and AluYAP Element Polymorphisms." *American Journal of Human Biology* 21 (3): 354–56.

Ribeiro, Gustavo Lins. 2005. "What Is Cosmopolitanism?" *Vibrant—Virtual Brazilian Anthropology* 2 (1/2). Accessed November 10, 2015. http://www.vibrant.org.br /issues/v2n1/gustavo-lins-ribeiro-what-is-cosmopolitanism/.

Ribeiro, Silvia. 2005. "La biopiratería humana como espectáculo." *La Jornada*, June 25.

————. 2009. "La farsa del mapa genómico de los mexicanos." *La Jornada*, May 23.

Ribeiro Corossacz, Valeria. 2015. "Whiteness, Maleness and Power: A Study in Rio de Janeiro." *Latin American and Caribbean Ethnic Studies* 10 (2): 157–79.

Richardson, Susan S., and Hallam Stevens, eds. 2015. *Postgenomics: Perspectives on Biology after the Genome*. Durham, NC: Duke University Press.

Risch, Neil, Esteban Burchard, Elad Ziv, et al. 2002. "Categorization of Humans in Biomedical Research: Genes, Race and Disease." *Genome Biology* 3 (7): comment 2007.1–2007.12.

Ritvo, Harriet. 1997. *The Platypus and the Mermaid and Other Figments of the Classifying Imagination*. Cambridge, MA: Harvard University Press.

Rivera-Servera, Ramón. 2012. *Performing Queer Latinidad: Dance, Sexuality, Politics*. Ann Arbor: University of Michigan Press.

Roberts, Dorothy. 2011. *Fatal Invention: How Science, Politics, and Big Business Re-Create Race in the Twenty-First Century*. New York: New Press.

Roberts, Elizabeth F. S. 2012. *God's Laboratory: Assisted Reproduction in the Andes*. Berkeley: University of California Press.

Rodríguez, Clara E. 2000. *Changing Race: Latinos, the Census, and the History of Ethnicity in the United States*. New York: New York University Press.

Rodriguez, Hector, Elisa de Rodriguez, Alvar Loria, et al. 1963. "Studies on Several Genetic Hematological Traits of the Mexican Population. V: Distribution of Blood Group Antigens in Nahuas, Yaquis, Tarahumaras, Tarascos and Mixtecos." *Human Biology* 35 (3): 350–60.

Rodríguez, José Vicente. 2004. *La antropología forense en la identificación humana*. Bogotá: Universidad Nacional.

Rodríguez, Miguel. 2004. *Celebración de "la Raza": Una historia comparativa del 12 de octubre*. Mexico City: Universidad Iberoamericana.

Rodriguez, Richard. 2002. *Brown: The Last Discovery of America*. New York: Viking.

Rodríguez Garavito, César, Tatiana Alfonso Sierra, and Isabel Cavelier Adarve. 2009. *Raza y derechos humanos en Colombia: Informe sobre discriminación racial y derechos de la población afrocolombiana*. Bogotá: Universidad de los Andes, Facultad de Derecho, Centro de Investigaciones Sociojurídicas (CIJUS), Observatorio de Discriminación Racial, Ediciones Uniandes.

Rojas, Winston, María Victoria Parra, Omer Campo, et al. 2010. "Genetic Make Up and Structure of Colombian Populations by Means of Uniparental and Biparental DNA Markers." *American Journal of Physical Anthropology* 143 (1): 13–20.

Rose, Nikolas 2007. *The Politics of Life Itself: Biomedicine, Power and Subjectivity in the Twenty-First Century*. Princeton, NJ: Princeton University Press.

Rose, Nikolas, and Peter Miller. 2008. *Governing the Present: Administering Economic, Social and Personal Life*. Cambridge: Polity.

Rose, Nikolas, and Carlos Novas. 2005. "Biological Citizenship." In *Global Assemblages: Technology, Politics, and Ethics as Anthropological Problems*, edited by Aihwa Ong and Stephen J. Collier, 439–63. Oxford: Blackwell Publishing.

Rubi-Castellanos, Rodrigo, Gabriela Martínez-Cortés, José Francisco Muñoz-Valle, et al. 2009. "Pre-Hispanic Mesoamerican Demography Approximates the Present-Day Ancestry of Mestizos throughout the Territory of Mexico." *American Journal of Physical Anthropology* 139 (3): 284–94.

Rubicz, Rohina C., Phillip Melton, and Michael H. Crawford. 2006. "Molecular Markers in Anthropological Genetic Studies." In *Anthropological Genetics: Theory, Methods and Applications*, edited by Michael H. Crawford, 141–86. Cambridge: Cambridge University Press.

Ruiz Linares, Andrés. 2014. "How Genes Have Illuminated the History of Early Americans and Latino Americans." In *Human Variation: A Genetic Perspective on Diversity, Race, and Medicine*, edited by Aravinda Chakravarti, 87–96. Cold Spring Harbor, NY: Cold Spring Harbor Laboratory Press.

Ruiz-Linares, Andrés, Kaustubh Adhikari, Victor Acuña-Alonzo, et al. 2014. "Admixture in Latin America: Geographic Structure, Phenotypic Diversity and Self-Perception of Ancestry Based on 7,342 Individuals." *PLoS Genetics* 10 (9): e1004572.

Safford, Frank, and Marco Palacios. 2002. *Colombia: Fragmented Land, Divided Society*. Oxford: Oxford University Press.

Salazar-Flores, J., F. Zuñiga-Chiquette, R. Rubi-Castellanos, et al. 2015. "Admixture and Genetic Relationships of Mexican Mestizos Regarding Latin American and Caribbean Populations Based on 13 CODIS-STRs." *HOMO—Journal of Comparative Human Biology* 66 (1): 44–59.

Saldaña-Tejeda, Abril. 2012. " 'Why Should I Not Take an Apple or a Fruit if I Wash Their Underwear?' Food, Social Classification and Paid Domestic Work in Mexico." *Journal of Intercultural Studies* 33 (2): 121–37.

Saldanha, P. H. 1957. "Gene Flow from White into Negro Populations in Brazil." *American Journal of Human Genetics* 9 (4): 299–309.

———. 1962. "Race Mixture among Northeastern Brazilian Populations." *American Anthropologist* 64 (4): 751–59.

Saldívar, Emiko. 2011. "Everyday Practices of Indigenismo: An Ethnography of Anthropology and the State in Mexico." *Journal of Latin American and Caribbean Anthropology* 16 (1): 67–89.

———. 2014. " 'It's Not Race, It's Culture': Untangling Racial Politics in Mexico." *Latin American and Caribbean Ethnic Studies* 9 (1): 89–108.

Salek, Silvia. 2007. BBC *Delves into Brazilians' Roots.* BBC News. Accessed February 20, 2015. http://news.bbc.co.uk/1/hi/6284806.stm.

Salinas Abdala, Yamile. 2014. "Los derechos territoriales de los grupos étnicos: ¿Un compromiso social, una obligación constitucional o una obligación constitucional o una tarea hecha a medias?" *Punto de Encuentro* 67:1–39.

Salzano, Francisco M., and Maria Cátira Bortolini. 2002. *The Evolution and Genetics of Latin American Populations.* Cambridge: Cambridge University Press.

Salzano, Francisco Mauro, and Newton Freire-Maia. 1970. *Problems in Human Biology: A Study of Brazilian Populations.* Detroit: Wayne State University Press.

Samper, José María. 1861. *Ensayo sobre las revoluciones políticas y la condición social de las repúblicas colombianas (hispano-americanas): Con un apéndice sobre la orografía y la población de la Confederación Granadina.* Paris: Imprenta de E. Thunot y Cia.

———. 1980. "Un viaje completo." In *Crónica grande del río de la Magdalena,* edited by Aníbal Noguera Mendoza, 87–100. Bogotá: Sol y Luna.

Sanchez, Margarita, and Maurice Bryan. 2003. "Afro-Descendants, Discrimination and Economic Exclusion in Latin America." London: Minority Rights Group.

Sanders, James E. 2004. *Contentious Republicans: Popular Politics, Race, and Class in Nineteenth-Century Colombia.* Durham, NC: Duke University Press.

———. 2014. *The Vanguard of the Atlantic World: Creating Modernity, Nation, and Democracy in Nineteenth-Century Latin America.* Durham, NC: Duke University Press.

Sandoval, Carlos, Antonio De la Hoz, and Emilio Yunis. 1993. "Estructura genética de la población colombiana: Análisis del mestizaje." *Revista de la Facultad de Medicina, Universidad Nacional de Colombia* 41 (1): 3–14.

Santos, Josenaide Engracia dos, and Giovanna Cristina Siqueira Santos. 2013. "Narrativas dos profissionais da atenção primária sobre a política nacional de saúde integral da população negra." *Saúde em Debate* 37:563–70.

Santos, Ricardo Ventura. 1996. "Da morfología ás moléculas, de raça a populacão: Trajetórias conceituais em antropologia física no século XX." In *Raça, ciência e sociedade,* edited by Marcos Chor Maio and Ricardo Ventura Santos, 125–40. Rio de Janeiro: Editora Fiocruz.

————. 2002. "Indigenous Peoples, Postcolonial Contexts and Genomic Research in the Late 20th Century: A View from Amazonia (1960–2000)." *Critique of Anthropology* 22 (1): 81–104.

Santos, Ricardo Ventura, Peter H. Fry, Simone Monteiro, et al. 2009. "Color, Race and Genomic Ancestry in Brazil: Dialogues between Anthropology and Genetics." *Current Anthropology* 50 (6): 787–819.

Santos, Ricardo Ventura, Michael Kent, and Verlan Valle Gaspar Neto. 2014. "From 'Degeneration' to 'Meeting Point': Historical Views on Race, Mixture and the Biological Diversity of the Brazilian population." In *Mestizo Genomics: Race Mixture, Nation, and Science in Latin America*, edited by Peter Wade, Carlos López Beltrán, Eduardo Restrepo, and Ricardo Ventura Santos, 33–54. Durham NC: Duke University Press.

Santos, Ricardo Ventura, Susan Lindee, and Vanderlei Sebastião de Souza. 2014. "Varieties of the Primitive: Human Biological Diversity Studies in Cold War Brazil (1962–1970)." *American Anthropologist* 116 (4): 723–35.

Santos, Ricardo Ventura, and Marcos Chor Maio. 2005. "Anthropology, Race, and the Dilemmas of Identity in the Age of Genomics." *História, Ciências, Saúde—Manguinhos* 12 (2): 1–22.

Santos, Ricardo Ventura, Glaucia Oliveira da Silva, and Sahra Gibbon. 2015. "Pharmacogenomics, Human Genetic Diversity and the Incorporation and Rejection of Color/Race in Brazil." *BioSocieties* 10:48–69.

Schaffer, Gavin. 2008. *Racial Science and British Society, 1930–62*. Basingstoke, UK: Palgrave Macmillan.

Schramm, Katharina, David Skinner, and Richard Rottenburg, eds. 2012. *Identity Politics and the New Genetics: Re/Creating Categories of Difference and Belonging*. Oxford: Berghahn Books.

Schwarcz, Lilia Moritz. 1999. *The Spectacle of the Races: Scientists, Institutions, and the Race Question in Brazil, 1870–1930*. Translated by Lilia Guyer. New York: Farrar, Straus and Giroux.

Schwartz Marín, Ernesto. 2011a. "Genomic Sovereignty and the Mexican Genome: An Ethnography of Postcolonial Biopolitics." PhD diss., University of Exeter, Exeter.

————. 2011b. "Protegiendo el 'mextizaje': El INMEGEN y la construcción de la soberanía genómica. In *Genes (&) mestizos: Genómica y raza en la biomedicina mexicana*, edited by Carlos López Beltrán, 155–84. Mexico City: Ficticia Editorial.

Schwartz-Marín, Ernesto, and Eduardo Restrepo. 2013. "Biocoloniality, Governance, and the Protection of 'Genetic Identities' in Mexico and Colombia." *Sociology* 47 (5): 993–1010.

Schwartz-Marín, Ernesto, and Peter Wade. 2015. "Explaining the Visible and the Invisible: Lay Knowledge of Genetics, Ancestry, Physical Appearance and Race in Colombia." *Social Studies of Science* 45 (6): 886–906.

Schwartz-Marín, Ernesto, Peter Wade, Arely Cruz-Santiago, et al. 2015. "Colombian Forensic Genetics as a Form of Public Science: The Role of Race, Nation and Common Sense in the Stabilization of DNA Populations." *Social Studies of Science* 45 (6): 862–85.

Seguín, Béatrice, Billie-Jo Hardy, Peter A. Singer, et al. 2008. "Genomics, Public Health and Developing Countries: The Case of the Mexican National Institute of Genomic Medicine (INMEGEN)." *Nature Reviews Genetics* 9 (Supplements): s5–s9.

Seigel, Micol. 2005. "Beyond Compare: Comparative Method after the Transnational Turn." *Radical History Review* 2005 (91): 62–90.

———. 2009. *Uneven Encounters: Making Race and Nation in Brazil and the United States.* Durham, NC: Duke University Press.

Seitler, Dana. 2008. *Atavistic Tendencies: The Culture of Science in American Modernity.* Minneapolis: University of Minnesota Press.

Seldin, Michael F. 2007. "Admixture Mapping as a Tool in Gene Discovery." *Current Opinion in Genetics and Development* 17 (3): 177–81.

Sexton, Jared. 2008. *Amalgamation Schemes: Antiblackness and the Critique of Multiracialism.* Minneapolis: University of Minnesota Press.

Sheriff, Robin E. 2003. "Embracing Race: Deconstructing Mestiçagem in Rio de Janeiro." *Journal of Latin American Anthropology* 8 (1): 86–115.

Sieder, Rachel. 2002a. "Recognising Indigenous Law and the Politics of State Formation in Mesoamerica." In *Multiculturalism in Latin America: Indigenous Rights, Diversity and Democracy,* edited by Rachel Sieder, 184–207. Basingstoke, UK: Palgrave Macmillan.

———, ed. 2002b. *Multiculturalism in Latin America: Indigenous Rights, Diversity and Democracy.* Basingstoke, UK: Palgrave Macmillan.

SIGMA Type 2 Diabetes Consortium. 2014. "Sequence Variants in SLC16A11 Are a Common Risk Factor for Type 2 Diabetes in Mexico." *Nature* 506 (7486): 97–101.

Silva, Nelson do Valle. 1985. "Updating the Cost of Not Being White in Brazil." In *Race, Class and Power in Brazil,* edited by Pierre-Michel Fontaine, 42–55. Los Angeles: Center of Afro-American Studies, University of California.

Silva-Zolezzi, Irma, Alfredo Hidalgo-Miranda, Jesus Estrada-Gil, et al. 2009. "Analysis of Genomic Diversity in Mexican Mestizo Populations to Develop Genomic Medicine in Mexico." *Proceedings of the National Academy of Sciences* 106 (21): 8611–16.

Simpson, Amelia. 1993. *Xuxa: The Mega-Marketing of Gender, Race and Modernity.* Philadelphia: Temple University Press.

Skidmore, Thomas. 1974. *Black into White: Race and Nationality in Brazilian Thought.* New York: Oxford University Press.

———. 1993. "Bi-Racial USA vs. Multi-Racial Brazil: Is the Contrast Still Valid?" *Journal of Latin American Studies* 25 (2): 373–86.

Skoglund, Pontus, Swapan Mallick, Maria Catira Bortolini, et al. 2015. "Genetic Evidence for Two Founding Populations of the Americas." *Nature* 525 (7567): 104–8.

Smart, Andrew. 2005. "Practical Concerns That Arise from Using Race/Ethnicity as 'The Most Reliable Proxy Available.'" *Critical Public Health* 15 (1): 75–76.

Smart, Andrew, Richard Tutton, Paul Martin, et al. 2008. "The Standardization of Race and Ethnicity in Biomedical Science Editorials and UK Biobanks. *Social Studies of Science* 38 (3): 407–23.

Smedley, Audrey. 1993. *Race in North America: Origin and Evolution of a Worldview*. Boulder, CO: Westview Press.

Smith, Carol A. 1997. "The Symbolics of Blood: Mestizaje in the Americas." *Identities: Global Studies in Power and Culture* 3 (4): 495–521.

Smith, Lindsay. 2013. " 'Genetics Is a Study in Faith': Forensic DNA, Kinship Analysis, and the Ethics of Care in Post-Conflict Latin America." *Scholar and Feminist Online* 11 (3). Accessed November 6, 2015. http://sfonline.barnard.edu/life-un-ltd -feminism-bioscience-race/genetics-is-a-study-in-faith-forensic-dna-kinship -analysis-and-the-ethics-of-care-in-post-conflict-latin-america/.

Smith, T. Lynn. 1966. "The Racial Composition of Colombia." *Journal of Inter-American Studies* 8:213–35.

Sommer, Doris. 1991. *Foundational Fictions: The National Romances of Latin America*. Berkeley: University of California Press.

Sommer, Marianne. 2012. " 'It's a Living History, Told by the Real Survivors of the Times—DNA': Anthropological Genetics in the Tradition of Biology as Applied History." In *Genetics and the Unsettled Past: The Collision of DNA, Race, and History*, edited by Keith Wailoo, Alondra Nelson, and Catherine Lee, 225–46. New Brunswick, NJ: Rutgers University Press.

———. 2015. "Population-Genetic Trees, Maps, and Narratives of the Great Human Diasporas." *History of the Human Sciences* 28 (5): 108–45.

Souza, Vanderlei Sebastião de, and Ricardo Ventura Santos. 2014. "The Emergence of Human Population Genetics and Narratives about the Formation of the Brazilian Nation (1950–1960)." *Studies in History and Philosophy of Science Part C: Studies in History and Philosophy of Biological and Biomedical Sciences* 47 (Part A): 97–107.

Speed, Shannon. 2005. "Dangerous Discourses: Human Rights and Multiculturalism in Neoliberal Mexico." *PoLAR: Political and Legal Anthropology Review* 28 (1): 29–51.

Speed, Shannon, and Xochitl Leyva Solano. 2008. "Global Discourses on the Local Terrain: Human Rights in Chiapas." In *Human Rights in the Maya Region: Global Politics, Cultural Contentions and Moral Engagements*, edited by Pedro Pitarch, Shannon Speed, and Xochitl Leyva Solano, 207–31. Durham, NC: Duke University Press.

Stack, Sarah. 2008. "DNA Tests to Reveal if Men Descend from Warlord Niall." *Metro*, June 13.

Stepan, Nancy. 1982. *The Idea of Race in Science: Great Britain, 1800–1960*. London: Macmillan in association with St Antony's College, Oxford.

Stepan, Nancy Leys. 1991. " 'The Hour of Eugenics': Race, Gender and Nation in Latin America*. Ithaca, NY: Cornell University Press.

Stern, Alexandra Minna. 2003. "From Mestizophilia to Biotypology: Racialization and Science in Mexico, 1920–1960." In *Race and Nation in Modern Latin America*, edited by Nancy Appelbaum, Anne S. Macpherson, and Karin A. Rosemblatt, 187–210. Chapel Hill, NC: University of North Carolina Press.

———. 2009. "Eugenics and Racial Classification in Modern Mexican America." In *Race and Classification: The Case of Mexican America*, edited by Ilona Katzew and Susan Deans-Smith, 151–73. Stanford, CA: Stanford University Press.

———. 2011. " 'The Hour of Eugenics' in Veracruz, Mexico: Radical Politics, Public Health, and Latin America's Only Sterilization Law." *Hispanic American Historical Review* 91 (3): 431–43.

Stocking, George. 1982. *Race, Culture and Evolution: Essays on the History of Anthropology*. 2nd ed. Chicago: University of Chicago Press.

Stolcke, Verena. 1995. "Talking Culture: New Boundaries, New Rhetorics of Exclusion in Europe." *Current Anthropology* 36 (1): 1–23.

Stoler, Ann Laura. 1995. *Race and the Education of Desire: Foucault's History of Sexuality and the Colonial Order of Things*. Durham, NC: Duke University Press.

———. 2001. "Tense and Tender Ties: The Politics of Comparison in North American History and (Post) Colonial Studies." *Journal of American History* 88 (3): 829–65.

———. 2002. *Carnal Knowledge and Imperial Power: Race and the Intimate in Colonial Rule*. Berkeley: University of California Press.

Strathern, Marilyn. 1992. *After Nature: English Kinship in the Late Twentieth Century*. Cambridge: Cambridge University Press.

Stutzman, Ronald. 1981. "El Mestizaje: An All-Inclusive Ideology of Exclusion." In *Cultural Transformations and Ethnicity in Modern Ecuador*, edited by Norman E. Whitten, 45–94. Urbana: University of Illinois Press.

Suárez-Díaz, Edna. 2014. "Indigenous Populations in Mexico: Medical Anthropology in the Work of Ruben Lisker in the 1960s." *Studies in History and Philosophy of Science Part C: Studies in History and Philosophy of Biological and Biomedical Sciences* 47 (Part A): 108–17.

Suárez Díaz, Edna, and Ana Barahona. 2011. "La nueva ciencia de la nación mestiza: Sangre y genética humana en la posrrevolución mexicana (1945–1967)." In *Genes (&) mestizos: Genómica y raza en la biomedicina mexicana*, edited by Carlos López Beltrán, 65–96. Mexico City: Ficticia Editorial.

———. 2013. "Postwar and Post-Revolution: Medical Genetics and Social Anthropology in Mexico (1945–1970)." In *Human Heredity in the Twentieth Century*, edited by Bernd Gausemeier, Staffan Müller-Wille, and Edmund Ramsden, 101–12. London: Pickering and Chatto.

Suárez Díaz, Reynaldo. 1973. *El hombre, ese recién llegado: Ensayo de antropología física*. Bucaramanga: Universidad Industrial Santander.

Suarez-Kurtz, Guilherme. 2011. "Pharmacogenetics in the Brazilian Population." In *Racial Identities, Genetic Ancestry, and Health in South America: Argentina, Brazil, Colombia, and Uruguay*, edited by Sahra Gibbon, Ricardo Ventura Santos, and Mónica Sans, 121–35. New York: Palgrave Macmillan.

Suarez-Kurtz, Guilherme, and Sergio D. Pena. 2006. "Pharmacogenomics in the Americas: The Impact of Genetic Admixture." *Current Drug Targets* 7 (12): 1649–58.

Suarez-Kurtz, Guilherme, Daniela D. Vargens, Claudio J. Struchiner, et al. 2007. "Self-Reported Skin Color, Genomic Ancestry and the Distribution of GST Polymorphisms." *Pharmacogenetics and Genomics* 17 (9): 765–71.

Sue, Christina A. 2013. *Land of the Cosmic Race: Race Mixture, Racism, and Blackness in Mexico*. New York: Oxford University Press.

Taguieff, Pierre-André. 1990. "The New Cultural Racism in France." *Telos* 83:109–22.

TallBear, Kim. 2007. "Narratives of Race and Indigeneity in the Genographic Project." *Journal of Law, Medicine and Ethics* 35 (3): 412–24.

Tapper, Melbourne. 1999. *In the Blood: Sickle Cell Anemia and the Politics of Race*. Philadelphia: University of Pennsylvania Press.

Tate, Shirley Anne, and Ian Law. 2015. *Caribbean Racisms: Connections and Complexities in the Racialization of the Caribbean Region*. Basingstoke, UK: Palgrave Macmillan.

Taussig, Karen-Sue. 2009. *Ordinary Genomes: Science, Citizenship, and Genetic Identities*. Durham, NC: Duke University Press.

Taylor, Charles, and Amy Gutmann. 1994. *Multiculturalism and "the Politics of Recognition."* Princeton, NJ: Princeton University Press.

Taylor-Alexander, Samuel, and Ernesto Schwartz-Marín. 2013. "Bioprophecy and the Politics of the Present: Notes on the Establishment of Mexico's National Genomics Institute (INMEGEN)." *New Genetics and Society* 32 (4): 333–49.

Telles, Edward E. 2004. *Race in Another America: The Significance of Skin Color in Brazil*. Princeton, NJ: Princeton University Press.

Telles, Edward E., and René Flores. 2013. "Not Just Color: Whiteness, Nation and Status in Latin America." *Hispanic American Historical Review* 93 (3): 411–49.

Telles, Edward E., and Project on Ethnicity and Race in Latin America. 2014. *Pigmentocracies: Ethnicity, Race, and Color in Latin America*. Chapel Hill: University of North Carolina Press.

Templeton, Alan R. 2012. "Gene Flow, Haplotype Patterns and Modern Human Origins." *eLS*. Accessed December 8, 2015. http://dx.doi.org/10.1002/9780470015902.a0020795.pub2.

Thompson, Charis. 2005. *Making Parents: The Ontological Choreography of Reproductive Technologies*. Cambridge, MA: MIT Press.

Todo Colombia. 2005. *Etnias de Colombia*. Accessed May 26, 2015. http://www.todacolombia.com/etnias/etniasdecolombia.html.

Triana, Gloria. 1990. *Aluna: Imagen y memoria de las Jornadas Regionales de Cultura Popular*. Bogotá: Presidencia de la República, Instituto Colombiano de Cultura.

Turner, Jimmy. 2013. "The Tight-Rope between Vulgarity and Chastity: How Middle-Class White Women in the South of Brazil Construct 'Modern' Sexual Identities." *Journal of Gender Studies* 23 (1): 81–92.

———. 2014. "Uma Cultura Atrasada: The Luso-Baroque Manezinha, Hyper-Whiteness, and the Modern Middle Classes in Florianópolis, Brazil." *Journal of Latin American and Caribbean Anthropology* 19 (1): 84–102.

Tutton, Richard. 2007. "Opening the White Box: Exploring the Study of Whiteness in Contemporary Genetics Research." *Ethnic and Racial Studies* 30 (4): 557–69.

Twinam, Ann. 1980. "From Jew to Basque: Ethnic Myths and Antioqueño Entrepreneurship." *Journal of Inter-American Studies* 22:81–107.

———. 1999. *Public Lives, Private Secrets: Gender, Honor, Sexuality and Illegitimacy in Colonial Spanish America.* Stanford, CA: Stanford University Press.

Twine, France Winddance. 1998. *Racism in a Racial Democracy: The Maintenance of White Supremacy in Brazil.* New Brunswick, NJ: Rutgers University Press.

Tyler, Katharine. 2007. "Race, Genetics and Inheritance: Reflections upon the Birth of 'Black' Twins to a 'White' IVF Mother." In *Race, Ethnicity and Nation: Perspectives from Kinship and Genetics*, edited by Peter Wade, 33–51. Oxford: Berghahn Books.

UNESCO. 1950. "The Race Question." Accessed November 6, 2014. http://unesdoc .unesco.org/images/0012/001282/128291eo.pdf.

———. 1952. *The Race Concept: Results of an Inquiry.* Paris: UNESCO.

University of Adelaide. 2016. "Ancient DNA Shows European Wipe-Out of Early Americans." *Science Daily.* Accessed April 3, 2016. https://www.sciencedaily.com /releases/2016/04/160401144502.htm.

Uribe Vergara, Jorge. 2008. "Sociología biológica, eugenesia y biotipología en Colombia y Argentina (1918–1939)." In *Genealogías de la colombianidad: Formaciones discursivas y tecnologías de gobierno en los siglos XIX y XX*, edited by Santiago Castro-Gómez and Eduardo Restrepo, 204–21. Bogotá: Pontificia Universidad Javeriana.

Van Cott, Donna Lee. 2000. *The Friendly Liquidation of the Past: The Politics of Diversity in Latin America.* Pittsburgh: University of Pittsburgh Press.

———. 2006. "Multiculturalism versus Neoliberalism in Latin America." In *Multiculturalism and the Welfare State: Recognition and Redistribution in Contemporary Democracies*, edited by Keith Banting and Will Kymlicka, 272–96. Oxford: Oxford University Press.

van den Berghe, Pierre. 1979. *The Ethnic Phenomenon.* New York: Elsevier.

Vasconcelos, José. [1925] 1997. *The Cosmic Race: A Bilingual Edition.* Translated by Didier T. Jaén. Baltimore: Johns Hopkins University Press.

Velásquez Cepeda, María Cristina. 2000. "Frontiers of Municipal Governability of Oaxaca, Mexico: The Legal Recognition of Usos Y Costumbres in the Election of Indigenous Authorities." In *The Challenge of Diversity: Indigenous Peoples and Reform of the State in Latin America*, edited by Willem Assies, Gemma van der Haar, and André Hoekema, 165–79. Amsterdam: Thela-Thesis.

Velásquez Gómez, Ramiro. 2006. *Los antioqueños son europeos en un 80%.* MedellinStyle .com. Accessed May 7, 2015. http://medellinstyle.com/los-antioquenos-son -europeos.htm.

Vergara Silva, Francisco. 2013. " 'Un asunto de sangre': Juan Comas, el evolucionismo bio-info-molecularizado y las nuevas vidas de la ideología indigenista en México." In *Miradas plurales al fenómeno humano*, edited by Josefina Mansilla Lory and Xabier Lizárraga Cruchaga, 235–65. Mexico City: Instituto Nacional de Antropología e Historia.

Villalobos-Comparán, Marisela, M. Teresa Flores-Dorantes, M. Teresa Villarreal-Molina, et al. 2008. "The FTO Gene Is Associated with Adulthood Obesity in the Mexican Population." *Obesity* 16 (10): 2296–2301.

Villegas, Álvaro. 2014. "El valle del río Magdalena en los discursos letrados de la segunda mitad del siglo XIX: Territorio, enfermedad y trabajo." *Folios* 39:149–59.

Villegas Vélez, Alvaro Andrés. 2005. "Raza y nación en el pensamiento de Luis López de Mesa: Colombia, 1920–1940." *Estudios Políticos* 26:209–32.

Vimieiro-Gomes, Ana Carolina. 2012. "A emergência da biotipologia no Brasil: Medir e classificar a morfologia, a fisiologia e o temperamento do brasileiro na década de 1930." *Boletim do Museu Paraense Emílio Goeldi. Ciências Humanas* 7 (3): 705–19.

Vinson, Ben, III, and Matthew Restall, eds. 2009. *Black Mexico: Race and Society from Colonial to Modern Times.* Albuquerque: University of New Mexico Press.

Viveros Vigoya, Mara. 2002. "Dionysian Blacks: Sexuality, Body, and Racial Order in Colombia." *Latin American Perspectives* 29 (2): 60–77.

———. 2006. "Políticas de sexualidad juvenil y diferencias étnico-raciales en Colombia." *Revista Estudos Feministas* 14 (1): 149–69.

Viveros Vigoya, Mara, and Franklin Gil Hernández. 2006. "De las desigualdades sociales a las diferencias culturales: Género, 'raza' y etnicidad en la Salud Sexual y Reproductiva en Colombia." In *Saberes, culturas y derechos sexuales en Colombia,* edited by Mara Viveros Vigoya, 87–108. Bogotá: Centro de Estudios Sociales, Universidad Nacional de Colombia, Tercer Mundo Editores.

Wade, Peter. 1993. *Blackness and Race Mixture: The Dynamics of Racial Identity in Colombia.* Baltimore: Johns Hopkins University Press.

———. 1995. "The Cultural Politics of Blackness in Colombia." *American Ethnologist* 22 (2): 342–58.

———. 1999. "Representations of Blackness in Colombian Popular Music." In *Representations of Blackness and the Performance of Identities,* edited by Jean M. Rahier, 173–91. Westport, CT: Greenwood Press.

———. 2000. *Music, Race and Nation: Música Tropical in Colombia.* Chicago: University of Chicago Press.

———. 2002a. "The Colombian Pacific in Perspective." *Journal of Latin American Anthropology* 7 (2): 2–33.

———. 2002b. *Race, Nature and Culture: An Anthropological Perspective.* London: Pluto Press.

———. 2004. "Images of Latin American Mestizaje and the Politics of Comparison." *Bulletin of Latin American Research* 23 (1): 355–66.

———. 2005a. "Hybridity Theory and Kinship Thinking." *Cultural Studies* 19 (5): 602–21.

———. 2005b. "Rethinking Mestizaje: Ideology and Lived Experience." *Journal of Latin American Studies* 37:1–19.

———, ed. 2007. *Race, Ethnicity and Nation: Perspectives from Kinship and Genetics.* Oxford: Berghahn Books.

————. 2009. *Race and Sex in Latin America*. London: Pluto Press.

————. 2010. *Race and Ethnicity in Latin America*. 2nd ed. London: Pluto Press.

————. 2011. "Multiculturalismo y racismo." *Revista Colombiana de Antropología* 47 (2): 15–35.

————. 2012a. "Afro-Colombian Social Movements." In *Comparative Perspectives on Afro-Latin America*, edited by Kwame Dixon and John Burdick, 135–55. Gainesville: University Press of Florida.

————. 2012b. "Race, Kinship and the Ambivalence of Identity." In *Identity Politics and the New Genetics: Re/Creating Categories of Difference and Belonging*, edited by Katharina Schramm, David Skinner, and Richard Rottenburg, 79–96. Oxford: Berghahn Books.

————. 2013a. "Articulations of Eroticism and Race: Domestic Service in Latin America." *Feminist Theory* 14 (2): 187–202.

————. 2013b. "Blackness, Indigeneity, Multiculturalism and Genomics in Brazil, Colombia and Mexico." *Journal of Latin American Studies* 45 (2): 205–33.

————. 2013c. "Brazil and Colombia: Comparative Race Relations in South America." In *Racism and Ethnic Relations in the Portuguese-Speaking World*, edited by Francisco Bethencourt and Adrian Pearce, 35–48. Oxford: Oxford University Press, British Academy.

————. 2014. "Conclusion: Race, Multiculturalism, and Genomics in Latin America." In *Mestizo Genomics: Race Mixture, Nation, and Science in Latin America*, edited by Peter Wade, Carlos López Beltrán, Eduardo Restrepo, and Ricardo Ventura Santos, 211–40. Durham, NC: Duke Unversity Press.

————. 2015. *Race: An Introduction*. Cambridge: Cambridge University Press.

Wade, Peter, Vivette García Deister, Michael Kent, and María Fernanda Olarte Sierra. 2014. "Social Categories and Laboratory Practices in Brazil, Colombia, and Mexico: A Comparative Overview." In *Mestizo Genomics: Race Mixture, Nation, and Science in Latin America*, edited by Peter Wade, Carlos López Beltrán, Eduardo Restrepo, and Ricardo Ventura Santos, 183–209. Durham, NC: Duke University Press.

Wade, Peter, Vivette García Deister, Michael Kent, María Fernanda Olarte Sierra, and Adriana Díaz del Castillo Hernández. 2014. "Nation and the Absent Presence of Race in Latin American Genomics." *Current Anthropology* 55 (4): 497–522.

Wade, Peter, Carlos López Beltrán, Eduardo Restrepo, and Ricardo Ventura Santos, eds. 2014. *Mestizo Genomics: Race Mixture, Nation, and Science in Latin America*. Durham, NC: Duke University Press.

Wailoo, Keith, Alondra Nelson, and Catherine Lee, eds. 2012. *Genetics and the Unsettled Past: The Collision of DNA, Race, and History*. New Brunswick, NJ: Rutgers University Press.

Wailoo, Keith, and Stephen Pemberton. 2006. *The Troubled Dream of Genetic Medicine: Ethnicity and Innovation in Tay-Sachs, Cystic Fibrosis, and Sickle Cell Disease*. Baltimore: Johns Hopkins University Press.

Wang, Qian, Goran Štrkalj, and Li Sun. 2003. "On the Concept of Race in Chinese Biological Anthropology: Alive and Well." *Current Anthropology* 44 (3): 403.

Wang, Sijia, Cecil M. Lewis Jr., Mattias Jakobsson, et al. 2007. "Genetic Variation and Population Structure in Native Americans." *PLoS Genetics* 3 (11): e185.

Wang, Sijia, Nicolas Ray, Winston Rojas, et al. 2008. "Geographic Patterns of Genome Admixture in Latin American Mestizos." *PLoS Genetics* 4 (3): e1000037.

Weinstein, Barbara. 2015. *The Color of Modernity: São Paulo and the Making of Race and Nation in Brazil.* Durham, NC: Duke University Press.

Weismantel, Mary. 2001. *Cholas and Pishtacos: Stories of Race and Sex in the Andes.* Chicago: University of Chicago Press.

Weiss, Kenneth M., and Brian W. Lambert. 2014. "What Type of Person Are You? Old-Fashioned Thinking Even in Modern Science." In *Human Variation: A Genetic Perspective on Diversity, Race, and Medicine,* edited by Aravinda Chakravarti, 15–28. Cold Spring Harbor, NY: Cold Spring Harbor Laboratory Press.

Werbner, Pnina. 2006. "Vernacular Cosmopolitanism." *Theory, Culture and Society* 23 (2–3): 496–98.

Winkler, Cheryl A., George W. Nelson, and Michael W. Smith. 2010. "Admixture Mapping Comes of Age." *Annual Review of Genomics and Human Genetics* 11 (1): 65–89.

Wood, Stephanie. 1998. "Sexual Violation in the Conquest of the Americas." In *Sex and Sexuality in Early America,* edited by Merrill D. Smith, 9–34. New York: New York University Press.

Woolgar, Steve, and Javier Lezaun. 2013. "The Wrong Bin Bag: A Turn to Ontology in Science and Technology Studies?" *Social Studies of Science* 43 (3): 321–40.

Xu, Shuhua. 2012. "Human Population Admixture in Asia." *Genomics and Informatics* 10 (3): 133–44.

Young, Robert. 1995. *Colonial Desire: Hybridity in Theory, Culture and Race.* London: Routledge.

Yudell, Michael. 2014. *Race Unmasked: Biology and Race in the Twentieth Century.* New York: Columbia University Press.

Yunis, Juan J., Luis E. Acevedo, David S. Campo, and Emilio J. Yunis. 2005. "Population Data of Y-STR Minimal Haplotypes in a Sample of Caucasian-Mestizo and African Descent Individuals of Colombia." *Forensic Science International* 151 (2–3): 307–13.

Yunis, Juan J., Luis E. Acevedo, David S. Campo, and Emilio J. Yunis. 2013. "Geno-Geographic Origin of Y-Specific STR Haplotypes in a Sample of Caucasian-Mestizo and African-Descent Male Individuals from Colombia." *Biomédica* 33:459–67.

Yunis, Juan J., and Emilio Yunis. 1999. "DNA Typing in Colombia—Previous Experiences and Future Outlook." Paper read at 10th International Symposium on Human Identification, September 29–October 2, Coronado Springs Resort, Orlando, Florida. http://www.promega.com/~/media/files/resources/conference%20proceedings/ishi%2010/oral%20presentations/18yunis.pdf.

Yunis Turbay, Emilio. 2006. *¡Somos así!* Bogotá: Editorial Bruna.

―――. 2009. *¿Por qué somos así? ¿Qué pasó en Colombia? Análisis del mestizaje.* 2nd ed. Bogotá: Editorial Temis.

Zack, Naomi. 2002. *Philosophy of Science and Race.* New York: Routledge.

Zambrano, Fabio, and Olivier Bernard. 1993. *Ciudad y territorio: El proceso del poblamiento en Colombia.* Bogotá: Universidad Nacional de Colombia.

Zorzett, Ricardo, and Maria Guimarães. 2007. "A África nos genes do povo brasileiro." *Pesquisa* FAPESP 134:37–41.

INDEX

AAFESP (Sickle Cell Anemia Association of the State of São Paulo), 138

affirmative action: multiculturalist policies and, 139; race and, 125–26, 128–30; on racial inequalities, 137–38

African ancestry, 43, 80, 108, 111, 113, 159, 203, 208, 216, 235, 252; African ancestry index (AAI), 125; African-derived populations, 136, 137, 169; in Brazil, 130–31, 134, 137, 138–39, 140; multiculturalism, genomics and, 174, 182, 184

African genetic ancestry: health disorders and, 134, 138–39; race-color classification and, 140

Afro-Brazilian, as category, 20, 132–33, 174, 178, 217, 235

Afro-Brazilian roots project, 131, 137

Afro-Colombians, 101–2, 104, 109, 114, 119–20

Afro-mestizo, 78, 96

Afro-Mexican, 164

alterity, structures of, 174

América Negra, 100, 101

American Journal of Physical Anthropology, 57

Amerindian ancestry, 42, 108, 111, 128, 140, 208, 216, 221, 246, 265; in Mexico, 150, 151, 152–53, 157, 158, 159, 162, 163, 164; multiculturalism, genomics and, 172, 176–77

ancestral populations, 224; Colombia, ancestral founding populations in, 109–10; concept of, DNA ancestry testing and, 33–34, 172; race, mixture and, 170–71

ancestry: ancestry informative markers (AIMS), 33, 86, 151; appearances and, 233–35; continental ancestral population, idea of, 33–34; diversity and, data about, 224; geneticization, ancestry testing

and, 249–53; genomic versions of, 257; in Mexico, 150; mixture and, 2–3; testing in Brazil, 131–32

Antioquia, Colombia, 9, 20, 108, 110–13, 121, 209, 217, 238

anti-quota manifesto in Brazil, 132, 137

antiracism, 220–21; comparison, 180; genomics and, 260, 263–64; postwar turn toward, 28–29

antiracism, global transitions to, 54–59; biological anthropology, 57; biological determinism, 54–55, 56–57; biological "populations," idea of, 59; cultural racism, 59; cultural relativism, 56; culture, separation of biology and, 59; eugenics, 55–56; human value, race and hierarchy of, 56; intelligence, "race" and, 58; race, UNESCO statements on (1950 and 1952), 56–57, 57–58, 257; racial consciousness as biological trait, 58–59; racial inequality, racism and, 56–57; racial types, 54; scientific racism, 55–56; social construction of "race," 57; sociobiological ideas, 58–59

Arocha, Jaime, 99–100

articulation, Hall's ideas about, 47

assemblage theory, 46–48; location within, significance of, 255–56; mestizo assemblage, 48–51; science, society and, 46–48

assimilation, mixture and, 182–83

asymmetric mating, 208–9

Australoid race, 28–29

authoritarian clientelism, 94

autosomal DNA, 37, 111, 157, 195, 214, 216

Basque ancestry, 113

Berardinelli, Waldemar, 64 ·

cultural fundamentalism, 59, 234
cultural identity, 15, 102, 268
cultural isolation, 57, 102–3
cultural process, 16
cultural racism, 20, 56, 58–59, 234
cultural relativism, 56
cultural selection, 112
cultural traditions, 12, 62, 65, 68
culture: culturalized biology, 142; entanglement of biology and, 82; separation of biology and, 59
Current Anthropology, 58

democracy: hierarchy and, 38–39; hierarchy and, relation of mixture to, 143–44; mixture and, link between, 7–8
diabetes, INMEGEN research on, 162–63
difference, proliferation of, 172
differentialist policies, support for, 130
discrimination and segregation, culture of, 106
disease: disease-causing genetic variants, differences in, 41; race and genetics and, 243–46
diversity: in Colombia, Yunis's presentation of, 106, 119–20, 121; dynamic view of, shift toward, 29–30; mixture and, 265–66; of population in Brazil, 60; of population in Colombia, 60; of population in Mexico, 60; racial and ethnic otherness and, 102
diversity of indigenous groups in: Mexico, 77–78
DNA: basic structure of, revelation of, 85; DNA sequencing, data analysis and, 49; "high-throughput" DNA sequencing, 85–86; indigenous DNA, fine-grained analysis of, 162; likelihood ratios in DNA identifications, 183; purification of, 85–86; reference populations in DNA identification, role of, 115
DNA ancestry testing, 33–38; admixture approaches, 34–35; ancestral populations, concept of, 33–34; ancestry informative markers (AIMs), 33; biocontinental evolutionary formations, 34; biogeographical ancestry (BGA), 33; continental ancestral population, idea of, 33–34; ethnic origin, 33; genetic ancestral origins, quantification of, 33; grid sampling, 35; "island

model" of insular populations, 33; out-of-Africa replacement model, 36; population differentiation, 34; "racial mixing," measures of, 33; reticulate models, 35–36, 37; rhizomic models, 35–36; spatiotemporal narrative, 34–35; tree metaphor, 35–38
Dobzhansky, Theodosius, 29, 56, 72, 76, 258
Du Bois, W. E. B., 55–56

educational programs, 94–95
Education and Citizenship of Afro-Descendants and the Poor (Educafro), 137
elites in Latin America, racial hierarchies and, 199
Equipo Argentino de Antropologia Forense (EAAF), 263
ethical sampling, 31
ethnicity: diversity in, racial and ethnic otherness, 102; ethnic origin, 33; ethnicization of blackness in Colombia, 89–90; ethno-racial groupings, 116–17; indigenous and Afro-Colombian (and Rom) ethnic identity, 90; interethnic admixture, 42–43, 127; multiethnicity, 100; sexual relations and, 198
eugenics, 18, 59–65; antiracism, global transitions to, 55–56; in Brazil, 59–65; in Colombia, 59–65; eugenic sanitation, 61–62; in Mexico, 10–11, 59–65; preventive eugenics, 61; racial difference and eugenic discourse, 62; tensions within, 64–65
European-African mixture, 43
European females, sexual agency and, 219
European genetic ancestry, 124, 141
European immigration, 124, 128
European men, sexual agency and, 215
everyday life, geneticization of race and diversity in, 22–23
exceptionalism of Latin America, 15
Expedición Humana (EH) in Colombia, 99–104, 119–20

family lineage, preservation of, 199
Federation Cynologique Internationale, 228
female sexual agency, 203–6
female sexuality, purity and, 198
focus group conversations: race and color in, 235–40; race and genetics in, 240–53

Ford Foundation, 97

forensic *peritos* (expert technicians) in Colombia, 115, 117–18, 119, 269n14

Foucault, Michel, 198

Frenk, Julio, 148

Freyre, Gilberto, 12, 63, 70, 131, 186, 205, 210

Friedemann, Nina de, 99–100

FUNSALUD (private health promotion institution) in Mexico, 147–48, 152

Galton, Francis, 55–56

Gamio, Manuel, 62

gender: genealogy and mixture, 22; genomics and gendered narratives of mixture, 207–20; honor in Latin America, gendered nature of, 199–200; race-gender politics, 192, 219–20, 222; sex and, *mestizaje* and, 221–22; social reproduction, gendered processes of, 198; uniparental DNA analysis, gender relations and, 195–98

genealogy, 4, 34, 38, 92, 156, 198, 225, 233, 251, 253, 257; genealogical purity, 199; genetic genealogies, 192–95, 196–98, 210–11, 214

genetic ancestry, 224; analysis of, 170–71; origins, quantification of, 33; research, 156–57

genetic data: in academic circulation, 135–36; deployment of, 146–47, 153–54; genomic practice and, 264; in health policy debates, 135; in moral and political debates, 130–33, 144; in public debates, 168

genetic geography, 171

genetic isolates in Antioquia, 110–11, 112–13

genetic knowledge, central message of, 256–57

genetic science: ancestry informative markers (AIMs), 86; basic structure of DNA, revelation of, 85; changes in genetic science, 85–87; conceptual schemata of, similarities in, 182–83; as directive for society, 139–40; forensic genetics and regional reference populations, 114–19; forensics and regional diversity of mestizos, 159–60; genetic reality, disavowal of race as, 173; genetic specificity, construction of idea of, 154; genetic traits, 87; genetic variants, identification of, 41; geneticization, trend toward, 87; genomics, evolutionary history and, 86; genomics,

impact on social life, 87; genomics, initiation of era of, 85–86; geography and, dynamic relationship between, 29–30; "high-throughput" DNA sequencing, 85–86; Human Genome Project, 86; human population genetics, 265; Latin American contexts for, comparison of, 97–98; mapping and visual techniques, 86; medical genetics, 99, 122, 126, 143, 167, 179–80, 183–84; in Mexico, development of, 77–78; national genetic particularity, idea of, 152–53; Pena and university racial quotas, 128–33; personalized medicine, 86; political context, changes in, 87–97; postwar genetics institutes, work of, 30; purification of DNA, 85–86; single nucleotide polymorphisms (SNPs), 86; social categories and labeling in, 264–65; structures of, 98; transformative impacts of, 226–28, 258

genetic uniqueness of Brazil, 124–25, 136

geneticization, 177–79; ancestry, genomic versions of, 257; ancestry and appearances, 233–35; ancestry testing, 249–53; assemblages, significance of location within, 255–56; blood type, 225; Brazil, 139–43; Brazil, genetic data in public debates in, 178; *Cicatrices* (Jairo Varela song), 229; collective and individual, 246–49; Colombia, focus group research in, 226–28; Colombia, genetic data in public debates in, 179; color and race as morally charged terms, 230–33; color and race as neutral terms, 228–30; color and race in everyday discourse, 228–35; color terms, categorization by, 231–32; contradictory tendencies in re-racialization and re-geneticization, 142–43; disease, race and genetics and, 243–46; Federation Cynologique Internationale, 228; focus group conversations, race and color in, 235–40; focus group conversations, race and genetics in, 240–53; genetic knowledge, central message of, 256–57; genetics, links between race and, 241–42; genetics, transformative impacts of, 226–28, 258; genomic sovereignty, 225; genomics, provision of new affordances by, 257; geography,

tically heritable health problems, 134; genetic data in health policy debates, 135; Health, amendment to General Law of (2008) in Mexico, 155; health care, potential for genomics in, 182–83; health for all, institutional agenda of, 164–65; inclusion agenda in health care, 38–39; inequalities in Brazil, 93; mestizo predisposition to ill health, 164; policy on, genetically logical balance in, 138–39; policy on, Pena and, 133–36; race, nation and, 161–63; race and, uncertain connections between, 243–46

hematological traits, 77

heterogeneity, 38, 40, 46, 72, 74, 76, 177; in Brazil, 139, 141; in Colombia, 108, 110, 120, 121; in Mexico, 151, 153, 163

HGDP-CEPH Diversity Panel, 170

hierarchy: democracy and, tension between, 6–7, 31, 180–81; equality and, tensions between, 17–18; genetic ancestry and, 257; mixture and, 4–5, 38–39; of value, tension between neutral biology and, 239; violence and, elision of, 211–14

Hippocratic humors, 48

human diversity: in Latin America, genetics research into, 180–81; scientific studies of, 53–54

human evolution, genetic isolates and, 112–13

Human Genome Diversity Project, 30–33, 38, 86; biocolonialism, 31; ethical sampling, 31; grid sampling, 32; hierarchy and democracy, tensions between, 31; insular populations, problem of, 32–33; isolated populations, concern with, 30–31; population, concept of, 32–33; sampling humans, problem of, 31–32

human value, race and hierarchy of, 56

Huxley, Julian, 56

hybridity, 15, 27–28, 35, 45, 62, 262; hybridization, migration and, 28–29; in Latin America, 16–17; optimistic visions of, critiques of, 16–17; rhizomic models of, 17; trihybrid populations, 72, 121, 212

identity: constitution of, 1, 17, 20; cultural identity, 15, 102, 268; genetic inheritance and, 247; identity politics, 2–3; indigenous and Afro-Colombian (and Rom)

ethnic identity, 90; national identity, 43, 62, 63, 164–65; racial identity, assignment of, 137–38; racial identity (and identification), 44, 133, 137, 140, 141, 219, 234; social identity, genetic criteria and, 141

ideology: ideologies of mixture, duality within, 17–18; mestizaje and indigenismo, ideologies of, 158; Mexico, ideological influences in, 146; race and, 238

immigration, 5, 6, 7, 10, 11, 60, 61, 111, 112, 124, 185, 218, 262; European immigration, 124, 200, 212; quota system in Brazil, 63–64

Independence, U.S. Declaration of, 5

indígena, 9, 78, 94–96, 101–2, 146, 155–58, 216, 229, 233. See also racial categories

indigeneity: African and indigenous females, sexual agency and, 215–17; Afro-Colombian and indigenous ethnic identity in Colombia, 90; black African and indigenous males in Brazil, sexual agency and, 217–19; black-white-indigenous triad, 69–70; blackness and, 173–75; blackness and, creation of space for, 13–14; diversity of indigenous groups in Mexico, 77–78; importance of indigenous peoples in Latin America, 39–40; indigenista agendas in Mexico, 76, 78; indigenous ancestry and genomics in Mexico, 168; indigenous rights legislation, 96; International Labour Organization [ILO] Indigenous and Tribal Peoples Convention (1989), 88, 97; mestizaje and indigenismo, ideological combination of, 78–79, 158

indigenous communities: in Colombia, 101; disestablishment of, attempts at, 200

indio. See indígena; racial categories

inheritance, soft theories of, 28

Institute of Family Welfare (ICBF) in Colombia, 105

Institute of Genomic Medicine (INMEGEN) in Mexico, 146, 147–52, 153, 154, 155, 157, 161–62, 163, 168–69

Institute of Land Reform (INCORA) in Colombia, 90

institutional racism, genetic data and, 135

Instituto Etnológico Nacional (IEN) in Colombia, 66, 67, 79

in, 192; racial democracy in, denting of idea of, 13; racial exceptionalism in, 260–63; reticulate models, 40; sexual exchanges, hierarchies of race and class and, 200; single nucleotide polymorphisms (SNPS), 41; slavery, abolition of, 200; social justice, racialization and pursuit of, 183–84; status and social order in, 199; "whitening" in, 200. *See also* Brazil; Colombia; Mexico

Latino populations, 15–16, 41, 163, 229, 236, 261–62, 263; global genomic map and, 167; in Mexico, diversity of, 151–52

Lévi-Strauss, Claude, 56

liberal political orders, 5; health care, inclusion agenda in, 38–39; hierarchy and democracy, tension between, 6–7; multiculturalism in, 14–15; sameness, liberal drive toward, 5–6; social life, institutionalization in, 44–45

Lisker, Rubén, 77–79, 149–50, 175, 180, 181

Livingstone, Frank, 56

Locke, John, 5

male sexual agency: in Latin America, 201–3; male power, sexual access and, 198

Mankind Quarterly, 58

Map of Genome of Mexican Populations, 152–53

mapping and visual techniques, 86

marriage patterns in Brazil, 73

Mayan mestizo, 162

medical genetics, 99, 122, 126, 143, 167, 179–80, 183–84

mestizaje, 1–3, 7, 8, 9, 13, 14–15, 18–19, 20, 21, 22, 51; as biological process, 54, 68–69; cultural exchange, centrality to, 191–92; duality of, 18, 170, 180, 233; eugenics and, 62; gender, genealogy and, 191–222; grammar of, reliance on, 97–98; hybridity and, 16; *indigenismo* and, ideological combination of, 17–18, 78–79, 94, 96, 144, 158, 180–81; measurement of, 67; mestizophilia and, 60; positive spin on, 144; process of, 81, 94; purity and, 39–44; sources of, 102–3; Yunis's analysis of, 104–8, 121, 186. *See also* mixture (*mestizaje/mestiçagem*)

mestizo and indígena, conceptual divide between, 146, 162

mestizo assemblage, 48–49, 51–52, 225; conceptual components of, 80–81; DNA sequencing, data analysis and, 49; Hippocratic humors, 48; topology, 51; transnational assemblages, 48. *See also* mixture (*mestizaje/mestiçagem*)

mestizo blood studies in Colombia, 68

mestizo figure, race and, 171–72

mestizo-indigenous distinction, 156–57, 159–60; ambivalence in, 158

mestizo liminality in Latin America, 15–16

mestizo majority in Colombia, 104, 119–20

mestizo modernity, 18, 78, 82, 170

mestizo populations: data from, 159–60; genetic work with, 172; MGDP focus on, 149, 151–52, 153–54; re-geneticization of social order for, 139, 141–42. *See also* mixture (*mestizaje/mestiçagem*)

Mexico, 21–22; admixture of groups in, 152, 153; Amerindian ancestry, 150, 151, 152–53, 157, 158; ancestry, 150; ancestry informative markers (AIMS), 151; asymmetric mating, 208–9; authoritarian clientelism, 94; autosomal DNA, 157; biocultural lineage, 156; biological diversity and mixture in, 75, 77–78; biopiracy, 149; biotypology, popularity in, 62–63; Black/African and indigenous males, sexual agency and, 217–19; blood studies in, 75–79; blood types, studies of, 75–76; Brazil and, comparison of human diversity studies, 74–75; Brazil and, contrasting practices in, 96–97; Brazil and, deployment of genetic data in, 146–47; categorization of populations in, 81–82; Catholic Church, influence in, 60; Colombia and, contrasting practices in, 96–97; Colombia and, deployment of genetic data in, 146–47; Combined DNA Index System (CODIS), 159, 160; Consortium for Promotion of Genomic Medicine Institute, 147–48; constructive miscegenation in, 60; diabetes, INMEGEN research on, 162–63; diversity of indigenous groups in, 77–78; diversity of population in, 60; educational programs, 94–95; eugenic sanitation in, 61–62; eugenics and race

Mexico (*continued*)

in, 10–11; eugenics in, 59–65; European females, sexual agency and, 219; European men, sexual agency and, 215; focus group research in, 226–28; forensics and regional diversity of mestizos, 159–60; FUNSALUD (private health promotion institution), 147–48, 152; genetic ancestry research, 156–57; genetic continuum of mestizo category, 157; genetic data, deployment of, 146–47, 153–54; genetic data in public debates in, 178–79; genetic specificity, construction of idea of, 154; genetics in, development of, 77–78; Genome Diversity Project (MGDP), 147–52, 152–54, 155, 156, 158, 161–62, 163–64; Genome Diversity Project (MGDP), public outreach for, 148–49; Genome Diversity Project (MGDP), research results, 151–52; Genome Project, genetic discrimination and, 253–55; genomic medicine, 151, 152; genomic patrimony, 153–54, 155; genomic profile, 158–59; genomic research in, 167–68; genomic sovereignty, disputes over concept of, 154–55; genomic sovereignty, unique mixtures and, 152–55; genomic studies in, 173–74, 175; genomics and gendered narratives of mixture in, 207–20; genomics in public debates, 164; Genotyping and Expression Analysis Unit at INMEGEN, 157; geographic genealogy, 156–57, 160; Gobernanza Forense Ciudadana (GFC) in, 263; Hapmap populations, 150, 151–52, 153; Health, amendment to General Law of (2008), 155; health, race and nation, 161–63; health for all, institutional agenda of, 164–65; hematological traits among indigenous people, 77; hierarchy and violence, elision of, 211–14; human diversity, scientific studies in, 54; ideological influences in, 146; *indigenista* agendas, 76, 78; indigenous ancestry and genomics in, 168; indigenous and African females, sexual agency and, 215–17; indigenous DNA, fine-grained analysis of, 162; indigenous rights legislation, 96; Institute of Genomic Medicine (INMEGEN), 146, 147–52, 153, 154, 155, 157, 161–62, 163, 168–69; institutionalization of indigene-

ity in, 184; Instituto Nacional Indigenista (INI), 77, 94–95; land ownership, 94; Latino populations, diversity of, 151; Map of Genome of Mexican Populations, 152–53; Mayan mestizo, 162; meanings of mixture in, 187; *mestizaje* and *indigenismo*, ideological combination of, 78–79, 146, 158; mestizo populations, data from, 159–60; mestizo populations, MGDP focus on, 149, 151–52, 153–54; mestizo predisposition to ill health, 164; mestizos, *indígenas* and race, 155–59; mestizos-indigenous distinction, 156–57; mestizos-indigenous distinction, ambivalence in, 158; mixture and democracy in, 9–11; mixture as core reality for, 191; modernization and reform in, 60; Molecular Genetics Laboratory at ENAH, 161; molecular variance analysis, 160; mothers and fathers in popular science, 209–10; multicultural reforms in, 166; multiculturalism in, 94; multiculturalist turn in, 146; National Autonomous University of Mexico (UNAM), 147–48, 155, 161; National Council for the Prevention of Discrimination (CONAPRED), 97; National Council of Science and Technology (CONACYT), 147; national genetic particularity, idea of, 152–53; national identity, 164–65; National School of Anthropology and History (ENAH), 161; National Zapatista Liberation Army (EZLN), 95; Native Mexican Diversity Panel, 161–62; political context of genetic science in, 94–97; population groupings, 160; post-MGDP genomic projects, 162; postcolonial racial situation, 155–56; preventive eugenics in, 61; preventive medicine, 150–51; private alleles, identification of, 153, 159; race, biological definition of, 76; race, debate on question of, 9–10; race, overt disavowal of, 155–56; race-gender politics today in, 219–20, 222; racial difference and eugenic discourse in, 62; regional diversity, multiple versions of, 160; Salvador Zubirán National Institute of Medical Sciences and Nutrition (INCMNSZ), 161; sampling indigenous peoples, 149–50, 154; sanitary challenges, 150–51; self-identification of mestizos in, 156–57; sexual agency, distribution of, 214–19; short tandem repeats (genetic markers, STRs), 159; single nucleotide polymorphisms (SNPS), 151; state-backed *indigenismo*, 94; telescoping time, 210–11; Yucatán, genomic studies in, 162; Zapotec sample, 149, 150, 151, 153, 156, 158, 169, 170–71

Mill, John Stuart, 5

miscegenation: constructive miscegenation, 60; social effects of, 12

mitochondrial DNA (mtDNA), 22, 37, 123–24, 207–8, 209, 216, 218–19; ancestry and, use of data on, 220–21; in Colombia, 111–12; genetic variants, 196–97; race, mixture and, 169, 172, 186, 192–95

mixture (*mestizaje/mestiçagem*): admixed populations in Latin America, 40–41; admixture approaches to DNA ancestry testing, 34–35; admixture mapping in Latin America, 41–42; ancestry and, 2–3; as biocultural process, 1; biopolitical connotations, 3–4; boundary crossing, mixture and prospects of, 6; concept of, 1; core reality of, 191; democracy and, 7–8, 8–9, 9–11, 11–12; diversity and, 265–66; duality within, 17–18; as genetic process, 1–2; genomics in Colombia and, 120–21; hierarchy and, 4–5, 38–39; ideologies of, duality within, 17–18; meanings of, 185–87; Mexico, admixture of groups in, 152, 153; modernization and, 182–83; optimistic visions of, critiques of, 16–17; purity and, relationship with, 28, 257; purity and, tensions between, 3–5, 18, 38–39; racial difference and, 259; roots of, 2–3; sexual reproduction and, 2–3; as sociocultural processes, 1–2; in United States, "hidden history" of, 15. *See also* race and mixture

modernization: mixture and, 182–83; reform and, 60

Molecular Genetics Laboratory at ENAH in Mexico, 161

molecularization of race, 170

"molecular portrait" of Brazil, 123, 124–25, 126, 127, 131, 185

molecular variance analysis, 160

Molina Enríquez, Andrés, 62

Mongoloid race, 28–29

Montagu, Ashley, 28–29

mortality and morbidity, effect of racial mixing, 74

Morton, Newton, 73–74

Movimento Negro Unificado in Brazil, 132

mulato, 61, 64, 71, 74, 169, 249

multiculturalism, 87–88, 143, 262–63; affirmative action and, 129–30; blackness and indigeneity, 173–75; in Brazil, genomic studies in, 173–75; in Colombia, 88–89, 91, 106–7; in Colombia, genomic studies and, 173–74; comparison, 180; genomics and, 166–87; Latin American multiculturalism, 88; liberal political orders and, 14–15; in Mexico, 94, 146; in Mexico, genomic studies and, 173–74, 175; multicultural reforms in Brazil, 92–93, 166; multicultural reforms in Colombia, 166; multicultural reforms in Colombia, national reconfiguration and, 103–4; multicultural reforms in Mexico, 166; multiculturalist reforms in Latin America, 13–15, 19; racial division and, 122

multiethnicity, 100

multiraciality, challenges to, 43–44

nation: as framing device, 184–85; origins in human diversity and mixture, 185; sexual relations and, 198

National Autonomous University of Mexico (UNAM), 147–48, 155, 161

National Council for the Prevention of Discrimination (CONAPRED) in Mexico, 97

National Council of La Raza, 229–30

National Council of Science and Technology (CONACYT) in Mexico, 147

national genetic particularity, idea of, 152–53

national hierarchy in Colombia, 103–4

national identity in Mexico, 164–65

National Institute of Legal Medicine and Forensic Sciences (INMLYCF) in Colombia, 114–15, 118, 119

National Policy on Health of Black Population in Brazil, 127, 133, 134, 135

National School of Anthropology and History (ENAH) in Mexico, 161

National Zapatista Liberation Army (EZLN) in Mexico, 95

Native American populations in Latin
America, 40
Native Mexican Diversity Panel in Mexico,
161–62
Nature Biotechnology, 155
"The Nature of Race and Race Differences"
(UNESCO, 1951), 29
Neel, James, 73–74
Negro. See racial categories
Negroid race, 28–29
networks: of connections, complexity of,
79–80; topology and, 50
nonracialist society in Brazil, 139–40

Ottensooser, Friedrich, 72

paisas of Colombia, 108, 195, 208, 217, 238;
as regional genetic isolate, 110–13, 167,
172–73
Palmares Foundation, 92
pardo, 71, 92, 130, 137, 174, 235. *See also preto*
Paredes, Manuel, 115–16, 117, 119, 176,
269n13
Paz, Octavio, 49, 187, 192, 267n3
pedigrees, 28
Pena, Sergio, 122–28, 128–33, 133–36
personalized medicine, 86
pharmacogenomics, 126–27, 128
phenotypes, 76, 86, 92, 117, 119, 125, 127, 171,
227, 232; genetics and, 248–49; inherited
phenotypes, 235–36; phenotypical appearances, 233–34, 241–42
Pijao people in Colombia, 81
politics: of comparison, 166–67; political
context for genetic science, changes in,
87–97
popular science, mothers and fathers in,
209–10
populations: concept of, 32–33; differentiation of, DNA testing and, 34; groupings of,
160; isolates and, 28–30
postcolonial period, social order in, 200
postcolonial racial situation in Mexico,
155–56
postraciality, challenges to, 43–44
preto, 92–93, 133, 137, 169, 174, 235. *See also
pardo*
private alleles, identification of, 153, 159

prodemocracy, 220–21
purity, 52; blood types and idea of, 68–69;
concept of, acceptance of, 27–28; cultural mixture/purity, correlation with
genetic, 81; cultural purity, 4, 68–69, 81;
fading of explicit language of, 181; female sexuality and, 198; "island model"
of insular populations, 38; isolation
and, 102; Latourian purification, 136;
maintenance of, 4–5; mestizo, purification and, 45; and mixture, concerns
about, 70; and mixture, dual perception
of, 73–74, 75; and mixture, genomic projects and tensions between, 39–44, 52;
and mixture, tensions between, 3–5, 18,
38–39; mixture and, relationship with,
28; relative purity, concept of, 27; relative
terms about, 238–39; scare quotes about,
80–81

raça, 93, 128; *brasileira*, 64; *negra*, 235
race: ambiguity in concept of, EH and, 103;
biocultural entity, 19; biological
definition of, 76, 136–37; as biological
reality, rejection of, 117–18; biological
variation and, 82; as biology and
culture, 239–40; in Colombian debate
on question of, 9; connectedness and,
198; debates on, employment of genetic
data in, 44; discourse on, explicit nature
of, 63–64; diversity and, public debate
about, 223–24; diversity in everyday life,
geneticization and, 223–57; genetic
validity of concept, 168–69; genetics
and ancestry, conceptions of links
between, 256; genetics and concept of,
258–59; in genomic science, move away
from references to, 181; genomics in
Latin America and, 183–84; as hierarchy
and discrimination, 237–39; language
of, 124; in Mexico, debate on question
of, 9–10; molecular reinscription of,
224; as neutral classification, 235–37;
overt disavowal of, 155–56; race-based
affirmative action in Brazil, 93–94;
race-based quotas in Brazil, 93;
race-gender politics in Latin America,
192, 219–20, 222; race-making in

sampling: of indigenous peoples in Mexico, 149–50, 154; problem of sampling humans, 31–32

sanitary challenges in Mexico, 150–51

science, society and, 44–48; articulation, Hall's ideas about, 47; assemblage theory, 46–48; biological and social, bringing together of, 81–82; categorization of populations, 81–82; connections, society and, 47–48; coproduction, theories of, 45; culture and biology, entanglement of, 82; funding of scientific research, 79; mestizo, purification and, 45; mestizos, modernity and, 82; networks of connections, complexity of, 79–80; ontological turn in social sciences, 45; race, biological variation and, 82; science and society, divide between, 45–46; scientific information, assimilation of, 224; separation of, 79; social life, institutionalization in liberal democracies, 44–45; society, concept of, 46–47; territorialization, processes of, 46

sexual agency, distribution of, 214–19

sexual boundaries, 198

sexual exchanges, hierarchies of race and class and, 200

sexual reproduction, mixture and, 2–3

short tandem repeats (genetic markers, STRS), 115, 117, 159

sickle-cell anemia (SCA): AAFESP (Sickle Cell Anemia Association of the State of São Paulo), 138; in Brazil, 134–35, 138–39, 142; sickle-cell trait, notion of, 71

Silva, Ernani, 71

Single Health System (SUS) in Brazil, 133–34

single nucleotide polymorphisms (SNPs), 41, 86, 151

slavery, abolition of, 200

Soberón Acevedo, Guillermo, 147

social and genetic categories: labeling in genetic science and, 264–65; race, mixture and, 169; social constructs as organizing categories, 224–25; tendency to alignment of, 182

social change, transformative potential for, 259–60

social justice: racialization and pursuit of, 183–84; social inequalities, redistribution policies, 129–30

social life, institutionalization in, 44–45

social orders constructed by mestizo assemblage, 221–22

Social Quotas, Law of (2012) in Brazil, 133

social relations, sexual relations and, 198

social reproduction, gendered processes of, 198

society, concept of, 46–47

sociobiological ideas, 58–59

space, fluid forms of, 50

Spanish Constitution (1812), 5

Spanish migration to Colombia, 111–12

Spivak, Gayatri, 16

state-backed indigenismo in Mexico, 94

status, social order and, 199

territorialization, processes of, 46

time, telescoping of, 210–11

topology, 49–51; invariant transformation, 50; map metaphor and, 49–50; mestizo assemblage, 51; networks, 50; race-making in Europe, 50; racial difference, racelessness and, 51; relationality, continuum and, 49; space, fluid forms of, 50; topological proximities, genetic reassembly and, 142

transformation: genetics, transformative impacts of, 226–28, 258; genomics and transformative potential for social change, 259–60; invariant transformation, 50; language of, 224

transnational assemblages, 48, 173

trihybrid populations, 72, 121

uniparental DNA analysis, 192–95; gender relations and, 195–98

United Nations Declaration on the Rights of Indigenous People, 97

United States, 10, 12, 16, 22, 56, 58, 97, 115, 166, 185, 193, 229; ancestry and appearances in, 233–34; biotypology, development in, 62–63; Brazil and, approaches to race in, 64, 70–71, 72–75, 82; Latin American racial exceptionalism and, 260, 261; Mexico and, approaches to race in, 153–54, 156; mixture in, "hidden history" of, 15; purity and mixture in human population genetics, 30, 38–39, 42; race and genomics in, 183–84